SCENIC DRIVING

COLORADO

STEWART M. GREEN

gpp

travel

Guilford, Connecticut

All interior photos by Stewart M. Green
Maps by Trailhead Graphics © Morris Book Publishing, LLC

ISSN 1544-8355
ISBN 978-0-7627-4791-7

Printed in the United States of America
10 9 8 7 6 5 4 3 2 1

CONTENTS

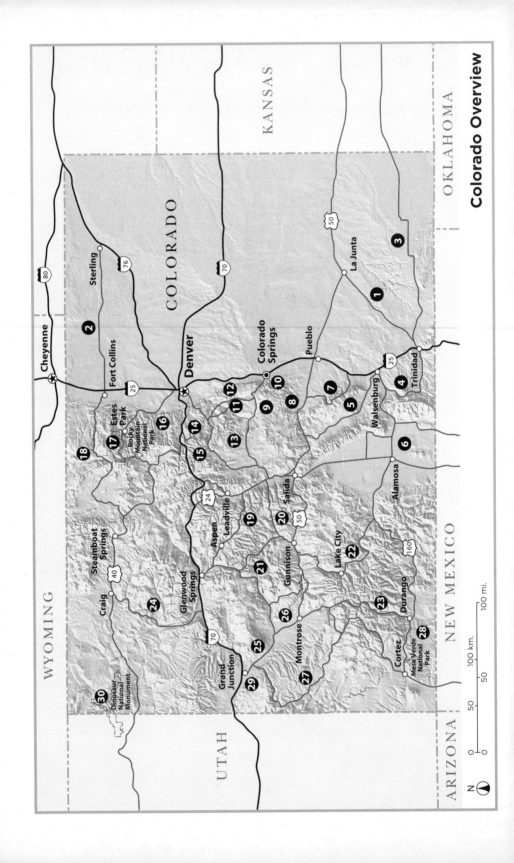

Colorado Overview

ACKNOWLEDGMENTS

Colorado, my home state, remains a place of beauty and mystery—for now. It's a place of pristine views and wide-open spaces. But it is also slowly shrinking. No longer is Colorado a great frontier and an enclave of wilderness. Now, like most of the American West, it's a collection of wilderness areas, a few untouched places, and uncluttered scenic views dismembered from a great eco-community. It's a special land that needs, more than ever before, to be loved, respected, and preserved. *Scenic Driving Colorado* celebrates Colorado's unique history.

Nature and guidebook writers have a serious responsibility to address environmental ethics, to interpret natural history, and to bring historical sensitivity to their subjects. By educating and sensitizing visitors, newcomers, and longtime residents to the beauty, wonder, and fragility of a place, a writer and a book can instill a sense of reverence, pride, and preservation in its users. *Scenic Driving Colorado* helps educate its readers by interpreting and caring for this wonderful place. Bring that respectful ethos with you as you travel its ribbons of highway and remember that we are a reflection of this world.

My thanks to Falcon Publishing for the opportunity to write and photograph the first edition of *Scenic Driving Colorado*—a book we had talked about doing for almost ten years—back in the early 1990s. And many thanks to The Globe Pequot Press for keeping the book in print, selling lots of copies, and bringing this new edition to the nation's bookshelves. Kudos to my first editor, Randall Green of Helena, Montana, for his excellent editing, comments, and direction. My sincere thanks and appreciation to the current editorial and art staff at Globe Pequot, especially editor Lynn Zelem, for all the work necessary to create this stunning third edition. A special thanks to the various United States Department of Agriculture (USDA), Forest Service, Bureau of Land Management, and National Park Service naturalists and rangers who reviewed and corrected portions of both the original and the revised manuscripts. Muchas gracias to Martha Morris for drawing maps, making corrections, offering editorial comments, driving drives, and taking notes. And finally, a special thanks to my sons Ian and Brett Green for the special relationship we have, the encouragement, the belays and beta on rock climbs, and the campfire wisdom and comedy. *Scenic Driving Colorado* was a great adventure.

Map Legend

Featured Route	▬▬▬▬▬
Interstate Highway	═══25═══
U.S. Highway	══27══
State Highway	──58──
County, Local, or Forest Road	──558──
Trail	- - - - - -
Railroad	┼┼┼┼┼┼┼
Point of Interest	▫
Campground	▲
Picnic Area	⊼
Pass	) (
Mountain, Peak, or Butte	▲
River, Creek, or Drainage	‾‾‾‾
Reservoir or Lake	⬬
State Line	COLORADO
Forest, or Other Federal Area	▢
Wilderness Area	▢

The rugged Indian Peaks loom beyond Red Rock Lake along the Peak to Peak Scenic and Historic Byway.

INTRODUCTION

Colorado—it's a state of majestic landscapes, startling panoramas, and an amazing ecological and topographical diversity. It's a land of uncompromising beauty, dominated by lofty, snow-capped peaks; creased by precipitous canyons and broad valleys; and rimmed by distant horizons, mesas, and buttes. Colorado offers a land of extreme contrasts—sere desert and verdant meadow; urban sprawl and rural solitude; granite cliff and aspen woodland; whitewater rivers and dissected arroyo. The timeless landscape out there, beyond the highway's edge, is filled with hidden places and undiscovered wonders.

Colorado, the eighth-largest state, stretches across North America's midsection. This giant, rectangular 104,091-square-mile state bestrides the Continental Divide, the great twisting spine that separates the Atlantic and Pacific watersheds. It's a land of immense topographical variety that ranges from a 3,350-foot low point on the Arkansas River near the Kansas border to the bouldery summit of 14,433-foot Mount Elbert high in the Sawatch Range. In between lies a stunning geography dominated and tempered by its majestic mountain ranges. Geographers divide Colorado into three main physiographic provinces—the Great Plains, the Rocky Mountains, and the Colorado Plateau. Each distinct province is defined by its geology or earth structure, which, coupled with different climates, dictates the state's diverse ecology, the complex web of relationships between plants and animals and the changing land.

Prairie, Peak, and Plateau

The Great Plains, covering 40 percent of Colorado, sweep eastward from the abrupt mountain escarpment to the Kansas border. It's a misnomer to call this region a plain. This lean land is characterized by undulating hills and interrupted by rock-rimmed mesas, buttes, and escarpments. The broad Arkansas and South Platte River valleys and angular canyons carved by the sparse Purgatoire, Apisapha, and Huerfano Rivers seam the shortgrass prairie. Wide fields, watered by snowmelt-laden rivers and groundwater aquifers, are planted with wheat, corn, sorghum, sugar beets, and other crops, while cattle and antelope roam the drier ranges.

The Rocky Mountains abruptly begin where the Great Plains end. The horizontal, 10,000-foot-thick sedimentary rock layers that floor the prairie sharply tilt into steep hogbacks like those seen at Garden of the Gods and Red Rocks along the eastern edge of the mountain uplift. Most Coloradans live in large cities scattered along this transition zone. The Continental Divide dominates Colorado's Rocky Mountains, part of the world's longest mountain chain. The Rockies twist from Alaska to Mexico but reach their climax in Colorado, with more than fifty separate mountain ranges that include fifty-four of America's sixty-seven 14,000-foot peaks and another 830 summits that top 11,000 feet. The mountains, mostly raised over the last seventy million years, were shaped by volcanism and earthquakes and sculpted by huge glaciers and swift rivers and streams. Colorado is the mother of rivers, with the Colorado, South and North Platte, Rio Grande, Yampa, Arkansas, San Juan, Gunnison, Dolores, and Purgatoire Rivers originating in snowy alpine cirques. Rich mineral deposits, including gold, silver, zinc, lead, copper, and molybdenum, lurk in the Rockies and lured nineteenth-century prospectors who left a historic legacy of roads, trails, mines, towns, and place-names on the mountains.

The plateau region, part of the 150,000-square-mile Colorado Plateau, covers roughly the western quarter of the state. It is a brilliantly colored land of horizontal sedimentary layers, dissected by erosion into canyons, mesas, and cuestas. Deep canyons carved by the Yampa, Green, Colorado, and Dolores Rivers slice through the layer-cake rocks. Folding and faulting created huge basins, rolling uplands, and rocky hogbacks in this arid area.

Colorado is an ecological melting pot, a place of unbelievable natural diversity, a place that thrills and startles the naturalist. Famed nature writer Edwin Way Teale wrote in his classic book *Journey into Summer,* "Before us now extended all of Colorado, a state that, like Florida and California, holds endless interest for the naturalist." The Rocky Mountains mold and temper the state's plants and animals, dictating their responses with variable temperatures, precipitation patterns, and elevations. Short-grass prairie, interrupted by a mosaic of farms, blankets the eastern plains. Verdant ribbons of cottonwoods, willows, tamarisk, and underbrush line sinuous rivers and creeks. Pygmy woodlands of piñon pine and juniper trees scatter over dry mesas and desert canyons. Dense evergreen forests of ponderosa pine, Engelmann spruce, lodgepole pine, and subalpine fir coat mountain slopes, while ancient bristlecone pines, dwarfed by wind and weather, huddle at timberline on snow-shrouded peaks. Immense golden groves of quaking aspen shimmer across the mountains under autumn's bright sun. Alpine tundra, a fragile ecosystem of grass and flowers akin to those of northern Canada and Alaska, lies on the harsh mountainsides above timberline, and above stretches a chilly world of shattered rock and endless winter.

Colorado offers the traveler not only incomparable scenery but also a host of natural wonders, historic sites, and outdoor recreation. The state boasts Rocky Mountain, Great Sand Dunes, Black Canyon, and Mesa Verde National Parks, some of the nation's most popular parklands, as well as Colorado, Dinosaur, Hovenweep, and Florissant Fossil Beds National Monuments, Curecanti and Arapaho

Morning clouds and a lonely highway traverse the prairie along the Comanche Grasslands scenic drive in southeastern Colorado.

National Recreation Areas, and Bent's Old Fort National Historic Site. Forty-three state parks are managed for both water and land-based recreation. Eleven national forests and two national grasslands spread across almost 14.5 million acres of public land, while the Bureau of Land Management offers an additional 8.3 million acres. More than 8,000 river-miles and 2,000 lakes yield watery opportunities for fishermen and rafters. The 469-mile-long Colorado Trail threads through seven national forests and six wilderness areas between Denver and Durango. Numerous rough roads invite mountain bikers and four-wheel-drive enthusiasts to sample the backcountry.

Scenic Driving Colorado finds the best of Colorado's majestic landscapes and recreational offerings. Its thirty drives traverse more than 2,300 miles of remote highways and off-the-beaten-track backroads that offer access to Colorado's magnificent landscape, ecological diversity, colorful history, and outdoor activities. Travelers cross lofty mountain passes on Independence Pass and Trail Ridge Road, twist through deep rock-walled canyons along the Dolores and Cache la Poudre Rivers, follow the historic Santa Fe Trail, marvel at Mesa Verde's long-deserted Anasazi cities, and climb to the lofty mountain aeries atop Pikes Peak and Mount Evans. On these drives travelers leave urban sprawl behind and take to the open road.

These drives are only the start of the adventure. Most of them are paved highways, but some are genuine backroads. Beyond the blacktop and the book hide more scenic drives. After exploring the prime roads detailed here, the intrepid traveler can seek out new tracks. Some of the best include Owl Creek Pass, Ophir Pass, Engineer Pass, the Divide Road on the crest of the Uncompahgre Plateau, Hagerman Pass, Boreas Pass, the twisting road between Buford and New Castle, the Deep Creek Road above Dotsero, and some of those lonely prairie roads like Colorado Highway 71 and the Elbert Highway.

All of the drives in *Scenic Driving Colorado* are the author's choice as the state's best scenic, recreational, steering-wheel adventures. Many of the drives or parts of the drives are designated as official Scenic Byways and Back Country Byways by the United States Department of Agriculture Forest Service and the Bureau of Land Management (BLM). Others are part of the state of Colorado's Scenic and Historic Byways program, established in 1989 to provide recreational, economic, and educational benefits to Coloradoans and visitors. These highways are nominated by local partnership groups and designated by the Colorado Scenic and Historic Byways Commission for their scenic, historic, cultural, recreational, and natural features. Two highways—the San Juan Skyway and Trail Ridge Road—are designated as All-American Byways and are among the most scenic drives in America, with only twenty-eight other highways nationwide receiving this honor. Another six Colorado roads are listed as National Scenic Byways.

Being Prepared

Be prepared when driving Colorado's scenic highways. Make sure your vehicle is in good working condition and the spare tire is properly inflated. Follow the speed limit, particularly on winding mountain roads, stay in your lane, and watch for blind corners. Maintain a safe speed and pull off to allow faster cars to pass. Fickle weather creates changeable driving conditions. Violent summer thunderstorms can impair vision and create hydroplaning situations. Snow and ice quickly slicken mountain highways. Carry tire chains, a snow shovel, and extra clothes when traveling in winter. Many high passes require tire chains in winter. Hot summer temperatures and steep mountain slopes can overheat your car. It's

Golden aspens shimmer in the late September sun atop Wilkerson Pass on the South Park–Tarryall Loop scenic drive.

best to pull off the road and allow the engine to cool down. Carry extra water in case of breakdown. It's best to top off your gas tank before embarking on remote roads. Know your vehicle and its limits. And above all—use common sense.

The scenic drives cross a mosaic of public and private lands. Respect private property rights by not trespassing. Forest Service and BLM maps designate public lands. Federal laws protect paleontological, archaeological, and historic sites, including fossils and bones, Indian sites and artifacts, and historic buildings and structures. It's best to utilize existing campgrounds and campsites to mitigate human impact. Remember to douse all campfires and tote your trash out.

Colorado—it's a word that resounds with images as clear as a mountain stream. Snow-capped peaks sharply etched against an azure sky. A muddy river with a glassy surface that runs between dusky red sandstone cliffs. Dark whiskery forests that clot a shaded ravine. An abandoned prairie homestead open to the blazing sun. It's all out there, along the highway shoulder. Follow the roads and drive without destinations. Stop, look, and linger. Every highway bend, every scenic overlook, every canyon crook, and every alpine pass yields a glimpse into the beauty, wonder, and awe of Colorado's natural soul.

Santa Fe Trail Scenic Drive

La Junta to Trinidad

General description: This 80-mile-long scenic drive, following the old Santa Fe Trail, crosses the desolate high plains between La Junta and Trinidad.

Special attractions: Santa Fe Trail, Bent's Old Fort National Historic Site, Comanche National Grassland, Corazon de Trinidad National Historic District, Baca House–Bloom Mansion–Santa Fe Trail Museum (Trinidad), scenic views, hiking.

Location: Southeastern Colorado. The drive runs between La Junta and US 50 and Trinidad and I-25.

Drive route name and number: Santa Fe Trail Scenic and Historic Byway, US 350.

Travel season: Year-round.

Camping: No campgrounds lie along the drive. Primitive camping is permitted on the Comanche National Grassland. Nearby campgrounds are at Trinidad State Park and in San Isabel National Forest.

Services: All services are found in La Junta and Trinidad. No services are found along the drive.

Nearby attractions: Highway of Legends Scenic Byway, Raton Pass, Trinidad State Park, Stonewall Gap, Cokedale National Historic District, Spanish Peaks Wilderness Area, San Isabel National Forest, Ludlow Monument, Comanche Grasslands Scenic Drive, Purgatoire Canyon.

The Drive

The limitless prairie stretches out beneath the blazing sun to a distant line of mountains perched on the horizon. Dusty arroyos, chiseled by quick runoff from occasional thunderstorms, seam broad valleys flanked by rock-rimmed cuestas and undulating hills. A few intermittent creekbeds twist north to the Arkansas River, their water dwindling into sand and reappearing as occasional bitter pools nestled in sandstone canyons. Southeastern Colorado is a land of little rain, fierce temperature ranges, and a leaping vault of azure sky. It's a supple, muscular land, an arena of light and space that reminds us that untamed corners still exist.

These rolling plains are Colorado's underdog landscape, a lost place forgotten and almost unseen by those intent on greener mountain pastures. But this brown land south of the Arkansas River is blanketed by a sea of shortgrass prairie, a delicate and complex ecosystem, and a history older than the United States. Folsom hunters trod the land 10,000 years ago in pursuit of big game; Comanches and Pawnees battled over its buffalo and water holes; Spanish battalions crossed its bleak wastes in search of golden Cibola; and in the 1840s the caravan wheels of traders bent for Santa Fe creaked across this land. The Santa Fe Trail scenic drive, traversing 80 miles of U.S. Highway 350 between La Junta on the Arkansas River

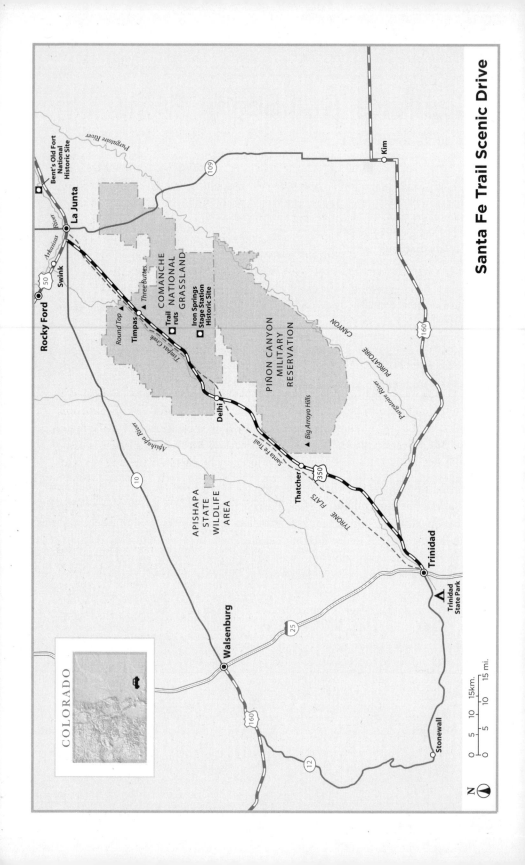

Santa Fe Trail Scenic Drive

and Trinidad at the foot of the Rockies, follows the old trail and explores this diverse and hidden Colorado corner.

Southeastern Colorado is indeed a land of little rain, and what rain does fall usually drops from violent summer thunderstorms that brew over distant mountains. Annual precipitation ranges between 12 and 15 inches. Summer brings hot weather, with daily highs climbing into the nineties and above. Carry water and wear a hat if you walk anywhere. Watch for the ubiquitous rattlesnakes; they teem among the area's boulders and bluffs. Late September begins the cooldown, although hot weather can persist into late October. Expect temperatures in the seventies and eighties. Winter is mild, with light snowfall, warm days, cold nights, and clear skies, although storms can lock in the land in a blizzard of white. Spring is unpredictable. A persistent wind gnaws at the high rangeland, sweeping clouds of dust across Timpas Creek and rattling dry grass on hummocky hills. Light showers dampen the ground, and by May, green grass sprinkled with wildflowers carpets the land. This exquisite bloom lasts but a few weeks before the blast of summer sun arrives to desiccate the prairie.

La Junta and Bent's Old Fort

La Junta, a small town straddling the Arkansas River 64 miles east of Pueblo, is at the junction of U.S. Highway 50 and US 350. La Junta, Spanish for "the junction," was founded in 1875 at the convergence of the Kansas Pacific and Santa Fe railway lines. But its history as a trading center goes back to Bent's Fort, a trading post established in 1834 just east of today's La Junta by brothers Charles and William Bent and Ceran St. Vrain.

Trade with Santa Fe and its remote Mexican colony began in 1821 with Mexico's secession from Spain and the fall of trade barriers. Missouri trader William Becknell crossed the prairie in 1821 to that lonely northern outpost of a newly independent nation and found an eager market for his trade goods. On his journey to Santa Fe, Becknell had followed the Arkansas River into Colorado and coaxed his mules over rocky Raton Pass, finding the route impractical for wagons. On his second trip he left the Arkansas and cut across waterless plains to the Cimarron River to establish the Cimarron cutoff. A Missouri resident later recalled Becknell's triumphant return: "When the rawhide thongs of the saddlebags were cut, the Spanish dollars rolled into the gutters, causing great excitement." Speculative traders soon found it was cheaper to ship goods to Santa Fe from Missouri than from Mexico City, and by 1827 the New Mexico trade had firmly established the 900-mile-long Santa Fe Trail, western America's great road of commerce.

The Bent brothers and St. Vrain cashed in on the lucrative Indian trade in eastern Colorado with their adobe castle perched on the cottonwood-lined banks of the Arkansas River. William Bent concentrated on Indian goods, while Charles

Bent and St. Vrain specialized in the lucrative Santa Fe and Taos trade. The Cimarron cutoff route on the Santa Fe Trail was fast and popular, but mounting Indian attacks and the lack of a reliable water supply forced an increasing number of merchants to follow the longer, but safer, Mountain Branch up the Arkansas River to Bent's Fort. Here they could rest and purchase supplies before heading southwest up arid Timpas Creek to the rough track over Raton Pass.

The Bent, St. Vrain & Company mercantile firm thrived until the late 1840s, when the enterprise began to unravel. Charles Bent, then the first American governor of the New Mexico Territory, was killed in the 1847 Taos Revolt by rioting Pueblo Indians, and shortly afterward a cholera epidemic swept along the river, decimating both Anglos and Indians. The U.S. Army, fighting a war with Mexico from 1846 to 1848, also requisitioned part of Bent's Fort, overgrazed surrounding pastures, and used up what little firewood remained around the fort. In frustration, William Bent abandoned and torched the fort in 1849 and moved downstream to build Bent's New Fort at Big Timber.

The old fort site lay open to the sun and sky until the mid-1970s, when the National Park Service, using original plans and scale drawings made in 1846 by army topographical engineer Lieutenant James W. Abert, rebuilt the massive adobe fort. Now open as **Bent's Old Fort National Historic Site,** the fort offers a glimpse of frontier life in the 1840s. At the fort, interpreters clad in period clothes, including a trader, blacksmith, Mexican laborer, and mountain man, keep the legacy of Bent's Fort and the Santa Fe Trail alive today. The fort lies a few miles northeast of La Junta on CO 194.

Along the Santa Fe Trail

The drive begins in western La Junta at the intersection of US 50 and US 350. Head south on quiet residential streets on US 350. The road bends southwest and leaves the town behind after a mile. US 350, nicknamed the National Old Trails Highway, was a major transcontinental highway between New York and Los Angeles in the days before the interstate system. The trace of the **Santa Fe Trail** itself, from Franklin, Missouri, to Santa Fe, New Mexico, is now preserved as a national historic trail. The 80-mile section between La Junta and Trinidad follows the Mountain Branch of the Santa Fe Trail. Here the old trail offered passage to trade caravans and later stage, freight, and mail lines, before the completion of the railroad in the 1870s. Travel along this segment generally took about four days.

The highway gradually ascends a tilted plain. Shortgrass coats the flat ground and only an occasional windmill marks the desolate plain. At about 5 miles an

Opposite: Bent's Old Fort National Historic Site, just outside La Junta, reconstructs the Santa Fe Trail's colorful history.

unassuming granite marker sits along the fence on the road's west side. This marker, one of many placed along the trail by the Daughters of the American Revolution (DAR), indicates where the trail crossed today's highway. Sharp eyes can discern wagon wheel ruts etched into the ground west of the marker. **Trail ruts,** found along much of the drive, appear as long, furrowed depressions and are usually heavily vegetated. When traveling flat country like this, wagon caravans spread out three and four abreast, creating wide rutted areas. In 1844 teamster Josiah Gregg wrote, "The wagons marched slowly in four parallel columns, in broken lines, often at intervals of many rods between. The unceasing 'crack, crack,' of the wagoners' whips, resembling the frequent reports of distant guns, almost made one believe that a skirmish was actually taking place between two hostile parties." Wagons traveled single file on steep ascents, gouging deep swales into hillsides that have eroded into sharp arroyos.

Unlike other Santa Fe Trail sections in Colorado and Kansas, the trail stretch followed by this drive remains much as it did when wagons inched across the wide expanse. Eighteen-year-old Susan Shelby Magoffin traveled the trail from Independence, Missouri, to Santa Fe with her trader husband Samuel Magoffin in 1846, a boom year when more than one million dollars in goods was hauled over the trail. Magoffin kept a journal recounting her daily experiences that has become a classic tale of the Santa Fe Trail. On Saturday, August 8, she wrote about the trail section southwest of the fort: "The dust is very great, and the vegetation so perfectly parched by the sun that not a blade of *green* grass is to be seen."

After 13 miles the highway drops over a tawny bluff above **Timpas Creek,** its dry meanders dotted with cottonwoods. Both the highway and Santa Fe Trail follow the Timpas Creek drainage to its headwaters, some 40 miles to the southwest. Distant views unfold west from the bluff top. The Wet Mountains and Spanish Peaks, over 70 miles away, float on the shimmering horizon like far-off blue clouds. The twin Spanish Peaks, called *Wahatoya* ("Breasts of the World") by the Ute Indians, were long a crucial landmark for the Indians, Spanish, and Santa Fe Trail travelers. **The Three Buttes,** another trail landmark, lift pointed summits above the cluster of trees marking the abandoned town site of Timpas. Susan Magoffin traveled here on Sunday, August 9, noting, "Mountains are coming in sight this morning—we are winding about among large stone hills which finally run into mountains, two of which appear in the distance. . . ." You can find this view by turning north on CO 71 and driving for a half mile to a parking area for Sierra Vista Overlook. A short walk leads to the overlook atop a bluff and a commanding view of the country along the Santa Fe Trail as it runs southwest. From here you can hike a 3-mile section of the Santa Fe National Historic Trail marked with stone posts to Timpas Picnic Area.

Timpas and Comanche National Grassland

The road begins a gradual descent into the broad Timpas Creek valley and enters the Timpas Unit of **Comanche National Grassland,** with over 440,000 acres. The area, a patchwork of public and private lands, encompasses a diversity of habitats within the grassland ecosystem. The grassland, managed by the USDA Forest Service, spreads across southeastern Colorado. The area, originally Comanche Indian territory, was overgrazed by early cattle barons and later divided by homesteaders into forty-acre tracts. But dry soil and bad farming and conservation practices created the Dust Bowl here and in surrounding states in the 1930s. In 1938 the federal government began reacquiring the homesteads and retiring them from cultivation. Today the Forest Service has reclaimed much of the grassland. Plentiful animals inhabit the high plains—including both mule and whitetail deer, pronghorn, black bear, opossum, mountain lion, black-tailed prairie dog, jackrabbit, snapping turtle, Texas short-horned lizard, and prairie, massasauga, and pygmy rattlesnakes. The area offers excellent bird habitats, with more than 235 bird species recorded. Common birds seen on the drive include turkey vulture, red-tailed hawk, American kestrel, western meadowlark, and raven.

The highway passes the ghost town of **Timpas,** an old stage station and railroad stop established in 1868. Clusters of elms and cottonwoods surround its abandoned school, houses, and weather-beaten stockyard. You can explore the area at Timpas Picnic Area by turning right or northwest on County Road 16.5. After crossing the railroad tracks, turn right into the parking area. Several covered picnic tables make a good lunch stop. Timpas Creek was the first water source encountered on this trail section after leaving the Arkansas River. A short trail loops out to the creek, passing stone markers that indicate the trace of the Santa Fe Trail. You can also hike 3 miles up to Sierra Vista Overlook.

The drive runs up the valley flank, cresting a low hill north of the Three Buttes. Soft, rolling hills broken by arroyos and shallow canyons surround a roadside overlook. A sandstone rim fringes distant bluffs, and junipers scatter across their talus slopes. The Southern Overland Mail Company stagecoach route threaded through the Three Buttes, leaving eroded ruts below the gap. Another DAR trail marker sits a couple miles down the road near milepost 51.

Following the valley floor, the highway dips across Lone Tree Arroyo, Hoe Ranch Arroyo, and Sheep Canyon Arroyo. Eleven miles from Timpas the drive intersects Iron Springs Road (County Road 9). The Santa Fe Trail crosses this gravel side road a half mile south. **Iron Springs Stage Station Historic Site** sits a little farther south by two stock tanks. Iron Springs, capped by a concrete box, supplies water to the tanks. Nearby lies the foundation of the station barn, a low mound marking the adobe remains of the station itself, and the stubby outline of

Clumps of grass and scattered junipers adorn stony hills along the Santa Fe Trail scenic drive.

the stage corral. The station, built in 1862 by Henry C. Withers, was burned by Cheyenne Indians in 1864. The stage station allowed for a change of horses and a chance for passengers to stretch their legs and get a meal. One early traveler, Episcopal bishop Joseph Talbot, arrived here at four in the morning after a ten-hour night ride from Bent's Fort. He noted, after dining on a "greasy breakfast of antelope," that the station was a "miserable, dirty place." Trail ruts are still visible west of the parking area.

In 1872 the Atchinson, Topeka, and Santa Fe Railroad came through, replacing the old stage route. The Iron Springs Station closed and Bloom, a new railroad stop, arose just west along today's highway and railroad. The town, a cattle shipping point, was named for a Trinidad banker and son-in-law of M. D. Thatcher, a prominent Colorado cattleman. After the post office closed in 1938, the town's fortunes sagged. Today it's a ghost town, with fallen houses surrounded by leafy trees and a roadside store with shattered windows.

Past Bloom the highway bends south, crosses Taylor Arroyo, and leaves Comanche National Grassland. The road climbs away from Timpas Creek to the almost deserted railroad town of **Delhi.** Cresting the hill, the road again enters the broad Timpas valley. High cuestas edged with sandstone and darkly dotted with junipers flank the highway. The Spanish Peaks and the snowcapped Culebra Range loom straight ahead.

Thatcher, the next ruined town encountered, began as a stage station called Hole-in-the-Rock and became a bustling railroad town after the Atcheson, Topeka, and Santa Fe Railroad pushed through in 1872. The town flourished as a cow town and was named for M. D. Thatcher, a well-known southern Colorado rancher and banker. The town's fortunes soared in the early twentieth century after a helium plant was built near local helium wells. The gas, used to inflate dirigibles, took orders from around the world until airplanes made them obsolete. After that, the town slowly declined. The lavish train depot closed in 1965 and shortly afterward the post office shut its doors. Now the town basks under the hot sun, empty but for a few remaining residents. Wind sifts through open doors and broken windows, and adobe walls crumble, unprotected from years of rain. Rusted car doors, a prone refrigerator, and sagging fences are scattered across weed-filled front yards. The town high school, once full of promise, lies in ruins. The gymnasium roof caved in a few years back and the front doors sit ajar.

A short side trip turns west at the only intersection in Thatcher. Head down the gravel road past the school to a narrow wooden bridge spanning Timpas Creek. Look north up the shallow rocky canyon. Hidden there is one of the prominent Santa Fe Trail landmarks on the highway—**Hole-in-the-Rock.** This deep tinaja, carved by flash floods into solid bedrock, kept water through even the driest times and was a welcome sight in trail days. Susan Magoffin wrote, "This road is very badly supplied with water." Her party camped here for a couple of days after their cattle ran off. She described the well as "a large 'hole in a rock' filled with clear, cold water, and to which a bottom has never as yet been found." The hole, on private property, is now dry and filled with sand. A ruined stone barn at the ranch just east of the bridge is the remains of the Hole-in-the-Rock Overland Stage Station's barn.

Thatcher to Trinidad

The highway runs southwest from Thatcher up a broadening valley among undulating hills. Fisher Mesa, a flat-topped landmark, rises beyond the road. The drive reaches a wide-rounded ridge above the Timpas Creek headwaters and heads down a gently tilted plain covered with short-grass prairie. The highway sweeps through a couple more mostly abandoned towns—Tyrone and Model—before dropping down into the Purgatoire River valley. The 240,000-acre **Piñon Canyon Military Reservation,** lying east of Tyrone and Thatcher, is used by the U.S. Army for tank and military training.

The drive's last 15 miles border the **Purgatoire River,** passing pastures and fields of pinto beans, alfalfa, and sugar beets. The Purgatoire River, running 150 miles from the Culebra Range to the Arkansas River, is a river of history and character. The river's original name, *El Rio de las Animas Perdidas en Purgatorio* (the River of Lost Souls in Purgatory), was shortened by Anglos to Purgatoire River and given a French spelling. Cowboys mangled it to Picketwire. The river, after passing Trinidad, hastens through its lonely redrock Purgatoire Canyon east of the drive.

Above the river US 350 intersects U.S. Highway 160, and 5 miles later enters 6,025-foot-high **Trinidad.** The road bends through the town's old downtown before ending at I-25. The summit of Raton Pass and the New Mexico state line lie 13 miles to the south, while Walsenburg sits 37 miles to the north. The Highway of Legends Scenic Byway (see Drive 4) begins on Trinidad's west side.

Trinidad, lying at the foot of Fisher's Peak, was an important Santa Fe Trail town. Founded in 1859 at the base of rough Raton Pass, the community was named *Santisima Trinidad*, or "Most Holy Trinity." Sheepherder Gabriel Gutierrez first settled here on the river's south bank and soon other settlers drifted in. Trinidad, a favorite haunt of mountain men and desperadoes, acquired a rowdy reputation that was reinforced after the Battle of Trinidad on Christmas Day, 1867. Racial friction between Anglo and Hispanic settlers escalated from a wrestling match to an all-out riot. Soldiers, called in from Fort Lyon, quelled the violence and imposed martial law. Later the town flourished when the vast coal reserves along the river to the west were mined for Pueblo's steel plant. Much of downtown Trinidad, with its narrow, bricked streets, is preserved as **El Corazon del Trinidad National Historic District.** The Baca House–Bloom Mansion–Sante Fe Trail Museum depicts life in pioneer Trinidad and displays wagons used on the Santa Fe Trail. The Louden-Henritze Archeology Museum at Trinidad State Junior College illustrates the area's diverse archaeological resources and shows Indian artifacts.

2

Pawnee Grasslands Scenic Drive

Ault to Sterling

General description: This 125-mile-long drive traverses the Pawnee National Grassland, passing ranch lands, abandoned homesteads, and undulating high plains.

Special attractions: Pawnee National Grassland, Pawnee Buttes, Crow Valley Recreation Area, Sterling Overland Trail Museum, wide views, photography, bird-watching, hiking, mountain biking, camping.

Location: Northeastern Colorado. The drive begins in Ault, 14 miles east of Fort Collins and I-25, and ends at Sterling and I-76.

Drive route name and numbers: Pawnee Pioneer Trails Scenic Byway. CO 14; Weld County Roads 77, 120, 390, 112, 111, 107, 110, 113, 110 1/2, 115, 127, and 129; Grasslands Road 685.

Camping: Crow Valley Recreation Area, 24 miles west of Ault at Briggsdale, is the only developed campground along the drive. Primitive camping is permitted elsewhere on the grassland. Watch for high winds and flash flood areas.

Services: All services in Fort Collins, Ault, and Sterling. Limited services in Raymer.

Nearby attractions: Fort Collins, Cache la Poudre National Wild and Scenic River, Lory State Park, Roosevelt National Forest, Rocky Mountain National Park, Estes Park, Trail Ridge Road, Cheyenne (Wyoming), Fort Morgan Museum, Fort Vasquez State Historic Site, Centennial Village (Greeley).

The Drive

Northeastern Colorado is a spare, austere landscape, a sparsely populated province of undulating hills that break into badlands, short-grass prairie that recedes to a flat eastern horizon, and trickling streams that dwindle into sand, only to reappear later in occasional muddy pools surrounded by cottonwoods. Indians once roamed its vastness, camping along the meager creeks and hunting vast buffalo herds. Later homesteaders tilled the dry soil but grew only loneliness and frustration. Still the prairie remains a refuge from today's urban sprawl and a place of exquisite beauty. Its buttes and mesa rims gleam white in summer's noonday sun; dancing heat waves shimmer across the plain revealing rumpled sky mirages. Evening brings smoky shadows and immense, billowing thunderheads tinged pink and rose with sunset. Out here the prairie traveler develops a new appreciation for simple forms and a devoted adoration of this elemental earth of clay, sky, and wind song.

Fickle, unpredictable weather dominates along the drive. Summer days are hot, with highs ranging into the nineties and above. Heavy thunderstorms,

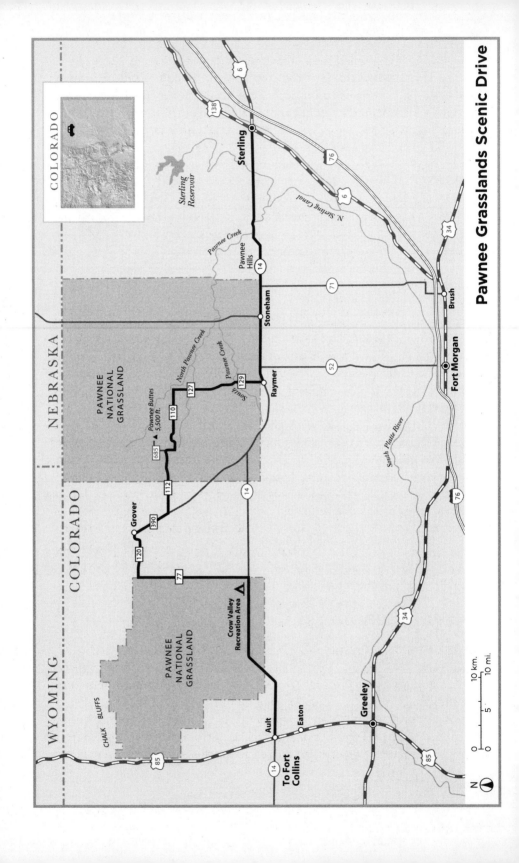

Pawnee Grasslands Scenic Drive

coupled with hail, regularly occur on summer afternoons. Rain makes the drive's dirt backroads temporarily impassable, muddy, and slippery. Watch for lightning on the exposed, higher elevations such as the Pawnee Buttes Overlook and trail parking area. Autumn days, from mid-September to early November, are pleasant and warm. Winter brings snow. Severe blizzards cause deep drifts along the backroads, and melting snow closes dirt roads. Check with the grassland office for road conditions and closures. Long warm periods in midwinter melt the snow, dry the roads, and make for excellent traveling conditions. Spring, beginning by late March, is characterized by rainstorms, heavy spring snows, high winds, and warming temperatures. Much of the prairie's 12 to 15 inches of annual precipitation falls between April and June. May, with greening grass and carpets of wildflowers, makes an excellent travel time across the grassland.

Ault to Pawnee National Grassland

The Pawnee National Grassland scenic drive begins in **Ault,** 14 miles west of Fort Collins and Interstate 25 on CO 14. Take I-25 exit 269A for CO 14 east. Ault, established in 1888 and named for Fort Collins miller Alexander Ault, has long been an agricultural town. It is a friendly, unassuming place with neat frame homes along tree-lined side streets, and tall grain silos that line the railroad tracks on the east side of town.

Ault, elevation 4,950 feet, sits at the junction of U.S. Highway 85 and CO 14. Scenic drivers head east on CO 14 from the intersection. The drive's first leg runs east for 24 miles to Briggsdale. The first 5 miles run across gentle farmland seamed by the sleepy meanders of Spring, Lone Tree, and Owl Creeks. Corn and wheat fields, interrupted by white farmhouses and windbreaks of cottonwoods, elms, and Russian olives, form a pastoral roadside border. After 5 miles the highway tilts up a long hillside and leaves the farmland behind. Ahead stretch tawny, rolling hills blanketed by shortgrass and subdivided by long fence lines. The highway bends northeast for 6 miles and then restraightens eastward. At just over 13 miles the blacktop enters Pawnee National Grassland.

Pawnee National Grassland

Pawnee National Grassland is an immense (193,060-acre) swath of prairie managed by the USDA Forest Service. This remote land was first inhabited by prehistoric big-game hunters some 11,000 years ago. Later nomadic plains tribes—the Pawnee, Apache, Arapaho, and Cheyenne Indians—traversed the plains while hunting bison. The first known European to visit the area, Don Pedro de Villasur, arrived in 1720, and French fur trappers regularly crossed it while trading with local Indians. Anglo homesteaders arrived here in the late 1800s, after the 1862

A weathered barn door at an abandoned homestead in Crow Valley on the Pawnee Grasslands scenic drive.

Homestead Act opened western lands to any able-bodied American willing to work 160-acre tracts. Early settlers plowed lands along the few perennial rivers and streams, while latecomers homesteaded the marginal dry land. The dryland farmers, initially successful, suffered after 1920 because of low wheat prices, drought, and bad farming practices. The Dust Bowl and Great Depression of the 1930s forced the mass migration of homesteaders from their 160-acre dream parcels. The federal government began buying back the damaged lands and restoring them with a semblance of their original grass cover. The recovered lands were returned to cultivation and grazing or administered as multiple-use National Grasslands by the Forest Service.

The Pawnee National Grassland, divided into two large units, is a patchwork of both public and private land. A Forest Service map, detailing the different lands, is a necessity for exploring beyond the area's gridwork of county roads. Be sure you are on public land; otherwise, obtain permission from the landowner. Most of the grassland is managed for livestock grazing as well as wildlife habitat. Oil and gas deposits, tapped by over fifty producing wells, underlie the grassland, particularly at the Keota Oil Field south of Grover and a small field north of Raymer. The U.S. Department of Agriculture also operates the 15,600-acre Central Plains Experimental Range for research on grassland ecology, range cattle nutrition, and the use of fertilizers and herbicides.

After entering the grassland, CO 14 rolls east, dipping through dry arroyos walled with clay. Wind-driven tumbleweeds stack against barbed-wire fences, lonely windmills rise against the sky, and elms shade the occasional ranch house. The road drops into broad Crow Valley and reaches Briggsdale, an almost deserted town of a half dozen streets south of the highway. Frank Briggs, a local real estate man and farmer, platted the town site in 1909. **The Briggsdale Museum,** housed in the old school house, depicts the area's homestead history. The drive turns north here on paved County Road 77.

Crow Valley to Grover

Crow Valley Recreation Area, the only developed camp and picnic ground along the drive, sits 0.2 mile up County Road 77. Shady campsites are scattered among cottonwoods and elms. The area also offers restrooms, water, a ballfield, and a group picnic area. A fenced display features antique farm machinery, including various plows and a windmill. The campground makes a good base to explore the surrounding grasslands on foot and mountain bike. An auto birding tour route threads along Crow Creek in the shallow valley.

Pawnee National Grassland, sitting on the edge of the Central Flyway, offers excellent birding opportunities, particularly in May and June when numerous migrant species nest in the varied habitats. Noted ornithologist Roger Tory Peterson called the grassland his favorite Colorado birding area. More than 225 species, including golden eagle, horned lark, black-billed magpie, western meadowlark, American goldfinch, burrowing owl, and the lark bunting, Colorado's state bird, live on the area's grassy plains, sandstone cliffs, moist creek bottoms, and wooded draws. Grassland mammals also thrive here. Common species are pronghorn and mule deer, coyote, badger, prairie dog, and jackrabbit. Hikers should watch for rattlesnakes. They commonly inhabit dry, rocky slopes on buttes and mesas, often sunning on ledges and boulders.

The narrow road runs due north up the edge of shallow Crow Valley. Ancient cottonwoods line the creek bed and ranches and farms scatter over the rolling hills. The snow-capped Front Range rims the western horizon with sculpted peaks. Flat-topped Longs Peak, high point of Rocky Mountain National Park, looms in the southwest sky. After 10 miles a low-browed escarpment of sandy cliffs fringed by green forest etches the eastern valley rim. The road passes an abandoned farm, its weather-beaten house and barn now the haunt of owls and lizards. An upturned, rusted refrigerator lies on the ground amid elms and tall grass.

The drive turns east on paved County Road 120 15 miles north of Briggsdale and passes an empty two-story house surrounded by junked cars and a plowed field. County Road 120 bends north and east past farmland in wide Crow Valley, and 7 miles later rolls into **Grover,** "Home of the Pawnee Jackrabbit."

Grover to the Pawnee Buttes

Shady gravel streets fill Grover, an off-the-beaten-track village. A small museum in the old railroad station houses displays of local artifacts and grassland ecology. On the far eastern edge of Grover, County Road 120 dead-ends into County Road 390. Turn right, or southeast, on this gravel road. The drive assumes a new character for the next 40 miles to Raymer, threading eccentrically along numerous dirt roads that criss-cross the prairie. Keep a careful eye on the road signs and you'll keep on the drive route. If you blunder off, however, it's hard to get lost. Almost all the roads run north and south or east and west, eventually intersecting some major road.

County Road 390 runs southeast alongside the abandoned Chicago, Burlington & Quincy Railroad right-of-way. The railway, originally a branch line between Cheyenne, Wyoming, and Sterling, came through in the late 1880s. During the halcyon days before World War I and the Dust Bowl, the towns and homesteaders along the track flourished with the railroad. Grover and neighboring Keota to the south offered daily passenger service, and the railroad shipped area grain to market. Locals even planned to chisel a new county called Pawnee out of eastern Weld County in 1912, but Grover and Keota argued so bitterly over which would be county seat that the entire proposal was scrapped. Oil wells, part of the Keota Oil Field, dot grass fields along the road. A wall of tumbled bluffs, the edge of an eroded upland called the High Plains Escarpment, looms to the east. Just past a low hill 6 miles southeast of Grover, the road intersects County Road 112. Turn east on County Road 112.

The new road, passing a ranch, twists through dry hills. After 2 miles it climbs onto a broad ridge studded with prickly pear cacti and yucca. Sligo Cemetery sits atop the rounded shoulder. Numerous pioneer graves dating from the early 1900s spread over this lovely hillock. Mostly young children and toddlers make up the cemetery's residents. Nameless plastic markers from Adamson Mortuary designate their remote graves. A purple cloth rose, torn and tattered by the ceaseless wind, lies half-buried in dust beside one faded plaque.

The road dips east from the cemetery ridge and enters the southern edge of a broad valley. Cliffs and deep ravines fringed with juniper stretch along its flat-topped rim. The valley narrows as the road runs east. Five miles from the graveyard, County Road 112 intersects County Road 107. Jog south and east on County Road 107 over steep hills. After almost 2 miles the road intersects Grasslands Road

A sandstone overlook, offering one of Colorado's best prairie vistas, views the twin Pawnee Buttes at the Pawnee Grasslands.

685. This marked route heads north onto a wide, rolling ridge for 1.5 miles to the **Pawnee Buttes Trailhead.** An overlook, another 0.5 mile farther north, yields one of eastern Colorado's most dramatic views.

The Pawnee Buttes to Raymer

The monolithic Pawnee Buttes, forming distinctive landmarks, rise out of North Pawnee Creek's broad, grass-filled valley. James Michener renamed them the Rattlesnake Buttes in his Colorado-based novel *Centennial* and called them the "two sentinels of the plains." Sandstone deposited on an ancient seafloor some 125 million years ago forms the horizontal layers on the 300-foot-high twin buttes. Over the last ten million years, wind and water erosion attacked soft sediments between the overlook's rimrock pedestal and the buttes a mile to the east, chiseling these towering monuments from the soft rock. The Arikaree Formation, a layer of sandstone and conglomerate, makes an erosion-resistant cap atop the softer clay-like Brule Formation beneath. The area surrounding the buttes and overlook is a well-known fossil locale. As early as 1871 paleontologists came to dig fossil mammal skeletons dating from Miocene and Oligocene times, some thirty million years ago, in the area's deep arroyos and steep mesa slopes. The fossils here, similar to those in South Dakota's Badlands, include small hooved animals, giant megafauna such as the rhinoceroslike *Titanothere* and the clawed, horselike mammal *Chalicothere*, other ancestral horses, and turtles. The Denver Museum of Natural History displays several mammal skeletons found here.

The Pawnee Buttes Trail, winding a mile and a half down from the trailhead to the base of the west butte, offers an excellent introduction to the grassland ecology. While much of the short-grass prairie was altered by decades of overgrazing, much has returned and resembles the historic grassland that was once the hunting ground of the Pawnee Indians. Blue grama and buffalo grasses dominate the dry prairie, while taller grasses still flourish in moist ravines unreached by grazing cattle. Prickly pear cacti scatter in clumps along the trail, and junipers cloak rocky hillsides. A stand of limber pines, probably a relic from wetter, glacial times, grows in Dave's Draw west of the buttes. The trail makes a good mountain bike excursion, although it's all uphill coming back.

The drive returns to County Road 112, which immediately bends south on County Road 111. The drive jogs around for the next few miles, following a single road that changes numbers almost every mile. After a mile, turn east on County Road 110 for another mile, north on County Road 113, and then east on County Road 110 1/2 for a mile. Turn south on County Road 115 and after a half-mile east again on County Road 110. The drive runs straight east, skirting rolling hills and dropping across dry swales. The Pawnee Buttes play hide-and-seek behind a broken bluff to the north for a few miles before the road breaks into the open on a broad valley edge. County Road 110 dead-ends into County Road 127 a few miles later. An abandoned homestead, surrounded by gangly elms, sits on the lonely corner. The drive turns south on County Road 127. The dirt road sweeps over the undulating landscape, dipping through Igo Creek's valley and climbing over sandstone rimrock. Scattered oil wells and windmills fringe the hillsides, and the buttes poke above the northwestern horizon. Deep grass and shallow pools of water fill South Pawnee Creek's lush valley before the track ascends a rise and reaches Raymer and CO 14.

Raymer to Sterling

Raymer is another one of those old homestead supply towns that prospered at the turn of the twentieth century. The town, platted by the Lincoln Land Company, was named for Burlington Railroad engineer George Raymer. The U.S. Post Office and Zip Code directory calls it New Raymer to avoid confusion with Ramah to the south, while the state highway map still calls it Raymer.

The drive turns east on paved CO 14 and traverses open grasslands and fenced farm fields. **Stoneham,** an 1888 railroad town, lies 11 miles from Raymer. Grain elevators, two churches, and a few houses mark this roadside hamlet. The drive leaves the Pawnee National Grassland almost 5 miles east of Stoneham and climbs over a low broken mesa called the **Pawnee Hills.** The road descends sharply through littered sandstone blocks to the broad Pawnee Valley. The sandy creek bed, lined with cottonwoods, winds southeast to the South Platte River. After gently climbing out of the valley, the highway enters farm fields irrigated by Platte water. Fields of corn and bright sunflowers border the blacktop.

The road tilts downward, crosses the North Sterling Canal, and enters the 3,935-foot-high town of **Sterling.** This pleasant town, on the fertile South Platte River floodplain, is an agricultural hub. The town started as a post office on rancher David Leavitt's property in 1872. He named it for his Illinois hometown. Sterling grew quickly a few years later after the Union Pacific Railroad pushed through to Denver. The **Overland Trail Museum,** just east of town by Interstate 76, is a worthwhile stop. The museum interprets the trail's colorful history and displays artifacts including branding irons, horse-drawn farm machinery, and a stone duplicate of old Fort Sedgewick. The drive ends in Sterling. Continue east from town over the river to exit 125 on I-76.

Comanche Grasslands Scenic Drive

Trinidad to Springfield

3

General description: This 192-mile-long drive explores the Comanche National Grassland and the scenic prairie and mesa country between Trinidad and Springfield.

Special attractions: Comanche National Grassland, Picture Canyon, Carrizo Picnic Ground, Mesa de Maya, short-grass prairie ecosystems, birding, wildlife observation, hiking, camping, mountain biking.

Location: Southeastern Colorado. The drive begins just east of Trinidad and I-25 at the junction of US 350 and US 160, and heads east on US 160 to Springfield. It turns south on US 287/385 to Campo and heads west on a series of gravel county and grassland roads back to Kim and US 160.

Drive route numbers: US 160 and US 287/385; Baca County Roads J, 13, M, 8, P, 3, and Q, and Las Animas County Roads 30.0, 211, 34.0, and 36.0.

Travel season: Year-round. The drive's gravel backroads between Campo and Kim can become impassable after heavy summer thunderstorms and when winter snow melts. Watch for thick mud and slippery roads. Inquire at the Springfield USDA Forest Service office for current road conditions.

Camping: No designated campgrounds are along the drive. Limited camping is permitted, however, at the parking areas at Carrizo Creek and Picture Canyon picnic grounds.

Services: All services are found in Trinidad and Springfield. Limited services are in Kim and Campo.

Nearby attractions: Corazon de Trinidad National Historic District, Trinidad State Park, San Isabel National Forest, Spanish Peaks, Santa Fe Trail, Purgatoire Canyon, El Capulin National Monument (New Mexico), Bent's Old Fort National Historic Site.

The Drive

The undulating plains stretch eastward across southeastern Colorado from the bold, snowy escarpment of the Culebra Range. The swelling land rolls with a lean musculature, lifting into rounded hills and low-browed mesas or breaking into sharp arroyos and sinuous hidden canyons. Out there on the tawny prairie lies the land of the flattened horizon, the land of the rising sun. It's a minimalist landscape. Everything is spare and lean, stripped of its veneer and laid bare under the blazing sun. Brittle grasses huddle in windswept clumps, prickly pear cacti clench together like tightly closed fists, and cottonwoods rustle along intermittent creeks. Under the yawning sprawl of sky and space, the prairie is reduced to simple forms—straight-arrow horizons, roads bordered by three strands of barbed wire that recede into the distance, and flat-topped tablelands, their sloped edges fringed

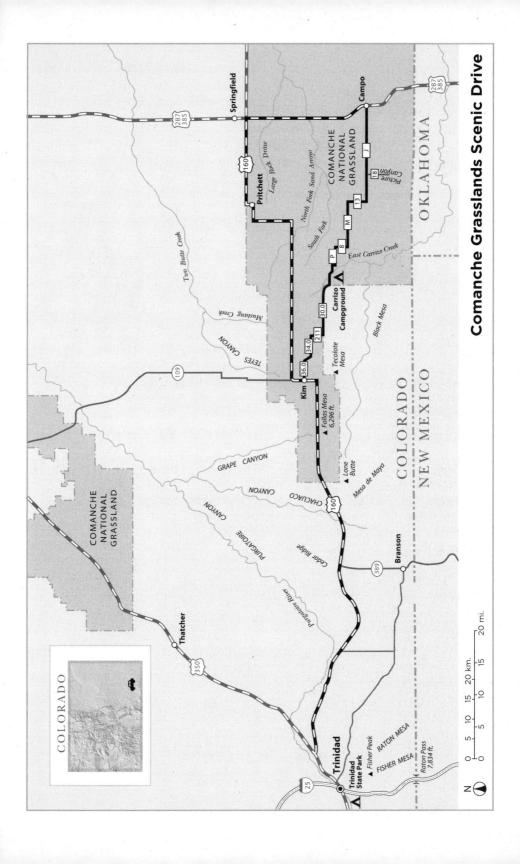

Comanche Grasslands Scenic Drive

in juniper, that bump against the azure sky like worn pillows. The 192-mile-long Comanche Grassland scenic drive explores this remote quarter of Colorado, crossing sun-baked prairie, dipping through shallow canyons, and finding its secret places.

Southeast Colorado is an arid land, with chilly winters and hot summers. Annual precipitation is low, bordering on desert amounts in some areas. The Springfield area receives 15 inches of rain annually. Much of the precipitation comes in intense summer thunderstorms, with the swift runoff flooding down arroyos and canyons. Gravel backroads on the drive during or after thunderstorms can become muddy and impassable. Summers are hot. Expect daily highs in the nineties and above. Autumn and spring are more reasonable times to drive the roads. Temperatures range between sixty and ninety degrees. Wind often tempers spring days. Winters are cool and dry, with occasional heavy snowstorms that quickly melt. High temperatures range from thirty to sixty degrees with cold nights. Use caution when driving the gravel backroads in winter. Blizzard conditions arise during swift-moving storms and melting snow and ice can turn gravel into impassable mud.

The Purgatoire to Comanche National Grassland

The drive begins 5 miles east of Trinidad at Beshoar Junction at the intersection of US 350 and US 160. Turn east on US 160. Springfield, the end of the drive's first leg, lies 114 miles away. The vanished town of Beshoar, named for an early Trinidad resident, sat here along the Colorado and Southern Railroad at the turn of the twentieth century. The paved highway runs east through low hills. Occasional pastures, hayfields, and ranch houses border the blacktop. **Fisher Peak** and **Raton Mesa,** dark with evergreen forest, form a broad escarpment to the south. This long, high mesa, reaching heights of 9,500 feet, is capped by eleven layers of erosion-resistant lava.

After 6 miles the highway swings southeast past the Mooney Hills, a low, rounded mesa etched with arroyos. Three miles later the road sweeps past the hills and across a broad basin seamed with Frijole Creek, an intermittent stream arising on the mesa flank to the south. **Mesa de Maya** huddles darkly on the eastern horizon.

The road winds over Frijole Creek, a tamarisk-lined thread of muddy water in a brown clay arroyo, and parallels the **Purgatoire River** for a few miles. The 150-mile-long Purgatoire River courses across southeastern Colorado from its source high on the crest of the Culebra Range west of Trinidad. The river keeps the French spelling of its name, a reminder of the itinerant fur trappers that traversed this wild country in the nineteenth century. The river's original name—*El Rio de Las Animas Perdidas en Purgatorio* ("River of Lost Souls in Purgatory")—was acquired after the members of a sixteenth-century Spanish expedition, murdered

The lofty Culebra Range towers beyond US 160 and the short-grass prairie near the start of the Comanche Grasslands scenic drive.

by Indians on the river bank, died without the last rites of their Catholic faith. Cowboys later corrupted the Spanish to "Picketwire," a name applied to part of the river's 40-mile-long canyon that slices across the prairie north of the drive. The river twists through low hills, passing occasional cottonwoods on its banks, a half mile north of the highway. After a couple miles the river bends northeast and enters Purgatoire Canyon through abrupt portals of Dakota sandstone. A piñon pine and juniper woodland fills the canyon and spills onto the rim.

The highway ascends a gradual rise onto a broad, barren plain. It dips across Salt Creek's shallow valley at 19 miles, passing black sandstone boulders mirrored in pools of clear water. Trinchera Creek, draining north to the Purgatoire like the other creeks here, lies a couple of miles farther east; it's a deep canyon sharp with cliffs and coated by sparsely spaced junipers. The road climbs northeast onto a high tableland, with expansive views back west to the long ridge of the Culebra Range and the twin Spanish Peaks to the northwest. After crossing Trementina Creek, another canyon filled with cliffs, water, and thick grass, the highway ascends through a juniper forest and reaches its junction with CO 389 at a place dubbed Walt's Corner. A store, surrounded by marvelous views and a few trees, sits at this lonely intersection on a rolling grass plain.

The dark bulk of Mesa de Maya dominates the highway view as it runs east. Cliffs of basalt deposited as lava flows cap the high flat-topped mesa, and a forest of juniper and piñon pine spills over its ragged flanks. No roads traverse this mostly wild upland, the home of mule deer, coyotes, and range cattle. Early Indians inhabited the mesa and the canyons along the drive beginning some 6,000 years ago. Traces of their passage include rock art panels pecked onto smooth rock slabs, projectile points and stone tools, broken pottery shards, and manos used for grinding seeds. Meadows of tall buffalo and grama grass blanketed the mesa top and its shallow valleys more than 100 years ago, attracting cattlemen to its lush pastures in this land of little rain in the 1870s.

The highway runs over undulating plains before dropping into abrupt Chacuaco Canyon. Chacuaco Creek, rising from mesas on the New Mexico state line to the south, excavated this long cliff-lined gorge. Water trickles through the wild canyon almost all year, creating a haven for mammals and birds. The asphalt climbs out of the canyon onto another dry plain and arches northeast around Mesa de Maya. The road dips through several dry, rocky canyons that drain north from the mesa. A ghost village of abandoned stone houses sits on a canyon rim below the mesa, cattle poking through their empty rooms. Distant views unfold west from here. Rows of mountains—the Culebra Range, Spanish Peaks, Raton Mesa, Sierra Blanca, and the Wet Mountains—parade across the horizon, their snowcapped summits gleaming in the sun like whitewashed castles.

Comanche National Grassland

The highway enters the **Comanche National Grassland,** a sprawling spread of more than 440,000 acres managed by the USDA Forest Service and divided into the Timpas Unit south of La Junta (see Drive 1) and the Carrizo Unit along this scenic drive. The story of the national grassland began in 1884 when Baca County's first homestead patent was granted. Thousands of homestead patents in southeast Colorado were issued from 1884 to 1926, with the homesteaders required to plow forty acres of each 160-acre homestead. The homesteader's plow, along with farming marginal agricultural lands and severe overgrazing in this semiarid region, caused the Dust Bowl of the early 1930s here and in neighboring states. The federal government began buying back damaged farms and ranches, retiring the land from cultivation and allowing families to relocate in other areas. More than eleven million acres were acquired and rehabilitated, with four million acres designated as national grassland in 1960 and assigned to the Forest Service. Crumbling stone homesteads, abandoned windmills, and empty crossroads stores are all that remain of Colorado's homestead era on today's Comanche Grassland.

The highway bends straight east after entering the grassland. The ruins of Tobe sit in the field to the north. The town, established in 1910 and named for resident Tobe Benavides, was more of a post office than a town. When the filling station–post office closed its doors in 1960, Tobe folded. The only remnants now are stone foundations scattered among grass and cacti.

The long, low rim of Mesa de Maya looms south of the road as it runs due east across a featureless plain coated with short grasses. Six miles from Tobe the drive passes 6,296-foot-high **Fallas Mesa,** a barren escarpment riddled with ravines. Dalerose Mesa, broken by canyons and cliffs, lies farther south, while broad **Tecolote Mesa** sits to the southeast. The drive turns north at 65 miles and enters Kim a mile later.

An alert jackrabbit prowls the prairie near Picture Canyon in southeastern Colorado's Comanche National Grassland.

Kim to Springfield

Kim, named for Rudyard Kipling's orphan boy hero, was established in 1918 by Olin D. Simpson when he built a general store and post office on the corner of his homestead. The 5,690-foot-high town now serves as a ranching and agricultural center. Frame houses line neat side streets, cattle graze on the edge of town, and a cemetery makes a final resting place. The town offers an RV park, cafe, the Trail's End Bar, gas, and groceries. Picnic tables sit in a roadside park.

The drive continues north along U.S. Highway 160 and swings east after a couple of miles. CO 109 intersects the drive here and continues north to La Junta.

US 160 travels 50 miles from here to Springfield, passing over a mixture of federal and private land. This is flat, dry country, broken by fences and occasional irrigated fields. **Pritchett,** the only real town along this section, sits 36 miles east of Kim. The town rises out of the plain like a mirage, its skyline of trees and house-tops dominated by three towering grain elevators. Boarded-up shops line the main street, a reminder of more prosperous times. The town, established in 1920, marked the western end of an Atchison, Topeka, and Santa Fe Railroad branch. It was named for railway director Dr. Henry Pritchett. The highway goes east from Pritchett past farms and ranches and reaches U.S. Highway 287/385 14 miles later. A roadside picnic area sits at the junction.

Springfield lies a mile to the north, looming as Pritchett does above the endless prairie. Grain elevators again form the highest point for miles around. Elms, maples, and cottonwoods shade the town streets. Springfield, the seat of Baca County, was established in 1887 by the Windsor Town Company and named for town site owner Andrew Harrison's hometown of Springfield, Missouri. The town has since flourished as an agricultural hub. A National Forest Service office, lying just north of the highway intersection, dispenses information and directions to points of interest on the Comanche Grassland.

Springfield to Campo

The journey's next leg runs south 20 miles from Springfield to Campo on US 287/385. The road crosses a high plain divided into farms and ranches. A clutch of houses huddles along the highway in **Campo,** an old farming community aptly named with the Spanish word for "field."

For the drive's last leg, turn west on Baca County Road J at the drugstore in Campo. The road bumps across railroad tracks, passes a grain elevator, and turns to gravel. The drive's last 53 miles follow numerous gravel backroads over the grassland back to Kim and US 160. The dusty road courses west past farms, fields, pastures, cattle, and windmills. Baca County Road 18 intersects County Road J after 10 miles. Turn south for a side trip to **Picture Canyon,** one of southeastern Colorado's hidden treasures.

A dry swale rimmed with sandstone bluffs hides in upper Picture Canyon.

Picture Canyon

Follow County Road 18 south for 5 miles and turn right down a marked lane into upper Picture Canyon. The road winds down the broad canyon and after a couple of miles reaches the road's end. A picnic area with three covered tables spreads along the base of tall sandstone cliffs. A 2.6-mile hiking trail, following an old road, drops down into the canyon. Ragged cliffs, forming abrupt canyon walls, are broken by side ravines and eroded into promontories, buttresses, and arêtes. After 0.5 mile the canyon makes a sharp bend west. Pools of water surrounded by tall grass and cottonwoods spread along the creek bed. A couple of panels of Indian petroglyphs, marred by modern vandalism, sit along the shaded cliff base. The Picture Canyon trail continues north up a side canyon, scales its slope onto a low mesa, and heads west to a spur of Holt Canyon and a natural arch. The trail wends east and drops through Hell's Half Acre back to Picture Canyon. Watch for rattlesnakes in the grass and on the rocky canyon sides when hiking.

Picture Canyon, along with other southeast Colorado canyons, has long attracted settlers. Early Indians found shelter in shallow caves, harvested the area's diverse plants, and hunted game. Indian campsites from the Late Archaic Period (A.D. 1–500) scatter under the canyon's overhanging shelters. Later inhabitants, the Apishapa culture, lived here after A.D. 1000, planting crops on the moist canyon floor and building small villages atop the canyon rims. The rock art that gave the canyon its name probably came from nomadic plains tribes like the Apaches and Comanches.

Clues to one of Colorado archaeology's most puzzling mysteries sit on the canyon's west side south of the bend. Here, etched onto the soft sandstone wall, is a series of vertical lines incised into the rock. Some ancient-language scholars say the lines are Ogam, a type of Celtic writing used as long ago as 2000 B.C. in the British Isles. This strange writing is found at more than fifty sites in southeastern Colorado and the Oklahoma panhandle. Some of the translated writings include compasses, sun dials, traveler's messages and directions, and information about the area's latitude, equinoxes, and planting seasons. One theory holds that Irish monks traveled to Iceland, eastern Canada, and even Mexico over a thousand years ago, lending some credence to the idea that early Celtic wanderers roamed across this area. Most archaeologists, however, are skeptical about the Celtic influence, saying not enough evidence exists to substantiate the theory. And so the Ogam writings remain a tantalizing, unsolved mystery.

Carrizo Mesa to Kim

Head back north to Baca County Road J and continue west on it. The rest of the drive crosses grassland, broken by shallow ravines, windmills, and occasional cottonwood-lined watercourses. After 5 miles turn north on County Road 13 and at 3 miles turn west on Baca County Road M. This runs west 5 miles to Baca County Road 8. At this lonely intersection sits the old Kirkwell Post Office, now used for storage by the Kirkwell Cattle Company. The post office operated from 1917 to 1921. Turn north on County Road 8 and after a couple of miles head west on Baca County Road P. **Carrizo Mesa,** a low-slung tableland rimmed by shattered basalt cliffs, sits to the west. Canyons dark with junipers and piñon pine slice into the mesa, and Potato Butte forms a sharp summit atop the flat mesa. Baca County Road P dead-ends at Baca County Road 3 above Carrizo Creek. Turn north on County Road 3 for 0.5 mile and then west on Baca County Road Q.

County Road Q twists over a low ridge and dips down alongside Carrizo Creek in a wide valley. Rounded hills studded with juniper and cliff bands line the creek. Immense cottonwoods shade the trickle of water. Cottonwoods are the tree of the plains. These tall, broad-trunked trees, growing along creeks, signified water, shade, and firewood to early pioneers and Indians. Indian children made toy tepees with the wide triangular leaves, and the sweet inner bark was used as winter horse feed. Cottonwood bark also had medicinal uses, particularly for upset stomach from bad water—an occupational hazard cowboys called the "gypwater quickstep." Nineteenth-century cattle baron Charles Goodnight, whose empire stretched into southeastern Colorado, called the bark tea "a hell of a drink, a wonderful astringent, and a bitter dose. But it is a sure shot."

The drive wends up along the creek's arroyo and passes a ranch house and barn shaded by huge cottonwood trees. The road bends northwest, edging along below Carrizo Mesa. It becomes a single-lane track for a couple of miles before joining improved Las Animas County Road 30.0. This narrow road rolls west from the mesa over prairie toward Tecolote Mesa. This mesa, also rimmed with cliffs, stretches darkly on the west horizon. County Road 30.0 ends and bends north on Las Animas County Road 211. The drive jogs north and west for 10 miles, following County Road 211 past Pintada Creek's bouldery valley and over broad dry ridges to Kim. The drive ends back on US 160 at Kim's cemetery. A left turn heads 65 miles back to Trinidad and Interstate 25, while a right turn goes to Springfield via US 160 or La Junta on CO 109.

4

Highway of Legends Scenic Byway

Walsenburg to Trinidad

General description: The Highway of Legends Scenic Byway forms a 117-mile-long open loop between Walsenburg and Trinidad on the eastern slope of the Culebra Range.

Special attractions: Lathrop State Park, La Veta, Fort Francisco Museum, Great Dikes of the Spanish Peaks, Spanish Peaks Wilderness Area, Cucharas Pass, Culebra Range, Cordova Pass, Monument Lake, Stonewall, Picketwire Valley, Cokedale National Historic District, Trinidad State Park, Trinidad historic sites, camping, fishing, hiking, scenic views.

Location: South-central Colorado. The drive begins in Walsenburg, off I-25, runs west on US 160 and south on CO 12 to La Veta. The byway continues on CO 12 to Trinidad and I-25. A spur road goes over Cordova Pass to Aguilar.

Drive route name and numbers: Scenic Highway of Legends, US 160, CO 12, Forest Road 415.

Travel season: Year-round.

Camping: Four San Isabel National Forest campgrounds—Cuchara, Blue Lake, Bear Lake, and Purgatoire—lie just off the drive. Lathrop State Park has a 103-site campground, while Trinidad State Park offers a spacious sixty-two-site campground on the lake's north shore. The Monument Lake Campground is owned and operated by the city of Trinidad.

Services: All services are found in Walsenburg, La Veta, and Trinidad. Limited services are in Stonewall and Cuchara.

Nearby attractions: Santa Fe Trail scenic drive (see Drive 1), Wet Mountain Valley, Comanche National Grassland, Capulin National Monument, San Luis Valley, Great Sand Dunes National Park, Wet Mountains scenic drive (see Drive 7), Graneros Gorge.

The Drive

The 117-mile-long Highway of Legends Scenic Byway skirts the wooded eastern flank of the Culebra Range in southern Colorado. The twisting crest of the Culebras imposes a lofty barrier between the sweep of prairie to the east and the San Luis Valley, a broad intermontane basin, to the west. The range, even still untraversed by any roads, is mostly private land, the remaining legacy of sprawling early Spanish land grants. The area's numerous Spanish place-names also linger on the land. Culebra, the Spanish word for "snake," was first applied to a creek on the range's western slope, and later given to the mountain range. The scenic drive, beginning in Walsenburg, ascends the fertile Cuchara Valley to the 9,941-foot summit of Cucharas Pass before dropping south through forests and meadows on

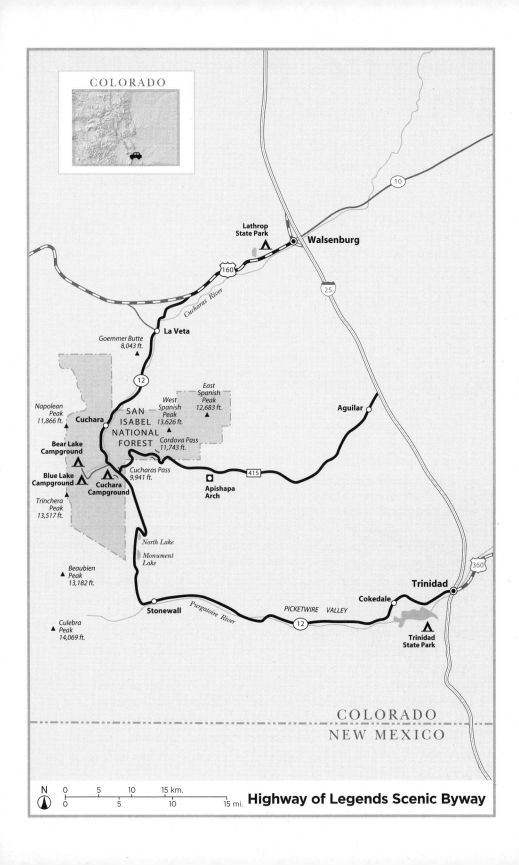

COLORADO

10

Lathrop
State Park
Walsenburg

160

25

Cucharas River

La Veta

*Goemmer Butte
8,043 ft.*

12

*East
Spanish
Peak
12,683 ft.*

*Napolean
Peak
11,866 ft.*

Cuchara

SAN
ISABEL
NATIONAL
FOREST

*West
Spanish
Peak
13,626 ft.*

Aguilar

**Bear Lake
Campground**

*Cordova Pass
11,743 ft.*

**Blue Lake
Campground**

**Cuchara
Campground**

*Cucharas Pass
9,941 ft.*

415

**Apishapa
Arch**

*Trinchera
Peak
13,517 ft.*

North Lake

*Monument
Lake*

*Beaubien
Peak
13,182 ft.*

360

*Culebra
Peak
14,069 ft.*

Trinidad

Cokedale

Stonewall

Purgatoire River

PICKETWIRE VALLEY

12

**Trinidad
State Park**

COLORADO
NEW MEXICO

N

0   5   10   15 km.
0   5   10   15 mi.

Highway of Legends Scenic Byway

the range flank to the Purgatoire River's broad valley west of Trinidad. A spur segment of the drive travels over Cordova Pass to Aguilar.

The highway is open year-round, with each season lending a distinctive flavor to the drive experience. Summers are pleasant, with high temperatures ranging from seventy to ninety degrees along the drive. Afternoon thunderstorms regularly build above the mountains, dousing the road with heavy rain and hail. September and October, the autumn months, bring warm days and cool nights. Expect golden aspen groves in late September and occasional rain showers through October. Temperatures can be hot on the drive's lower elevations. Winter days are chilly, with highs in the thirties and forties. Snow falls heavily in the upper Cuchara valley and on the pass. The lesser amounts in the low valleys quickly melt under the warm winter sun. Spring begins in April with warming days and melting snow. Look for breezy afternoons and rain or sleet storms.

Walsenburg and Lathrop State Park

The Highway of Legends, a national forest scenic byway, begins in **Walsenburg** just off Interstate 25. The town is nestled in the Cucharas River's broad valley amid dusty, piñon pine–covered hills. Walsenburg began in 1859 as an early Mexican hamlet, named *La Plaza de los Leones* ("Square of the Lions") for prominent early settler Don Miguel Antonio Leon. When the pueblo incorporated in 1873, citizens renamed it for local shopkeeper Fred Walsen. After the Denver & Rio Grande Railroad pushed through in 1876, Walsenburg boomed as one of Colorado's largest coal producers. The remains of over fifty mines still litter the area. Town points of interest include the historic Huerfano County Courthouse, built with limestone blocks in 1904, and the nearby **Walsenburg Mining Museum,** with exhibits detailing the coal miner's life and the replica of a mine shaft.

The drive begins in downtown Walsenburg. Head west on U.S. Highway 160, the Navajo Trail. After passing houses, and the town park and swimming pool, the highway swings past slag heaps and abandoned mining ruins. The road crosses the Cucharas River, climbs a steep hill, and after 3 miles reaches **Lathrop State Park.** This small state park, with 1,594 land acres and 320 water acres in Martin and Horseshoe Lakes, offers 103 sites in Piñon and Yucca Campgrounds, picnic facilities, a nine-hole golf course leased to Walsenburg, boating, swimming, and fishing. The lakes yield trout, crappie, bass, channel catfish, and perch to anglers. A hiking trail loops north from Martin Lake for almost 2 miles, climbing onto a scrubby volcanic hogback. Gnarled junipers spring from the bedrock amid barrel cacti, yucca, and rabbitbrush. Distant views unfold along the ridgeline—Pikes Peak, almost 100 miles to the north, lifts its broad shoulders beyond the Wet Mountains; the barren prairie sweeps eastward to a Kansas horizon; and to the south loom the Spanish Peaks.

Boaters paddle across Horseshoe Lake at Lathrop State Park west of Walsenburg along the Highway of Legends.

The highway runs west from Lathrop along the northern edge of the broad Cuchara valley. Low hills, coated with a pygmy forest of piñon pine and juniper, flank the road on the north, while the wide valley stretches south to forested foot-hills below the Spanish Peaks. Open rangelands, broken only by fence lines and a twisting grove of cottonwoods along the river banks, fill the valley floor. Perennial blue grama and needle-and-thread grasses sod the spacious pastures, while shrubby saltbush, snakeweed, and rabbitbrush cover the drier slopes. A small roadside Cath-olic shrine, with a statue of the Virgin Mary and many votive candles, is tucked into a sandstone alcove at 6 miles. The drive turns southwest onto CO 12 a few miles farther west. US 160 continues west over La Veta Pass to the San Luis Valley.

The Spanish Peaks and La Veta

CO 12 follows an undulating, grassy bench sprinkled with ranches and grazing cattle above the Cucharas River. **The Spanish Peaks** continue to dominate the southern skyline. The Spanish Peaks, designated as a National Natural Landmark, are preserved in a 17,855-acre wilderness area. The higher west peak reaches 13,626 feet, while the east peak is 12,683 feet.

These jutting twin peaks were conspicuous landmarks to travelers on the great plains. Early explorers often confused the Spanish Peaks with Pikes Peak far to the north. Jacob Fowler noted them in 1821: "We Head a full view of the mountains, this must be the place Whare Pike first discovered the mountains Heare I took the bareing of two that ware the Highest." Indians, Spaniards, French trappers, and Santa Fe Trail traders called them a host of names—Pikes Peak, Las Cumbres Espanoles, Las Dos Hermanas, The Two Sisters, Les Tetons, Les Mamelles, and Wahatoyeh or Huajatolla. *Wahatoyeh,* a Pueblo Indian word still used, loosely translates as "Breasts of the World."

The wild Spanish Peaks host an improbable fable of a lost gold mine. The legend originates with Coronado's 1541 trek across southeastern Colorado in search of mythical Quivara. Three priests were left behind to convert the natives, and two died at their hands as martyrs. The third, Fray Juan de la Cruz, journeyed to Huajatolla after hearing of wealthy Indian mines there. According to the legend, he found the gold, enslaved Indians to remove it from the hidden passages, and journeyed south to Mexico with gold-laden mules. The priest and his treasure, however, disappeared, never to be seen again. Persistent rumors of the lost Spanish gold echoed across southern Colorado for the next three centuries, but no trace of the gold or the fabulous mine was ever uncovered. Indeed, no geologic evidence suggests that the Spanish Peaks or their immediate neighbors ever yielded any precious metals.

After 4 miles the blacktop drops down to the river bottomlands and a mile later enters the town of **La Veta.** This lovely village spreads among ranch land at the feet of the Spanish Peaks. The town was originally established as a trading post and fort by Colonel John Francisco and Henry Daigre in 1862. A post office opened at the site, known as Francisco Plaza, in 1871, and when the Denver & Rio Grande Railroad came through in 1876 the town of La Veta arose. The name means "the vein" in Spanish and probably refers to the numerous volcanic dikes slicing across the Spanish Peaks.

The Fort Francisco Museum, operated by the Huerfano County Historical Society at the original site, makes an informative stop in downtown La Veta. The museum displays coal mining equipment, an old saloon, a barbershop with poker-playing dummies, a medical office, a blacksmith shop, and an excellent collection of historical documents and letters, including an 1853 letter by practicing attorney Abraham Lincoln and Kit Carson's will. La Veta offers a variety of visitor accommodations and a couple of restaurants.

La Veta to Cuchara

The drive leaves La Veta on the south and runs along the Cucharas River. Goemmer Butte, an 8,043-foot-high volcanic plug or conduit of a long-extinct volcano, rears to the west. Its cliffed summit rises 500 feet above the valley floor. The road descends into the grassy valley, crosses the river at Three Bridges, and swings southwest below scrub oak–covered slopes. Six miles from La Veta the highway passes under **Devil's Stairsteps,** an abrupt volcanic rock dike that stair-steps south from the highway. This dike, as well as prominent Profile Rock to the east and other rock walls, is part of the Spanish Peaks' great dike system. The buff-colored igneous rock dikes formed, along with the Spanish Peaks, some thirty-five million years ago. During that period of geologic unrest when the Rocky Mountains began to rise, two blisters of molten rock pushed their way upward, buckling the sedimentary surface layers. As the strata bulged, long cracks radiated out from the molten blisters like spokes on a bicycle wheel. Liquid magma filled the cracks before the entire mass slowly cooled into classic volcanic rocks like the granite and granodorite that compose the Spanish Peaks. Erosion later attacked the old sedimentary layers and exposed the harder, more erosion-resistant igneous rocks, leaving the page of geologic history seen today. More than 400 separate dikes fan out from the peaks, with the longest stretching 14 miles. The dikes range up to 100 feet high and vary in width from 1 foot to 100 feet.

As the highway runs southwest, the valley slowly narrows with high ridges looming overhead. The snowcapped **Culebra Range** towers to the west. After a few miles the road passes through a gap cut through the Dakota Wall, a sandstone hogback that stretches along the Front Range from Wyoming to New Mexico. The highway roughly follows the hogback from here to Stonewall. New Mexican locust trees, Colorado's only native locust, line the asphalt and offer colorful pink blossoms in early summer. The road enters San Isabel National Forest and a couple of miles later rolls into 8,650-foot high Cuchara.

Cuchara and Cucharas Pass

Cuchara, established in 1916, is something of a ghost town today. The village sits near the head of a spectacular valley, surrounded by thick forests of spruce, pine, and fir. This spoon-shaped valley gave the name Cuchara ("spoon" in Spanish) to the town, river, and valley. Cuchara thrived in the 1980s until the savings-and-loan scandal, and the local ski resort closed. Much of the town folded up with the resort, leaving only a few cafes and lodges. Vacation cabins are sprinkled throughout the valley around Cuchara. Spring Creek Picnic Area lies on the south side of Cuchara.

The drive steadily climbs the valley south of Cuchara and after a couple of miles reaches Forest Road 413. This short dirt road climbs west along the Cucharas River to a pair of forest-lined lakes cupped in a basin beneath the Culebra Range crest. Cuchara Campground sits a quarter-mile up the road, and fifteen-site Blue Lake and fourteen-site Bear Lake Campgrounds lie at road's end beside their respective lakes. An excellent 2-mile trail climbs south from the spruce and fir forest at 10,500-foot Blue Lake to the alpine tundra atop the rounded summit of 13,517-foot Trinchera Peak.

The highway twists up steep, aspen-blanketed slopes above the South Fork of the Cucharas River and reaches 9,941-foot **Cucharas Pass.** The dense forest along this drive section yields a great example of plant succession. The thick transitional aspen woodland is slowly being replaced by a climax spruce-fir forest. Autumn is gorgeous along here, with dark spruce sprinkled among golden groves of quaking aspen. Meadows, ringed by dark woods, surround the highway and a stock corral on the broad pass summit. Henry Daigre, one of La Veta's founders, built a road from La Veta to Stonewall along an old Indian path in 1865. Today's highway follows his old track over the pass, but it wasn't paved until the 1960s.

The Cordova Pass Segment

A 35-mile-long arm of the Highway of Legends runs east from the top of Cucharas Pass to **Cordova Pass,** and then down to I-25 at Aguilar. This road segment, added to the scenic byway in 2002, is a welcome addition to the Highway of Legends as an alternate route with different views and beauty than the main scenic drive. To drive this route, head east from Cucharas Pass on Forest Road 415. The unpaved road climbs 6 miles to the summit of 11,743-foot Cordova Pass. A picnic area with restrooms is located here, along with some short, easy-going trails that explore the subalpine environment. A longer trail leaves the parking area and meanders through grassy meadows and woods of lodgepole pine and Engelmann spruce on a ridge to a timberline lookout below West Spanish Peak. Intrepid hikers can continue up the steep west ridge another mile to the peak's 13,626-foot summit and its grandiose view of mountain and prairie.

Cordova Pass was named for Jose de Jesus Cordova, a prominent southern Colorado citizen in the early twentieth century. Cordova, a three-term Las Animas County commissioner, pushed for funding to build a road between Cuchara and Aguilar. It was finally approved in 1928 and was finished in 1934 by the Works Progress Administration and the Civilian Conservation Corps. Cordova died in 1929 and didn't see the road completed, although it was dedicated to his memory.

From the summit you can either return to the main scenic highway or continue east to I-25. This winding road runs another 29 miles along the Apishapa River. One of its best features is **Apishapa Arch,** an immense stone archway spanning the road that was blasted through one of the volcanic dikes that radiates from the Spanish Peaks. The lower road section twists past ranches along the willow and cottonwood-lined river. It's especially pretty in early October when the golden leaves color the stream corridor.

Cuchara to Stonewall

CO 12 runs south from the pass along the Culebra Range's eastern flank, traversing rolling hills and dipping through shallow valleys. A variety of ecosystems cover the hillsides, with mixed fir and spruce forest blanketing the moist, north-facing slopes and ponderosa and limber pines and Gambel oak covering the drier, south-facing hills. Open aspen-lined meadows break the woodland mosaic. The road horseshoes around **North Lake,** a state wildlife area and reservoir, 7 miles from the pass. Peaks of the Culebra Range—13,488-foot Cuatro Peak, 13,406-foot Mariquita Peak, and 13,350-foot De Anza Peak—lift snowy ridges to the west. The Dakota Hogback forms an abrupt wall above the lake and highway. North Lake, with a boat ramp at its north end, offers fishing and boating.

Just past the lake, Forest Road 411 heads 4.5 miles west up the North Fork of the **Purgatoire River** to twenty-three-site Purgatoire Campground. This pleasant camping area is tucked into a valley filled with spruce, corkbark fir, and quaking aspen at the foot of the Culebras. **Monument Lake** lies in a shallow valley a mile farther south. A turn at the southern end of the narrow, mile-long reservoir leads to Monument Lake Campground, operated by the city of Trinidad. This popular recreation area offers camping, an adobe lodge, a restaurant, trout fishing, boating, and hiking. The drive continues south, crossing Whiskey and Romain Creeks before dropping down Wilkins Creek to **Stonewall** and the upper Purgatoire River canyon.

Stonewall, at 7,460 feet, is a quiet ranching and vacation village settled in 1867 by early rancher Juan Guitterez. The town is named for an immense stone wall of Dakota sandstone. This tilted hogback, part of the Dakota Hogback seen near La Veta, was deposited along ancient beaches some seventy million years ago during the Cretaceous period. The formation, widespread over much of Colorado, was later uplifted during the rise of the Rocky Mountains. **Culebra Peak,** the range high point at 14,069 feet, forms Stonewall's western skyline. CO 12, upon entering Stonewall, swings past a cliff and passes through a gap that breaches the sandstone escarpment.

Picketwire Valley to Trinidad

The drive turns east at Stonewall and enters Stonewall Valley and then **Picketwire Valley,** a broad swale carved by the Purgatoire River. The name "Picketwire" is a bastardized version of the river's French name, Purgatoire. The Spanish first named the muddy river *El Rio de las Animas Perdidas en Purgatorio,* or "River of the Lost Souls in Purgatory." The 150-mile-long Purgatoire, originating on the Culebra divide west of Stonewall, twists east and northeast onto the prairie before merging with the Arkansas River near Las Animas.

The drive's 30-mile leg from Stonewall to Trinidad crosses dusty plateau country. Low rock-rimmed mesas, creased with shallow canyons and dry arroyos, loom above the valley.

Culebra Peak, the high point of the Culebra Range, looms above the Highway of Legends and cottonwoods in Stonewall Valley.

The drive passes through a succession of old Hispanic villages and home-steads. Vigil Plaza lies 5 miles east of Stonewall. Weston, first called Los Sisneros, started as an 1880s ranch and was later renamed for pioneer farmer Sam Weston. An adobe structure on the town's east side is part of the original Sisneros Ranch. Farther east are the ruins of Cordova, Medina, and Valasquez plazas and San Juan, all old family communities. Segundo, a mostly abandoned town of old stone buildings and low-slung adobe houses, sits along the river. Valdez sits a mile east. It headquartered the Frederick Mine, which, with over 30 miles of tunnels, was one of Colorado's largest underground mines until it closed in 1960. Huge piles of red mine tailings are heaped alongside the road.

A few miles east of Valdez, the highway turns north from Picketwire Valley and climbs through low hills to Reilly Canyon and **Cokedale National Historic District.** Cokedale, spread over hillsides amid colored tailings, was established in

1906 as a company town by the Carbon Coal and Coke Company. Numerous historic homes and buildings are scattered throughout the hamlet, and lines of coke ovens lie south of the highway. Coke, a refined form of coal that burns hotter, was shipped from the town ovens to Leadville and other smelters.

The drive climbs through low hills and drops past **Trinidad State Park.** The park's centerpiece is a 900-acre, 3-mile-long reservoir built for irrigation and flood control. Archaeological sites include a tepee ring, a circle of stones that once surrounded a nomad's tent, at Carpios Ridge Picnic Area. Forty-eight archaeological sites lie beneath the lake and on surrounding ridges, while six mining towns lie submerged under the lake's green waters. The reservoir offers great fishing, as well as boating, water-skiing, board-sailing, and camping.

Trinidad, the drive's end, is 3 miles east of the reservoir. The highway drops back into the Purgatoire's valley and passes through Jansen, a town that was the eastern terminus of the Colorado & Wyoming Railroad during the area's mining heyday. Trinidad, one of Colorado's oldest and most historic communities, sits at the foot of Raton Pass. The town sprang up as a stop on the Mountain Branch of the old Santa Fe Trail. Wagon trains could rest here before climbing over the steep, rough pass into New Mexico. Gabriel Gutierrez, the town's first settler, built a cabin on the river's south bank in 1859. The town later flourished as a ranching and transportation center fueled by years of prosperous coal mining. The town, protected as **El Corazon del Trinidad National Historic District,** boasts several excellent historic sites, including the Baca and Bloom houses and Sante Fe Trail Museum. Trinidad offers all visitor services and is the gateway to the Comanche National Grassland to the east (see Drive 3).

5

Sangre de Cristo Scenic Drive

Texas Creek to Walsenburg

General description: This 86-mile-long highway runs south along Texas Creek from the Arkansas River into the Wet Mountain Valley and the historic town of Westcliffe. The drive, bordering the rugged Sangre de Cristo Mountains, continues south into the broad sagebrush-covered Huerfano River valley before ending at Walsenburg.

Special attractions: Arkansas River, McIntyre Hills Wilderness Study Area, Wet Mountain Valley, Westcliffe, Silver Cliff, Sangre de Cristo Mountains, ghost towns, Huerfano River valley, Walsenburg, scenic views, fishing, hiking, wildlife.

Location: South-central Colorado. The drive on CO 69 runs from US 50 and the Arkansas River 26 miles west of Cañon City southeast to Walsenburg and I-25.

Drive route number: CO 69.

Travel season: Year-round. Severe winter storms and blizzards can temporarily close the highway. It's advisable to carry chains and a shovel if the weather is threatening.

Camping: No public campgrounds lie along the highway itself. Numerous campgrounds are found in the surrounding San Isabel National Forest, including Lake Creek Campground west of Hillside and Alvarado Campground southwest of Westcliffe. Other forest campgrounds are found in the Wet Mountains. Public camping is at Lake de Weese and primitive camp areas are found in the national forest.

Services: All services are found in Westcliffe and Walsenburg. Limited services in Texas Creek, Hillside, and Gardner.

Nearby attractions: South Colony Lakes, Crestone Peak and Needle, Hermit Pass, Arkansas Headwaters State Recreation Area, Grape Creek Wilderness Study Area, Cañon City, Temple Canon, Hardscrabble Pass, Marble Cave, Sierra Blanca, Medano Pass, Highway of Legends Scenic Byway, Great Sand Dunes National Park.

The Drive

CO 69 rolls down the broad Wet Mountain and Huerfano River valleys for 86 miles from the Arkansas River to Walsenburg on the western rim of the Great Plains. The excellent route, flanked by the lofty Sangre de Cristo Mountains on the west and the swelling Wet Mountains on the east, travels an unpopulated land rich in spectacular views, lush with verdant grasslands and pastures, and alive with early Spanish and mining history. The highway is a friendly backroad, used mostly by locals who salute oncoming traffic with a wave.

The Sangre de Cristo Mountains, one of the longest ranges in the Rocky Mountains, stretches over 150 miles from Salida to Santa Fe in New Mexico. The

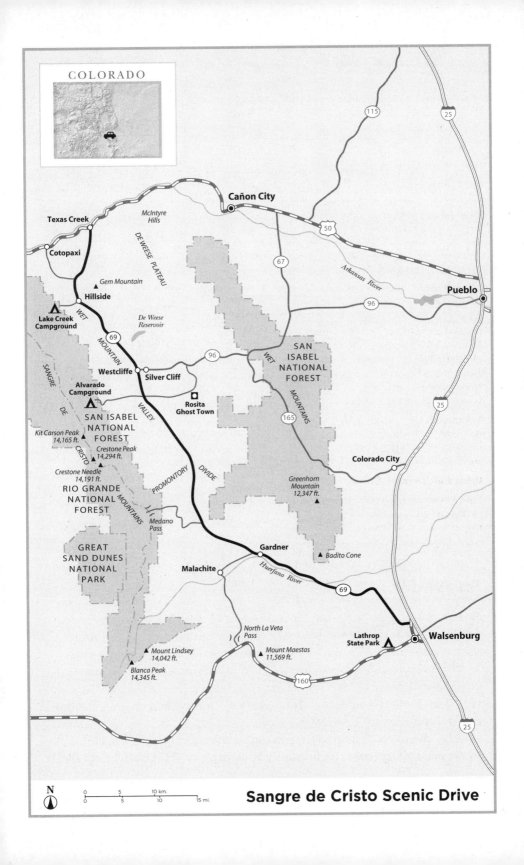

COLORADO

Cañon City

Texas Creek

McIntyre
Hills

Cotopaxi

DE WEESE PLATEAU

Gem Mountain

Hillside

Lake Creek
Campground

*De Weese
Reservoir*

WET MOUNTAIN

Arkansas River

Pueblo

50

67

96

96

69

Westcliffe   Silver Cliff

SAN
ISABEL
NATIONAL
FOREST

WET MOUNTAINS

Alvarado
Campground

SANGRE DE CRISTO MOUNTAINS

Rosita
Ghost Town

VALLEY

165

25

*Kit Carson Peak
14,165 ft.*

SAN ISABEL
NATIONAL
FOREST

*Crestone Peak
14,294 ft.*

*Crestone Needle
14,191 ft.*

RIO GRANDE
NATIONAL
FOREST

PROMONTORY DIVIDE

Colorado City

*Greenhorn
Mountain
12,347 ft.*

*Medano
Pass*

GREAT
SAND
DUNES
NATIONAL
PARK

Gardner

Badito Cone

Malachite

Huerfano River

69

*North La Veta
Pass*

Lathrop
State Park

Walsenburg

*Mount Lindsey
14,042 ft.*

*Mount Maestas
11,569 ft.*

*Blanca Peak
14,345 ft.*

160

25

N

0   5   10 km.
0   5   10   15 mi.

Sangre de Cristo Scenic Drive

sierra's midsection in southern Colorado is called the Culebra Range. Above the scenic drive and the Wet Mountain Valley, the Sangre de Cristos form an awesome escarpment of sawtoothed peaks that soar into the azure sky. Four 14,000-foot peaks—Crestone Needle, Crestone Peak, Humboldt Peak, and Kit Carson Peak—cluster along the skyline southwest of Westcliffe. Sierra Blanca, an abrupt massif containing another four "fourteeners," sits farther south. Although the Sangres are only 20 miles wide, no highways cross their rugged crests. The few passable gaps, including Medano, Mosca, and Hermit Passes, have been well-traveled routes for centuries. The range supposedly received its Spanish name *Sangre de Cristo,* or "Blood of Christ," from the Spanish explorer Valverde, who upon sighting the peaks bathed in morning alpenglow fervently exclaimed, "Sangre de Cristo." Most of the range is protected in the 226,455-acre Sangre de Cristo Wilderness Area. This area, the third largest in Colorado, was established in 1993.

Summer and fall are ideal times to drive the route. Summer days are warm, with temperatures ranging from ninety degrees near Walsenburg to the seventies at Westcliffe. Heavy thunderstorms regularly build up over the mountains and douse the valleys on summer afternoons. September and October bring a succession of clear, crisp days. Warm temperatures are occasionally broken by rain and low clouds. Winters are long and cold, with snow lasting from November to April. Expect chilly temperatures and wind. Bad road conditions, including ice and whiteouts, occur during severe winter storms. The highway is a glorious drive after a winter storm. The sun glimmers in the clear sky, fresh snow blankets the valley floor, and wind sweeps gossamers of snow off the high mountain ridges. Spring is cool and breezy. Daily high temperatures range from thirty to sixty degrees, and unsettled weather brings frequent storms.

Texas Creek

The drive begins 26 miles west of Cañon City at Texas Creek, the junction of U.S. Highway 50 and CO 69. Turn south on CO 69. The highway climbs south alongside Texas Creek in a steep-walled canyon broken by jumbled boulders and a scattered piñon pine and juniper woodland. The abandoned railbed of the Westcliffe Branch of the Denver & Rio Grande Railroad parallels the highway in the canyon. The line, built in 1900, served Westcliffe and its prospering ranches. A previous narrow gauge line that hauled silver ore down Grape Creek was torn up by the Denver & Rio Grande in 1890 after a series of disasters and a downturn in the area's silver boom.

The road steadily climbs up the canyon, passing placid beaver dams. The first view of the Sangre de Cristo Range is 2 miles up the drive. The rough **McIntyre Hills** rise east of the highway, forming a rugged maze of deep canyons and sharp peaks. This remote region, traversed only by a few trails, was studied for possible wilderness designation by the Bureau of Land Management but finally rejected. The hills offer excellent hiking adventures with abrupt stair-stepped canyons and plentiful wildlife including mule deer, bighorn sheep, and mountain lion.

By 6 miles, ponderosa pine begin mixing in the piñon forest, lifting their rounded crowns above the low piñons. A mile later the highway climbs away from the creek onto the northern **Wet Mountain Valley,** a high sagebrush plain dotted with ponderosa and piñon pines below the looming mountain escarpment. At 10 miles the drive reaches green pastures filled with grazing cattle and wide hay fields.

The Wet Mountain Valley

The Wet Mountain Valley, considered one of Colorado's prime ranch lands, flanks the Sangre de Cristos for over 30 miles from here to Promontory Divide. The broad valley, reaching 15 miles in width, is drained by Grape and Texas Creeks. The valley is rich in history. The Ute Indians frequented the valley, drawn by plentiful game and a salubrious summer climate. One early prospector remembered that "many a howling war dance has disturbed the midnight air of this pleasant valley." Spanish explorers and miners scouted the region, leaving legends of mysterious lost gold mines and treasure troves hidden in mountain caverns. In 1806 Lieutenant Zebulon Pike, on his quest to explore the southern Louisiana Purchase, traversed the valley en route to the Rio Grande and his capture by the Spanish. The first Anglo settlers were a group of 397 German immigrants who colonized the valley on a communal basis. These farmers and artisans failed due to inexperience at irrigation and at high-altitude farming. Most left for Denver and Pueblo, but those who hung on to their land eventually prospered. Descendants of these early immigrants still live and ranch in the valley.

After entering the northern Wet Mountain Valley, the highway passes Hillside, now a one-store town with gas and a post office, and swings back along Texas Creek on the valley's east edge. Just past **Hillside,** County Road 198 climbs west to eleven-site Lake Creek Campground in **San Isabel National Forest.** The drive continues south through a shallow canyon lined with volcanic cliff bands and ranches. Dense willow thickets border the tumbling creek, and pines coat low surrounding hills. After 5 miles the highway emerges onto the valley floor. A spectacular panorama opens to the south—the Wet Mountains rim the valley on the southeast; the landmark Spanish Peaks poke their snowy heads above the southern horizon; and the Sangre de Cristo Mountains march across the western skyline. The high peaks of the southern Sawatch Range on the Continental Divide glimmer to the north. The highway runs past 8,549-foot Beckwith Mountain, an abrupt hogback broken by cliffs east of the asphalt, and after a few miles crosses meandering Grape Creek, the valley's main drainage. Westcliffe, at 7,888 feet, sits 3 miles south on a rounded bluff above the creek.

The snowcapped Sangre de Cristo Mountains tower beyond a ranch and grazing cattle in the northern Wet Mountain Valley.

Westcliffe and Rosita

Westcliffe was founded in 1885 by local landowner Dr. J. W. Bell, who named the picturesque community for Westcliffe-on-the-Sea, his English birthplace. The town, seat of Custer County, has long outlived its neighbors Silver Cliff, Querida, and Rosita. All three were mining boom towns in the late nineteenth century. Westcliffe, however, grew and thrived as a supply center for area ranchers and as a railhead. After the great Silver Crash of 1893, Westcliffe still prospered while its neighbors faded away. The Denver & Rio Grande Railroad came to town in 1900 but was abandoned in 1937. Westcliffe today is the county's center of commerce and offers all services to travelers.

CO 69 runs south from Westcliffe past verdant ranches. After 3 miles the highway intersects Schoolfield Road. A turn west leads 6 miles straight across the valley into the Sangre de Cristo Mountains and forty-seven-site Alvarado Campground. This 9,000-foot-high campground makes a cool summer base camp for exploring the valley and mountains. Trails lead west up forested valleys to alpine lakes and high peaks.

A turn east heads to the ghost town of **Rosita,** nestled among summer cabins and ranchettes in the scrubby hills east of the valley. Silver was found here in 1870; by 1872, when rich claims that yielded as much as 145 ounces of silver to the ton were found, the silver rush was on. Rosita, along with nearby Querida and Silver Cliff, arose around rich mines and lived and died by their earthen fortunes.

Rosita epitomizes the boom and bust mining cycle. Founded after a rich find in the winter of 1872–1873, Rosita quickly became one of the Colorado Territory's largest towns. Rosita swelled with miners who dug the ore and teamsters who hauled the silver through deep canyons to Pueblo and the nearest railhead. By 1875 the town boasted a population of 1,500, a two-story school, Townsend's Brewery, three churches, a bank, the Pennsylvania Reduction Works for ore milling, a newspaper, a post office, hotels, as well as doctor and real estate offices. The mines began a slow decline in 1876, and Rosita was usurped by a new boom town, Querida, a few miles north. The decline furthered in 1878 when horn silver was discovered in Silver Cliff. Much of Rosita was destroyed in an 1881 fire and never recovered. The town lingered on as a well-preserved ghost of its former self well into the 1960s, when the post office was finally closed down. Rosita, used as a film set for a few movies, including *Saddle the Wind, Cat Ballou,* and *Continental Divide,* is now a forgotten, windswept corner of Colorado's colorful history. Only a few crumbling buildings remain of this faded rose along the dusty backroad. The Rosita Cemetery tells the poignant story of the town's rise and fall.

Sangre de Cristo Mountains

The 17-mile-long highway section through the upper Wet Mountain Valley from Westcliffe to the crest of the Promontory Divide is simply spectacular. The broad valley, criss-crossed by arrow-straight side roads, is divided by barbed-wire fences into ranches dotted with grazing cattle. The Sangre de Cristo range pierces the western skyline, its abrupt escarpment of ragged peaks broken by plunging glacier-carved cirques and thickly wooded canyons. Four 14,000-foot peaks dominate the range here—14,294-foot Crestone Peak, 14,191-foot Crestone Needle, 14,165-foot Kit Carson Peak, and 14,064-foot Humboldt Peak. The Crestone peaks, named for their resemblance to a cock's comb, were the last of Colorado's fifty-four "fourteeners" to be ascended, when Albert Ellingwood and Eleanor Davis climbed them in 1916. Kit Carson Peak is named for the famed western scout and Humboldt Peak for Alexander von Humboldt, a renowned nineteenth-century geographer. The peaks are usually approached from the Wet Mountain Valley via South Colony

Road and Forest Road 313 up South Colony Creek. Uplifted 270-million-year-old Paleozoic sediments including sandstone, shale, conglomerate, and limestone compose the bulk of the range, although ancient granite forms the Sierra Blanca section.

The Sangre de Cristo Mountains, besides being an enclave of wildlife and wilderness, are rife with legends. One of the best concerns **Marble Cave,** called by the Spanish *El Caverna del Oro* or "The Cavern of Gold," a deep cave high above the timberline on the windswept flanks of Marble Mountain south of the Crestones. Myth relates that Spanish conquistadores used the cave as a stash for ill-gotten gold mined by Indian slaves. An old Maltese cross painted on a rock wall marks the cave's entrance. The cave makes an unpleasant exploration, reaching a depth of 300 feet including a vertical 80-foot pit, a year-round average temperature of thirty-four degrees, 95 percent humidity, and snowdrifts that reach far into the cave. The first explorers in 1929 found a crude ladder and hand-forged hammer thought to be at least 200 years old. The gold, if it was there at all, vanished long before.

CO 69 runs south on gravel benches above meandering Grape Creek and gently climbs toward 8,500-foot Promontory Divide, a low ridge that separates the Wet Mountain Valley from the Huerfano River drainage. As the road climbs the surrounding country dries, with sagebrush hills replacing the fertile valley floor. Wild country stretches in every direction from atop the divide. The highway drops south from the divide along Muddy Creek, a shallow trickle lined with willows and cottonwoods in a shallow valley. Piñon pine–covered hills flank the valley. Eight miles from the divide summit the drive passes Medano Road, a four-wheel-drive track that climbs over 9,950-foot Medano Pass and drops down to the Great Sand Dunes and the San Luis Valley. Past the turn the highway bends southeast down Muddy Creek's broad valley. The creek meanders through deep flash flood–carved arroyos on the valley floor. Low mesas studded with piñon pine and juniper flank the drive.

Gardner to Walsenburg

At 59 miles the highway reaches **Gardner,** an old southwestern settlement perched at the confluence of Muddy Creek and the Huerfano River. The town, named for pioneer farmer Herbert Gardner, retains a frontier spirit with old adobe houses shaded by towering cottonwoods. A spur road, County Road 550, heads southwest up the river through Malachite and Redwing and climbs up a four-wheel-drive trail to the San Isabel National Forest boundary and 14,345-foot Blanca Peak. Another side road ascends to the summit of 9,750-foot Mosca Pass. An old Ute Indian trail drops west to the Great Sand Dunes.

Gardner Butte, a rough volcanic plug broken by cliff bands, looms just east of Gardner. The Wet Mountains, topped by 12,347-foot Greenhorn Mountain, tower to the north. Long outwash plains, cloaked with sagebrush and piñon, sweep up to the

CO 69 crosses the broad Huerfano Valley beneath the wintry escarpment of the Sangre de Cristo Mountains.

range's steep forested slopes. Greenhorn Mountain is named for a Comanche chief killed in a violent battle between the Comanches and the Spanish in 1779. The mountain's southern flank is a wilderness area of remote, rugged canyons and ridges.

The drive follows benches above the Huerfano River, passing through the old Mexican town of Farista. The town, originally called Fort Talpa, was established in 1820. A few miles east the highway runs through the abandoned town Badito at the far southern edge of the Wet Mountains. The range terminus is topped by distinctive Badito Cone, a volcanic vent. The road twists through a narrow gap carved through uplifted sandstone layers by the muddy Huerfano River below the cone. The old Taos Trail, a path used by American traders and Spanish soldiers, cuts through Badito en route to Sangre de Cristo Pass and Taos. A Spanish fort was built a few miles south of here in 1819 to protect the pass from American invasion. Past the gap the highway climbs away from the river and onto the edge of the treeless Great Plains. The drive's last 15 miles roll across short-grass prairie, over piñon-dotted mesas, and past an old bituminous coal mine. The drive drops down to I-25 just north of Walsenburg.

6

Los Caminos Antiguos Scenic Byway

Alamosa to Cumbres Pass

General description: This 152-mile-long scenic byway traverses the San Luis Valley between Alamosa and Cumbres Pass. The drive passes historic sites, the Rio Grande, the Great Sand Dunes, desert hills, valley farms, and aspen forests.

Special attractions: Alamosa, Great Sand Dunes National Park, San Luis Lakes State Park and Wildlife Area, Zapata Falls, Medano-Zapata Ranch, Fort Garland State Museum, San Luis Museum and Cultural Center, Stations of the Cross, Jack Dempsey Museum, Rio Grande, Pike's Stockade, Cumbres and Toltec Scenic Railroad, Cumbres Pass, Rio Grande National Forest, autumn colors, fishing, hiking, scenic views, camping.

Location: Southern Colorado. The drive begins in Alamosa and travels north on CO 17, then east on Six Mile Lane and south on CO 150 to US 160. It then goes east on 160 to Fort Garland, south on CO 159 to San Luis, and west on CO 142 to Romeo. It turns south on US 285 for 7 miles to Antonito and then west on CO 17 to Cumbres Pass and the New Mexico border.

Drive route name and numbers: Los Caminos Antiguos Scenic Byway; CO 150, 159, 142, and 17; US 285 and 160; Six Mile Lane.

Travel season: Year-round. Heavy snow can temporarily close the highway over La Manga and Cumbres Passes.

Camping: Mogote, Aspen Glade, Elk Creek, and Trujillo Meadows campgrounds lie along Co 17 west of Antonito in Rio Grande National Forest. Campgrounds are also at San Luis Lakes State Park and Great Sand Dunes National Park on the northern part of the drive.

Services: All services are found in Alamosa, Blanca, Fort Garland, San Luis, and Antonito. Limited services are in Manassa and Romeo.

Nearby attractions: Sierra Blanca, Penitente Canyon climbing area, San Isabel National Forest, Spanish Peaks, South San Juan Wilderness Area, Monte Vista National Wildlife Refuge, Alamosa National Wildlife Refuge, Silver Thread Scenic Byway, Pike's Stockade, Taos, Chama, Rio Grande Gorge, Carson National Forest (New Mexico).

The Drive

The 152-mile Los Caminos Antiguos drive, a Colorado scenic byway, traverses the San Luis Valley between Alamosa and Cumbres Pass in southern Colorado. The San Luis Valley, an intermontane basin roughly 100 miles long and 60 miles wide, reaches from Poncha Pass to the New Mexico border. The valley, three times the size of Delaware, rolls out to the mountain horizon like a giant carpet patterned with fields, pastures, and sagebrush flats. The Sangre de Cristo and Culebra Ranges wall in the valley on the east. The jagged escarpment, including

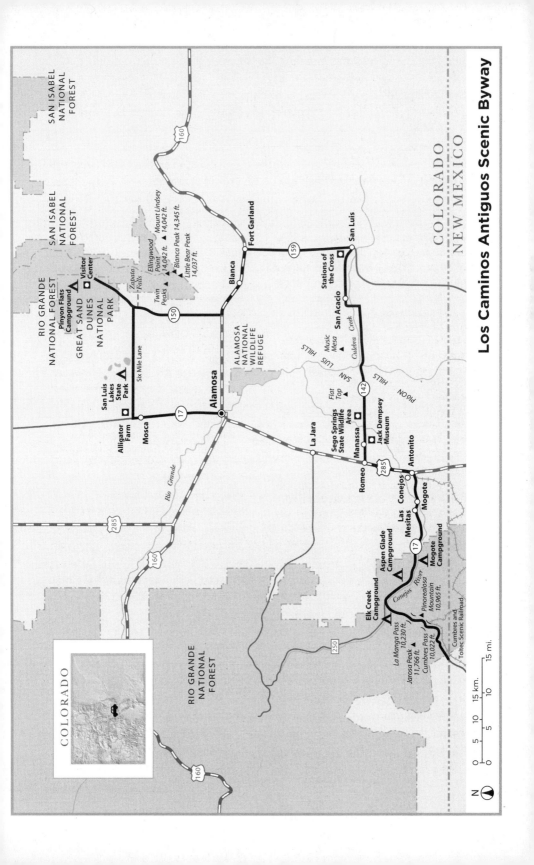

Los Caminos Antiguos Scenic Byway

nine 14,000-foot peaks, makes a formidable barrier that is crossed by only one paved road and two four-wheel-drive tracks. The San Juan Mountains form a lower but equally impassable barrier to the west. The Rio Grande, southern Colorado's river of history and character, breaks from the San Juans at Del Norte and meanders across the San Luis Valley between banks thick with cottonwoods and willows, before plunging down a wild gorge into New Mexico. This superb drive passes old towns and historic sites, skirts the Great Sand Dunes, threads over volcanic hills, follows the sparkling Conejos River, and climbs through fir and spruce forests to the summit of 10,022-foot Cumbres Pass, a stone's throw from New Mexico.

The San Luis Valley, lying at elevations above 7,500 feet, is classified as desert, with an average precipitation of only 10 inches. The valley, the driest part of Colorado, lies in the rain shadow of the San Juan Mountains. Storms laden with Pacific moisture unload on the San Juans, but by the time the clouds reach the valley most rain has already been wrung out. The bulk of the year's meager moisture generally falls in torrential afternoon thunderstorms during July and August. The San Juans west of the valley are Colorado's wettest region. Heavy snows fall on the mountains, including an average 267 inches atop Cumbres Pass. In contrast, the town of Manassa to the east receives only 18 inches of snow each winter. Summer and fall are the best times to travel the highways. Summer days are warm and sunny, with highs generally in the seventies and eighties. Autumn brings cooler days and bright skies. Winters are frigid, with temperatures often falling below zero and snow lingering on the valley floor. Spring months are cool and windy, with occasional rain showers.

Alamosa to San Luis Lakes

The drive begins on the east side of Alamosa in the center of the San Luis Valley at the junction of U.S. Highway 160 and CO 17. **Alamosa,** the largest city in the valley, was established in 1878 as a railroad town. It was named for the large cottonwood groves along the Rio Grande. It flourished with the railroad, becoming the region's main agricultural and mining center. The town's economy depended on freight. As the temporary end of the railroad, shipments of goods reached out to Santa Fe and northern New Mexico as well as the mining areas in the San Juan Mountains to the west. After the railroad extended westward, Alamosa became the center of a prosperous farming and ranching economy, which continues today.

Two of the best nearby points of interest are the 11,169-acre **Alamosa National Wildlife Refuge** and the 14,804-acre **Monte Vista National Wildlife Refuge.** The two large wetland areas are rich habitat for migratory waterfowl. Many bird species, including whooping cranes, sandhill cranes, snow geese, egrets, and bald eagles, either stop or nest at the refuges. Self-guided tours can be taken year-round. A visitor center is located at the Alamosa refuge, which is 3 miles east of Alamosa on El Rancho Road off US 160.

From Alamosa head north on CO 17 through agricultural land dotted with fields and houses. After almost 14 miles you reach the village of **Mosca,** a small community named for Mosca Pass in the Sangre de Cristo Mountains to the east. Turn right (east) here on Six Mile Lane (County Road LN6N), following signs for the Great Sand Dunes National Park. Three miles north of this turn on CO 17 is the **San Luis Valley Alligator Farm,** one of Colorado's most unusual ranches. Warm water, spewing at 87 degrees from geothermal wells, allows alligators to flourish here in several man-made pools. A small admission fee is charged.

Drive east on Six Mile Lane toward the tawny sand dunes. At 8 miles you reach the turnoff to **San Luis Lakes State Park and Wildlife Area.** This quiet 2,054-acre state parkland is comprised of a couple of lakes surrounded by low sand dunes stabilized with rabbitbrush and saltbush. The park's main geographic feature is shallow, 890-acre San Luis Lake, a popular summer recreation area for fishermen and boaters. To the north is a wildlife area with marshy wetlands and Head Lake. Both provide valuable wildlife habitat. The lake, one of the largest in the San Luis Valley, is significant as a resting point for migrating shorebirds, water birds, gulls, and terns. Over 150 bird species have been identified at the park, including sandhill and whooping cranes, grebes, avocets, snowy egrets, white-faced ibis, herons, and bald and golden eagles. For recreationists, the park offers picnic sites, a boat ramp, waterskiing, windsurfing, swimming, 9 miles of hiking and biking trails, and pleasant fifty-one-site Mosca Campground. Spectacular views of the Sangre de Cristo Mountains abound from the park and its lakes.

Medano-Zapata Ranch

Continue driving east on Six Mile Lane. The land surrounding the road is part of the **Medano-Zapata Ranch,** 100,000 acres of mostly undeveloped countryside that eventually will become part of the Great Sand Dunes National Park. The area, one of the largest biologically intact undeveloped landscapes remaining in Colorado, is an important repository of natural diversity and beauty. The Nature Conservancy acquired the land in 1999 at a price well below market value because the land's owner wanted that biodiversity protected. The arid terrain belies the abundant groundwater that helps support a wealth of plant and animal life, including a free-roaming herd of some 2,000 bison, more than 200 bird species, deer, elk, pronghorn, and some rare and endemic insect species, including the circus beetle, the antlike flower beetle, and the Great Sand Dunes tiger beetle.

North of the Great Sand Dunes National Monument is the 97,036-acre **Baca Ranch,** another piece of the national park puzzle that was acquired by the Nature

Conservancy in 2002. With more than 151 square miles, the ranch encompasses a large part of the Sangre de Cristo Range, including 14,165-foot Kit Carson Peak. The Baca Ranch, part of the Luis Maria Baca Grant No. 4, an 1824 Mexican land grant, is part of the largest land preservation effort in Colorado. When federal funds become available, the Baca Ranch will be combined with the Medano-Zapata Ranch and the Great Sand Dunes National Monument to create the Great Sand Dunes National Park and Preserve and the Baca National Wildlife Refuge.

Near the end of the road is a kiosk on the south side. This makes a good orientation stop to the ranch and sand dunes area. The display details Folsom man's habitation of the San Luis Valley as well as information on the San Luis Lakes, Zapata Falls, and the bison herd.

Great Sand Dunes National Park

Continue east on Six Mile Lane until it dead-ends at CO 150. Take a left turn to visit **Great Sand Dunes National Park** and one of America's most unusual dune fields. The highway runs north across scrubland and enters the park after a couple of miles. Continue past the fee station and through an area that was burned by fire in April 2000. The human-caused fire burned 3,120 acres, but only 200 acres of forest. Stop at the park visitor center on the left for orientation, interpretive displays, and maps.

Great Sand Dunes National Park, nestled in a deep alcove on the eastern edge of the San Luis Valley, holds the tallest sand dunes in the Western Hemisphere. The dunes, rising over 700 feet above the valley floor, have a sandy volume estimated at 8 cubic miles, enough sand that it would be almost 5 inches deep if evenly spread across Colorado's 103,766 square miles. The dune field, covering 39 square miles, has an oval shape that is kept from advancing eastward by the abrupt mountain scarp and Medano Creek.

The San Luis Valley receives less than 10 inches of annual rainfall, making it a true desert as well as Colorado's driest region. The dune field began to form 20,000 years ago, when great ice sheets marched south across North America. During that period glaciers were scraping out Colorado's peaks and valleys, and snowmelt-laden rivers rushed into the San Luis Valley. As the climate warmed and dried up, glacial sand and silt were deposited along the Rio Grande. Wind and time did the rest of the work, with centuries of brisk wind scouring the valley floor and sweeping the sand across the valley into a natural pocket below the mountains. The wind, forced to rise over Medano and Mosca Passes, dropped its load of sand. The dunes today are still part of this ongoing process. The dune field now, however, is growing in volume rather than size.

The Great Sand Dunes are also a fascinating study in natural history. The dunes are not nearly as lifeless as they appear at first sight. Sunflowers spring from

A lone hiker walks over wind-rippled sand at Great Sand Dunes National Park.

the sand in August. Indian ricegrass wavers under the ripple of wind. Cottonwood trees, half buried in sand, avoid suffocation by sending out new roots. A delicate tracery of beetle tracks thread across the dunes. And kangaroo rats, which never drink water, plug their burrow entrances with sand to avoid midday heat and await the cool of nightfall. Insects are among the brave creatures that choose to live among the inhospitable dunes. Three species—the circus beetle, Great Sand Dunes tiger beetle, and giant sand treader camel cricket—live only on the dunes and in the eastern San Luis Valley.

The dunes are an exhilarating playground for park visitors. Many clamber to the highest ridges, High Dune and Star Dune, before bounding back down in giant steps. Some put on skis and schuss down the gritty slopes. Others splash about in Medano Creek. If you do climb the dunes, remember to wear shoes because surface temperatures can soar to over 140 degrees—hot enough to burn your soles. Also bring sunscreen, a hat, and plenty of water in summer. You can pick your own path; there are no trails across the dunes. Hiking up the ridgelines is much easier than hiking in a straight line up steep slopes. If you have the time and inclination, it's worthwhile to get a free overnight permit and camp out among the dune hollows, especially during the full moon.

There are other trails in the park, including the Montville Nature Trail (0.5 mile), the historic Mosca Pass Trail (3.5 miles), Castle Creek Trail (2.5 miles), and Little Medano Creek Trail (5.5 miles), which explores "escape dunes" east of the creek and a ghost forest of smothered trees. Since the dune field is a wilderness area, there is no motorized recreation except for a four-wheel-drive track that follows Medano Creek up to Medano Pass. No off-road driving is allowed. Campers at the eighty-eight-site Pinyon Flats Campground enjoy marvelous views of the dunes. Other activities include a visitor center and ranger-led talks and walks. Check at the center for scheduled activities.

Sand Dunes to Fort Garland

The next drive section heads south from the national park along CO 150. South of the park on the west is the historic **Zapata Ranch.** This area, listed on the national historic register in 1993, is owned by the Nature Conservancy and is slated for inclusion in the Great Sand Dunes National Park. The ranch, established in 1879, included a stagecoach station, store, and post office. The ranch has one of Colorado's largest bison herds, as well as a golf course, hiking trails, and a hotel that hosts workshops, field trips, students, and researchers.

Zapata Falls hides in a deep cleft in South Zapata Creek's narrow canyon east of the byway. Turn east on the marked dirt road at mile marker 10.5 and drive about 4 miles to a parking area and trailhead. A half-mile hike leads up through a piñon pine and juniper woodland to the falls, which cascades down a series of cliffs. The falls formed as water from a retreating glacier pooled behind a rock dike. Eventually a weakness was created in the dike and the water eroded its way through the rock, leaving today's waterfall. Besides the falls, you find excellent views of the sand dunes and the valley from this lofty height.

Continue south on CO 150 along a broad sagebrush-covered apron below the mountain massif of the Sierra Blanca. This massif soars more than 7,000 feet above the flat valley to airy ridges and rocky summits. **Blanca Peak,** a sacred mountain of the Navajo Indians, is the range's high point and Colorado's fourth highest peak at 14,345 feet. The other "fourteeners" in this group are 14,037-foot Little Bear Peak, 14,042-foot Mount Lindsey, and 14,042-foot Ellingwood Point, named for pioneer climber Albert Ellingwood. Blanca, Little Bear, and Ellingwood are usually climbed from Lake Como on the west side of the range. It's accessed via an unmarked dirt road that begins on CO 150 3 miles north of US 160. The dirt road eventually becomes an axle-breaking,

Blanca Peak, Colorado's fourth highest peak, dominates the view from Los Caminos Antiguos Scenic Byway north of San Luis.

rock-filled four-wheel-drive route that has been called Colorado's roughest road.

When CO 150 reaches US 160, turn east and drive 10 miles to **Fort Garland.** The drive passes through **Blanca,** a small community of old adobe and stucco buildings. The town was founded after a land drawing in 1908 brought a mass of people here with the chance to draw for large lots of land. Problems with water rights and unproductive soil have kept the village from growing. Fort Garland, 47 miles west of Walsenburg, sits at the intersection of US 160 and CO 159.

Fort Garland, now a sleepy little crossroads, started out in 1858 as an army fort to protect settlers from marauding bands of Ute Indians. Colorado's first permanent settlements, established in the early 1850s in the San Luis Valley, lay on newly acquired territory ceded by Mexico after the Mexican–American War. The military built Fort Massachusetts, Colorado's first military post, in 1852 northeast of Fort Garland. The poor location and stagnant water, however, prompted the army to relocate the garrison to Fort Garland a few years later. The new fort, named for Brigadier General John Garland, maintained order in the valley until the Utes were moved westward in 1880. The post was abandoned in 1883. Famed scout, Indian fighter, and soldier Kit Carson commanded the fort in 1866–1867 before dying two years later at Fort Lyon.

Soldiers considered a post at remote Fort Garland to be a type of involuntary exile. One visitor wrote that he was "struck with commiseration for all the unfortunate officers and men condemned to live in so desolate a place." The old fort, a grassy parade ground surrounded by low adobe buildings, is now open year-round as a state historic site that preserves a slice of Colorado's colorful past. Exhibits include a re-creation of the commandant's quarters during Carson's tenure and displays of military life and Hispanic folk art from the San Luis Valley.

Fort Garland to San Luis

From Fort Garland, drive south on CO 159, passing farmland watered by deep artesian wells and wide sagebrush-covered flats. Scrubby, broken mesas rimmed by ancient lava flows border the drive to the east, forming low foothills below the alpine crest of the Culebra Range. Most of these hills were subdivided as part of the Forbes Trinchera Ranch, but they were originally part of the million-acre Sangre de Cristo Land Grant given by the Mexican government to Stephen Lee and thirteen-year-old Narciso Beaubien for eventual colonization in 1843. After the two were murdered during a Taos Indian uprising two years later, the land passed to Beaubien's father, Charles, owner of the Maxwell Land Grant near Trinidad. Much of the grant was acquired in 1863 by William Gilpin, Colorado's first territorial governor and a land speculator, and used for grazing.

The Culebra Range forms a ragged mountain wall east of the scenic drive. This 32-mile-long range twists south from La Veta Pass into New Mexico. Much of the range, topped by 14,069-foot Culebra Peak, remains wild, uninhabited country where visitors are unwelcome. The Maxwell and Sangre de Cristo land grants kept the mountains out of the public domain and even today most of the Culebra Range is private property. Hikers pay for the privilege of crossing the private land to climb Culebra Peak.

After 15 miles the highway drops down into Culebra Creek's broad, shallow valley and reaches **San Luis,** Colorado's oldest town. Historians acknowledge the community as the first continuously occupied town in today's Colorado, although Taos resident George Gould established a nearby settlement in 1842. The original San Luis, called San Luis de Culebra, was built three-quarters of a mile south of today's town on the Sangre de Cristo land grant in 1851 by six Spanish families. The original town was a collection of low-slung adobe buildings huddled around a central plaza for protection from Indians; the surrounding arable land was divided into ranches and farms. A canal diverted water from Culebra Creek, establishing Colorado's first water right.

Today San Luis, part of the Plaza de San Luis de la Rio Culebra National Historic District, boasts strong civic pride and a sense of community. Many local ranchers and farmers descended from the original settlers. The excellent **San Luis Museum and Cultural Center** displays southern Colorado's classic Hispanic culture and includes a brilliant collection of santos, or carved religious icons. The Stations of the Cross Shrine, following a 1.4-mile trail up a dark mesa just northwest of town, depicts the last hours of Christ's life in a series of dramatic bronze sculptures by sculptor Huberto Maestas. The trail ends at the beautiful, domed Capilla de Todos los Santos, or All Saints Chapel, atop the mesa. The shrine attracts numerous pilgrims who walk the path and ruminate on their faith.

The Rio Grande, San Luis Hills, and Manassa

The drive turns west onto CO 142 at the Stations of the Cross trailhead. The road runs alongside a low mesa rimmed with basalt blocks and coated with sagebrush. Verdant hay fields, watered by Culebra Creek, fill the wide valley south of the blacktop. After 8 miles the highway passes through **San Acacio.** Only a few houses and abandoned buildings remain in this town, founded in 1853. Early settlers battled the Utes here in the name of San Acacio, a Spanish soldier canonized as Saint Acacius. A mile past the town the drive bends south and runs across a creek floodplain for 2 miles before turning west again on an almost arrow-straight road. The **San Luis Hills,** rough volcanic knobs, hills, and mesas, rear up to the north and west, forming a wall gray with sagebrush and mottled with piñon pines and junipers. The highway heads across brushy flats toward the hills for 9 miles and reaches the Rio Grande tucked into a shallow cliffed canyon.

The Rio Grande, the second longest river in the United States at 1,887 miles, arises on the Continental Divide west of the San Luis Valley. The river winds across the valley to this crossing, where it begins cutting into basalt layers. Farther south it enters a deep gorge and plunges into New Mexico. This upper section offers good canoeing through quiet, steep-sided canyons. The cliffs and open spaces attract numerous raptors, including bald eagles, common winter residents.

The highway crosses the Rio Grande on a long bridge and begins climbing over rolling benchlands to a wide saddle between the Piñon Hills on the south and Flat Top, a mesa to the north. Several connected groups of low, barren mountains—South Piñon Hills, Piñon Hills, Flat Top, and Brownie Hills—compose the San Luis Hills. The hills, rising as much as 1,000 feet over the surrounding valley, are the eroded remnants of the volcanic deposits that form the San Juan Mountains. The steep slopes are blanketed in sagebrush, saltbush, and rabbitbrush and dotted with piñon pines and junipers; they house numerous wildlife species, including mule deer, pronghorns, coyotes, bobcats, and eagles. Pristine grasslands thrive on the upper elevations. Hikers can park anywhere along the highway here or take one of the side roads to access the backcountry. A good hike climbs to Flat Top's broad summit and yields marvelous views of the valley and surrounding ranges.

The highway crests the saddle and begins a gradual descent to the Conejos River valley. After 4 miles the road reaches the valley floor and crosses Rio San Antonio, a small stream densely lined with narrow-leaf cottonwoods and willows. The highway swings around a low hill and crosses the **Conejos River** a mile later. Farms and hayfields cover the moist floodplain, with cattails and sunflowers lining marshland along the highway. A dirt road goes north for 0.5 mile to **Sego Springs State Wildlife Area.** Past that turnoff, the drive enters **Manassa,** a well-kept rural community with wide streets and orderly clapboard houses. The town, established in 1878 by Mormon colonists, is famed as the 1895 birthplace and childhood home of heavyweight boxing champion Jack Dempsey. Dempsey, who fought as a teenager in surrounding mining camps as "Kid Blackie," won the crown at age twenty-four. Nicknamed "The Manassa Mauler," Dempsey is considered the best heavyweight in the first half of the twentieth century. The **Jack Dempsey Museum,** a one-room cabin where he grew up on Main Street, displays boxing memorabilia and family photos.

Two miles west of Manassa, the drive enters Romeo and intersects U.S. Highway 285. Just a few miles north of the drive and this intersection is **Pike's Stockade** at Sanford, off CO 159 East. The stockade is a replica of the fort built by Lieutenant Zebulon Pike and his soldiers in January 1807 while exploring today's southern Colorado, including the San Luis Valley. The group, after crossing Medano Pass, passed the Great Sand Dunes, and explored south along the Rio Grande and Conejos Rivers. They built the makeshift fort as protection from the severe winter weather and against Indians. The American flag was raised above the fort on January 31. The stockade, however, was on Spanish soil and within a month the group was arrested by Spanish dragoons and escorted to Santa Fe and then Chihuahua, Mexico; they were released after a year. The replica fort, made of cottonwood logs, measures 36 feet square with 12-foot-high walls and has projecting pickets and a moat for added security. The replica was built by the Colorado Historical Society using notes from Pike's expedition diary.

Conejos, Antonito, and Las Mesitas

From Romeo, US 285 runs south over farmland, crosses the Conejos River again, passes the turnoff to Conejos, and reaches Antonito after 6 miles. **Conejos** is well worth a visit. The town, first settled by Major Lafayette Head and eighty-four

Opposite: The beautiful La Nuestra Señora de Guadalupe Church sits in San Luis, Colorado's oldest town.

Hispanic families in 1854, soon rivaled San Luis with numerous settlers, productive farms, and Colorado's first church, dedicated by Bishop Lamy of Santa Fe in 1863. The beautiful Our Lady of Guadalupe Church dominates the town with its twin domed towers. Conejos thrived as a commercial center until 1881, when the Denver & Rio Grande Railroad bypassed the town and founded Antonito just down the road. Conejos became a footnote in Colorado history when the state's last hanging took place there on July 16, 1889.

Antonito began in 1881 as a railroad stop. The line originally planned on stopping at Conejos, but high land prices and difficulty in obtaining a right-of-way prompted the Denver & Rio Grande to build a new town. The narrow gauge railroad, now known as the **Cumbres and Toltec Scenic Railroad,** ran from Alamosa through Antonito and west over Cumbres Pass to Durango. A branch called the Chile Line went south from Antonito to Espanola. The town quickly became the south valley's business hub, with warehouses, hotels, saloons, bordellos, and banks. Antonito retains its old charm and remains a ranching and farming community. Its most popular attraction is the 64-mile railroad between Antonito and Chama. The Cumbres and Toltec Railroad, America's longest narrow gauge line, twists along the Colorado and New Mexico border and passes through scenic Toltec Gorge. The train runs daily from early summer to late fall.

At the train station on Antonito's south side, US 285 turns south toward New Mexico. The scenic drive continues west on CO 17. Past Antonito, the road runs through a succession of small, old towns—Paisaje, Mogote, and Las Mesitas. All began in the 1850s as settlers spread out from Conejos across the fertile bottomlands along the Conejos River.

Paisaje is best remembered as the home of the crazy Espinosa brothers. The duo, Felipe and Julian, claimed that a vision told them to kill "gringos." In the spring of 1863 they went on a brutal rampage, murdering numerous Anglos in the South Park area. A posse surprised the pair near Cripple Creek, and Felipe was killed in a shootout. In his diary they found an entry revealing that the brothers had sworn to kill 600 men. A $2,500 bounty was put on the escaped Julian, and soldiers at Fort Garland mobilized to find him, dead or alive. In September army scout Thomas Tobin tracked Espinosa and his nephew to Cucharas Pass, where he shot them at their evening campfire. Tobin collected his reward after bringing the outlaw's head to the fort commandant.

After crossing the Conejos River, the highway swings through **Las Mesitas.** Adobe houses and small ranches mark the town today, along with the gutted roadside ruins of San Isadore church. The church burned down in 1975, leaving its massive walls open to the sun and rain. From here the canyon narrows and the road runs west beneath a high mesa. Scattered piñon pines and junipers mix with sagebrush on its steep slopes. The highway passes through Fox Creek and a mile later enters **Rio Grande National Forest.** Mogote Campground, with nine sites at 8,300 feet, nestles among ponderosa pines and tall cottonwoods along the Conejos River.

Conejos River to Cumbres Pass

The highway runs alongside the river for the next 10 miles, passing into a deep canyon lined with volcanic cliffs and dense forests. The Conejos River, draining from 13,172-foot Conejos Peak, is one of Colorado's least known yet wildest rivers. Excellent trout fishing, great wildlife habitat, and its undammed flow provide recreation for anglers, kayakers, and naturalists. Aspen Glade Campground, with twenty-seven sites, sits just past the first roadside aspen grove. Numerous stands of golden aspens gild the hillsides along the drive in late September. Keep an eye out for wildlife, including bighorn sheep, elk, and mule deer. The canyon widens into a broad, glaciated valley 20 miles from Antonito. Forest Road 250 continues up the valley, passing several campgrounds and lakes to Platoro, an old 1880s mining ghost town. The scenic drive crosses the river, passes the turnoff to thirty-one-site Elk Creek Campground, and begins the final climb.

Today's highway follows an old Indian trail over La Manga and Cumbres Passes. The Overlook wayside site makes a great stop with its scenic viewpoint after the highway begins its steep climb out of the valley. The road switchbacks up through aspen and spruce forest on the western flank of 10,561-foot McIntyre Mountain and after a few miles follows La Manga Creek to the grassy 10,230-foot summit of La Manga Pass. The highway drops south along a creek to Rio de Los Pinos in a broad valley, swings around Neff Mountain above the railroad tracks, and climbs to the summit of 10,022-foot Cumbres Pass. Just before the summit, a road heads northwest to Trujillo Meadows Reservoir and Campground. A small railroad station sits in the spruce forest atop the pass. The low mountains between La Manga and Cumbres Passes offer excellent cross-country skiing in winter, with plentiful snow and gorgeous scenery. The drive continues southwest, dropping over rolling hills studded with crags and covered with meadows and forest before quietly ending at the Colorado–New Mexico border. Chama, a picturesque New Mexico town, sits 8 miles south of the byway.

7

Wet Mountains Scenic Drive

Florence to Colorado City

General description: This 58-mile drive traverses the Wet Mountains between Florence and Colorado City, passing historic sites, ragged canyons, and recreational areas.

Special attractions: Florence, San Isabel National Forest, Hardscrabble Canyon, Bishop Castle, Lake Isabel, Greenhorn Mountain, camping, hiking, fishing, aspen colors, rock climbing.

Location: South-central Colorado. The drive begins in Florence 5 miles south of US 50 at the junction of CO 115 and 67. The highway runs south, joins CO 96 in Wetmore, and intersects CO 165 at McKenzie Junction. The drive ends in Colorado City at exit 74 on I-25 south of Pueblo.

Drive route name and numbers: The Greenhorn Highway; CO 67, 96, and 165.

Travel season: Year-round.

Camping: Three national forest campgrounds—Ophir, Davenport, and Lake Isabel—lie along the drive. Primitive camping is also permitted on forest land. Greenhorn Meadows Park in Colorado City offers camping.

Services: All services are found in Florence and Colorado City. Limited services are in Wetmore, San Isabel, and Rye.

Nearby attractions: Sangre de Cristo Wilderness Area, Westcliffe, Cañon City attractions, Gold Belt Tour Back Country Byway, Royal Gorge, Pueblo area attractions, Lake Pueblo State Park, Lathrop State Park, La Veta, Spanish Peaks, Highway of Legends Scenic Byway.

The Drive

Far away, across the dusty prairie, the Wet Mountains lift above the western horizon like a humpbacked, blue cloud. Early pioneers, inching across the Great Plains in wagon caravans, saw a promise in those dreamlike mountains. Up there, beyond the dry land of shortgrass, yucca, and rattlesnakes, lay a cool oasis lush with wind-ruffled pine forests, wildflower-dotted meadows, and sparkling streams of clear water. A party of early Mormon emigrants, on reaching this mountain outpost, reveled in the wooded slopes and rain-laden clouds after their months-long trek over what was then called "The Great American Desert." They named them the Wet Mountains—oddly enough, a name also given by the Spanish and Indians.

The Wet Mountains, the southern vestige of the Front Range, makes a broad arc from the Arkansas River west of Cañon City to the Huerfano River at Badito. The range, composed of Precambrian granite and metamorphic rocks, formed when a fault uplifted those old rocks and thrust them onto younger sedimentary layers. The range summits are from 9,000 to over 12,000 feet, with 12,349-foot

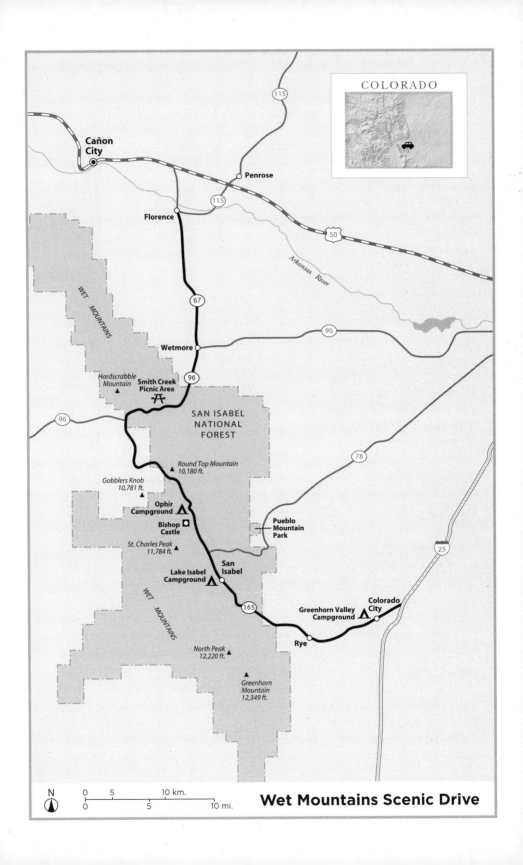

COLORADO

115

Cañon
City

Penrose

115

Florence

50

Arkansas River

67

96

Wetmore

96

Hardscrabble
Mountain ▲

Smith Creek
Picnic Area
⛱

SAN ISABEL
NATIONAL
FOREST

96

78

Round Top Mountain
10,180 ft. ▲

Gobblers Knob
10,781 ft. ▲

Ophir
Campground △

Bishop
Castle ◻

Pueblo
Mountain
Park

St. Charles Peak
11,784 ft. ▲

25

Lake Isabel
Campground △

San
Isabel

WET

MOUNTAINS

165

Greenhorn Valley
Campground △

Colorado
City

Rye

North Peak
12,220 ft. ▲

Greenhorn
Mountain
12,349 ft. ▲

WET

MOUNTAINS

N

0   5   10 km.

0   5   10 mi.

Wet Mountains Scenic Drive

Greenhorn Mountain the highest point. Creeks slice into the ancient bedrock creating abrupt, cliff-lined canyons and shallow, grassy valleys.

The Wet Mountain scenic drive, part of the Frontier Pathways Scenic Byway, begins in Florence in the Arkansas River valley and wends through the canyons and valleys for 58 miles before emptying onto the prairie at Colorado City. Weather along the drive is generally pleasant year-round. Summer temperatures range from the nineties at the lower elevations at Florence and Colorado City to the seventies in the mountains. Immense thunderstorms build over the Wet Mountains and the neighboring Sangre de Cristo Mountains on summer afternoons. Expect localized heavy rain. Autumn days are warm and clear, with golden aspens sprinkled on the hillsides. Winter sets in by early November, and snow locks the upper reaches until April. Spring is short and unpredictable, with periods of rain, snow, and sun.

Florence to Wetmore

Florence is 5 miles southwest of U.S. Highway 50 and Penrose and 10 miles east of Cañon City at the intersection of CO 115 and 67. The town lies on the south bank of the Arkansas River in a broad, arid valley hemmed in by the Pikes Peak massif to the north and the Wet Mountains to the south. The river, after bursting from the mountains and the Royal Gorge at Cañon City, gently braids across a wide channel lined with cottonwoods. Florence, founded in 1860, was first named Frazerville for Joe Frazer, who developed coal mines south of town and planted the first apple orchards here. The town was renamed for the daughter of local oilman James McCandless in the 1870s. Besides seams of coal, oil deposits underlie the Florence area. A. M. Cassiday drilled the first well in 1862 in nearby Oil Canyon, where an oil spring bubbled to the surface. The oil field, called the Florence Pool, is the second oldest in the United States. Well No. 42, considered the oldest continuously operating oil well in the world, has pumped out over a million gallons of crude since it was drilled in 1889.

The drive starts just east of downtown Florence on CO 67, heading south. The straight road runs across a gently tilting plain seamed with shallow valleys and scarred by deep arroyos. The highway crosses a succession of dry creekbeds— Cocklebur, Newlin, and Mineral Creeks.

Cottonwoods, indicating underground water, border the creek beds, and low scrubby mesas, fringed with tawny rimrock and scattered junipers, form low ramparts. Round-shouldered Pikes Peak looms to the north above the wide Arkansas River valley. After 7 miles the road climbs onto a flat, barren bench surrounded by low-browed hills. The Wet Mountains, a high escarpment of green forested peaks and canyons, towers to the west and south.

A state historic marker at 9.5 miles commemorates the area's earliest settlements. The first was El Cuervo ("The Raven"), an Indian trading post built by

Maurice LeDuc a mile west of the marker near the mountain base at the junction of Adobe and Mineral Creeks. Colonel Henry Dodge of the First Regiment of United States Dragoons noted a camp of sixty Arapaho tepees at the post in 1835. The pueblo of Hardscrabble was established in 1844 at the confluence of Adobe and Hardscrabble Creeks a few miles north of the marker and used as a trading post for Indians and trappers. The village was visited by explorer John C. Fremont in 1845. Twenty-five trappers with Indian wives and children lived there. Fremont stopped by again in late November 1848 during his disastrous fourth expedition in search of a transcontinental railroad route along the thirty-eighth parallel. Few people inhabited the village, most having moved to Pueblo after Indian attacks. Richard Kern, an expedition member, described Hardscrabble in his journal as the "summer resort of hunters." The expedition lingered only two days, buying and shelling 130 bushels of corn and dining on chicken and pumpkin before heading west to the San Juan Mountains.

The highway continues south, passing a lone ponderosa pine and running 2 miles to Wetmore on Hardscrabble Creek's gravel banks. Frances and William Wetmore bought an old homestead here and surveyed, named, and established the town around 1880. It served as a stagecoach station on the line between Pueblo and the Wet Mountain Valley. CO 67 dead-ends here at CO 96. Turn west on CO 96.

Hardscrabble Creek

The highway bends south onto a bench above Hardscrabble Creek in a broad valley. The valley edge gently rises west toward the mountains, where tilted sandstone layers form rocky hogbacks against a soaring mountain wall. Rounded hills cloaked in oak and pine flank the valley's east side. As the road runs south the valley narrows and deep forests of scrub oak and ponderosa pine mix with open meadows. Tall cottonwoods shelter the creek below the road.

At 15 miles the drive enters San Isabel National Forest. A half-mile later the road swings west into North Hardscrabble Canyon's abrupt defile. Forest Road 306 begins here and runs south and west up South Hardscrabble Creek. Near this road junction sits a rock face inscribed with famed frontiersman Kit Carson's name and his wife Josefa Jaramillo's initials.

The highway heads west up the canyon, cutting through sandstone hogbacks and passing steep side canyons. Bighorn sheep and mule deer graze in open meadows along the drive. As the road climbs, the canyon steepens and narrows. Ponderosa pine, piñon pine, and juniper scatter over the warm north slopes, while deep forests of spruce and fir darken the south side. A picnic area sits partway up the canyon along the creek. Peaks, including rough Hardscrabble Mountain, tower above the canyon floor. Tilted layers of metamorphic rock form bands

Hardscrabble Mountain lifts its rocky ramparts high above the Wet Mountains scenic drive.

of cliffs and break into sharp buttresses, pointed pyramids, and blocky castles. The origins of the name "Hardscrabble" are lost, but local legend says the name came after Ute Indians massacred settlers in Pueblo on Christmas Day 1855. The Indians, pursued by soldiers, fled up the creek and had a "hard scrabble" to elude capture.

At 19 miles the canyon narrows and the highway twists through roadcuts. The creek below tumbles over boulders, forming frothy cascades. A pulloff at Rattlesnake Gulch is a good picnic stop. A trail climbs the steep gulch, passing numerous climbing crags and boulders. The canyon widens above the gulch, the road grade abates, and narrow-leaf cottonwoods densely line the creek. McKenzie Junction, the intersection of CO 96 and 165, sits in the widening, grassy valley. The drive turns south on CO 165, while CO 96 heads west 16 miles to Westcliffe.

Greenhorn Highway and Bishop Castle

CO 165, the Greenhorn Highway, runs 35 miles from the CO 96 junction to Colorado City. The road climbs south up Hardscrabble Creek's South Fork, a shallow valley fringed with pine and fir forest, aspen groves, and meadows. The road steadily ascends and reaches 9,379-foot Wixson Divide after 5 miles. This broad saddle, surrounded by grassland and open forests, lies below Wixson Mountain. The drive drops down another valley, crosses South Hardscrabble Creek, and begins climbing another shallow valley to the summit of Bigelow Divide. Edging south above Bigelow Creek, the drive passes old ranch buildings and bends west up Middle Creek. Ophir Creek Campground, with thirty-one sites, is tucked into a wooded valley along the creek, where the highway makes a hairpin turn. Forest Road 400 heads west up Ophir Creek here and reaches the Wet Mountains range crest. Forest Road 403 winds along the crest to a point just west of Greenhorn Mountain's summit.

The drive climbs out of the valley, slices through several roadcuts, and reaches **Bishop Castle.** The castle, a marvelous stone building rising out of the forest above the highway, is testimony to the ingenuity and labor of Jim Bishop. Bishop, starting in 1969, began building the castle from his imagination. Today, without blueprints, he continues to craft arches, turrets, towers, and huge rooms from local cobbles and mortar. The main tower soars 160 feet into the sky. This marvelous structure, looking less like a traditional medieval castle and more like a storybook fantasy, attracts more than 60,000 travelers a year. Jim, a wiry man with strong hands, calls the castle "the largest one-man project in the world," and says it's "a tourist attraction without being a tourist trap." The castle, owned by the nonprofit Bishop Castle Foundation, donates money raised from donations for newborn heart surgery. Admission is free and the castle and a gift shop are open year-round.

Past Bishop Castle the highway runs south, across Davenport Creek, over Greenhill Divide, and into Willow Creek valley. At the valley base sits **San Isabel,** a small resort with lodging, restaurants, and supplies. Lake Isabel nestles in the broad valley beyond the town, its deep blue water attracting anglers. The lake, formed by St. Charles Dam, impounds the St. Charles River. High forested ridges and rounded peaks studded with granite crags loom above the aspen-fringed lake. A parking area on the highway allows angler and hiker access. A turn south of the lake leads to the national forest's Lake Isabel Recreation Area with fifty-two sites in three campgrounds and a large picnic area.

The drive intersects the twisting Old San Isabel Road a mile past the lake. Here the highway begins winding downward, dipping through shallow canyons and passing groves of aspen. Greenhorn Mountain, its south summit reaching 12,349 feet, towers above the drive. Steep ridges and slopes, scaled with conifer forest, rise above. This wild land of woods and canyons is part of the 22,040-acre Greenhorn Mountain Wilderness Area.

Rye to Colorado City

As the road descends the mountain flank, the vegetation changes from spruce, fir, and aspen forest to a drier woodland of ponderosa pine and scrub oak. The highway leaves the national forest 6 miles from San Isabel and traverses high, rolling foothills coated with scrub oak and open grassland. Sandstone-rimmed cuestas or upturned mesas seamed with canyons break from the hills and drop eastward. After a few miles the road passes grazing cattle and pastures and bends into **Rye.** This quiet town, established in 1882, was named for surrounding grain fields. It serves today as a ranching center.

The drive runs east from Rye along the north side of the Greenhorn Creek valley. Fields scattered with hay bales and cattle lie along the creek. Higher mesas rimmed with Dakota sandstone and covered with pine and oak rise north of the asphalt. The road and creek continue descending eastward, and the climate and hills steadily dry. By the time the road reaches the valley floor, shortgrass, yucca, and cactus dominate this Upper Sonoran life zone. Greenhorn Meadows Park, with a cottonwood-shaded campground, sits along the creek. The nearby Cuerno Verde monument memorializes the Indian chief killed here.

Passing over low, scrubby hills, the highway climbs up to **Colorado City,** one of the state's newer communities. The town, called Crow Junction in the 1880s, was founded in 1963 as a resort and commercial enterprise and named for the Colorado City Development Company. Now it's a placid crossroads with visitor

Opposite: The unique turrets and towers at Bishop Castle rise above Greenhorn Highway along the Wet Mountains scenic drive.

services, a golf course, and Beckwith Reservoir, offering fishing and boating. The drive ends at Interstate 25's exit 74. Pueblo lies almost 25 miles to the north, while Walsenburg sits 24 miles to the south. Graneros Gorge, just south of the interchange, is a spectacular canyon sliced into grassy hills.

8

Phantom Canyon and Shelf Roads

Cañon City to Cripple Creek

General description: This 64-mile-long open loop drive follows Phantom Canyon and Shelf Roads through precipitous canyons on the south slope of Pikes Peak.

Special attractions: Indian Springs Trace Fossil Site, Beaver Creek Wilderness Study Area, Cripple Creek and Victor National Historic Districts, Cripple Creek & Victor Narrow Gauge Railroad, Window Rock, Shelf Road Climbing Area, Garden Park Fossil Area, Red Cañon Park, Cañon City attractions, hiking, rock climbing, camping, fishing, wildlife, mine ruins, photography.

Location: Central Colorado. The drive follows Shelf Road north from Cañon City to Cripple Creek, then turns south on CO 67 to Victor and down Phantom Canyon Road to US 50 near Florence.

Drive route names and numbers: Shelf Road, Phantom Canyon Road, CO 67, Fremont County Road 9, Teller County Road 88.

Travel season: Year-round. Snow and mud may temporarily close the roads during winter. Watch for slick roads after heavy summer thunderstorms. Both roads are very narrow—often only one lane wide with tight turns. Vehicles over 25 feet wide, including motor homes, large campers, and travel trailers, should not be used for the drive.

Camping: Private campgrounds are in the Cripple Creek and Cañon City areas and at Indian Springs. A couple of campgrounds operated by the Bureau of Land Management (BLM) are at the Shelf Road Climbing Area. National Forest campgrounds are in nearby Pike National Forest.

Services: All services in Cañon City, Cripple Creek, Victor, and Florence.

Nearby attractions: Royal Gorge Park, Temple Canyon Park, Arkansas Headwaters State Recreation Area, Mueller State Park, Florissant Fossil Beds National Monument, Pikes Peak, Beaver Creek State Wildlife Area, Elevenmile Canyon, Colorado Springs attractions, Lake Pueblo State Park.

The Drive

Pikes Peak, towering to 14,110 feet, anchors the southern Front Range and forms a distinctive landmark for travelers. Canyons slice into its bedrock southern slopes, forming deep defiles separated by high, forested ridges. This rugged country remains one of the Front Range's wildest and least-accessible landscapes. It's a bold, sculpted land overlooked by pink granite bastions and inhabited by bighorn sheep, mountain lions, falcons, and rattlesnakes. This 64-mile-long scenic drive makes an open loop between Cañon City and Cripple Creek on two narrow gravel roads—Shelf Road and Phantom Canyon Road—that thread through precipitous canyons on Pikes Peak's southern slope.

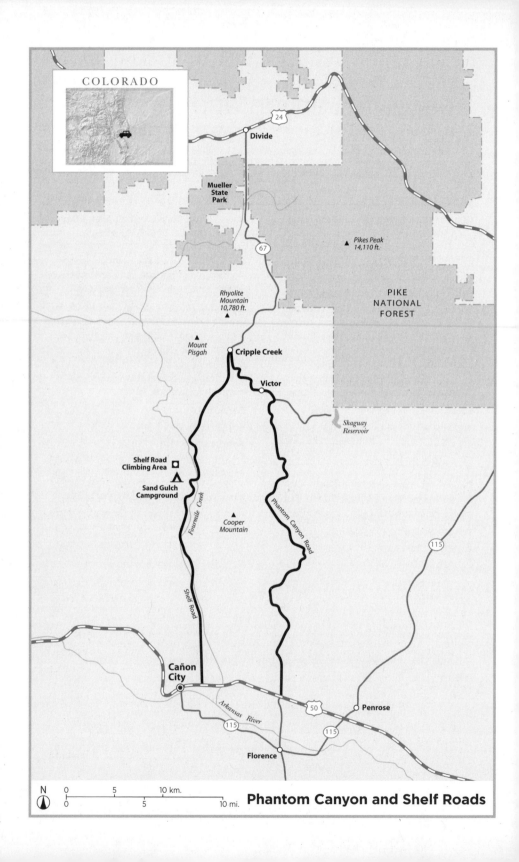

COLORADO

Divide

Mueller
State
Park

Pikes Peak
14,110 ft.

Rhyolite
Mountain
10,780 ft.

PIKE
NATIONAL
FOREST

Mount
Pisgah

Cripple Creek

Victor

Skaguay
Reservoir

Shelf Road
Climbing Area

Sand Gulch
Campground

Fourmile Creek

Cooper
Mountain

Phantom Canyon Road

Shelf Road

115

Cañon
City

Arkansas River

Penrose

50

115

115

Florence

N

0   5   10 km.
0   5   10 mi.

Phantom Canyon and Shelf Roads

The roads, part of the Bureau of Land Management's Gold Belt Tour Back Country Byway, offer an out-of-the-ordinary scenic driving experience. Both are winding dirt and gravel tracks that often narrow to a single lane for miles at a time in deep canyons or on exposed slopes. Frequent pullouts allow passing on narrow sections. Neither road is well maintained, and each is often rough and corrugated, particularly after heavy rain. The Shelf Road's shelf section should not be driven after rain or during snowmelt; its clay surface becomes extremely slippery and there is no guardrail to stop a slip to oblivion. **Trailers, motor homes, or vehicles over 25 feet in length should not be used to travel either road.** Drive defensively on the roads. Always expect another car on blind corners, don't speed, and remember that uphill traffic has the right-of-way.

The drive is open year-round, with each season offering its own flavor. Summers tend to be hot in the lower elevations, with highs regularly climbing into the nineties near the Arkansas River valley. The pleasant upper elevation temperatures range from sixty to eighty degrees. Expect thunderstorms on summer afternoons. Autumn days are warm and clear, with occasional showers. Winter brings variable weather. Mild winter weather rules in the lower elevations, with days as warm as fifty degrees and light snowfall. Snowpack and ice slicken shaded road sections near Cripple Creek and Victor from November to February. Spring brings warm, breezy weather to the area along with rain and snow showers.

Morrison Formation and Garden Park Quarry

The Shelf Road drive segment begins in east Cañon City. Turn north on Raynolds Avenue from U.S. Highway 50. A Colorado state scenic drive sign marks the turn. Head north on Raynolds for 0.7 mile through a residential neighborhood. The street dead-ends. Bend left on Pear for 0.1 mile and then north of Fields through fenced pastures and scattered houses. The street, turning into Shelf Road, quickly leaves Cañon City behind and climbs a low hill. It crests the flat hill topped with homes and drops through shale hills into Fourmile Creek's canyon.

The roughly paved road swings past a small ranch and tall cottonwoods, and at 4.5 miles enters a cliffed portal carved through tilted Dakota sandstone cliffs by the creek. The canyon quickly deepens with the sandstone layer capping the canyon rim. Slopes below the rim cascade down to the road with a veneer of fallen boulders and scattered piñon pine, juniper, and rabbitbrush. The first oil well west of the Mississippi River was drilled in this canyon in 1862. The drive winds along benches on the creek's western margin. Indian petroglyphs decorate one roadside boulder. A BLM picnic area with an information kiosk sits partway up the canyon. The road, turning to gravel past the picnic tables, continues up the shallow canyon. Steep slopes of colored shale and mudstone stairstep back to the higher sandstone rim from the creek. These unassuming soft rock layers, called the **Morrison**

Formation, hold one of Colorado's most astounding natural wonders—a dinosaur graveyard.

The Morrison Formation, a thick widespread layer of sandstone, mudstone, siltstone, and shale, was deposited on a vast, swampy floodplain along the edge of a retreating sea during Jurassic times, almost 150 million years ago. Wide rivers and streams, flowing from distant mountains and volcanic peaks, sluggishly meandered across a broad basin. Trees lined the riverbanks and backwater ponds, and life flourished on the fertile, subtropical landscape. The most prominent residents of this ancient land were giant dinosaurs. The rivers and swamps swallowed their bones after death, slowly entombing, petrifying, and preserving the remains until small Fourmile Creek exhumed the bones in another age.

Dinosaur bones hide in the Morrison Formation all over Colorado and Utah, including Riggs Hill near Grand Junction, the famous quarry in Dinosaur National Monument, near Morrison outside Denver, and at the **Garden Park Quarry** along Shelf Road. The area's first finds came to local school superintendent O. W. Lucas in March 1877. Lucas, an amateur botanist studying local plants, found several fossil fragments, including a 5-foot-long leg bone weathering out of the strata. He sent off samples to eminent Philadelphia paleontologist Edward D. Cope, who promptly dispatched excavators to the Garden Park site. Over the next few years Cope and rival Yale scientist Othniel C. Marsh dug into the soft shale and mudstone slopes and found a staggering number of gigantic, almost complete dinosaur skeletons. The first stegosaur, the official Colorado state fossil, came from the Garden Park quarries, as well as camarasaur, diplodocus, and allosaur remains. The area also yielded bones from numerous small dinosaurs, plants, and trees. The Denver Museum of Natural History continues to probe the Garden Park Quarry. A state historic marker, sitting near the canyon's northern end, commemorates the Garden Park Quarry and its buried treasures.

The drive swings across Fourmile Creek beneath low bluffs and climbs into Garden Park, a long, broad valley flanked by rolling hills and steep mountains. The road traverses the valley for almost 5 miles, passing hayfields, fenced paddocks with grazing cattle and horses, and the cottonwood-lined creek. Mule deer and wild turkeys often congregate in the open fields along the creek in early evening. The drive passes the entrance to **Red Canyon Park,** a 600-acre Cañon City parkland, just after crossing the creek halfway up the valley. The park, a maze of upturned sandstone layers, fringes the base of Rice Mountain on Garden Park's western edge. This primitive, off-the-beaten-track park offers eroded hoodoos and spires, long sweeping escarpments chiseled from red sandstone, a maze of hiking trails that thread among the formations, and picnic tables.

Shelf Road to Cripple Creek

The road continues north past a couple of ranches into dry hills studded with piñons and junipers. At 12 miles the University Wall looms to the east, lifting its leaning limestone rampart above Fourmile Creek's shallow gorge. The road passes a stylish ranch house and climbs onto an almost level plain coated with shortgrass and surrounded by low woods. Just east of here inside the canyon rim lie two small caves—Marble and Fly Caves. Wilson Cave hides farther up Helena Canyon.

Prominent limestone cliff bands rim the low hills and canyons north of the road. These short, sharp cliffs comprise **Shelf Road Climbing Area,** one of Colorado's best sport climbing areas, with hundreds of established routes. Two turns lead to the best crags. The first goes through a gate and bumps northwest across a pasture to a campground and parking area for The Gallery and Sand Gulch. A tenth of a mile north is a marked BLM road that climbs north to The Bank and The Dark Side, two long cliff bands in Trail Gulch. Some of the area's best climbing routes, including Thunder Tactics, Heavy Weather, and Back to the Future, ascend The Bank's blond limestone walls. Almost all of the area's routes are protected with permanent bolts and anchors. A campground sits at the parking area above The Bank.

Shelf Road twists down a slight canyon with piñon pines, junipers, and boulders tacked to the hillside. The track emerges onto a 4-mile-long shelf hacked from a steep slope between cliff bands in Helena Canyon. This spectacular road section offers stunning scenery, dramatic drop-offs below the passenger windows, and a white-knuckle grip for inexperienced mountain drivers. Most of the road is single lane, with only the occasional outside pullout for passing. The road edges along the shelf, only leaving the main canyon to dip into Trail Gulch. Fourmile Creek, dashing over worn boulders and bedrock, riffles far below the road in a somber granite gorge. Above the shelf stretches a band of limestone broken into varnished black faces and tawny overhangs and arêtes. Steep slopes littered with boulders and cholla cacti cascade below the cliffs to the roadside. The Ordovician period sandstone deposited atop the Precambrian granite below the road preserves traces of some of the world's oldest known vertebrate life. Small blue dots are revealed through a microscope as fossilized platelets of *Agnathid* fish that swam here in an ancient ocean over five hundred million years ago.

The road follows the track of an 1892 toll stage road that ran from Cañon City to the new gold camp at Cripple Creek. The uphill ride took six hours and required eighteen horses in teams of six. Stages paid tolls on each rig's number of horses at both ends of the shelf itself. The lower tollkeeper's cabin ruin lies on a spacious bend on the canyon floor just after the shelf road begins.

After 3 miles the road begins a gentle descent through a mixed conifer forest and a mile later reaches the canyon floor and crosses the creek. The drive winds

Rocky Mountain bighorn sheep, the Colorado state animal, pause on granite bedrock below Window Rock along Shelf Road.

up the east side of the creek in a broadening canyon for a couple of miles before reaching a long stack of tailings excavated from the Carlton Drainage Tunnel. The 6-mile-long tunnel, bored in 1941, drained water from gold mines north of Victor. Past the tailings the drive turns away from Fourmile Creek and enters a steep canyon carved by Cripple Creek.

Shelf Road follows Cripple Creek for the next 8 miles. The road corkscrews up a deep canyon flanked by granite cliffs and talus and scrub oak–covered slopes. The creek trickles over boulders and past small quaking aspen groves. **Window Rock,** an unusual granite arch, towers over the road a couple of miles up-canyon. Bighorn sheep often graze along these boulder-strewn slopes. Higher up the canyon becomes a shallow, grassy valley and passes several old mines before intersecting CO 67 just south of the town of Cripple Creek.

Cripple Creek and Victor

Cripple Creek and its sister city, **Victor,** lie in the fabulously wealthy Cripple Creek Mining District, a collapsed volcanic caldera rimmed with gold. Local cowboy Bob Womack first found gold in nearby Poverty Gulch in 1890. His claim, the El Paso Lode, sparked a gold rush to the Pikes Peak region. Almost overnight a town sprang up and by 1900 more than 50,000 people lived in Cripple Creek, making it Colorado's fourth-largest city at the time. During the boom years the district's 500 mines yielded more than $340 million in gold at the prevailing price of $20.67 per ounce. The area mines eventually yielded more gold than the California and Alaska gold rushes combined. Today active mining continues, and geologists say a fortune in gold still lies underground. Cripple Creek, now preserved as a National Historic District, offers numerous attractions, including the Cripple Creek District Museum, the Cripple Creek & Victor Narrow Gauge Railroad, the Old Homestead brothel, and gambling houses.

The drive turns south on CO 67, winding 5 miles to Victor through aspen, spruce, and pine forests. Dramatic views unfold along this lofty highway stretch of the snowcapped Sangre de Cristo Range and the broad Arkansas River valley. The highway passes the Carlton Mill, part of the Cripple Creek and Victor Gold Mining Company. The road bends through a roadcut and enters 9,729-foot Victor, nicknamed the "city of mines." The slopes of Battle Mountain, looming north of town, are studded with colored mine tailings from famous mines like the Ajax, Portland, and Independence. The Gold Coin Mine operated within Victor itself. Victor, also a National Historic District, remains a mining town at heart, with old brick buildings, frame houses, and working-class ethic. The drive meanders through downtown Victor before bending onto the Phantom Canyon Road at the town's far southeast corner.

Head frames, old cabins, and mine tailings scatter across hillsides in the historic Cripple Creek Mining District between Cripple Creek and Victor.

Phantom Canyon Road

The unpaved Phantom Canyon Road runs 31 miles south to US 50. The road initially loops across high benches and rolling hills covered with meadows, aspen groves, and spruce and pine forests. A turn, just outside Victor, leads east 6 miles to eighty-four-acre Skaguay Reservoir, a popular state wildlife area with fishing and camping.

Phantom Canyon Road traverses the abandoned railbed of the old Florence and Cripple Creek Railroad, "The Gold Belt Line." The railroad carried raw ore from Cripple Creek's mines to nine reduction mills in Florence. At Alta Vista the road begins a slow descent for a few miles before dropping steeply into Phantom Canyon. The train originally climbed the Wilbur Loop on 4 percent grades out of the canyon with helper engines.

After reaching upper Phantom Canyon, the road bends south and follows the canyon floor past granite crags, aspens, and pine-covered hills. The road gently winds down, the canyon alternately widening and narrowing. Fifteen miles down, the canyon pinches off to a narrow slot, with Eightmile Creek and the road twisting below tall cliffs. Beyond the canyon widens and drops steeply below the road as it edges across dry mountain slopes. After crossing a steel bridge built in 1897, the road reaches a BLM information booth and the parking area for access to the adjoining Beaver Creek BLM Wilderness Study Area. This proposed 27,020-acre wilderness area, accessible via a trail by the bridge, encompasses the rugged canyons of East and West Beaver Creeks and a renowned cutthroat trout fishery.

The narrow road continues down-canyon past the abandoned town of Adelaide, a train watering stop. As the road descends, the canyon deepens and becomes drier. Piñon pine, juniper, cactus, and yucca replace the spruce, fir, and pine forests of higher elevations, and the creek slows to a trickle among cottonwoods. The road runs through two tunnels built in 1895 after floods destroyed the original track alignment. A mile past Tunnel #1 the canyon walls slacken, the mountains become rounded, and the drive runs through a narrow gate hemmed in by tall rock walls. The canyon widens and the road bends west along a sandstone hogback and then south into a broad valley flanked by the mountain uplift and the Dakota hogback. The road becomes paved and swings past the turn to **Indian Springs Trace Fossil Natural Area.**

This national natural landmark, on private land, exhibits surface trails on sandstone of 460-million-year-old arthropods. The area, once a mudflat in a tidal lagoon, preserves some twenty-five different kinds of markings left by diverse animals including a brachiopod; the walking, foraging, and burrowing tracks of an ancestral horseshoe crab; walking and swimming tracks from a giant trilobite; and evidence of a jawless armor-plated fish, one of the world's first known vertebrates. The site's owners conduct tours and offer a private campground.

The drive passes through a deep notch chiseled into the hogback, twists through a shallow canyon, and climbs onto a broad bench above Sixmile Creek. The road runs south through a typical Upper Sonoran ecosystem with short grass and cholla cacti, and stops a few miles later at US 50. Cañon City sits 4 miles to the west, while Florence lies 3 miles south on CO 67 along the Arkansas River.

9

Pikes Peak Highway

Cascade to the Summit of Pikes Peak

General description: This 20-mile-long paved and gravel toll road climbs to the summit of 14,115-foot Pikes Peak, Colorado's thirty-first highest peak.

Special attractions: Scenic views, hiking, rock climbing, Bottomless Pit, Glen Cove, tundra plants and above-timberline ecosystem, Barr Trail, Pikes Peak Cog Railroad, fishing.

Location: East-central Colorado. Pikes Peak towers over Colorado Springs and the surrounding Front Range 70 miles south of Denver. The scenic highway begins in Cascade off US 24 about 5 miles west of Manitou Springs.

Drive route name and number: Pikes Peak Highway, Forest Road 58.

Travel season: The road is usually open from May through October, depending on the weather and snow conditions. Call the tollgate for more information.

Camping: No camping is allowed along the highway. Many campgrounds are found in the surrounding Pike National Forest at the Crags, Elevenmile Canyon, north of Woodland Park on CO 67, and along the Rampart Range Road. Private campgrounds are in Colorado Springs.

Services: There are no services on the drive, except for food at Glen Cove and the Summit House. Limited services are available at Cascade and Green Mountain Falls at the highway's base. Complete visitor services are found in Colorado Springs, Manitou Springs, and Woodland Park.

Nearby attractions: Colorado Springs attractions, Air Force Academy, Garden of the Gods, North Cheyenne Canyon, Cripple Creek, Florissant Fossil Beds National Monument, Elevenmile Canyon, Pike National Forest, Lost Creek Wilderness Area, Mueller State Park, Royal Gorge, Gold Belt Tour Back Country Byway.

The Drive

Pikes Peak stands high above the tawny Colorado prairie like a strong, silent sentinel. From its base, the peak lifts over its low, forested neighbors, rising almost 8,000 feet from Colorado Springs to its snowcapped 14,115-foot summit.

The great peak has long been a beacon for travelers. Its distinctive outline, seen from over 100 miles away, was a landmark to the Ute Indians, early explorers and trappers, traders on the Santa Fe Trail, and prospectors and settlers heading west during the 1850s rush to northern Colorado's gold fields. The peak is perhaps America's most famous mountain. More people reach its sixty-acre summit—via Barr Trail, the Pikes Peak Cog Railroad, and the Pikes Peak Highway—than any other high peak in the United States. The highway, ascending 20 miles to the summit, is one of Colorado's highest and best drives. The paved and gravel road offers expansive views and dramatic scenery.

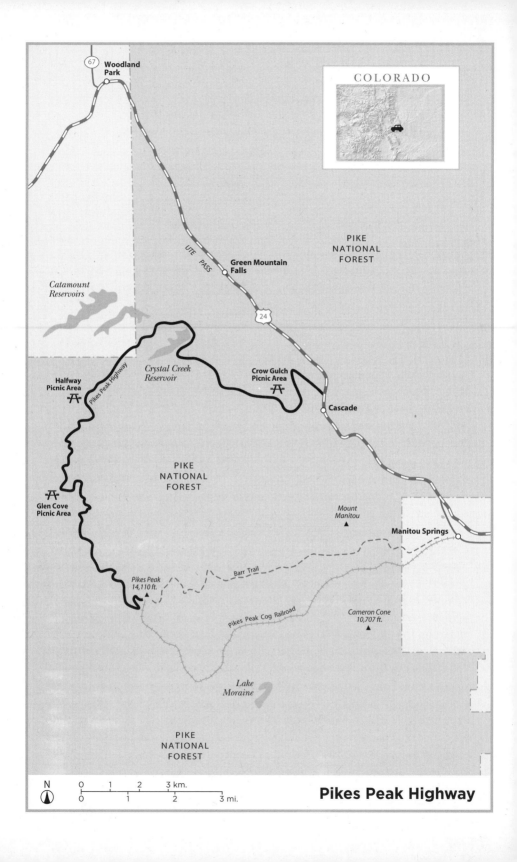

COLORADO

67 Woodland Park

PIKE NATIONAL FOREST

UTE PASS

Green Mountain Falls

Catamount Reservoirs

24

Crystal Creek Reservoir

Crow Gulch Picnic Area

Halfway Picnic Area

Pikes Peak Highway

Cascade

PIKE NATIONAL FOREST

Mount Manitou

Glen Cove Picnic Area

Manitou Springs

Barr Trail

Pikes Peak 14,110 ft.

Cameron Cone 10,707 ft.

Pikes Peak Cog Railroad

Lake Moraine

PIKE NATIONAL FOREST

N

0   1   2   3 km.
0   1   2   3 mi.

Pikes Peak Highway

Pikes Peak began attracting tourists in the 1870s, who trekked on foot or mule to its lofty summit above the new resort community of Colorado Springs. The first road, a 17-mile carriage road, reached the summit in 1889, allowing visitors to ride in comfort to the top. But the completion and popularity of the nearby Pikes Peak Cog Railroad in 1891 forced the wagon route to close by 1905.

In 1913 Cripple Creek mining magnate Spencer Penrose joined with Charles Noble, a retired railroad man, and petitioned the Department of Agriculture to build a new road for automobiles to the peak's summit. Naysayers said no automobile had enough power to climb the peak, but on July 17, 1913, two Denver men drove a Buick Bear Cat up the carriage road to the summit in four hours. In 1914 the federal government gave Penrose a permit to build the road, warning him it would cost as much as $25,000. The highway, completed in 1915, climbed 6,746 feet on an average 6 percent grade to the peak's apex and ended up costing over $250,000. Penrose started the Pikes Peak Hill Climb auto race, the world's highest auto race, in 1916 to give needed publicity to his expensive road. The race tradition continues every July on the highway's gravel section. The highway operated as a toll road until 1936, but Penrose never turned a profit on his investment due to the road's expensive maintenance. The deteriorating road was free until 1948, when Colorado Springs received a permit from the National Forest Service to operate the highway.

The Pikes Peak Highway is one of the most expensive roads to maintain in the United States. As much as 7 million cubic feet of snow is removed from the highway every spring. Melting snow also damages and erodes the road surface. Because of costly maintenance, the city of Colorado Springs, which operates the highway under permit from Pike National Forest, charges a toll for all travelers. Much of the road is being paved to control erosion and sediment deposition along the roadside.

Allow at least two hours for the 40-mile round trip. Drivers should make sure their vehicles are in excellent operating condition. Use lower gears when ascending and descending the peak to avoid overheating and riding the brakes. The Pikes Peak Patrol checks brakes at Glen Cove for excessive brake heat on busy days and weekends. Use the numerous highway pullouts for sightseeing and to allow faster traffic to pass. The highway is very narrow in places, clinging to steep slopes. Stay on your side of the road, do not cut corners, avoid passing on blind corners, and stay within the speed limit. Up-hill traffic has the right-of-way. The Pikes Peak Patrol regularly traverses the highway and provides road assistance. **Travelers with cardiac and respiratory problems should not make the ascent.**

The Pikes Peak Highway is generally open from May through October; depending on weather conditions and snowfall, it may open earlier and close later. Highway travelers should be prepared for all weather conditions. Snow often falls on the highway, leaving a muddy and slick surface. The weather atop the peak is usually cool and breezy. While summer temperatures in Cascade at the drive's start are often in the eighties, it can be as cold as thirty degrees on Pikes Peak's summit. Be prepared by bringing warm clothes and a raincoat. Autumn days are generally brisk and clear.

Ute Pass

The Pikes Peak Highway begins off U.S. Highway 24 in 7,400-foot-high Cascade, 5 miles west of Manitou Springs. Exit west off US 24 and follow the signs to the highway tollgate almost a mile from Cascade. The road begins climbing immediately up steep mountain slopes thickly clad in ponderosa pine, Douglas fir, and Engelmann spruce. The highway reaches **Camera Point,** the first overlook, just under a mile from the tollgate. This lofty point yields a spectacular view down Ute Pass to Colorado Springs and the distant prairie.

Ute Pass is not a pass at all, but rather an abrupt canyon sliced into the Front Range escarpment that separates the Pikes Peak massif from the Rampart Range. The canyon, carved by Fountain Creek, follows the weakened line of the almost 60-mile-long Ute Pass Fault. Ute Pass has long offered an easy passage from the plains into the mountains. The Ute Indians regularly followed a trail down the pass from their mountain strongholds to the mineral springs at Manitou Springs and the rich hunting grounds east of the Front Range. A freight road was built up the pass in 1872 to better serve the South Park mining camps, and the Colorado Midland Railroad, a standard gauge line between Colorado Springs and Aspen, was completed in 1887. The railroad, with tunnels and railbed still existing in Ute Pass, climbed 4 percent grades up the pass to Divide. The pass was a dangerous place in the 1860s, with numerous robberies and murders.

Cascade Creek to Glen Cove

The road swings west from the viewpoint and quickly enters Cascade Creek's hanging valley. The highway twists up a shallow canyon. Immense granite boulders, scattered hillsides of pine and fir, and groves of quaking aspen line the highway. A picnic ground with restrooms sits at Crow Gulch on the road's north side at 3 miles. Beyond, the highway climbs up and away from Cascade Creek, reaches 9,000 feet, and drops north above Crystal Creek Reservoir. Most of Pikes Peak is part of the Colorado Springs watershed. Numerous dams plug the mountain's creeks to form sparkling reservoirs. Trout fishing is allowed at Crystal Creek Reservoir. After crossing the reservoir spillway, the highway climbs rounded gravel ridges and at 7 miles the road surface becomes graded gravel.

Pikes Peak towers south of the highway, an abrupt wall of ragged cliffs, buttresses, cirques, and ridges. Steep gullies coated with snow and ice plunge down the peak's north face. Pikes Peak, composed of billion-year-old Pikes Peak granite, is a huge batholith, a mass of once-molten rock that cooled under the earth's crust as the core of a mountain range. The granite later lifted as part of the ancestral Rocky Mountains eroded, and then rose again as today's peak. Glaciers chiseled and sculpted Pikes Peak's distinctive features over the last million years. Thick glaciers perched on the mountainside, carving out huge cirques on the peak's east flank, including the Crater, North Pit, and Bottomless Pit. The last of the glaciers disappeared about 11,000 years ago.

Pikes Peak and the surrounding granite region is renowned for its exquisite minerals and gemstones. Some that have been found include smoky quartz, topaz, amethyst, amazonite, fluorite, and zircon crystals. Delicate blue topaz crystals are found on the steep cliffs above Glen Cove on the highway. Pikes Peak, while not a volcano, has had volcanic episodes on its western slopes. Rich gold deposits hide in the Cripple Creek mining district southwest of the peak in the caldera of a collapsed volcano.

The highway climbs southward over humpbacked ridges broken by shallow canyons toward the looming peak. At almost 10 miles the road reaches 10,000 feet and passes the **Halfway Picnic Area.** Past here the highway begins switchbacking across steep forested slopes and 3 miles later reaches the **Glen Cove Picnic Area** at 11,425 feet. Glen Cove, with limited services for travelers, lies in a north-facing alpine cirque carved by a hanging glacier. Granite crags and boulders litter the steep mountainsides above the cirque floor. Steep snow-filled couloirs attract extreme skiers in May and early June.

The drive reaches timberline just past Glen Cove. Timberline marks the upper limit of forest. This snowy, windswept transition zone between the subalpine spruce and fir forest and the treeless tundra is characterized by stunted, twisted trees including Engelmann spruce, subalpine fir, limber pine, and bristlecone pine. At this elevation, the trees grow slowly because of extreme temperatures and the short growing season.

Elk Park and Devils Playground

Past timberline the highway climbs steeply up a flattened ridge. **Elk Park,** a grassy knoll with a parking area, lies a mile past Glen Cove. A marvelous view of the peak's rugged north face and surrounding mountains and valleys spreads out below this timberline viewpoint. A trail, following an old road, heads southeast from here and drops into North Pit, an abrupt glacier-carved cirque.

The road edges up the mountain flank for the next 2 miles, gaining almost 1,000 feet of elevation on eight twisting switchbacks. This airy road section is particularly treacherous for both cars and drivers. Remember to keep to your side of the highway on the sharp turns. Use lower gears when ascending to keep a

The Pikes Peak Highway steeply switchbacks up rock-strewn slopes below Devils Playground.

constant speed and avoid overheating, and when descending to keep brakes from overheating. Pump the brakes to reduce speed rather than applying continuous pressure. At the top of the switchbacks sits 16-Mile Turnout. This overlook offers spacious views to the north across the South Platte River country. Beyond the river basin stretches the snowcapped Front Range, including Mount Evans and Mount Bierstadt. The Tarryall Range lifts its jagged brow of broken rock and rough summits to the northwest.

Devils Playground lies immediately south of the pullout. A good hike heads west along a rounded ridge to a couple of scenic viewpoints. This area is a great place to explore the delicate alpine tundra ecosystem. The climate and growing season on this ridge are the same as that in northern Canada and Alaska. Despite the climatic rigors, including a below-freezing mean annual temperature, a frost-free season that is at most two months long, and winds exceeding 100 miles per hour, numerous plants and shrubs thrive at this elevation. July and August bring a carpet of colorful wildflowers to these mountain heights—greenish-white Arctic gentians, yellow paintbrush, spiked elephant flowers, brilliant alpine sunflowers, and many others. More than 250 plant species grow above timberline in the Colorado Rockies. Most are small perennials that not only endure but also thrive in this stark land of never summer.

From the Devils Playground parking area the highway uncoils across Pikes Peak's long northern ridge. The road slowly climbs past 13,000 feet and passes a couple of great viewpoints. The first overlooks the deep chasm of North Pit, its steep walls littered with soaring granite crags and buttresses. Past the North Pit view the highway swings around a rocky knob and reaches the **Bottomless Pit** overlook at 13,200 feet. The cirque falls away below the viewpoint. Long rock ribs plunge north from the peak's summit to the distant cirque floor. Vertical cliffs, stained with snowmelt and cracked by ice, line the abyss far below.

The highway's final 2 miles slowly scale the boulder-strewn western slope of the peak's final rock pyramid, edging across precipitous slopes. After the last switchback and the last incline, the road ends on the peak's level 60-acre summit. This lofty sky-island sits more than two and a half miles above sea level at 14,115 feet.

Pikes Peak Summit

Pikes Peak was called "Long Mountain" by the Arapahoes. Black Elk, an Oglala Sioux medicine man, had a vision of the sacred peak at the age of nine as the cloud home of the six Grandfathers that represented *Wakantanka*, the Great Spirit of the Sioux religion.

Lieutenant Zebulon Pike first spotted the peak that bears his name from far out on the Colorado plains on November 15, 1806. He recorded the occasion in his journal: "At two o'clock I thought I could distinguish a mountain to our right, which appeared like a small blue cloud." Pike dubbed it Grand Peak and calculated its elevation at 18,851 feet. Pike and a small party of soldiers were dispatched by President Thomas Jefferson in 1806 to explore and determine the southern boundary of the newly acquired Louisiana Purchase, a vast swath of pristine land that swept from the Mississippi River to the Pacific coast.

Pike and three of his ill-equipped men later left their Arkansas River camp in today's Pueblo and attempted to scale Grand Peak. Freezing temperatures and a blizzard conspired to defeat the feeble effort. Pike noted in his journal that "the summit of the Grand Peak, which was entirely bare of vegetation and covered with snow, now appeared at the distance of fifteen to sixteen miles from us, and as high again as what we had ascended, and would have taken a whole day's march to have arrived at its base, when I believe no human being could have ascended to its pinnacle."

The peak was first ascended by Anglo-Americans on July 14, 1820, when botanist Dr. Edwin James and two companions from Major Stephen Long's "Expedition from Pittsburgh to the Rocky Mountains" ascended its east flank. In the process the trio started a major forest fire after leaving a smoldering campfire. In 1858 twenty-year-old Julia Archibald Holmes became the first white woman to ascend Pikes Peak. On the summit she penned a letter to her mother, saying: "In all probability I am the first woman who has ever stood upon the summit of this mountain and gazed upon this wondrous scene, which my eyes now behold . . . all, and everything, on which the eye can rest, fills the mind with infinitude, and sends the soul to God."

Not much has changed over the last 150 years; magnificent panoramas still spread out below the rocky summit in every direction. To the east, the peak's escarpment sweeps down to low forested mountains, jewel-like reservoirs and lakes nestled among ridges, and the urban sprawl of Colorado Springs. Beyond stretches the brown prairie, its grasslands reaching the Kansas horizon. The Spanish Peaks, twin landmarks on the Santa Fe Trail, and the serrated crest of the Sangre de Cristo Mountains glisten in the sunlight like alabaster towers in the south. The Continental Divide, Colorado's mountainous spine, marches across the western rim. Clear days yield marvelous views northward to Longs Peak in Rocky Mountain National Park more than 100 miles away, while Denver's skyscrapers huddle in a broad basin below the mountain uplift.

The breathtaking views from Pikes Peak's summit inspired "America the Beautiful," the nation's unofficial anthem. Katherine Lee Bates, a visiting eastern English professor at Colorado College, rode to the summit in a wagon in the summer of 1893. The view inspired her to write: "Oh beautiful for spacious skies, for amber waves of grain, for purple mountain majesties above the fruited plain. . . ." She later recalled, "The opening lines of the hymn floated into my mind as I was looking out over the sealike expanse of fertile country spreading away so far under those ample skies."

The Pikes Peak Summit House sits on the eastern edge of the summit, with a snack bar and gift shop. The **Barr Trail,** a 13-mile National Recreation Trail, drops east from the summit house, swinging down a broad face and over forested mountains to Manitou Springs almost 8,000 feet below. The strenuous Pikes Peak Marathon follows the trail every August. The **Pikes Peak Cog Railway,** the highest in the world, also ends at the Summit House. The 8.9-mile railway climbs to the acme on grades as steep as 25 percent.

Follow the highway back down the peak to Cascade, 20 miles away. Remember to let the auto's gears do the work, and don't ride the brakes.

North Cheyenne Cañon and Lower Gold Camp Roads

Colorado Springs

General description: A 9-mile drive through North Cheyenne Cañon Park and along Gold Camp Road in the mountains above Colorado Springs.

Special attractions: North Cheyenne Cañon Park, Starsmore Discovery Center, Columbine Trail, Mount Cutler Trail, Helen Hunt Falls, Silver Cascade Falls, High Drive, mountain biking, hiking, rock climbing, scenic views.

Location: East-central Colorado. The drive is in the Front Range on the southwest side of Colorado Springs. Begin at the junction of North and South Cheyenne Cañon Roads. To access the start from I-25, exit onto Tejon Street and head southwest up Tejon and then Cheyenne Boulevard. The canyon road entrance is well marked.

Drive route names: Lower Gold Camp Road, North Cheyenne Cañon Road.

Travel season: Year-round. North Cheyenne Cañon Road is sometimes closed in winter due to ice and snowfall.

Camping: No camping is allowed along the drive. The nearest public campground is at Cheyenne Mountain State Park off CO 115 south of Colorado Springs. Campgrounds also are found in Pike National Forest at the Crags, Elevenmile Canyon, north of Woodland Park on CO 67, and along the Rampart Range Road. Private campgrounds are in Colorado Springs.

Services: No services on the drive. Complete visitor services are found in Colorado Springs.

Nearby attractions: Colorado Springs attractions, Cheyenne Mountain Zoo, Seven Falls, Section 16 Trail, Garden of the Gods, Pike National Forest, Rampart Range Road scenic drive (see Drive 12), Pikes Peak Highway scenic drive (see Drive 9).

The Drive

The 9-mile-long North Cheyenne Cañon–Lower Gold Camp Roads scenic drive ascends a steep, rocky canyon carved into the Front Range southwest of Colorado Springs and then edges above the canyon back to the city and U.S. Highway 24. This short but lovely drive offers lofty viewpoints, a couple of waterfalls, solitude on the edge of one of Colorado's largest cities, and superb hiking trails. The canyon road segment is a paved, two-lane road. The Gold Camp Road segment is a narrow, gravel road. Numerous pullouts allow for safe passage around oncoming vehicles and for scenic views. Recreational vehicles or those towing a trailer should not be used for the drive. The drive is open year-round, except after severe winter storms, when the North Cheyenne Cañon Road is closed. Allow an hour to drive the route.

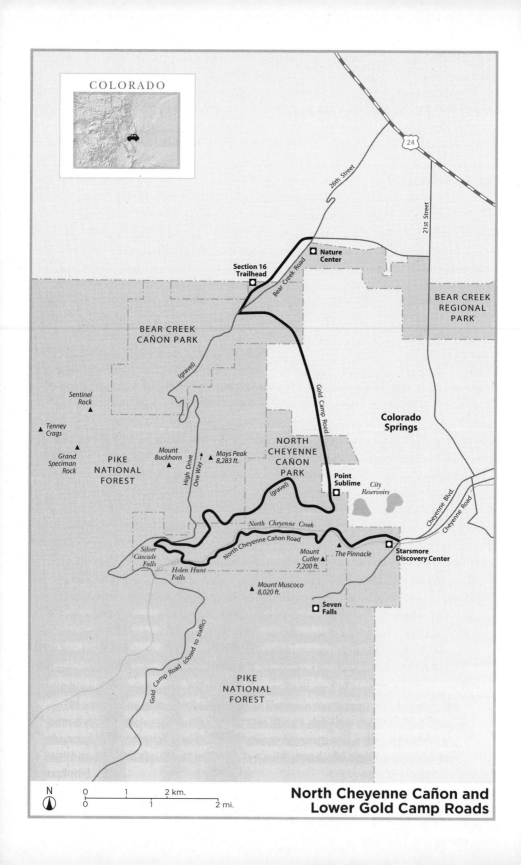

COLORADO

US 24

26th Street

21st Street

Nature Center

Section 16 Trailhead

Bear Creek Road

BEAR CREEK REGIONAL PARK

BEAR CREEK CAÑON PARK

(gravel)

Gold Camp Road

Colorado Springs

Sentinel Rock ▲

▲ Tenney Crags

▲ Grand Speciman Rock

PIKE NATIONAL FOREST

Mount Buckhorn ▲

High Drive

One Way →

▲ Mays Peak 8,283 ft.

NORTH CHEYENNE CAÑON PARK

(gravel)

Point Sublime

City Reservoirs

Cheyenne Blvd.

Cheyenne Road

North Cheyenne Creek

North Cheyenne Cañon Road

Silver Cascade Falls

Helen Hunt Falls

Mount Cutler ▲ 7,200 ft.

The Pinnacle ▲

Starsmore Discovery Center

▲ Mount Muscoco 8,020 ft.

Seven Falls

Gold Camp Road (closed to traffic)

PIKE NATIONAL FOREST

N

0   1   2 km.

0   1   2 mi.

North Cheyenne Cañon and Lower Gold Camp Roads

North Cheyenne Cañon Park

North Cheyenne Cañon Park, a spectacular Colorado Springs city park, is a deep cleft chiseled through pink granite cliffs by North Cheyenne Creek tumbling down from its headwaters on rounded Mount Almagre. The canyon has been a popular local destination since 1885, when Colorado Springs purchased 640 acres for a city park. Early residents often brought visitors here by carriage to marvel at the granite bastions and the raw natural beauty.

The 1,600-acre park, the largest in the Colorado Springs city park system, is tucked into the forested mountains on the southwest side of the city. The park, easily accessed by the paved road that winds up its twisting floor, offers more than a dozen miles of hiking and mountain biking trails, as well as two visitor centers and two waterfalls. North Cheyenne Cañon is renowned for the many hummingbirds that flit about in summer, so much so that the canyon is dubbed the Hummingbird Capital of Colorado.

The drive begins on the southwest edge of Colorado Springs at the junction of North and South Cheyenne Cañon Roads. The start is easily reached from Interstate 25 via Tejon Street and Cheyenne Boulevard. Before starting the drive, park your car in a lot just west up South Cheyenne Cañon Road and visit the **Starsmore Discovery Center.** This visitor center for North Cheyenne Cañon Park is housed in a historic stone house that originally sat at the corner of South Nevada Avenue and Cheyenne Road in Colorado Springs before being moved to its present location. The center offers park information and maps, an indoor climbing wall, dioramas, and a hands-on mineral exhibit, as well as nature programs and special events. The Lower Columbine Trail begins at the center and heads west parallel to the road. This 6-mile trail, open to hikers, bikers, and horses, is divided into three distinct segments. It finishes at **Helen Hunt Falls** in the upper canyon.

From the road junction, turn right onto North Cheyenne Cañon Road. The road twists west up the deepening canyon. Tall ponderosa pines, a few narrow-leaf cottonwoods, and thickets of scrub oak line the creek on the left. After 0.5 mile, the road makes the first of three wide, looping meanders beneath the north-facing cliffs of Mount Cutler, and after 0.8 mile it reaches a wide parking area next to Graduation Boulder, a massive, creekside boulder on the left. **The Pinnacle,** a looming granite precipice, towers to the south. This formation, along with surrounding rock pinnacles and faces, is popular with local rock climbers. Do not attempt to climb any of the rock formations without a rope and proper climbing hardware. The granite can be rotten and crumbly, and it's easy to scramble into dangerous places.

All the rock here and in the surrounding Pikes Peak Massif is Pikes Peak granite, a rough, pink, and coarse-grained granite originally deposited almost a billion years ago when it bubbled up under the earth's crust into an immense batholith. The rock slowly cooled into granite far underground over millions of years. This

Helen Hunt Falls, named for a famed nineteenth-century writer, tumbles over a granite cliff in North Cheyenne Cañon.

core of rock became part of the ancestral Rocky Mountains and later the Rocky Mountains. As the mountains rose, eons of erosion stripped away all the surface layers above, eventually exposing the ancient granite. Weathering, mostly water erosion and frost wedging in winter, has chiseled this relatively soft granite into today's canyon, cliffs, buttresses, and spires.

The road swings west beneath pointed Longfellow Pinnacle on the right and the west face of The Pinnacle to the left. At 1.1 miles is the parking area for the **Columbine Trail.** The trail climbs onto the canyon's dry northern slopes here and continues west to Helen Hunt Falls.

At 1.6 miles is the parking area on the left for the very popular 1-mile-long **Mount Cutler Trail.** The trail legs it uphill to the summit of 7,200-foot-high Mount Cutler and marvelous views across Colorado Springs. The trail is for hikers only.

The drive continues west up the floor of the canyon, passing granite monoliths jutting above hillside pines. The rocky summit of **Mount Muscoco** rises to the south as the road climbs Mine Hill at 2 miles. Several picnic areas with tables scatter along the road before it reaches Helen Hunt Falls at 2.7 miles. The Helen Hunt Visitor Center, housed in the old Bruin Inn beside Helen Hunt Falls, is open from Memorial Day to Labor Day. Helen Hunt Falls itself is a picturesque 40-foot-high waterfall named for Helen Hunt Jackson, a nineteenth-century writer who lived in the region. A short path climbs to a bridge above the falls. Continue hiking from here along a trail that switchbacks up to **Silver Cascade Falls,** a pretty waterfall spilling down a granite slab. It's best admired behind fenced overlooks. The slick, water-polished slabs are treacherous to walk across; more than thirty visitors who have ventured beyond the fences have been killed in falls. Above the cascade is Silver Cascade Slab, a large sweep of granite, and a section of the Gold Camp Road that is closed to auto traffic.

Just beyond the falls parking area at a tight switchback is the upper trailhead for the Columbine Trail. Continue up the paved road until it ends at 3.4 miles at a large parking lot and a three-way intersection.

Lower Gold Camp Road

At this point, there are two possible routes to take. The first option is a left turn onto **High Drive.** This narrow road leads north up to a pass between Mount Buckhorn and Mays Peak before dropping into the Bear Creek Cañon drainage. The 3.3-mile-long, one-way road offers some spectacular views of the towering rock formations called Grand Specimen Rock and Sentinel Rock. It also allows access to the Upper Bear Creek Canyon Trail. The road, closed in winter, ends at **Gold Camp Road.**

The other choice follows Lower Gold Camp Road for 6 miles to the west side of Colorado Springs. The dirt road heads east, edging above North Cheyenne Cañon. After 0.6 mile the road narrows down to one lane and plunges through

Tunnel #2. Note the tunnel roof is still black from locomotive smoke, a reminder of the tunnel's history.

Gold Camp Road, following an old railroad bed, meanders 31 miles along the south slopes of Pikes Peak between Colorado Springs and Cripple Creek. Cripple Creek was, in the 1890s, the world's richest gold camp. The mountainsides above the town yielded millions of dollars of gold ore that was hauled down to mills in the Colorado Springs and Cañon City area for refining. Three railroads served the booming gold district. The most famous of these lines to Cripple Creek was the Colorado Springs and Cripple Creek District Railway, otherwise dubbed The Short Line.

Many of the early Cripple Creek gold barons, living on Wood Avenue in Colorado Springs, were protective of their prosperous monopoly on Cripple Creek's commerce. So when Irving Howbert, president of the First National Bank in Colorado Springs, proposed a new railroad to Cripple Creek, it was not difficult to find interested investors. Thus in 1901 The Short Line was born. The line, also nicknamed "the gold-plated railroad," boasted the best rolling stock, track, and equipment available in its day. The railroad ran through nine tunnels on a 3.8 percent grade from the mill in Colorado City to the way station at Summit, making it one of the steepest standard gauge railways in the world.

Eventually the gold ran out. Competition with the Colorado Midland Railroad for haulage of the last reserves was too much, and The Short Line folded. The last train left the great gold camp in May 1920. Shortly thereafter businessman W. D. Corley saw the rail line's potential for tourism and paid $370,000 for the railbed. He promptly tore up the tracks and made it a toll road—the Gold Camp Road. The road became public in 1936.

The road between Colorado Springs and Cripple Creek still follows the original railroad bed, although the section between the top of the North Cheyenne Cañon Road and St. Peter's Dome is closed to vehicular traffic because of unstable tunnels. This section, accessed by parking at the large lot, is popular with hikers and mountain bikers.

Scenic views abound as you follow the drive above the canyon. When President Teddy Roosevelt rode the line, he stated theatrically that the trip "bankrupts the English language." Past the tunnel are good views south to Mount Muscoco, a rocky peak that rises above the canyon. You pass through Tunnel #1 after 1.6 miles and 0.5 mile later reach an overlook on the right that looks straight down into the rocky canyon below.

Past the view the road slims down to a single lane and edges around several sharp curves onto the east flank of Mays Peak. After the road widens and becomes paved there is another spectacular overlook offering a view of Colorado Springs and the prairie beyond. This is a great view in the early evening as the city lights twinkle below.

Drive north through copses of scrub oak and tall ponderosa pines. Secluded homes lie alongside the road. The road eventually bends west and travels into Bear Creek Cañon. At a three-way junction, keep straight on Gold Camp Road. The road passes a shallow canyon filled with granite buttresses and reaches the parking area on the left for the popular **Section 16 Trail.** A quarter-mile later it passes through the upturned sandstone layers of the Dakota hogback and then reaches a stop sign at the intersection of Gold Camp Road and Twenty-sixth Street marking the end of this drive. A left turn on Twenty-sixth Street leads 2.5 miles down to US 24 and the Old Colorado City Historic District. A right turn drops down to the Bear Creek Nature Center, a wonderful natural area that offers a good introduction to the ecology of the Pikes Peak region.

11

South Platte River Roads

Woodland Park to Pine Junction

General description: This 72-mile drive runs north from Woodland Park to Deckers, where the road divides and forms a loop that follows the South Platte River and the river's North Fork to the historic town of Buffalo Creek and the drive's end at Pine Junction.

Special attractions: Pike National Forest, Manitou Lake, South Platte River, Buffalo Creek, Pine, North Fork National Historic District, fishing, camping, picnicking, rock climbing, hiking, Colorado Trail, mountain biking, scenic views.

Location: Central Colorado. The drive's southern terminus begins in Woodland Park off US 24, 20 miles west of Colorado Springs. The northern access is via US 285 at Pine Junction some 25 miles west of Denver.

Drive route numbers: CO 67; Jefferson County Roads 126, 96, and 97; Douglas County Roads 40 and 67.

Travel season: Year-round. The drive is open all winter, although snow and ice accumulate in shaded areas.

Camping: Nine national forest campgrounds—Red Rocks, South Meadows, Colorado, Painted Rocks, Lone Rock, Wigwam, Kelsey, Platte River, and Bridge Crossing—are found along the drive.

Services: All services are found in Woodland Park. Limited services are at Pine Junction, Pine, Buffalo Creek, and Deckers.

Nearby attractions: Lost Creek Wilderness Area, Mount Evans Wilderness Area, Rampart Range Road, Devils Head, Mount Evans Scenic Byway, Guanella Pass Scenic Byway, Chatfield State Park, Denver area attractions, Colorado Springs area attractions, Cripple Creek, Florissant Fossil Beds, Pikes Peak Highway, Mueller State Park, Rampart Reservoir Recreation Area.

The Drive

The South Platte River, arising on the Continental Divide's snowy peaks above Fairplay, twists 360 miles across Colorado to the Nebraska border. The river, draining over 28,000 square miles, is Colorado's workhorse. The South Platte and its mountain tributaries irrigate the state's fertile northeastern corner and yield tap water for over 60 percent of Colorado's population, including Denver, Boulder, and Fort Collins. From the air, this working river looks like a string of watery pearls, with numerous reservoirs that impound its tumbling waters. Still, despite the dams and irrigation projects, the river retains a wild character through much of its rugged mountain course.

Some of the river's best scenery remains in deep, wooded canyons in the low mountains southwest of Denver, an area the Denver Water Board wants to change someday with its proposed Two Forks Dam. The 72-mile South Platte River scenic drive, following CO 67 and several county roads, explores these canyons and

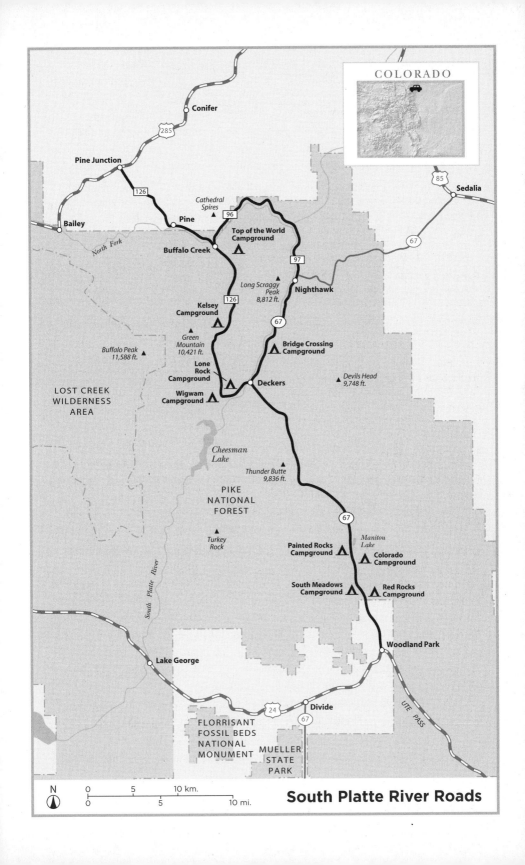

COLORADO

Conifer

285

Pine Junction

126

Bailey

North Fork

Pine

Cathedral Spires ▲

96

Top of the World Campground ⛺

Buffalo Creek

97

Long Scraggy Peak 8,812 ft. ▲

Nighthawk

Kelsey Campground ⛺

126

Green Mountain 10,421 ft. ▲

67

Bridge Crossing Campground ⛺

Buffalo Peak 11,588 ft. ▲

Lone Rock Campground ⛺

Devils Head 9,748 ft. ▲

Deckers

LOST CREEK WILDERNESS AREA

Wigwam Campground ⛺

Cheesman Lake

Thunder Butte 9,836 ft. ▲

PIKE NATIONAL FOREST

South Platte River

Turkey Rock ▲

67

Manitou Lake

Painted Rocks Campground ⛺

Colorado Campground ⛺

South Meadows Campground ⛺

Red Rocks Campground ⛺

Woodland Park

Lake George

UTE PASS

24

Divide

67

FLORISSANT FOSSIL BEDS NATIONAL MONUMENT

MUELLER STATE PARK

N

0   5   10 km.

0   5   10 mi.

South Platte River Roads

85

Sedalia

67

the surrounding piney mountains between Woodland Park and Pine Junction. The area, close to both Colorado Springs and Denver, is a popular destination for weekend campers and anglers.

Weather along the drive is generally pleasant year-round, although spring, summer, and fall are the preferred travel seasons. Spring days are mild and windy, with highs reaching sixty degrees with occasional rain. Summer highs range between sixty and eighty degrees, with afternoon thunderstorms usually falling somewhere along the drive. Summer at the drive's higher elevations gives welcome relief from flatland heat. Fall brings cooler but dry days until the first snow falls in November. Winter days can be very mild, with highs reaching into the fifties. Snow generally clings to cold north-facing slopes, but the roads are usually dry, with ice only in shaded spots.

Woodland Park to Deckers

The scenic drive begins at the intersection of U.S. Highway 24 and CO 67 on the west side of Woodland Park, 20 miles northwest of Colorado Springs. Woodland Park, a mountain community at 8,500 feet, spreads across a broad, wooded valley west of the Rampart Range. The town offers all traveler services.

The drive's first 23 miles, following CO 67, traverse lovely countryside with rolling hills, forested mountains, grassy valleys, and shallow canyons to Deckers on the South Platte River. This slice of landscape is more representative of Colorado's Front Range than the usual image of immense snowcapped peaks. It's a land of intimate views—a sweep of wind-rippled grass; cloud reflections in a serene beaver pond; aspen groves strewn with sky-blue columbines; the dusty smell of dry ponderosa pine needles on the forest floor.

The drive heads north on CO 67, leaves most of Woodland Park's suburban development behind after 2 miles, and enters Pike National Forest at 4 miles. Pike National Forest sprawls across 1.1 million acres of central Colorado's mountains and includes not only the South Platte's canyons but also the historic landmark Pikes Peak, Lost Creek Wilderness Area, and the Mosquito Range. Sixty-four-site South Meadows Campground, the second in a succession of national forest campgrounds scattered along the highway, is reached at 5 miles. Past the campground the road leaves the pine forest and skirts the east side of willow-lined Trout Creek in a broad valley. The highway passes Colorado Campground, with eighty-one sites, at almost 7 miles, crosses the creek, and reaches the turn to Painted Rocks Campground, a pleasant eighteen-site area just west of the drive. The Painted Rocks are small, eroded pinnacles nestled in the pine forest, the remains of downfaulted Paleozoic sandstone rocks that floor the valley north of Woodland Park. Both the highway and Trout Creek follow the Ute Pass Fault, a major Front Range fault that runs over 60 miles from south of Colorado Springs to north of Woodland Park.

Manitou Lake Picnic Area, with forty-two sites, sits alongside Manitou Lake, a small reservoir on Trout Creek. This popular recreation area offers fishing, canoeing, and hiking as well as picnicking. A paved, 2-mile-long bike/hike trail, bordering the highway, links the lake area with Colorado and South Meadows Campgrounds to the south.

The highway dips and rolls past Manitou Lake, running through open ponderosa pine woods and green meadows west of Trout Creek before turning away from the broad valley onto rounded ridges clad in spruce, fir, and aspen. At 13 miles the road crosses a divide, passes a pioneer cemetery, and drops down to West Creek's canyon. **Thunder Butte,** a ragged 9,836-foot mountain, dominates northwest of the drive, while domed Sheep's Nose, a premier rock climbing crag, and Bell Rock sit to the west. The drive turns north and follows West Creek through a shallow, winding canyon, lined with pine, spruce, and fir, that alternately widens and narrows for 9 miles to **Deckers** on the South Platte River.

Deckers, a small fishing resort with a restaurant and supplies, sits at a crossroads on the river. The town site, founded about 1885 as Daffodil, was renamed in 1912 for Steve Decker, who operated a store and saloon here.

Deckers to Buffalo Creek

The scenic drive makes a loop from here, heading north on Jefferson County Road 126 to Pine Junction on U.S. Highway 285 before backtracking to Buffalo Creek and following county roads along the North Fork and the South Platte River back to Deckers. The drive crosses the river at Deckers and heads west up County Road 126 along the north bank. This river section offers excellent fishing with flies and lures only. Lone Rock Campground, with nineteen sites, sits alongside the river just upstream from Deckers. The drive continues above the river, crossing gravel slopes studded with ponderosa pines.

About 2.5 miles from Deckers the road turns away from the river up Wigwam Creek and shortly afterward swings northward up Sixmile Creek. A side road turns off the main drive along Wigwam Creek and heads southwest past Cheesman Lake and Lost Creek Wilderness Area toward Lake George and US 24. Wigwam Campground, with ten walk-in sites, sits alongside the drive where it turns north. The paved road climbs steeply up Sixmile Creek's valley, widening to three lanes, and reaches a broad ridge crest after 3 miles. **Green Mountain,** its 10,421-foot summit wreathed in broken granite and forest green, looms to the west.

Kelsey Campground, with seventeen sites nestled in pine and aspen woods, sits a mile farther up the drive. The road bends around Little Scraggy Peak onto its east flank and reaches a scenic overlook. This point offers spectacular views eastward across the South Platte drainage—**Long Scraggy Peak** lifts its craggy ridge to the east while the river canyon hides in a maze of forest below. The Rampart

Range, dominated by **Devils Head,** rims the eastern horizon. The drive continues north along Little Scraggy's east slope onto a broad ridge. A roadside parking area here offers access to popular sections of the **Colorado Trail,** a 469-mile-long footpath that winds from Denver to Durango.

The road drops abruptly through pine forest and after 2 miles reaches the broad valley of the North Fork of the South Platte River and the picturesque community of **Buffalo Creek.** The town, mostly vacation cabins, is anchored by the Green Mercantile, an immense granite building perched on the riverbank alongside the drive. This old-fashioned country store, run by the same family since 1883, offers groceries and local chat. Buffalo Creek began as a railroad stop for area mines and lumber in 1880 on the now-abandoned Denver, South Park, and Pacific Railway.

Buffalo Creek to Pine Junction

The scenic drive forks at Buffalo Creek. A 10-mile spur continues north up County Road 126 to Pine Junction on US 285 west of Denver. This short road section, allowing drive access from Denver, is not to be missed. From Buffalo Creek the road twists through a granite-walled gorge. The river in early summer roars with mountain snowmelt alongside the drive. After a mile the road enters a wide, placid valley with the North Fork gently meandering between grassy banks. Grazing cattle and horses dot the meadows and complete the pastoral scene. Two miles later the road enters 6,738-foot-high Pine and the **North Fork National Historic District.** Pine, like its downstream neighbor, was established in the early 1880s as a railroad stop. This charming, historic community sits amid spectacular granite monoliths and bucolic meadows at Sphinx Park. Sphinx Rock, bearing a fanciful resemblance to its Egyptian namesake, looms east of town. Past Pine the drive twists up Pine Gulch through dry hills covered with ponderosa pine, mountain mahogany, and yucca and reaches Pine Junction and US 285 6 miles from Pine.

Along the South Platte River

To complete the scenic drive, backtrack to Buffalo Creek. The last leg of the scenic drive follows the South Platte River's **North Fork** and the **South Platte River** for 24 miles back to Deckers. Much of this drive section is unpaved and is intensively managed by Pike National Forest as the South Platte River Corridor. This river segment, lying close to Colorado's major metropolitan areas, is both used and abused. The forest's management plan addresses and alleviates use problems to create a positive recreational experience for visitors. The 15-mile road section from Buffalo Creek to Nighthawk is a day-use-only area. Parking is permitted only in designated parking areas. Camping is allowed on the Nighthawk-to-Deckers section only in designated campgrounds.

The drive's first 10 miles, following Jefferson County Road 96, heads northeast then southeast from Buffalo Creek to the confluence of the river's two forks at South Platte, following the abandoned railbed of the Denver, South Park, and Pacific Railway, a narrow gauge line that ran from Denver to the rich mining district of Fairplay and on to Buena Vista and Gunnison in the 1880s.

A couple of miles from Buffalo Creek, the drive passes under the **Cathedral Spires,** a collection of soaring granite pinnacles and slabs perched high above the road. The spires, including Cynical Pinnacle and The Dome, offer some of Colorado's best granite rock climbing. Downriver, the drive passes through Foxton, now a group of vacation cabins but once a railroad stop, and reaches Jefferson County Road 97, the Foxton Road, after another mile. Just up the road lies **Reynolds Ranch County Park,** part of Jefferson County's huge open space system, with hiking and picnicking among the pines.

The drive winds southeast from here, bordering the river and offering secluded fishing holes and picnic sites. A granite gravestone, inscribed "Tell my wife I died thinking of her," sits alongside the road among willows. After 10 snaking miles the road reaches the confluence of the North Fork and the South Platte Rivers at the old railroad stop of South Platte.

This confluence, called **Two Forks,** has long been a battleground between the Denver Water Board and Coloradans concerned with losing some of the Front Range's best recreational lands and one of the nation's prime trout fisheries. The water interests have long proposed putting a large dam here that would bury these scenic canyons under 500 feet of lake water. It would ostensibly provide boating recreation as well as both lawn and tap water to burgeoning Front Range cities. Below the forks, the South Platte tumbles down through wild Waterton Canyon before emptying into Chatfield Reservoir, a flood-control impoundment in the hills south of Denver.

At South Platte the drive crosses the river and bends southwest on Jefferson County Road 97. This river canyon is more gentle than its North Fork cousin, with bulging granite domes and rounded hills veneered with fir and pine trees. The river itself is also calmer, riffling over cobbled shoals and gliding past immense boulders. Designated parking areas allow anglers access to the river and hikers and mountain bikers access to canyon trails. Five miles from the forks the road intersects the Pine Creek Road, Douglas County Road 40. This road climbs over the flattened northern end of the Rampart Range and ends at Sedalia 17 miles to the east.

Nighthawk spreads across the broad valley just south of the road junction. Today it's a group of spread-out cabins, but in the 1890s it was a teeming gold mining settlement and lumber camp. The town, platted in 1896, included a hotel,

The Cathedral Spires edge the skyline above the North Fork of the South Platte River and the South Platte River Roads drive.

post office, general store, livery stable, blacksmith, and two newspapers, the *Mountain Echo* and the *West Creek Mining News.* A narrow gauge railroad ran through the canyon from 1904 to 1916.

The drive parallels the river for the next 10 miles to Deckers, passing a succession of picnic areas and campgrounds. Willow Bend and Scraggy View picnic grounds sit below the castellated ramparts of 8,812-foot Long Scraggy Peak that towers to the west. Fishing along this river section is by flies and lures only with a two-trout limit and 16-inch minimum. The road then passes the Ouzel camping area and Platte River Campground with walk-in sites. Past Bridge Crossing Picnic Area the canyon broadens with grass meadows and open ponderosa pine woodlands. A couple of miles later the canyon again narrows and the road twists alongside the river to an end at Deckers and CO 67.

12

Rampart Range Road

Garden of the Gods to Sedalia

General description: This 60-mile-long gravel road travels the forested crest of the Rampart Range from the Garden of the Gods near Colorado Springs to CO 67, 10 miles west of Sedalia.

Special attractions: Garden of the Gods, Queens Canyon, Rampart Reservoir Recreation Area, Devils Head National Recreation Trail, Devils Head Lookout, scenic views, fishing, camping, hiking, picnicking, rock climbing, mountain bike trails, motorized vehicle trails, cross-country skiing.

Location: East-central Colorado. The drive runs along the Rampart Range between Colorado Springs and southwest Denver. Access from the south is via Garden of the Gods park and US 24. The drive's northern terminus is reached from south Denver and I-25 via US 85. Turn west on CO 67 at Sedalia.

Drive route name and number: Rampart Range Road, Forest Road 300.

Travel season: Year-round. The lower section of the road, from Rampart Reservoir to Garden of the Gods, is unmaintained in winter. Snow blankets the upper reaches here. The northern section of the road, from 14 miles north of the Mount Herman Road to north of Devils Head, is closed in winter,

depending on snowfall and snowmelt. Travel at your own risk and carry chains and a shovel. Watch for icy spots in winter and slick sections after summer thunderstorms. Check with Pike National Forest for road closure information.

Camping: Seven forest campgrounds lie on or just off the drive. Thunder Ridge and Meadow Ridge at Rampart Reservoir Recreation Area offer forty sites on the lake's south shore. The campgrounds heading north from here are Springdale (fourteen sites), Jackson Creek (nine sites), Devils Head (twenty-two sites), Flat Rocks (twenty sites), and Indian Creek (eleven sites). Primitive camping is allowed on numerous side roads off Rampart Range Road.

Services: No services are found along the drive. Complete services are found in Colorado Springs, Woodland Park, and south Denver. Limited services in Sedalia, including gasoline.

Nearby attractions: Pikes Peak Highway, Colorado Springs attractions, Cave of the Winds, Florissant Fossil Beds National Monument, Mueller State Park, Lost Creek Wilderness Area, South Platte River roads (see Drive 11), Roxborough State Park, Chatfield State Park, Colorado Trail, Denver area attractions.

The Drive

Rampart Range Road, one of Colorado's best off-the-beaten track drives, traverses the crest of the Rampart Range for 60 miles between Colorado Springs and Sedalia. The scenic gravel road yields spectacular views of Pikes Peak, the prairie, and the rugged Front Range and Tarryall Mountains and offers quiet camping, diverse mountain biking and camping opportunities, and one of Colorado's last fire lookouts, atop Devils Head.

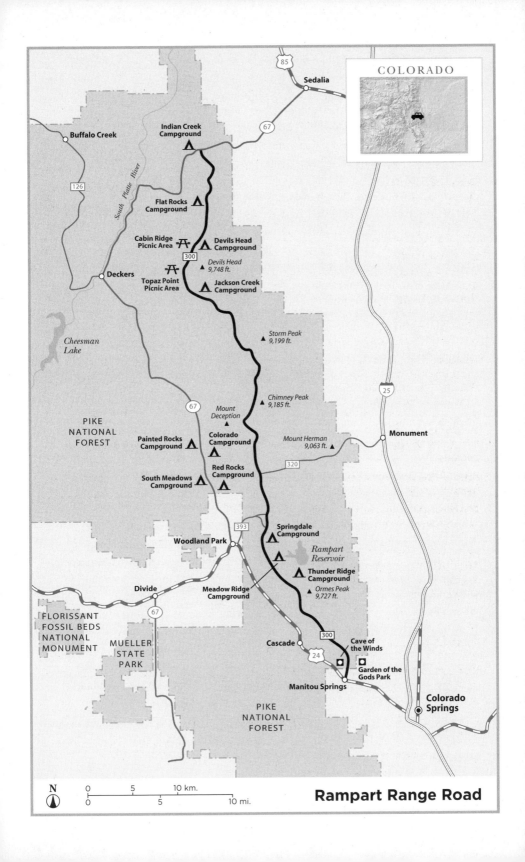

COLORADO

N

0   5   10 km.

0   5   10 mi.

Rampart Range Road

Sedalia

85

67

Buffalo Creek

Indian Creek
Campground

126

South Platte River

Flat Rocks
Campground

Cabin Ridge
Picnic Area

Devils Head
Campground

300

Devils Head
9,748 ft.

Deckers

Topaz Point
Picnic Area

Jackson Creek
Campground

Cheesman
Lake

Storm Peak
9,199 ft.

25

Chimney Peak
9,185 ft.

67

PIKE
NATIONAL
FOREST

Mount
Deception

Painted Rocks
Campground

Colorado
Campground

Mount Herman
9,063 ft.

Monument

320

South Meadows
Campground

Red Rocks
Campground

393

Springdale
Campground

Woodland Park

Rampart
Reservoir

Divide

Meadow Ridge
Campground

Thunder Ridge
Campground

Ormes Peak
9,727 ft.

67

FLORISSANT
FOSSIL BEDS
NATIONAL
MONUMENT

MUELLER
STATE
PARK

Cascade

300

Cave of
the Winds

24

Garden of the
Gods Park

Manitou Springs

Colorado
Springs

PIKE
NATIONAL
FOREST

Spring, summer, and fall are the best times to drive the road. Expect cool, breezy days in spring, with occasional showers and snowstorms. Summer days are pleasant and mild, with highs in the seventies and eighties. Severe thunderstorms occur almost daily somewhere along the drive on July and August afternoons. Mornings, however, are generally clear. Autumn offers colorful aspen foliage and a succession of bright, clear days with only occasional storms. Winter brings cold temperatures and deep snows that blanket the drive.

The road is plowed and maintained in winter from Rampart Reservoir Recreation Area to 14 miles north of Mount Herman Road. Drive with caution and watch for icy corners. The lower road section from the reservoir to Colorado Springs is unmaintained in winter. Drive at your own risk and carry chains and a shovel. By late March the lower road is generally passable to passenger cars. Inquire at the forest office for current road conditions. The lower road, running over corrugated sandstone bedrock, is rough year-round. The upper road section gets washboarded in summer after heavy rainstorms. Drive slowly to avoid vehicle damage.

Garden of the Gods

Rampart Range Road begins at the western end of the **Garden of the Gods,** a 1,391-acre Colorado Springs city park, just off U.S. Highway 24. The Garden of the Gods is a dramatic landscape, a place of soaring sandstone hogbacks nestled against the Rampart Range's southern flank in an outdoor sculpture garden. The strangely eroded rock formations have long attracted visitors. The Ute Indians often camped among the rocks. Nineteenth-century travelers bestowed fanciful names on the rocks—Montezuma's Tower, The Three Graces, Kissing Camels, and Weeping Indian. After Colorado Springs was established in 1871, the Garden became a tourist attraction. Writer and poet Helen Hunt Jackson wrote, "You wind among rocks of every conceivable and inconceivable shape and size . . . all bright red, all motionless and silent, with a strange look of having been just stopped and held back in the very climax of some supernatural catastrophe."

Rampart Range Road begins on the west edge of the Garden at 300-ton **Balanced Rock.** The rocks here are the gently tilting strata of Fountain Formation. This maroon formation, comprising alternating layers of sandstone, mudstone, and conglomerate, was deposited 300 million years ago as an alluvial apron by rushing streams and rivers below Frontrangia, an ancestral mountain range.

The dirt road turns north just east of Balanced Rock and begins climbing. Another balanced rock sits below the road past Balanced Rock, and after 0.3 mile the road swings north and bumps up a shallow canyon. A pygmy forest of piñon pine, juniper, and scrub oak lines the roadside.

Queens Canyon and Williams Canyon

The road's first couple of miles travel up rounded ridges west of the Garden of the Gods and after 4 miles reaches a good viewpoint above **Queens Canyon**. This canyon, draining southeast out of the Rampart Range, is lined with sharp granite precipices and buttresses. **Glen Eyrie,** Scottish for "Valley of the Eagle's Nest," sits at the canyon's entrance below the overlook. This Tudor-styled castle, built among soaring sandstone towers, was the home of General William Jackson Palmer, the founder of Colorado Springs. Queens Canyon is named for his wife, Queen Palmer. An abandoned gravel strip mine sits atop the ridge above Queens Canyon east of the overlook.

The road begins corkscrewing upward here, passing scrub oak copses and scattered ponderosa pines. The first 8 miles of road, passing over sandstone bedrock, has a rough, corrugated surface. Magnificent views of Pikes Peak and Colorado Springs unfold from the road as it slowly climbs the southern flank of the Rampart Range. At 6 miles the road traverses a ridge west of **Williams Canyon** and passes the South Rampart Shooting Range. A mile and a half later the drive passes a lofty viewpoint above upper Queens Canyon and then swings west above Williams Canyon. Upper Williams Canyon is a shallow gorge studded with granite crags. The lower canyon to the south is lined with white limestone cliffs and numerous caves, including the **Cave of the Winds.** By 8 miles the road encounters its first aspen grove tucked into a moist side canyon.

The drive climbs onto another lofty ridge and after 12 miles reaches the range crest and a spectacular fenced overlook perched atop granite crags. **Pikes Peak,** the 14,115-foot pioneer landmark of the Rockies, towers to the west. Far below the overlook stretches Ute Pass. The pass is not really a pass at all but an abrupt canyon that follows the Ute Pass Fault, a major fault eroded by Fountain Creek that separates the Rampart Range from the Pikes Peak massif. The canyon, offering relatively easy passage from the Great Plains into the mountains, was first used by the Ute Indians. Wagon roads and the Midland Railroad to the South Park and Cripple Creek mining areas later traversed the pass. US 24 now ascends Ute Pass from Manitou Springs to Woodland Park.

Another scenic viewpoint perches on the rim of Ute Pass another 0.3 mile farther north. A roadside monument here commemorates Rampart Range Road's dedication on June 19, 1938, and the USDA Forest Service and Civilian Conservation Corps workers who built the scenic drive.

The road twists north at an elevation of 9,000 feet along the western edge of the Rampart Range, dipping through shallow canyons densely lined with pine, fir, and spruce. Forest Road 303 is reached after 15 miles. This road allows access to 9,727-foot **Ormes Peak,** the range high point.

Pikes Peak, America's most famous mountain, looms beyond aspen glades and grassy meadows along Rampart Range Road.

Rampart Reservoir to Mt. Herman Road

Past Forest Road 303 Rampart Range Road improves dramatically, with a smooth gravel surface maintained by the city of Colorado Springs for access to its reservoirs. At almost 18 miles a turnoff leads east 3 miles to **Rampart Reservoir Recreation Area.** The 400-acre reservoir, part of the Colorado Springs watershed, is a popular recreation site managed by the Forest Service. Facilities include the Meadow Ridge and Thunder Ridge Campgrounds, Promontory Picnic Area, the barrier-free BPW Interpretive Trail, and a boat ramp. Lake Shore Trail, a popular 12-mile-long mountain bike and hiking path, circles the reservoir. Another popular trail, 1.2-mile Rainbow Gulch Trail, begins on Rampart Range Road a mile and a half north of the reservoir turnoff. The trail drops down to the reservoir through a ponderosa pine forest broken by open meadows.

Past Rainbow Gulch, the road climbs onto a grassland studded with pine groves. Great views unfold along this road section. The Sawatch Range and the Continental Divide poke above the far western horizon. The snowcapped summits of Mount Evans and Longs Peak are far to the north. Alert drivers can spot elk, mule deer, and wild turkey browsing in the meadows. Springdale Campground sits at 9,200 feet in an evergreen copse on the northern meadow edge. Past the grassland the drive intersects with Loy Creek Road, a short paved road that drops a couple of miles down to Woodland Park and US 24. Another spur road to Woodland Park sits 1.6 miles to the north. Woodland Park offers all services for travelers.

The road rolls north, hemmed in by thick forest. Occasional pullouts yield views across the range to distant peaks and the prairie. The Rampart Range, seen from the plains and surrounding high peaks, appears almost flat, with only occasional peaks rising above the level surface. Indeed, the range crest seldom climbs above 9,000 feet and only in eroded valleys does it drop below that elevation. The Rampart Range is what geologists call a pediment, or old erosional surface. Its granite hills are the worn down stubs of what were once great mountains. The pediment, once continuous with the high plains and extending over much of the Front Range, was uplifted some 28 million years ago.

Mount Herman Road (Forest Road 320) branches east 4 miles north of Loy Creek Road. This scenic road edges around 9,063-foot **Mount Herman** to Monument and Interstate 25. Rampart Range Road continues north, passing numerous side roads and Saylor Park, a popular cross-country skiing area. At the microwave towers, some 36 miles from the road's start, a gate is locked in winter, limiting access to the road. Past the gate the drive drops down a shallow canyon. A stream lined with aspen groves and beaver ponds borders the road. Beyond the canyon the road swings around a granite boulder-studded mountainside and twists northward. Forest Road 348, reached at 42 miles, heads west through Long Hollow to CO 67.

Devils Head

Devils Head, the 9,748-foot high point of the Rampart Range, dominates the northern section of the drive. The peak rears above the dusty road, its forested flanks broken by ragged granite crags and outcrops. The Forest Service's last Front Range fire lookout is stationed atop the peak. Since 1910 a spotter has been stationed here looking for forest fires. The 1.5-mile **Devils Head National Recreation Trail** threads up the peak's northern slopes to the fire lookout. The last trail section scales a series of staircases to the rocky summit. The view is astounding, taking in the entire Front Range from the Spanish Peaks almost 150 miles to the south to flat-topped Longs Peak to the north. The plains stretch eastward, while mountain ranges spread west. Denver's urban sprawl lies in the Denver Basin to the northwest, its glass buildings shimmering in the sun. Legend says that over $60,000 in gold coins was stashed somewhere on Devils Head's rough sides after an 1870s train robbery. Treasure hunters still canvas the mountain for the hidden gold.

Forest Road 507, reached at 44 miles, heads northeast down scenic Jackson Creek. Jackson Creek Campground sits 2 miles down the road. The scenic drive swings around the west side of Devils Head. Topaz Point Picnic Area and Viewpoint sits on a rocky knoll just west of the road. A short hike to the overlook yields a wide view of the South Platte River country from a weathered granite shelf. A display identifies the surrounding mountains.

Rampart Range Road climbs up and over the northern shoulder of Devils Head and after 2 miles reaches a spur road that leads 0.5 mile south to Devils Head Campground and the start of the Devils Head Trail. Cabin Ridge Picnic Area sits a mile farther north. The road begins steadily losing elevation past Cabin Ridge, passing from spruce and fir forest to a drier ponderosa pine woodland. Flat Rocks Campground and overlook sit another 4 miles up the road. The overlook offers views of wooded ridges and canyons, the flat-topped mesas around Castle Rock, and the plains. This upper road section is the Rampart Range Motorized Recreation Area, with 120 miles of all-terrain vehicle and motorcycle trails. The area is busy in the summer, especially on weekends. The drive ends on CO 67 at a Pike National Forest work center. Indian Creek Campground lies just west of the highway junction. A right turn runs down Jarre Canyon 10 miles to Sedalia and U.S. Highway 85, while a left turn drops down Douglas County Road 67 to the South Platte River and Deckers.

13

South Park–Tarryall Loop Scenic Drive

Lake George through South Park and back to Lake George

General description: This 121-mile loop drive follows Tarryall Creek along the Tarryall Mountains into South Park, traverses the park's western edge beneath the Park and Mosquito ranges, then turns east and crosses the park and Wilkerson Pass back to Lake George.

Special attractions: Pike National Forest, Lost Creek Wilderness Area, Puma Hills, Tarryall Creek, Tarryall Reservoir State Wildlife Area, South Park, Fairplay, Park Range, Como, South Park City, Mosquito Range, Antero Reservoir State Wildlife Area, Buffalo Peaks, Spinney Mountain State Park, Wilkerson Pass, hiking, backpacking, fishing, rock climbing, scenic views, picnicking.

Location: Central Colorado.

Drive route numbers: US 24 and US 285; Park County Road 77.

Travel season: Year-round. The highways are plowed in winter. Be prepared, however, for blowing and drifting snow during blizzards, icy roads, and hazardous driving conditions. Park County Road 77 can be temporarily closed in severe weather.

Camping: Several national forest campgrounds lie on or just off the drive. Happy Meadows Campground and Spruce Grove Campground are on Park County Road 77. Kenosha Pass, Aspen, Lodgepole, Jefferson Creek, Michigan Creek, Selkirk, Beaver Creek, Four Mile, Horseshoe, and Buffalo Springs campgrounds all sit on forest roads west of US 285 between Kenosha Pass and Antero Junction. Elevenmile State Park, 11 miles south of the drive in eastern South Park, offers a large state-run campground. Numerous forest campgrounds are found in Elevenmile Canyon south of Lake George at the drive's eastern terminus. Primitive camping is permitted on national forest lands, particularly in the Puma Hills. Practice low-impact camping and make sure your fire is out.

Services: All services are found in Fairplay. Limited services, including gas, in Jefferson, Hartsel, and Lake George.

Nearby attractions: Breckenridge, Boreas Pass, Brown's Canyon, Arkansas Headwaters State Recreation Area, Sawatch Range, San Isabel National Forest, Elevenmile Canyon, Cripple Creek, Florissant Fossil Beds National Monument, Bristlecone Scenic Area, Mosquito Pass, Guanella Pass Scenic and Historic Byway (see Drive 15), South Platte scenic drive (see Drive 11).

The Drive

The 121-mile-long South Park–Tarryall drive makes a spectacular loop through some of Colorado's most spacious scenery. The drive traverses the granite-studded canyons and valleys of Tarryall Creek and crosses the open, sweeping grasslands of South Park, a high intermontane basin that sits in the state's middle. This land of wide views and historic sites boasts a long human history, from the Ute Indians

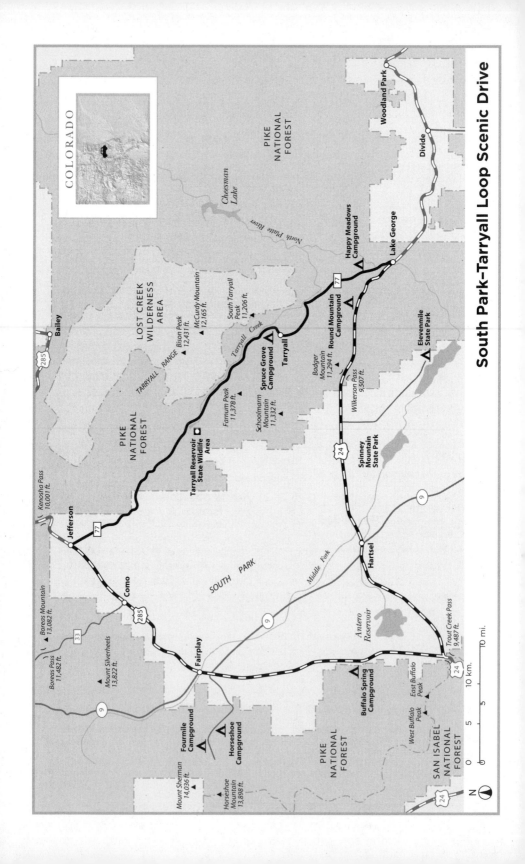

South Park-Tarryall Loop Scenic Drive

who hunted buffalo on the park's broad expanse, to silver and gold prospectors who mined around Fairplay, to sheep and cattle ranchers. Today this is a land of peace and quiet. Wind ruffles the surrounding pine forests, thunderstorms spread a veil of rain and lightning over the mountains, and shortgrass broken by fence lines and roads carpets the park floor.

South Park, lying at 9,000 feet, and the higher surrounding mountains are cool in summer and cold in winter. Summer days are generally clear; thunderstorms build up in the afternoon over the high peaks to the west. Expect heavy localized rain and lightning. Avoid being in the open or under trees during lightning storms. Autumn brings clear, warm days and a frosting of snow to the above-timberline ranges. Winters are cold and windy. Heavy snow blankets South Park and the Mosquito and Park ranges. Ground blizzard conditions are common during snowstorms. Temperatures are frigid, often dropping below zero, in South Park because cold air sinks onto the valley floor from adjacent higher slopes. Spring days are cool and often windy. The snow cover slowly melts away, leaving dry grass by April.

Tarryall

The drive begins 1 mile west of Lake George and 45 miles west of Colorado Springs along the South Platte River. Turn north off U.S. Highway 24 onto roughly paved Park County Road 77. This first leg of the byway journey ends 42 miles ahead in Jefferson on U.S. Highway 285. The road turns north along the river and follows a broad, grassy valley through rolling, ponderosa pine–clad hills. After a mile the river leaves the road and bends into a deep canyon that twists northeastward through the Front Range to Denver. A spur forest road follows the river for a mile to seven-site Happy Meadows Campground, a popular summer site for anglers.

After leaving the river, the road follows broad Tappan Gulch northward past small ranches and grassy meadows grazed by horses and cattle. Low granite hills, sparsely covered with ponderosa pines, line the valley floor. After 4 miles the road crosses a divide below 8,954-foot Tappan Mountain and drops into Tarryall Creek's scenic drainage. Tarryall Creek slices through a wide canyon that separates the rugged Tarryall Mountains to the northeast from the Puma Hills to the west. The creek meanders through a verdant valley here, swinging past wide meadows, hay fields, and gray granite crags. A mile after reaching the creek, the drive intersects Matukat Road, Forest Road 211. This scenic dirt road sweeps around the east flank of the Tarryalls and offers views into the South Platte River drainage. After another mile, the drive turns west away from the creek up Marksbury Gulch. The gulch is named for an early homesteader, buried in the Lake George cemetery, who was killed by Ute Indians after stealing an Indian pony. The China Wall, a long granite escarpment, parallels the dry arroyo on its north side. The road passes the boulder-strewn hillsides, climbs into rounded, grassy hills, crosses a divide, and drops into the historic town of **Tarryall** at 12 miles.

Tarryall, formerly called Puma City, got its start in 1859, when prospectors found gold nuggets "as big as watermelon seeds" in the creek below. The new town supposedly got its name when a miner remarked, "Let us tarry all." Those who came later, however, found the best placer sites claimed and derided the town as "Grab all" before starting the competing town of Hamilton on the opposite creek bank and heading across South Park and founding Fairplay.

Hamilton quickly surpassed its neighbor and boasted a transient population of 6,000 by 1860. The town offered saloons, casinos, its own newspaper, and a theater. Tarryall was officially laid out in 1861 and was the Park County seat for a short while. In the summer of 1861 miner John Parsons began his own mint, stamping out $2.50, $5.00, and $20.00 gold coins that are today worth more than $30,000. Slowly the placer claims were exhausted and miners left Tarryall and Hamilton for new strikes elsewhere. By 1875 the towns were mostly deserted.

Tarryall now is a small community of mostly rustic cabins. Still visible, however, is Whiskey Hole. This deep pit was set aside during the boom days for poor miners to pan enough gold to buy a shot of whiskey at local watering holes. The Tarryall School, listed in the National Register of Historic Places, sits on the roadside entering Tarryall. The elegant white clapboard building, with a steeple and bell, was built in 1922 and now serves as a town meeting hall. Nothing remains of Hamilton save a few mining scars.

The Tarryall Range

Just past Tarryall, the road becomes gravel and descends to Tarryall Creek. The drive parallels the creek through canyons and valleys for the next 12 miles to Tarryall Reservoir. The Puma Hills, a long ridge of timbered hills topped by 11,378-foot Farnum Peak, border this spectacular road section on the west, while the Tarryall Range, a 25-mile-long sierra studded with bold granite cliffs and deep forests of aspen and evergreen, lifts its serrated escarpment to the east.

The 119,790-acre **Lost Creek Wilderness Area** protects most of the Tarryall Range from encroaching civilization. Numerous hiking trails wend up ponderosa pine–covered slopes, passing trickling creeks lined with columbines and aspens, and switchbacking to the summit of 12,431-foot Bison Peak, the range high point. The Tarryalls are formed by Pikes Peak granite, a billion-year-old, pink, coarse-grained rock that formed after a massive underground reservoir of molten magma slowly cooled over millions of years. Eons of erosion chipped away at the granite, sculpting today's rocky wonderland of spires, flying buttresses, domes, castles, and rounded boulders. Besides being an excellent getaway for hiking and backpacking,

Abandoned ranch buildings weather under the blazing summer sun near the historic town of Tarryall.

the wilderness area offers rock climbing, fly-fishing in cold streams, and wildlife observation. The area is one of the best spots to see Rocky Mountain bighorn sheep. Any hiker scrambling to the cobbled summit of the high peaks here has a good chance of seeing these elegant, sure-footed mammals. Other wildlife includes mule deer, black bear, mountain lion, golden eagle, elk, turkey, porcupine, and raccoon. The wilderness is easily accessed from the scenic drive at Spruce Grove Campground, Twin Eagles Picnic Ground, and at Ute Creek. The Pike National Forest office in Colorado Springs offers detailed maps and trail descriptions.

Spruce Grove Campground, with twenty-seven sites at 8,600 feet, sits just off the drive a mile north of Tarryall. This lovely campground, surrounded by jagged cliffs, nestles among tall pines along the swift creek. Twin Eagles Picnic Area and Trailhead, a popular stop for anglers, lies 2 miles northward along a sharp creek bend. A broad valley, carpeted with green hay fields and dotted with grazing cattle, stretches away from the road just beyond the picnic area to the Tarryall Range.

The road follows the creek, passing grassy banks lined with dense willow thickets and dipping across dry drainages below timbered Farnum Peak. After almost 22 miles the drive reaches the **Ute Creek Trailhead,** a popular jumping-off point for backpackers trekking into Lost Creek Wilderness Area. The canyon broadens beyond Ute Creek, but steep mountain slopes clad in pine and granite continue to wall the canyon. Fishing along this section of Tarryall Creek is allowed with artificial flies and lures only.

At 23 miles the pavement begins again and views of the snow-capped Park Range unfold to the west. **Tarryall Reservoir State Wildlife Area** is 2 miles down the road.

The 700-acre lake is a glistening jewel nestled among treeless, rolling hills studded with brief rock outcrops. It's a popular destination for anglers who come to fish for trout and picnic on its shores.

South Park, Jefferson, and Como

The scenery dramatically changes beyond the reservoir as the drive ventures onto the hilly northeastern fringe of **South Park.** The road continues following Tarryall Creek northwestward, crossing dry Schoolhouse and Graveyard Gulches and passing abandoned cabins, a cemetery, and picturesque ranches. Scrubby forests scatter across the rolling hills, including 10,073-foot Observatory Rock, a prominent peak to the southwest.

Twelve miles from the reservoir, Michigan Creek and the drive enter South Park itself. A wide, lush grassland, watered by snowmelt from the peaks of the towering Park Range, stretches westward to the distant forest edge. The creek cuts through meadows enclosed by barbed-wire fences.

The drive's first leg ends 5 miles later in **Jefferson** at US 285. Jefferson was hastily erected in 1879 when the Denver, South Park & Pacific Railroad pushed across northern South Park in a race to reach Leadville before the rival Denver & Rio Grande did from Cañon City. The old railroad depot still stands alongside the highway. By 1881 the town boasted a post office and 300 residents. Jefferson became an important shipping and ranching center for area cattle and sheep outfits, a role it continues to play.

The drive's next leg runs south on US 285 along the western edge of South Park from Jefferson 16 miles to Fairplay and another 23 miles to Antero Junction at the park's southwestern corner. South Park is an intermontane basin 50 miles long and 35 miles wide with an area of more than 900 square miles, just slightly smaller than Rhode Island. Elevations range from 8,500 feet to higher than 10,000 feet. The park, covered with shortgrass, is broken by several long, forested hogbacks. The South Platte River, arising on the Continental Divide near Hoosier Pass, drains the valley and the surrounding mountains. Mountains rim South Park—the Puma Hills, bisected by Wilkerson Pass on the east; the dark rounded peaks of the old Thirty-Nine-Mile Volcanic Field to the south; and the lofty snowcapped Mosquito and Park Ranges on the west and north. The Mosquito range includes four peaks—Mounts Lincoln, Bross, Democrat, and Sherman—that top 14,000 feet. Mosquito Pass, Colorado's highest pass at 13,180 feet, crosses the range west of Fairplay en route to Leadville. South Park, one of Colorado's four mountain basins (the other ones being North Park, Middle Park, and the San Luis Valley), was originally named Valle Salada ("Salt Valley") for the white saline deposits left on flat, evaporated lake beds on the valley floor. One of the salts is sodium chloride, or common table salt.

From Jefferson, the drive crosses well-watered meadows covered with summer wildflowers, including sky-blue iris. West of the highway looms the snow-covered Park Range, an extension of the Front Range. The Continental Divide, separating the Pacific and Atlantic ocean drainages, meanders along the range crest over high peaks including 13,370-foot Mt. Guyot and 13,082-foot Boreas Mountain. Gravel roads climb west from the highway into Pike National Forest up Jefferson, Michigan, and Tarryall Creeks to alpine valleys, beaver ponds, and several forest campgrounds. The Boreas Pass Road, ascending Tarryall Creek from Como to 11,482-foot Boreas Pass, offers an excellent route to Breckenridge. The well-maintained gravel road generally follows the old narrow gauge Denver, South Park & Pacific Railroad grade. The railroad, in use from 1881 to 1937, climbed 4.5 percent grades and 435 curves on this stretch of track. Selkirk Campground, with fifteen sites, sits along the road at 10,500 feet.

The drive reaches **Como,** an old railroad town, 7 miles from Jefferson. Como, like neighboring Jefferson, was a boom town during the heady days of railroad construction, with a population of more than 6,000, most of whom lived in tents. The town also prospered with coal mining in the nearby hills. The dangerous

Como mines claimed numerous victims, including thirty-five Chinese miners in 1885 and twenty-five Italians in 1893. The mines closed in 1896 and Como began a quiet life as a railroad center.

The highway climbs a low, forested ridge southwest of Como, drops across Trout Creek, and steeply ascends to the summit of 9,943-foot Red Hill Pass. Red Hill is a long hogback of tilted Dakota sandstone that runs southward across South Park from here. The road descends the summit's western slope, runs across grassy benches, and enters Fairplay 3 miles later. The drive intersects CO 9 here, which runs north to Hoosier Pass and Breckenridge.

Fairplay

Fairplay, South Park's largest town and the seat of Park County, sits at 9,953 feet on gravel benches above the Middle Fork of the South Platte River in the park's extreme northwestern corner. Fairplay, once a brawling, boisterous mining camp, retains a quaint historic charm, with log cabins, gingerbread-adorned Victorian homes, and a friendly atmosphere. The town sprang up in 1859 at the core of a rich placer mining district by miners incensed by claim-grabbing at Tarryall across the valley. The frontier town slowly grew not only as a mining center, but also as a freight, transportation, and supply hub. By the 1870s Fairplay boasted hotels, a post office, a brewery, a stone courthouse, a newspaper, and of course several churches to minister to the miners. The **Sheldon Jackson Memorial Chapel,** named for the superintendent of the West's Presbyterian missions, was built in 1874. This elegant, white church, also called the South Park Community Church, is considered by some to be one of the nation's best examples of Timber Gothic architecture. Fairplay offers all services to visitors, including accommodations, dining, groceries, and gas.

Today old Fairplay lives in **South Park City Museum,** a living-history museum that preserves buildings and artifacts from the past. Real history is found in real people. Trod the dusty streets here, peer through shop windows, examine an old cabin, and study a miner's tools. South Park City gives the traveler a moment to experience history, to share in its making, to take a step backward in time to a place where every day is yesterday.

The Mosquito Range

The drive continues south on US 285 23 miles to Antero Junction. This highway section runs atop rolling hills and plains of stream-deposited glacial gravels on South Park's western margin beneath the rounded Mosquito Range, a high range

Opposite: The Sheldon Jackson Memorial Chapel in Fairplay is considered one of Colorado's best-preserved Timber Gothic churches.

that twists south from Hoosier Pass to Trout Creek Pass. Most of the range crest soars above timberline and includes four 14,000-foot peaks. The high peaks west of the drive—14,036-foot Mount Sherman, 13,898-foot Horseshoe Mountain, and 13,739-foot Ptarmigan Peak—are rounded bumps on the range crest. Glaciers contoured and smoothed the range's ancient sedimentary rock layers into broad valleys and steep-walled cirques. Most of the range names are of Civil War vintage, with miners naming Mount Lincoln for the president and Mounts Sherman and Sheridan for generals. Myth has it that the Mosquito Range acquired its name in 1861 when a mosquito was found pressed on the blank spot of a legal document where the name of a proposed mining district was to be written, giving the name to the district, pass, mountain, and range.

Several gravel roads head west from the drive onto the eastern flank of the Mosquitos. The Fourmile Creek Road, just south of Fairplay, twists up Fourmile Creek past nineteen-site Horseshoe and fourteen-site Fourmile Campgrounds to the abandoned ghost town site of Leavick. An easy trail climbs west from here to the summit of Mount Sherman, considered the easiest of Colorado's fourteeners to scale. The Weston Pass Road ascends to 11,921-foot Weston Pass. **The west side of the pass is four-wheel-drive only.**

The **Buffalo Peaks,** a twin-summited mountain of lava and volcanic ash, dominates the southern Mosquito Range and the drive. The peaks, in a 43,410-acre wilderness area, are densely forested and teem with wildlife, including bighorn sheep and elk. Access is via several forest roads. This drive section ends at Antero Junction at US 285's junction with US 24. US 285/24 continues west over Trout Creek Pass to Buena Vista. The drive, however, turns east on US 24 onto the treeless steppe of South Park.

Across South Park

The last segment of this drive runs east 39 miles across the park, over Wilkerson Pass, and on down to Lake George and the drive's starting point. The highway drops away from Antero Junction, crosses several dry arroyos, and reaches the old Colorado Midland Railroad grade after a couple of miles. The grade parallels the highway from here to Hartsel before heading east to Elevenmile Canyon. The Colorado Midland, built by Colorado Springs mining magnates with interests in the Leadville and Aspen mines in the 1880s, was the first standard gauge railroad into the Colorado Rockies. The railroad often ran "Wildflower Excursion" trains from Colorado Springs to South Park for passengers to collect colorful bouquets. The rail line was torn up in 1921.

The highway, running northeast, passes prominent Twin Peaks, swings down a dry, shallow valley, and reaches the turnoff to Antero Reservoir after almost 9 miles. **Antero Reservoir,** a popular fishing lake, was built in 1913 and supplies water to Denver. Numerous Indian sites line this road section, including a large campsite and battleground near Twin Peaks. South Park, with plentiful game, including buffalo and deer, was a popular summer hunting ground for the Ute, Comanche, Cheyenne, Kiowa, and Arapaho Indians. Legendary scout and trailblazer Kit Carson witnessed a three-day battle between the Comanches and Utes in eastern South Park in 1844. The Utes were defeated on the third day after forty braves were killed and more than 100 Ute horses were taken as battle spoils.

Hartsel sits on the South Platte River in the middle of the park, 13 miles from Antero Junction. The town, named for early rancher Sam Hartsel, once thrived as a mini-resort on the Colorado Midland line. A small hot spring, with 134-degree water, attracted visitors who stayed overnight at a hotel. The bathhouse, now abandoned, sits just south of town above the riverbank. A more modest bathtub now graces the hot spring and allows weary travelers a moment's respite in what has been called "Colorado's hottest hot spring"—the radon-laden water is radioactive. Ask in town for permission to bathe here.

US 24, after intersecting CO 9, which runs north to Fairplay and south to Cañon City, crosses the South Platte River. The drive continues east, skirting several low mountains, and passes the turnoff for Elevenmile State Park after 11 miles. The 3,300-acre reservoir, built in 1932 as part of Denver's water supply, is one of Colorado's most popular mountain lakes. Trophy-sized trout, kokanee salmon, and northern pike are regularly pulled from its chilly waters. The highway climbs into the Puma Hills beneath 11,294-foot Badger Mountain and snakes up to the summit of 9,507-foot **Wilkerson Pass.** Imaginative eyes can spot an Indian head composed of metamorphic cliff bands on Badger Mountain's western slope.

Wilkerson Pass, with a rest area and Forest Service visitor center, offers spectacular views to the west of South Park, the Mosquito Range, and beyond to the Sawatch Range. To the east towers bulky 14,115-foot Pikes Peak, surrounded by a green forest mantle. The highway winds down the Puma Hills' gentle east flank, passes sixteen-site Round Mountain Campground, and twists down Pulver Gulch to the South Platte River, Lake George, and the drive's eastern terminus. Colorado Springs lies another 45 miles to the east.

14

Mount Evans Scenic Byway

Idaho Springs to the Summit of Mount Evans

General description: The 28-mile Mount Evans Highway, the nation's highest automobile road and a National Forest Scenic Byway, climbs from Idaho Springs to the 14,264-foot summit of Mount Evans.

Special attractions: Pike National Forest, Arapaho National Forest, Mount Evans Wilderness Area, Echo Lake, Mount Goliath Natural Area, Summit Lake, camping, picnicking, fishing, rock climbing, wildlife observation, spring skiing, hiking, bristlecone pines, scenic views.

Location: Central Colorado. The drive is in the Front Range just west of Denver.

Drive route name and numbers: Mount Evans Highway, CO 103 and 5.

Travel season: Summer only. The road to the summit, CO 5, usually opens to Summit Lake by Memorial Day and all the way to the summit by late June, depending on the winter's snowfall depth. The road closes on Labor Day. The lower-elevation highway is open year-round. Expect severe driving conditions on the upper mountain in summer, with possible heavy thunderstorms and even snow. The road can become slick and icy.

Camping: Two national forest campgrounds—sixteen-site West Chicago Creek and eighteen-site Echo Lake—lie along the drive. Three picnic areas are found on the drive.

Services: All services are found in Idaho Springs.

Nearby attractions: Guanella Pass Scenic Byway (see Drive 15), Oh My God Road, Central City, Georgetown National Historic District, Georgetown Loop Railroad, Loveland Basin Ski Area, Arapaho Basin Ski Area, Golden Gate Canyon State Park, Clear Creek Canyon, Mount Evans State Wildlife Area, Evergreen, Buffalo Bill Grave, Red Rocks Park, Denver area attractions.

The Drive

Colorado's Front Range lifts its snow-flecked peaks high above the parched eastern plains. The sawtoothed mountains cut across the horizon, the old, sturdy summits etched against an azure sky. While the procession of seasons alters the mountain garb—carpets of summer wildflowers, emerald green forests in spring, aspen leaves that flutter like newly minted gold coins in autumn, and winter's blanket of dazzling snow—the peaks seem unchanging, silent, and even aloof. The Front Range escarpment fronting the prairie is dominated by three massive peaks that lift above their neighbors—Pikes Peak, Longs Peak, and Mount Evans.

Mount Evans, rising to 14,264 feet, is Denver's mountain. It's always visible from the city streets—glistening in the sun like an alabaster castle or its ridges obscured by windswept clouds. Its conspicuous presence is a reminder that out there, beyond the urban gridlock, is a wild, wonderful world waiting to be explored.

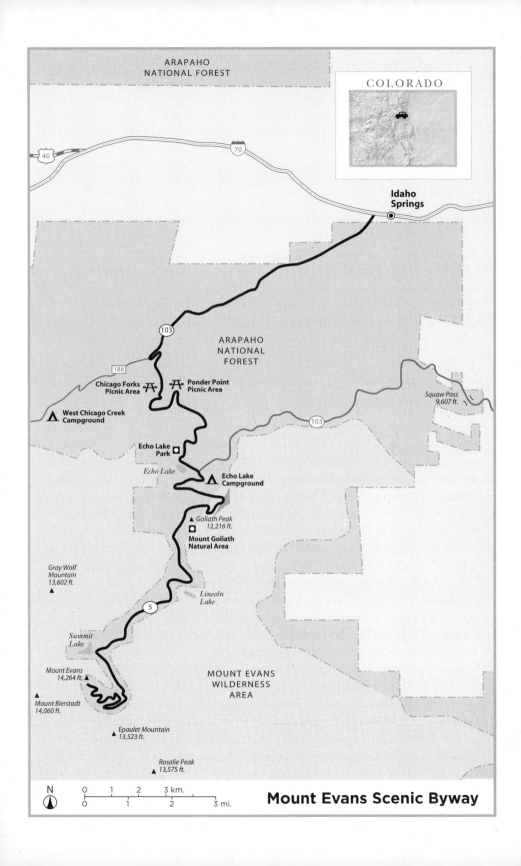

ARAPAHO
NATIONAL FOREST

COLORADO

Idaho
Springs

40

70

103

ARAPAHO
NATIONAL
FOREST

188

Squaw Pass
9,607 ft.

Chicago Forks
Picnic Area

Ponder Point
Picnic Area

West Chicago Creek
Campground

103

Echo Lake
Park

Echo Lake

Echo Lake
Campground

Goliath Peak
12,216 ft.

Mount Goliath
Natural Area

Gray Wolf
Mountain
13,602 ft.

Lincoln
Lake

5

Summit
Lake

Mount Evans
14,264 ft.

MOUNT EVANS
WILDERNESS
AREA

Mount Bierstadt
14,060 ft.

Epaulet Mountain
13,523 ft.

Rosalie Peak
13,575 ft.

N

0   1   2   3 km.

0   1   2   3 mi.

Mount Evans Scenic Byway

The 28-mile-long Mount Evans scenic drive, a National Forest Scenic Byway, explores this lofty peak. The paved highway, beginning off Interstate 70 in Idaho Springs, twists and winds up canyons and across ridges, passes ancient bristlecone pine forests and clear alpine lakes, and ends with spectacular views that encompass all of central Colorado.

The road to Mount Evans's summit, CO 5, is open only in summer from Memorial Day to Labor Day. The lower drive section above Idaho Springs is open year-round. The summer weather on Mount Evans, like any high Colorado peak, is fickle. Expect clear skies in the morning and clouds and possible thunderstorms in the afternoon. Summer temperatures range from the eighties at Idaho Springs to the thirties atop the mountain. Snow, below-freezing temperatures, and high winds can occur on any summer day. Be prepared by bringing warm clothes, including long pants and a raincoat. Beware of lingering on the summit or high ridges during lightning storms. The road surface can be slick with rain, snow, and ice during and after storms—drive cautiously. Many visitors will experience altitude sickness from the quick elevation gain. The rarefied air offers less oxygen than lower elevations. The best remedy is to descend from the upper heights.

Idaho Springs

The drive begins at exit 240 on I-70 in Idaho Springs 30 miles west of Denver. Idaho Springs, at 7,540 feet, stretches along narrow Clear Creek Canyon among dry, steep-walled mountains. Idaho Springs was the site of Colorado's first important gold strike. In January 1865, George Jackson, a prospector and cousin of scout Kit Carson, descended Chicago Creek alone on a hunting trip. He camped at the confluence of Chicago Creek and Clear Creek just south of today's exit 240 and kept warm with a campfire. The next morning he "removed the embers and panned out eight treaty cups of dirt, and found nothing but fine colors; with one cup I got a nugget of gold." Jackson marked his claim and returned later in the spring to pan out thousands of dollars' worth of gold, and the stampede was on.

Miner Street in Idaho Springs quickly became a wall-to-wall tent city, with a population of 12,000. Its less-populous eastern neighbor, Denver, had only 2,000 residents. The placer deposits were soon exhausted, but the discovery of rich ore veins in the surrounding metamorphic gneiss and schist rock kept the town alive. In 1868 the local hot springs began attracting tourists, and Idaho Springs discovered new wealth as a spa. Visitors still come to Idaho Springs to soak in the hot springs as well as to visit downtown Idaho Springs, a registered National Historic District dotted with picturesque Victorian homes and buildings. The town is also the gateway to central Colorado's ski areas. A good backroad drive heads 8 miles north from town up Russell Gulch to Central City. This twisting road, nicknamed the Oh My God Road, follows the treacherous old trail between the two mining camps.

The Continental Divide rises behind a cyclist laboring up the flank of Goliath Peak on the Mount Evans Highway.

Chicago Creek to Echo Lake

At Idaho Springs, turn south on CO 103 from I-70. Arapaho National Forest's Clear Creek Ranger Station sits just south of the highway junction. The visitor center here, open from 8:00 a.m. to 8:00 p.m. from Memorial Day to Labor Day, dispenses forest maps, guidebooks, and free information about the national forest and surrounding communities. CO 103 runs southwest up Chicago Creek in a deep, broad canyon. Groves of juniper and thickets of mountain mahogany and skunkbush line the dry, south-facing slopes, while mature ponderosa pines lift stately crowns above the moister, north-facing hillsides. As the road climbs, the forest changes, with ponderosas lining the northern walls and dense fir and spruce forest shrouding the southern slopes. Willows and aspen groves line the tumbling creek. Numerous houses and abandoned mines lie along Chicago Creek.

After 6.5 miles the highway turns south from Chicago Creek and begins climbing steep, wooded slopes above the creek. Forest Road 188 continues up

West Chicago Creek for 3 miles to eleven-site West Chicago Creek Campground. The scenic drive, with steep grades and sharp curves, ascends past Chicago Forks and Ponder Point Picnic Areas. Ponder Point, perched above a hairpin turn, offers the first view of Mount Evans to the southwest.

The road continues climbing and by 13 miles reaches **Echo Lake** and the Echo Lake Picnic Area at 10,600 feet. Scenic Echo Lake, part of Denver's city park system, is a popular stopover for picnickers and anglers. The road bends southeast from the lake and 0.5 mile later reaches the junction of CO 103 and 5. Echo Lake Lodge, a large three-story log building, sits at the intersection. The lodge, which opened in 1927, has been a hunting lodge, brothel, Army winter survival base in World War II, and is now a popular restaurant. Arapaho National Forest's eighteen-site Echo Lake Campground sits south of the lodge. This wooded campground makes an excellent overnight stopover for highway travelers.

Echo Lake to Summit Lake

The scenic drive turns west at the campground and lodge on CO 5. The roadway narrows and begins sharply ascending through a thick subalpine forest on the northern slopes of Goliath Peak, a 12,216-foot spur of Mount Evans. Lodgepole pine, a straight tree favored by Indians for teepee poles, dominates the forest, along with subalpine fir and Engelmann spruce. After a couple of miles the highway swings onto Goliath's southern slope and marvelous views begin to unfold of the surrounding lower mountains and valleys. Here at tree line, at an elevation just above 11,000 feet, grows a limber pine and bristlecone pine woodland, one of Colorado's most unique forests. These trees, unable to compete with the vigorous spruce, fir, and pine forests of lower elevations, thrive on exposed rocky slopes at timberline with high winds, long, snowy winters, and fierce temperature ranges. The twisted, windswept bristlecones, among Colorado's oldest living trees, are more than 1,000 years old. A parking area allows hikers to explore the bristlecone forest. The bristlecone forest and the alpine tundra on Goliath Peak are protected by the **Mount Goliath Natural Area,** a 160-acre preserve that spreads across the rounded mountain.

The highway switchbacks and climbs north past timberline onto Goliath's north slopes. A roadside pullout allows marvelous views northward to the snow-covered Continental Divide. Echo Lake glistens far below in the forest. The road edges westward and after 1.5 miles crosses a 12,152-foot saddle. The **Alpine Garden Trail** begins at a small parking area here. This half-mile loop explores the alpine tundra and lichen-covered boulders.

This site is an outstanding example of the land above the trees, a land of punishing climatic extremes. Driving up the highway to this airy garden is like taking a compressed journey to northern Alaska beyond the Arctic Circle. Indeed,

Colorado's tundra shares many of the same plants found in the Arctic, as well as a similar climate with a brief growing season—few frost-free nights, fierce winds, shallow soils, and humidity so low that the land is a high-altitude desert. Primitive plants—lichens and mosses—dot the granite boulders, while dwarfed, slow-growing perennials hug the ground and avoid the desiccating wind. The alpine sunflower, the largest plant found here, is full grown at 6 inches high. Other flowers include alpine avens, bistorts, alpine forget-me-nots, alpine phlox, and snow buttercups. These delicate alpine plant communities are extremely sensitive to disturbance; stay on the trail and don't pick any flowers. The Mount Goliath Trail also begins at the parking area and drops 1.1 miles down through bristlecone pines and subalpine firs to Mount Evans Road.

The road runs west for a few miles along the southern slopes of 13,391-foot Rogers Peak and 13,291-foot Mount Warren, high points on a long spur ridge of Mount Evans. The shelflike road swings across the top of a huge glacier-carved cirque. Far below at timberline, nestled behind a glacial moraine, lies Lincoln Lake. Deep snow drifts and cornices line this road section in early summer. Past the lake the drive traverses gentler tundra and willow-clad slopes on Summit Lake Flats before arriving at 12,850-foot **Summit Lake.** This alpine lake, tucked into a lofty, cliff-rimmed basin scoured by glaciers, is the gem of Denver's mountain park system. After the ice melts off the lake in July, the Colorado Division of Wildlife stocks it with cutthroat trout for anglers. Picnickers and hikers also enjoy this scenic alpine lake. A short hike northeast from the parking area leads to a divide and a magnificent view down the glaciated, U-shaped valley of Chicago Creek.

Summit Lake to Mount Evans Summit

The road begins its final ascent of Mount Evans from Summit Lake, bending abruptly south and switchbacking up steep, bouldery slopes for 5 miles to the summit. This final section of highway was completed on October 10, 1930. Work began on the road at Echo Lake in 1922. Mount Evans, originally named Rosalie by pioneer painter Albert Bierstadt in 1863 for his wife, was renamed in 1895 for John Evans, Colorado's second territorial governor.

Mountain goats and bighorn sheep often graze along the drive's upper sections. The goats thrive on Mount Evans, with the herd numbering about sixty. A few hunting licenses are sold each year to cull the population. Visitors are asked not to feed or molest the seemingly tame, roadside mountain goats. A Division of Wildlife study indicates that those goats fed by humans produce fewer offspring and have thinner coats. Other above-timberline wildlife includes pikas, marmots, and white-tailed ptarmigans. The ptarmigan changes the color of its plumage to fit the season—brilliant white in winter and mottled brown in summer.

A mountain goat relaxes in the snow alongside the Mount Evans Scenic Byway.

The Mount Evans Highway corridor, from Echo Lake to the summit, is surrounded by the 74,401-acre **Mount Evans Wilderness Area.** This wilderness, spread across parts of Arapaho and Pike National Forests, encompasses both Mount Evans and neighboring 14,060-foot Mount Bierstadt, an almost pristine swath of alpine country, and deep canyons and ridges matted with dense woodlands.

After slowly switchbacking up Mount Evans's southeast flank, the highway reaches its end at a parking lot at 14,150 feet. A short trail climbs north to the peak's rocky 14,264-foot summit. The parking area is small and may be filled on busy weekend days. Restrooms and the burned remains of the old Crest House are found at road's end. Nearby sits the University of Denver's High Altitude Laboratory for research in astronomy, physiology, weather, and biochemistry. There is a 24-inch telescope in the observatory.

The view from atop Mount Evans is breathtaking. Visibility on clear days reaches almost 200 miles. To the west towers Mount Bierstadt's summit pyramid, and beyond stretches the Continental Divide, the nation's backbone that separates the Pacific and Atlantic Ocean watersheds. The famed Mount of the Holy Cross and the rounded summits of the Sawatch range, including 14,433-foot Mount Elbert, Colorado's high point, run across the horizon. South Park, an immense intermontane basin, spreads between snowy ranges to the southwest. Pikes Peak lifts its bulk in the southern sky, framed by the distant Wet Mountains and the jagged ridge of the Sangre de Cristo Mountains. The high summits of Rocky Mountain National Park loom to the north, while the prairie stretches east from Denver's glimmering streets to a flat Kansas horizon.

15

Guanella Pass Scenic and Historic Byway

Georgetown to Grant

General description: This 22-mile paved and gravel road, a National Forest Scenic Byway, climbs from Georgetown over 11,669-foot Guanella Pass to Grant in the Front Range.

Special attractions: Pike National Forest, Arapaho National Forest, Georgetown National Historic District, Mount Evans Wilderness Area, hiking, backpacking, camping, fishing, scenic views, cross-country skiing, historic sites, aspen colors.

Location: Central Colorado. The drive begins in Georgetown off I-70 west of Denver and ends at Grant on US 285 just east of Kenosha Pass.

Drive route numbers: Clear Creek County Road 381, Forest Road 118.

Travel season: Year-round. The drive is regularly plowed in winter, although heavy snow may temporarily close it. Carry chains, a shovel, and warm clothes in winter. The drive is not recommended for oversized RVs or trailers.

Camping: Five national forest campgrounds lie along the drive. Clear Lake and Guanella Pass Campgrounds sit north of the pass summit, while Geneva Park, Burning Bear, and Whiteside Campgrounds lie south of the pass along Geneva Creek.

Services: All services are found in Georgetown.

Nearby attractions: Lost Creek Wilderness Area, Colorado Trail, Kenosha Pass, Fairplay, Como, Boreas Pass, South Park, South Platte River, Silver Plume, Mount Evans Scenic Byway (see Drive 14), Mount Goliath Natural Area, Grays and Torreys Peaks, Arapaho Basin Ski Area, Central City and Blackhawk National Historic District, Golden Gate Canyon State Park, Winter Park and Mary Jane ski areas.

The Drive

The Guanella Pass scenic drive traverses 22 miles of the Front Range, passing abandoned silver mines, sweeping across swatches of alpine tundra littered with wildflowers and willow thickets, dropping down glaciated valleys and abrupt canyons, and exploring the range's geologic history. The Front Range, the Rocky Mountains' easternmost range, forms a lofty escarpment that soars over the rolling plains from Cañon City into Wyoming. This long, twisting spine, including part of the Continental Divide, is formed by ancient granite, gneiss, and schist rocks that were once the roots of another mountain range over a billion years ago. Repeated faulting, folding, heat, pressure, a final uplifting during the Laramide Orogeny some sixty million years ago, and a final excavation by recent glaciers sculpted the range into its present shape.

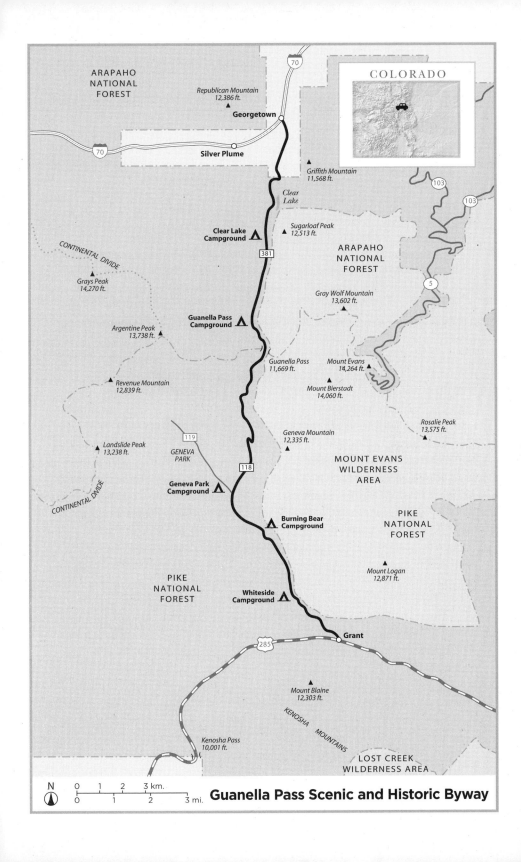

ARAPAHO
NATIONAL
FOREST

Republican Mountain
12,386 ft.
▲

Georgetown

○ **Silver Plume**

70

COLORADO

Griffith Mountain
11,568 ft.
▲

Clear
Lake

Clear Lake
Campground △

Sugarloaf Peak
12,513 ft.
▲

381

ARAPAHO
NATIONAL
FOREST

103

103

5

CONTINENTAL DIVIDE

Grays Peak
14,270 ft.
▲

Gray Wolf Mountain
13,602 ft.
▲

Guanella Pass
Campground △

Argentine Peak
13,738 ft. ▲

Guanella Pass
11,669 ft.

Mount Evans
14,264 ft.
▲

Revenue Mountain
12,839 ft.
▲

Mount Bierstadt
14,060 ft.
▲

Rosalie Peak
13,575 ft.
▲

Landslide Peak
13,238 ft.
▲

119

GENEVA
PARK

Geneva Mountain
12,335 ft.
▲

MOUNT EVANS
WILDERNESS
AREA

CONTINENTAL DIVIDE

118

Geneva Park
Campground △

PIKE
NATIONAL
FOREST

△ **Burning Bear**
Campground

Mount Logan
12,871 ft.
▲

PIKE
NATIONAL
FOREST

Whiteside
Campground △

○ **Grant**

285

Mount Blaine
12,303 ft.
▲

KENOSHA MOUNTAINS

Kenosha Pass
10,001 ft.

LOST CREEK
WILDERNESS AREA

N

0   1   2   3 km.
0   1   2   3 mi.

Guanella Pass Scenic and Historic Byway

Summer and autumn remain the best times to drive over Guanella Pass. Daily summer highs reach the sixties and seventies, while cooler temperatures prevail atop the timberline pass summit. Expect afternoon thunderstorms with heavy rain and lightning. Autumn brings a succession of warm, clear days, chilled nights, and spectacular displays of changing aspen leaves. The first snow usually falls in October and lasts until late May, making an easily accessible wonderland for cross-country skiers. Spring comes slowly to the high country, but with warmer days the snow fields recede from the woodlands by early June.

Georgetown

The Guanella Pass drive, a National Forest and Colorado Scenic Byway, begins in **Georgetown** off Interstate 70 west of Denver. Take exit 228 off I-70 and follow scenic byway signs through Georgetown to the drive's start on the town's south edge. Georgetown, nestled in Clear Creek's wide upper valley at 8,519 feet, is the centerpiece of the **Georgetown–Silver Plume National Historic District,** which preserves the area's unique architectural and mining attributes. Picturesque Georgetown still remains one of Colorado's richest mining towns, with over $200 million of silver and gold dug from the surrounding mountains.

The town got its start in June 1859, when George and David Griffith, two Kentucky brothers, heard the siren of gold and plodded westward to claim their fortune. These late arrivers found the best claims already taken at Central City and Idaho Springs, so they trekked farther west up Clear Creek Canyon to the confluence of Clear Creek and South Clear Creek in today's downtown Georgetown. Here George's pan revealed specks of gold. The brothers staked their claim and established the Griffith Mining District. George Griffith was named District Recorder and his name affixed to the huddle of cabins along the creek. George's town grew to 2,000 residents by the mid-1860s, but the best gold was soon exhausted. Silver, however, was plentiful and for the next twenty years Georgetown and Silver Plume, its upstream neighbor, thrived on the silver boom. Only Leadville, the "Silver King," outshone Georgetown, the "Silver Queen." The town quickly became the commercial hub of the huge mining district, with mills, a brick schoolhouse, numerous churches to minister to the heathen miners, luxurious hotels like the acclaimed Hotel de Paris, four fire companies, saloons and brothels, two newspapers, and, in 1877, the Colorado Central Railroad that linked Georgetown to Denver.

The railroad, operating until 1939 and now rebuilt as a historic attraction, climbed west from Georgetown through rocky Devil's Gate to Silver Plume, 2 miles west but 638 feet higher. To climb this menacing grade, railroad engineer Robert Blickensderfer designed 4 miles of track at a 4 percent grade that spiraled upward on sharp curves and one huge loop, where the track crossed back over itself via a 300-foot-long wooden trestle. This grand railroad stretch, called the Georgetown Loop, became a famed tourist attraction due to pioneer photographer William Henry Jackson's promotional photographs. The line was abandoned and demolished in 1939 to make room for the new automobile road, U.S. Highway 6. The railroad was rebuilt and reopened in 1984 to interpret Georgetown's rich mining legacy. The **Georgetown Loop Historic Mining and Railroad Park,** operated by the Colorado State Historical Society, runs daily train rides along the historic track from Memorial Day to Labor Day.

Georgetown grew until Congress repealed the Sherman Silver Purchase Act in 1893. Overnight the price of silver plummeted and the great mining era ended for the town. By the 1930s only 200 residents lived here amid boarded-up and decaying buildings. In the post–World War II period, easy access to the burgeoning Front Range communities brought new life to Georgetown as a quaint mountain community. Today the town's historical character and heritage is well preserved. A walking tour reveals classic architecture, including the Griffith Mine, the Old Missouri Firehouse, numerous excellent examples of "Gothic Revival" residences, the old 1860s stone jail, and the elegant Hotel de Paris, an exquisite hotel that once charmed President Ulysses S. Grant and others with fine cuisine and rare wines. Georgetown offers all visitor services and prospers as the gateway to the Summit County ski resorts.

Georgetown to Guanella Pass

From Georgetown, the drive switchbacks steeply up an abrupt mountainside. An excellent view of Georgetown and the broad, U-shaped glaciated valley of Clear Creek is found at a pullout almost a mile up the road. The drive climbs into a hanging valley and after 1.5 miles passes the ghost site of Silverdale at the junction of Leavenworth and South Clear Creeks. Nothing remains here now, but this area once housed silver miners who worked the Equator, Tilden, Colorado Central, Robinson, and Curtly mines on the slopes above the creek. The town boasted its own post office, but rarely exceeded a population of 100. An overlook at 2.6 miles views Leavenworth Creek tumbling through an abandoned mine tunnel. Forest Road 248 begins just to the south. This rough road, best followed in a high-clearance vehicle, ascends 7 miles up the abandoned railroad grade of the Argentine Central, the world's highest steam railroad, along Leavenworth Creek to the ghost town of Waldorf at 11,666 feet. Beginning in 1868 Waldorf's mines yielded millions in gold and silver. Early tourists also discovered the thrilling train ride and flocked up its spectacular, curving track. Today, jeeps and mountain bikes can continue up a four-wheel-drive road to almost 13,000 feet on the long ridged summit of Mount McClellan. The view from this vantage point is simply marvelous, encompassing one-sixth of Colorado and

176 peaks from Longs Peak in the north to the distant Sangre de Cristos in the south.

The drive continues south along South Clear Creek, enters Arapaho National Forest, and passes a string of lakes. Green Lake, framed by NO TRESPASSING signs, formed when a rock slide dammed the creek. Clear Lake, a deep lake originally excavated by glaciers, makes a good recreation stop. The lake, offering shoreline access only, gives good fishing for rainbow trout and offers a shady picnic area. Lower Cabin Creek Reservoir straddles the valley just beyond Clear Lake. This fenced reservoir, along with Upper Cabin Creek Reservoir to the west, is part of a massive hydroelectric project that pumps water from the lower lake to the upper one and uses the resulting energy to create electricity for Denver.

At 5.5 miles the byway passes eight-site Clear Lake Campground. Beyond here the valley broadens, with South Clear Creek meandering through still beaver ponds and dense willow thickets. Anglers can wade out into the silent currents to catch both rainbow and brown trout. This lush valley is a good place to study mountain riparian ecosystems. This valley, like most upper-elevation Colorado valleys, was sculpted by glaciers that left depressions that formed lakes and ponds as they retreated with the warming climate. These shallow lakes slowly filled with sediment, leaving bogs of rich soil behind. Today, streams braid across these wide valleys, providing a lush and diverse habitat for many animal species, including the beaver—the ubiquitous denizen of high country valleys. Beavers, North America's largest rodent, build dams that flood the bottomlands and create excellent conditions for quaking aspen and willow, the beaver's preferred food and building materials. The dams also fill with silt and slowly turn the moist bogs into mountain meadows. Aspen groves, showy with gold in autumn, line the roadside, while dense forests of blue and Engelmann spruce and subalpine fir mat the mountainsides above.

Guanella Pass Campground, with sixteen sites, sits in the forest below the final ascent to timberline and the pass summit at 10,800 feet. A nearby foot trail climbs 1 mile west to Silver Dollar, Naylor, and Murray Lakes, all glacial lakes tucked into a high cirque below 13,738-foot Argentine Peak. The road begins switchbacking up steep slopes from here. Great views unfold as the road ascends 14,060-foot Mount Bierstadt and its Sawtooth Ridge to the east. The drive passes wind-twisted subalpine fir, called krummholz, at timberline and reaches the broad 11,669-foot-high summit of Guanella Pass. The pass is named for Byron Guanella, who supervised the road's construction in 1952.

The pass summit offers not only scenic views but easy access to a broad swath of beautiful high country that includes the 74,401-acre **Mount Evans Wilderness Area.** This is a magnificent landscape. Melting snow fields whiten steep slopes and shallow alpine tarns reflect the open sky. Tundra, a delicate carpet of grasses and

Mount Bierstadt, named for pioneer painter Albert Bierstadt, dominates the view above the Guanella Pass Road.

wildflowers, spreads a mantle of green across the lower peaks, while jumbled granite boulders and cliffs reach to lofty summits. Mount Bierstadt, named for pioneer nineteenth century painter Albert Bierstadt, dominates the view to the east. One of the Front Range's finest wilderness experiences is climbing Bierstadt's broad west face to a high summit that yields superb views. A moderate hike, gaining almost 3,000 feet of elevation, begins at the pass parking lot, heads east through willowy bogs, and then up a rough trail through tundra and granite. Other good hikes include the Rosalie Trail and a trail that runs west to Square Top Lakes. The rolling land surrounding the pass summit makes excellent cross-country ski terrain in winter.

Geneva Park and Geneva Creek

The drive descends south from the pass, skirting a rounded ridge and reaching timberline in 0.5 mile. A mile later the road reaches privately owned Duck Lake, nestled behind a glacial moraine. Grassy slopes of the now-defunct Geneva Basin Ski Area slice into the forest west of the drive. Past the lake the road edges down the west flank of 12,335-foot Geneva Mountain through spruce forest and reaches Duck Creek in a U-shaped glacial valley. The creek, bordering the drive, winds through deep beaver ponds and willows.

At 17 miles the road drops into 9,700-foot-high Geneva Park, a broad grassy basin excavated by ancient glaciers. Geneva Creek, originating to the west on the Continental Divide, meanders among willow-clad banks and grazing cattle. Forest Road 119 heads northwest up the creek, passing twenty-six-site Geneva Park Campground and Duck Creek Picnic Ground. Bruno Creek, a tributary of Geneva Creek, supports endangered Colorado greenback trout and is closed to fishing. Continuing on Forest Road 118, Burning Bear Campground spreads its thirteen sites among open lodgepole pine forest on the southeast corner of Geneva Park. This pleasant campground makes a good overnight stay for wildlife watchers. A walk down to the park's edge in the evening often reveals a wealth of wildlife, including mule deer, elk, and occasional bighorn sheep.

The drive's character changes abruptly past Burning Bear Campground. The road reaches a bouldery terminal moraine left by massive glaciers that formed Geneva Park and switchbacks steeply down Falls Hill into Geneva Creek's steep, V-shaped canyon. The rushing creek tumbles in misty cascades over boulders and bedrock below the road. After a 1-mile descent the road again reaches the creek and the pavement ends. The drive's last 4 miles follow the canyon southward through lush aspen and willow woodlands along the creek. Primitive camping is found along the creek and at five-site Whiteside

Campground. Geneva Creek Picnic Ground is a popular lunch spot for byway travelers and anglers. The drive ends on U.S. Highway 285 at Grant, a small hamlet named for former president and Civil War hero Ulysses S. Grant. Denver lies almost 60 miles to the east, and Fairplay, via Kenosha Pass, sits 28 miles to the southwest.

16

Peak to Peak Scenic and Historic Byway

Central City to Estes Park

General description: This 63-mile-long drive parallels the forested east flank of the Front Range between Central City and Estes Park.

Special attractions: Clear Creek Canyon, Central City–Black Hawk National Historic District, Golden Gate Canyon State Park, Ward, Roosevelt National Forest, Brainard Lake Recreation Area, Indian Peaks Wilderness Area, Rocky Mountain National Park, Longs Peak, Enos Mills Cabin, Estes Park, hiking, camping, backpacking, rock climbing, historic sites, fishing, scenic views, autumn aspens.

Location: North-central Colorado. The drive begins at the junction of US 6 and CO 119 west of Golden and travels north via CO 72 and 7 to Estes Park east of Rocky Mountain National Park.

Drive route name and numbers: Peak to Peak Highway; CO 119, 72, and 7.

Travel season: Year-round.

Camping: National forest campgrounds along the way, south to north, are Cold Springs, Kelly Dahl, Pawnee, Peaceful Valley, Camp Dick, and Olive Ridge. Longs Peak Campground, tents only, is in Rocky Mountain National Park. Two campgrounds lie in Golden Gate Canyon State Park.

Services: All services are in Central City, Black Hawk, Nederland, and Estes Park. Limited services in Lone Pine, Rollinsville, and Ward.

Nearby attractions: Mount Evans Scenic Byway (see Drive 14), Guanella Pass Scenic and Historic Byway (see Drive 15), Georgetown, Golden, Arapaho National Forest, Rollins Pass, White Ranch Park, Eldorado Canyon State Park, Boulder, Trail Ridge Road, Never Summer Wilderness Area, Arapaho National Recreation Area.

The Drive

The Peak to Peak Highway, a National Forest Scenic Byway, unfurls for 63 miles between Clear Creek Canyon and Estes Park. The drive offers calendar-caliber scenery, with gorgeous views of the Continental Divide, high wooded hills, exhilarating canyons and valleys, and the dun-colored prairie to the east. The drive, lying within Roosevelt National Forest, is bordered by the Indian Peaks Wilderness Area and Rocky Mountain National Park.

The highway, although open year-round, is best driven in summer or autumn, when the fall colors peak. Summer temperatures vary according to elevation and range from the forties to the upper eighties. Expect warm days, cool nights, and regular afternoon thunderstorms. September can bring almost perfect

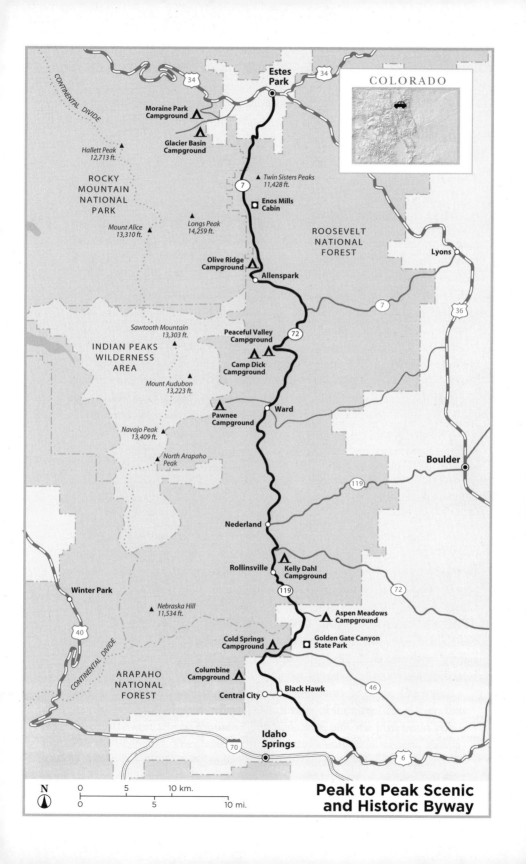

COLORADO

Estes Park

34
34

Moraine Park Campground

Glacier Basin Campground

Hallett Peak
12,713 ft.

ROCKY MOUNTAIN NATIONAL PARK

CONTINENTAL DIVIDE

7

Twin Sisters Peaks
11,428 ft.

Enos Mills Cabin

Mount Alice
13,310 ft.

Longs Peak
14,259 ft.

ROOSEVELT NATIONAL FOREST

Lyons

Olive Ridge Campground

Allenspark

7

36

Sawtooth Mountain
13,303 ft.

Peaceful Valley Campground

72

INDIAN PEAKS WILDERNESS AREA

Camp Dick Campground

Mount Audubon
13,223 ft.

Pawnee Campground

Ward

Navajo Peak
13,409 ft.

North Arapaho Peak

Boulder

119

Nederland

Winter Park

Rollinsville

Kelly Dahl Campground

119

72

40

Nebraska Hill
11,534 ft.

CONTINENTAL DIVIDE

Aspen Meadows Campground

Cold Springs Campground

Golden Gate Canyon State Park

ARAPAHO NATIONAL FOREST

Columbine Campground

Central City   Black Hawk

46

Idaho Springs

70

6

N

0   5   10 km.

0   5   10 mi.

Peak to Peak Scenic and Historic Byway

weather, with warm, clear days and spectacular aspen golds. October begins the cooldown with unpredictable weather. Snow lingers on the cooler slopes in late October, and by November the upper elevations are clothed in a mantle of white. Winters are cold and often windy. Days can be warm with highs climbing to the forties, but nighttime temperatures often fall to zero degrees. Spring days are windy and cool. The winter snowpack melts off below timberline in May.

Central City and Black Hawk

The drive begins at the junction of U.S. Highway 6 and CO 119 12 miles west of Golden. US 6 twists up Clear Creek Canyon, a precipitous gorge that slices through the lower Front Range escarpment. The same highway junction can be reached two miles east from Interstate 70's exit 244. The drive, heading northeast up CO 119 alongside North Clear Creek, gently ascends a slicing, dry-walled canyon. Mine tailings, a reminder of the area's golden history, line the creek bank. Occasional placer claims are still being worked by weekend prospectors.

After 6.5 miles the highway enters the **Central City–Black Hawk National Historic District** and 0.5 mile later enters Black Hawk. The town, along with Central City lying one mile west up Gregory Gulch, sits in what early miners dubbed "the richest square mile on earth." The story began in early 1859, when John Gregory, a Georgia prospector working Cherry Creek's placer gravels in today's Denver, trod up a snowy canyon and found promising color. Gregory had stumbled onto a veritable treasure trove and took out more gold in his first week than all of Cherry Creek had yielded the previous summer. Word spread quickly and Colorado's first gold rush was on. More than 5,000 miners teemed into Gregory's Diggings over the next few months, and several camps scattered over the mountain slopes. Two of the camps grew into burgeoning mining towns—Black Hawk, named for the trademark of an early mining company, and Central City, dubbed for the town's central location among the mining camps. By the mid-1860s Central City's population surpassed 15,000 and the community boasted a diverse, cultured, and cosmopolitan air. The famed Central City Opera House, still active today, offered its first production, *Camille* in 1861. A darker side existed as well. An 1861 election hosted "217 fistfights, 97 revolver fights, 11 Bowie knife fights, and 1 dog fight." Despite those frightening statistics, no one was killed. The Colorado Territory's first legal hanging occurred here in January 1864.

Central City and Black Hawk thrived on the riches extracted from the surrounding mountains and gulches. Numerous prospectors struck the mother

Opposite: Visitors stroll down a picturesque street in Central City, one of Colorado's most famous mining towns.

lode and basked in wealth and power. Other millionaires, besides Gregory, included future U.S. senator Henry Teller and Jeremiah Lee, a twenty-nine-year-old ex-slave of Robert E. Lee. The fabulous Argentine Lode was found in Lee's OK Mine. Teller built the stone Teller House, a town landmark, in 1872. When President Ulysses S. Grant stayed here in 1873, he found the path from his carriage to the Teller House bricked with silver bars. With the rise of the silver towns in the 1880s, the area's fortunes sagged and by 1900 the towns settled into retirement. The Opera House, refurbished and reopened in 1932, brought music lovers and tourists to the quaint towns. Writer Jack Kerouac penned his 1950s Central City experience in his classic novel *On The Road:* "Central City is two miles high; at first you get drunk on the altitude, then you get tired, and there's a fever in your soul. We approached the lights around the opera house down the narrow dark street; then we took a sharp right and hit some old saloons with swinging doors."

Central City and Black Hawk, today preserved in a National Historic District, offer many attractions. The **Gilpin County Historical Museum** displays community history. Tours are given at the Teller House and Opera House. The Central City Opera, the nation's oldest summer opera company, offers excellent productions every summer. Most folks come now for the gambling, which became legal here in 1991. Be prepared in summer and on weekends for traffic congestion and parking problems.

Golden Gate Canyon State Park

The drive continues up North Clear Creek Canyon past Black Hawk, the steep slopes coated in a mixed pine and fir forest and pockmarked with abandoned mine adits and tailings. After a couple of miles the highway leaves the drainage and climbs north onto high wooded ridges. The Roosevelt National Forest boundary lies at almost 12 miles. A look back reveals Mount Evans, its snowy 14,264-foot bulk outlined against the southern sky. Atop a ridge crest the drive intersects CO 46. This scenic backroad drops east down Ralston Creek to **Golden Gate Canyon State Park** and meanders on to Golden.

The park, also accessible via a turnoff on CO 119 at 16 miles, makes a good stopover. The 12,000-acre parkland is ideal for hiking, with 60 miles of trails threading the backcountry. Good hikes include 4.6-mile Mule Deer Trail and 2.1-mile Eagle Trail up City Lights Ridge. The evening view from the ridge is marvelous, with bits and pieces of the Denver sprawl glimmering in the twilight. Panorama Point, accessible by car on Tremont Mountain's north flank, overlooks the Indian Peaks stretching north to flat-topped Longs Peak. Thirty-five-site Aspen Meadows (tents only) and ninety-seven-site Reverend's Ridge campgrounds sit on the park's north side just east of the drive.

Rollinsville and Nederland

The road continues north from the state park, dipping through shallow valleys at South Beaver Creek and Lump Gulch before spiraling down Gamble Gulch to Rollinsville. This town, founded in 1873 by John Quincy Adams Rollins, allowed no casinos, dance halls, or saloons. Besides purchasing mines, Rollins built a toll road over 11,671-foot Rollins Pass on the Continental Divide to Middle Park. Later the Denver, Northwestern and Pacific Railroad acquired the right-of-way and built a temporary track with thirty-three tunnels along the route. The line remains the highest altitude reached by an American railroad. The abandoned railbed, converted into a jeep road in 1956, is now one of Colorado's most popular backroad excursions. The jeep road heads west from Rollinsville up South Boulder Creek.

The drive ambles north from Rollinsville and passes the forty-six-site Kelly Dahl Campground. The road swings around 8,922-foot Tungsten Mountain and drops down to 8,236-foot-high Nederland and Middle Boulder Creek. **Nederland** spreads across a broad valley above Barker Reservoir and Boulder Canyon and below the Continental Divide. The town, established in 1877, once boomed with gold, silver, and tungsten mining and now serves as a gateway to the Indian Peaks Wilderness and a getaway for Boulder residents. Author Helen Hunt Jackson described 1870s Nederland as a "dismal little mining town," but now it's a venerable, cozy village with an unpretentious charm. The town works hard at preserving its quiet atmosphere by not becoming a tourist trap or a Boulder bedroom community. It still functions as a regional supply center with a hardware store, auto parts shop, a printer, doctors, and veterinarians. It also offers numerous stores for visitors, including a marvelous rock shop, and twelve restaurants, and is home to several activist groups, like Amnesty International. Eldora Ski Area, west of town, offers 210 acres for skiers and one of Colorado's largest cross-country ski areas. CO 119, beginning in Nederland, heads northeast into Boulder Canyon, a popular rock climbing and hiking area, 17 miles to Boulder, home of the University of Colorado.

Ward and Indian Peaks

The Peak to Peak Highway, now following CO 72, climbs north from Nederland. For 9 miles the road twists and curls over forested ridges and through shallow canyons before swinging onto the eastern flank of 11,471-foot Niwot Mountain. Vast views unfold from the road. Lower mountains recede east to the great plains and the flat horizon. **Ward** sits below the drive above upper Lefthand Canyon. Ward, established in 1865, is another mining camp that settled into peaceful retirement after its gold heyday. Calvin Ward discovered the golden Ward Lode here in 1860. The "Switzerland Trail of America"—the now-defunct Denver, Boulder & Western Railroad—served the town after 1898. A fire in 1910 destroyed fifty-three buildings in Ward. Ward marks the northern boundary of the Colorado Mineral Belt, a 50-mile-wide swath that runs from here to southwestern Colorado and contains most of the state's mineral wealth.

As a side journey, take Forest Road 112 to Brainard Lake 0.1 mile past the Ward turnoff. This paved road climbs 5 miles past picturesque Red Rock Lake to **Brainard Lake Recreation Area** on the eastern edge of the 76,586-acre **Indian Peaks Wilderness Area.** The Indian Peaks, including Pawnee, Shoshoni, Navajo, and Arikaree Peaks, form a spectacular escarpment along the Continental Divide above the 10,345-foot-high lake. Snowfields and small glaciers cling to the serrated peaks through much of the summer. Glaciers excavated these spiked, weather-beaten mountains and their alpine cirques. The wilderness area, established in 1978, preserves some of Colorado's best mountain scenery. Its unfortunate proximity to the state's major population centers, however, has caused severe overuse. The USDA Forest Service now imposes restrictions to protect and rehabilitate the area's fragile alpine ecosystems. Permits are needed for overnight camping, and there are limitations on fires and pack animals. Bicycles and motorized vehicles are prohibited.

The Brainard Lake Recreation Area, at road's end, makes a good jumping-off point for day hikers and mountain climbers. Mount Audubon, the round-shouldered, 13,223-foot peak to the northwest, makes a good climb via a marked 4-mile trail. Numerous facilities are around the lake, including three picnic areas and the fifty-five-site Pawnee Campground. Night temperatures can be frigid at the campground during its May through September season. Snowdrifts often linger in the forest well into July. Both Brainard Lake and Red Rock Lake offer excellent trout fishing.

From Ward the drive continues north over wooded ridges before steeply dipping into Peaceful Valley along Middle St. Vrain Creek. The fifteen-site Peaceful Valley Campground sits just west of the hairpin turn at the canyon bottom. The highway runs down the sharp canyon, its walls studded with towering granite cliffs, before climbing out to its junction with CO 7 from Lyons. CO 72 ends here. The drive turns west on CO 7.

The new highway crosses rolling hills seamed by shallow, grassy valleys. A ponderosa pine woodland covers the land. Aspen groves tuck into moist ravines and willow thickets border trickling creeks. Ponderosa pine forests dominate Colorado's mid-elevation mountains. These open forests congregate on warm, south-facing slopes, where temperatures can be as much as twenty degrees warmer than on north-facing slopes. Acidic needles in the springy pine duff on the forest floor inhibit the growth of a shrub and grass understory, allowing the trees to retain all the precious moisture.

A scenic overlook 3 miles from the junction faces north to Mount Meeker and the Wild Basin in Rocky Mountain National Park. The turn to **Allenspark** sits

The Indian Peaks loom above Red Rock Lake along the Peak to Peak Scenic Byway.

0.5 mile farther. The town, named for 1859 homesteader Alonzo Allen, caters to visitors with several restaurants, shops, and motels. Olive Ridge Campground, a pleasant fifty-six-site area a couple of miles up the road, sits just west of the highway and makes a good base camp for forays into the Wild Basin area.

Rocky Mountain National Park and Longs Peak

From Olive Ridge to Estes Park, the highway parallels the eastern boundary of **Rocky Mountain National Park.** This immense parkland spreads across 414 square miles of almost pristine high country, including the Continental Divide. The park, Colorado's largest, boasts 104 peaks above 10,000 feet and seventy-one reaching above 12,000 feet. Flat-topped Longs Peak is the park's high point at 14,259 feet.

The road drops from Olive Ridge and crosses North St. Vrain Creek. Past the creek a turn west leads to Wild Basin, a rugged backcountry cirque in the park's remote southern reaches. Numerous trails lace the basin, threading along sparkling streams to tantalizing above-timberline tarns like Ouzel, Bluebird, Thunder, and Sandbeach Lakes. The highway runs north below bulky **Mount Meeker,** a towering pile of granite rubble, and through Meeker Park, a small hamlet with stables, a lodge, and cabins. Meeker Park Picnic Area lies a mile beyond. As the drive passes Mount Meeker the precipitous east face of **Longs Peak** monopolizes the view.

Longs Peak, named for 1820 explorer Major Stephen Long, dominates the Front Range like no other mountain save Pikes Peak to the south. Its flat summit, long a pioneer landmark, gleams like an alabaster tower above the sere prairie. The Arapaho Indians called the peak, along with Mount Meeker, "The Two Guides," and early French trappers named them "The Two Ears." An awesome 2,000-foot-high granite wall sliced by glaciers forms the east face of Longs Peak. Mount Meeker and Mount Lady Washington flank the peak. The Diamond, the peak's bold upper face, offers some of North America's best alpine rock climbing.

After traversing into Tahosa Valley between the Longs Peak massif and the Twin Sisters, the highway reaches the Longs Peak trailhead. A short road leads west to twenty-six-site Longs Peak Campground, a tents-only area, and the trailhead. The trail climbs the peak via the Keyhole Route, the peak's only nontechnical climb. The trail ascends 7.5 miles and 4,850 feet to the summit. Allow at least twelve hours for the round trip. The park service advises starting the hike by 3:00 a.m. to avoid the almost daily summer thunderstorms and to carry proper rain gear and extra clothes.

Enos Mills

A half-mile past the trailhead sits a monument to Enos Mills, Rocky Mountain National Park's founding father. A side road just up the highway bumps back to his one-room log cabin nestled among pines and wildflowers. Enos Mills came to Longs Peak in 1884, a sickly Kansas lad in search of better health among the clean mountains. He first climbed the peak the following year, homesteaded at its base, and began a lifelong career as an alpine guide and nature writer. He dubbed Longs Peak "the king of the Rocky Mountains" and made 297 ascents. In 1889 nineteen-year-old Mills met naturalist John Muir in San Francisco and began a friendship with the elder conservationist. In 1902 Mills built rustic Longs Peak Inn in the meadows across today's highway from his cabin and began writing numerous classic books like *Spell of the Rockies* that detailed his wilderness experiences and the joy of outdoor adventure. Mills wrote, "He who feels the spell of the wild, the rhythmic melody of falling water, the echoes among the crags, the bird songs, the wind in the pines . . . is in tune with the universe."

Mills, a firm believer in the national park idea and in the preservation of America's wildlands, advocated the creation of a national park surrounding Longs Peak and lectured tirelessly across the country promoting the preserve. In 1915 his dedication bore fruit when Rocky Mountain National Park was created. Mills died in 1922. The **Enos Mills Homestead Cabin,** run by the Mills family, keeps the memory and writings of this legendary Colorado naturalist alive. The cabin displays Mills's photographs, camera, climbing equipment, specimen collections, and original book editions and documents.

Lily Lake to Estes Park

Twin Sisters Trailhead sits just past the cabin. The trail spirals upward to the top of 11,428-foot Twin Sisters. Excellent views of Longs Peak and the Tahosa Valley stretch to the west. The drive continues north, crosses a broad divide, and begins dropping toward Estes Park. Popular **Lily Lake** tucks against Lily Mountain along the road. The highway twists down Lily Mountain's steep eastern slope, dropping past rough rock outcrops and scattered ponderosa pines. The road levels out on a wide bench beside Marys Lake before making its final plunge around Prospect Mountain and entering **Estes Park** and the drive's end at its junction with U.S. Highway 36.

Estes Park forms the eastern gateway to Rocky Mountain National Park. The town, named for the area's first homesteader—Joel Estes, who settled here in 1859—fills the wooded valley with homes, shops, hotels, restaurants, and tourist traps. The setting is, despite unbridled growth, enchanting, with snow-capped peaks and wooded ridges surrounding the town and valley. English traveler Isabella Bird, the first woman to ascend Longs Peak, wrote in 1873: "Never, nowhere, have I seen anything to equal the view into Estes Park." The Beaver Meadows and Fall Creek entrances to the national park lie just west of town. Several park campgrounds sit close to town and Trail Ridge Road, another magnificent scenic drive (see Drive 17), begins at Deer Ridge Junction. Lumpy Ridge, called by the Arapaho Indians *Thath-aa-ai-atah* or "The mountain of little lumps," walls in Estes Park on the north. This high ridge, studded with superb granite crags, offers excellent rock climbing. At the drive's end, the junction of CO 7 and US 36, a turn east leads to Lyons while a west turn eases through downtown Estes Park and on to the park.

17

Trail Ridge Road All-American Byway

Estes Park to Grand Lake

General description: Trail Ridge Road, one of Colorado's most spectacular and popular scenic drives, traverses glaciated valleys and above-timberline Trail Ridge in Rocky Mountain National Park for 45 miles.

Special attractions: Rocky Mountain National Park, Horseshoe Park, Trail Ridge, Tundra Nature Trail, Alpine Visitor Center, Fall River Pass, Milner Pass, Kawuneeche Valley, camping, hiking, scenic views, overlooks, wildlife, fishing, photography, wildflowers.

Location: North-central Colorado. The drive connects Estes Park and Grand Lake.

Drive route name and number: Trail Ridge Road, US 34.

Travel season: May through October. The exact opening and closing dates vary every year due to snow removal in spring and the first big winter snowstorms. Check with the park for current road information, conditions, and closures.

Camping: Five campgrounds are located in Rocky Mountain National Park, includ-ing two along the drive. Aspenglen Campground, open on a first-come, first-served basis, sits near the Fall River entrance 5 miles from Estes Park. Timber Creek Campground, a shaded 100-site campground, lies on the drive's western slope in the Kawuneeche Valley and also operates on a first-come basis. Moraine Park and Glacier Basin Campgrounds, both on the reservation system in summer, are near the Beaver Meadows Entrance just south of the drive. Longs Peak Campground, a tents-only area, is 11 miles south of Estes Park off CO 7.

Services: All services are found in Estes Park, Grand Lake, and Granby.

Nearby attractions: Peak to Peak Scenic and Historic Byway (see Drive 16), Roosevelt National Forest, Arapaho National Recreation Area, Cache la Poudre–North Park Scenic Byway (see Drive 18), Colorado State Forest, Never Summer Wilderness Area, Indian Peaks Wilderness Area, Wild Basin, Longs Peak, Enos Mills Cabin, Bear Lake, Glacier Gorge, Boulder attractions, Arapaho National Forest.

The Drive

Rocky Mountain National Park, one of Colorado's most spectacular natural areas, protects an immense swath of pristine high country along the Continental Divide. The divide, the literal roof of the Rockies, twists down North America's mountain backbone, splitting the Atlantic and Pacific watersheds. Jagged peaks march along the divide in the park, lifting glacier-carved ridges and summits into the sky. The 45-mile-long Trail Ridge Road drive, the highest continuous auto road in the United States, traverses this superlative parkland—crossing broad valleys with

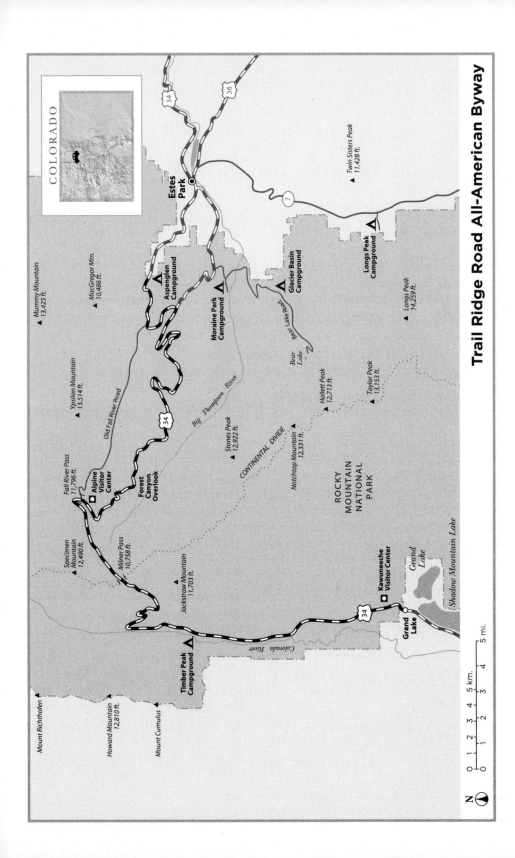

Trail Ridge Road All-American Byway

COLORADO

Mummy Mountain
13,425 ft.

MacGregor Mtn.
10,486 ft.

Twin Sisters Peak
11,428 ft.

Estes Park

Aspenglen Campground

Ypsilon Mountain
13,514 ft.

Moraine Park Campground

Glacier Basin Campground

Longs Peak Campground

Old Fall River Road

Bear Lake Road

Bear Lake

Longs Peak
14,259 ft.

Big Thompson River

Hallett Peak
12,713 ft.

Taylor Peak
13,153 ft.

Fall River Pass
11,796 ft.

Alpine Visitor Center

Forest Canyon Overlook

Stones Peak
12,922 ft.

CONTINENTAL DIVIDE

Notchtop Mountain
12,331 ft.

Specimen Mountain
12,490 ft.

Milner Pass
10,758 ft.

Jackstraw Mountain
11,703 ft.

ROCKY MOUNTAIN NATIONAL PARK

Mount Richthofen

Howard Mountain
12,810 ft.

Mount Cumulus

Timber Peak Campground

Colorado River

Kawuneeche Visitor Center

Grand Lake

Grand Lake

Shadow Mountain Lake

0 1 2 3 4 5 km.

0 1 2 3 4 5 mi.

N

meandering rivers, passing herds of elk, deer, and bighorn sheep, climbing forest-clad slopes, and winding along lofty Trail Ridge.

The 415-square-mile park encompasses 113 named peaks above 10,000 feet, seventy-one over 12,000 feet, and Longs Peak, the park's high point, which soars 14,259 feet above sea level. Two small ranges—the Never Summer Mountains and Mummy Range—split from the divide and the Front Range in the park's northwest corner. Besides being a place of mountain splendor, Rocky Mountain National Park is a land of valleys, rivers, and lakes. The park holds more than 150 lakes, and almost 500 miles of streams thread its valleys and canyons. The park is a mother of rivers, with four major rivers arising on the Continental Divide—the Cache la Poudre, Big Thompson, and St. Vrain Rivers on the eastern slope and the Colorado River on the western side. Rocky Mountain National Park is also the land above the trees. One-third of the park lies in the alpine zone above timber-line, a cold, windswept land where summer visits for a brief two months.

Trail Ridge Road is only the latest in a series of range crossings from the eastern plains to Middle Park's lush grasslands. Trail Ridge, with its gentle contours, forms a natural route over the otherwise cliffed and rugged Continental Divide. Indian hunters used the Ute Trail as early as 12,000 years ago. A Clovis spear point found on Trail Ridge confirms their ancient presence. Later Indians built low rock walls to funnel game to hidden hunters. Eagle traps, low pits covered with an animal skin, also dotted the broad ridge. The Ute and Arapaho Indians, settlers, and prospectors regularly crossed the ridge during the nineteenth century. Trail Ridge Road, built in three years, opened in 1932 and bypassed the dangerous Fall River Road.

Trail Ridge Road, the pathway to the high tundra, is America's highest through highway. It runs above 12,000 feet for 4 miles and above 11,000 feet for 11 miles. The road, climbing almost 5,000 vertical feet from Estes Park to the ridge's high point, journeys through three life zones in 20 miles to an alpine climate similar to that in northern Alaska and Canada. Each 1,000 feet ascended is the equivalent of a 600-mile trip northward. No other road in the Colorado Rockies offers such a unique opportunity to study, explore, and appreciate the delicate but rigorous world above tree line.

Trail Ridge Road opens in late May, depending on snow removal, and usually closes by late October after the first major snowfall. Unpredictable weather rules during summer and autumn on the drive. Mornings are usually clear, calm, and warm. Temperatures vary from the seventies and eighties in the lower elevations to the forties and fifties above timberline. Expect afternoon thunderstorms along the road, with localized heavy rain, hail, and snow. High winds usually accompany the storms. Winds exceeding 150 miles per hour have been clocked on Trail Ridge. Snow can fall during any month on the upper elevations. Be prepared by bringing warm clothes, rain gear, and sun protection. Lightning is a serious hazard along Trail Ridge. Keep off exposed ridges and trails before and during thunderstorms.

Estes Park to Horseshoe Park

The drive begins 5 miles northwest of Estes Park, where U.S. Highway 34 enters Rocky Mountain National Park at the Fall River Entrance Station. The park's other entrance at Beaver Meadows lies southwest of Estes Park via U.S. Highway 36 and leads to Moraine Park Museum, Glacier Basin and Moraine Park Campgrounds, and the Bear Lake area. US 36 also climbs from the Beaver Meadows entrance to a junction with US 34 and Trail Ridge Road at Deer Ridge Junction.

The highway runs west from the entrance station in an open ponderosa and limber pine forest. Aspenglen Campground, with fifty-four sites, sits at 8,230 feet near the Fall River just past the park boundary. The campground operates on a first-come, first-served basis. The road heads up a granite-studded canyon between MacGregor Mountain on the north and Deer Mountain to the south and climbs into **Horseshoe Park.** A great valley glacier, spilling down today's Fall River drainage from Trail Ridge, excavated this broad U-shaped valley during three ice advances. The last glacial period—the Pinedale—melted away some 12,000 years ago. Lateral moraines, piles of jumbled boulders, edge the valley, while a giant terminal moraine, marking the glacier's farthest advance, blocks the valley's eastern end. This terminal moraine also dammed the valley, forming a large, shallow lake. Erosion eventually sedimented the lake, leaving a level, marshy valley floor with the Fall River looping across it.

The road continues west on the valley's north edge and soon reaches the Sheep Lakes Information Station on the road's south side. The Sheep Lakes, four small glacier-formed kettle lakes, sit in the valley. A couple of pulloffs in Horseshoe Park make good stops to view wildlife. Mule deer, elk, and bighorn sheep regularly graze in the meadows and willow thickets along the Fall River. The mammals are best viewed during early morning or evening when feeding in the park. Elk herds, driven to lower elevations by deep snow pack, congregate in Horseshoe Park in spring, winter, and fall. The autumn rutting period is spectacular when the bull elk bugle their mating calls, vie for herd dominance, and gather harems of females. Two bighorn sheep flocks, totaling between 300 and 500 animals, inhabit Rocky Mountain National Park. While they usually keep to the high country, the Mummy Range flock occasionally descends Bighorn Mountain to natural salt licks in Horseshoe Park. The bighorn sheep road crossing in Horseshoe Park, just past the information station, is closely regulated to protect Colorado's state animal. Sheep, of course, have the right-of-way, and there is no roadside parking except in designated lots. Visitors are also advised not to approach any wild animals. Mature elk weigh more than 1,000 pounds and are unpredictably aggressive during mating

Elk graze in Horseshoe Park's meadows along Trail Ridge Road in Rocky Mountain National Park.

season. It's best to view them from the parking areas with field glasses and long telephoto lenses.

The 9-mile-long **Old Fall River Road** climbs from western Horseshoe Park up Fall River's glacier gorge to 11,796-foot Fall River Pass on Trail Ridge's northern end. The road, two-lane and paved to Endovalley Picnic Area and then dirt and one-way to its terminus, makes a spectacular side trip. It passes numerous glacial features, 25-foot-high Chasm Falls, and ancient subalpine spruce and fir forests. Old Fall River Road, a property on the National Register of Historic Places, follows an old Arapaho path called the "Dog's Trail." The road, the national park's first high drive, opened in 1920 but saw little use after Trail Ridge Road opened in 1932 because of landslides, avalanches, and 16-percent grades.

Trail Ridge Road loops south across Horseshoe Park, crosses a hilly moraine with aspens, willows, and Colorado blue spruce, and ascends the valley's southern flank. The **Horseshoe Park Overlook** offers views into the park below. The Mummy Range, a 20-mile-long Front Range spur, towers to the northwest. A row of jagged peaks, including 13,514-foot Ypsilon Mountain and 13,502-foot Fairchild Mountain, loom above Horseshoe Park.

The viewpoint also offers a look at one of the national park's newest geologic features. **Lawn Lake,** a small natural lake nestled in the heart of the Mummy Range, was enlarged in 1903 to provide irrigation water for farms near Loveland. In the early morning hours of July 15, 1982, the lake brimmed with snowmelt that slowly seeped around a damaged outlet valve. The water quickly eroded into the earthen dam and at 5:30 a.m. the levee gave way, plunging 674 acre-feet of water down Roaring River's narrow canyon. The 30-foot-deep deluge scoured the canyon floor, breached Horseshoe Park's north lateral moraine, and deposited a huge alluvial fan near the park's head with up to 44 feet of debris and boulders weighing more than 400 tons. The relentless water continued toward Estes Park. Horseshoe Park's wetlands, however, slowed the advance and allowed for the evacuation of downtown Estes Park. The flood buried the town's main street under 6 feet of mud. Three park campers, two in Aspenglen Campground, died in the flood.

The road climbs uphill and reaches **Deer Mountain Overlook** after 0.6 mile. This point gives great views of the Mummy Range, granite domes on MacGregor Mountain's flank, Little Horseshoe Park below, and 10,013-foot Deer Mountain to the east. Deer Ridge Junction, the intersection of US 34, US 36 from Moraine Park, and Trail Ridge Road, sits just ahead. A resort, Deer Ridge Chalet, once sat here, but the Park Service acquired the place in 1960, tore the buildings down, and restored the natural ecosystem.

Hidden Valley

The drive runs northwest and bends into Hidden Valley. The shallow valley, formed by the south lateral moraine of the Fall River glacier on its north side, is a lush, hidden oasis. Dense willow thickets and meadows of grasses and sedges line twisting Hidden Valley Creek. Silted-in beaver ponds form meadows in the east part of the valley. After a couple of miles the road reaches active beaver ponds. A wooden boardwalk offers a way to explore the ponds, traversing out among willows and fresh-cut aspen, a favorite beaver food. Look for these forest engineers swimming in their pools during morning and evening. Hidden Valley Creek also harbors a reintroduced population of threatened greenback cutthroat trout, a Colorado native. This trout, surviving only in isolated lakes and rivers in Colorado's Rockies, almost became extinct due to habitat loss, interbreeding with other trout species, and competition from nonnative fish. The downsteam moraine here blocks nonnative trout from living in Hidden Valley, allowing the greenback cutthroat trout to flourish. Fishing for greenback trout is on a strict catch-and-release program. A picnic area sits by the parking area.

The drive continues up Hidden Valley and after 0.5 mile loops southeast. The road climbs southeast through a mixed forest of aspen, lodgepole pine, subalpine fir, and Engelmann spruce and reaches the **Many Parks Curve** viewpoint in 1.5

miles. The overlook yields dramatic views into several large grassy parks tucked into the Front Range, including Horseshoe Park, Moraine Park, Beaver Meadows, and Estes Park. Forested lateral moraines left by retreating glaciers border the open grasslands. Coarse alluvium, deposited by the Lawn Lake flood, forms a small lake in Horseshoe Park to the north.

The highway bends onto a steep mountainside above upper Hidden Valley, steadily climbing through old-growth spruce and subalpine fir woods. A parking area in the upper valley gives views of the ski area and of open slopes carpeted with summer wildflowers. Melting snow irrigates marsh marigolds, paintbrush, lousewort, chiming bells, delphinium, and a forest of spruce and white-barked subalpine fir. The drive continues ascending and after another mile reaches 10,829-foot Rainbow Curve, a lofty viewpoint poised on a ridge over 2 miles high. Trail Ridge's humped shoulder looms to the south, verdant Horseshoe Park and the twisting highway in Hidden Valley lie far below, and the snowy Mummy Range stretches along the northern horizon. Early mountaineer William Hallett named the range for its fanciful resemblance to a reclining Egyptian mummy.

The road edges west across the north slope of Knife's Edge, a narrow rocky ridgeline. A scattered forest of weathered lodgepole pine and spruce spreads over the hillside. As the road climbs toward timberline, the forest becomes stunted and dwarfed. Severe winds, gusting over Trail Ridge, force the trees to hug the ground or form tree islands. Distinctive "banner trees" form when the branches grow on the tree's eastern or leeward side, out of the wind. Timberline, the elevation that marks the forest boundary, occurs between 10,000 and 11,500 feet in Rocky Mountain National Park. Beyond lies grassy alpine tundra—the land above the trees.

Trail Ridge

As the highway nears timberline, it passes a small glacier-carved cirque. This amphitheater, the headwaters of Sundance Creek, exhibits a cirque's distinctive features—a moraine of loose rubble, a rocky headwall dissected by the glacier, and a semicircular shape. Past the cirque, the drive crosses a low timberline gap onto **Trail Ridge** itself. This 11,440-foot pass, called Ute Crossing, marks the highway's junction with the old Ute Trail that traverses the ridge. The 15-mile-long trail, called *Taieonbaa* or "Child's Trail" by Native Americans, begins in Beaver Meadows, threads along the ridgetop, and drops down to Kawuneeche Valley on the west.

The drive twists along Trail Ridge for the next 7 miles to Fall River Pass. Several excellent viewpoints and points of interest sit along the road. **Forest Canyon Overlook,** at 11,716 feet, perches high above Forest Canyon. Huge glaciers chiseled this deep U-shaped valley along a major fault line now followed by the Big

A passing storm veils the Never Summer Range beyond the alpine meadows atop Trail Ridge Road.

Thompson River. Ragged peaks, including Mount Ida, Terra Tomah Mountain, and Sprague Mountain, line the Continental Divide's serrated ridge across the abyss. Three small glaciers still tuck under the divide's escarpment. Hanging valleys and cirques hide numerous lakes and tarns below soaring rock buttresses, cliffs, and snow fields. Keep on the paved trail to the overlook to avoid damaging fragile tundra plants.

Almost 2 miles later the road reaches **Rock Cut Overlook,** a spectacular 12,110-foot point just past a road cut. The excellent 0.5-mile Tundra Communities Trail climbs east from the parking area to the rounded ridge crest and offers a great introduction to alpine ecology. The tundra inhabitants have superbly adapted to its rigorous climate and short growing season. A scant six- to ten-week growing season, wind speeds as high as 170 miles per hour, intense ultraviolet radiation, desiccating air, low soil moisture, and intense sunlight all conspire against life. Yet despite the rigors, life not only survives but also flourishes atop Trail Ridge. Meadows with thick, wiry grasses spread over the ridge, and perennial flowers and herbs huddle against the ground. More than 185 flowering plants grow here, including alpine sunflowers, alpine avens, bistort, moss campion, lousewort, marsh marigold, dwarf clover, and phlox.

Hikers need to keep on the paved walkway and other existing tundra trails. The fragile tundra has almost no carrying capacity, and any human use quickly affects the plants. The National Park Service established "tundra protection areas" along Trail Ridge Road to preserve the alpine grassland from being loved to death.

The highway drops north from Rock Cut Overlook to the 11,827-foot Iceberg Pass and then climbs up the Tundra Curves to a lookout above Lava Cliff cirque. Tall cliffs of welded volcanic tuff form the cirque's abrupt wall. The road continues climbing and in 0.8-mile passes Trail Ridge Road's 12,183-foot high point. Edging along immense grassy slopes, the drive gently descends to **Gore Range Overlook.** This viewpoint, sitting above the head of Forest Canyon, offers expansive views of the **Never Summer Range** to the west and the Gore Range some 75 miles distant. Longs Peak, a pioneer landmark of the northern Front Range, lifts steep slopes broken by granite cliffs to its flat-topped summit. The road swings northeast and steadily drops another mile to 11,796-foot Fall River Pass and the Alpine Visitor Center.

Fall River Pass to Grand Lake

Fall River Pass, the terminus of Old Fall River Road, divides the Cache la Poudre and Fall River drainages. At the pass is the popular **Alpine Visitor Center,** which dispenses park information, sells books and maps, and offers exhibits on tundra ecology and geology. A nearby store sells gifts and lunches. Outside the center are spectacular views into Forest Canyon.

From here, Trail Ridge Road begins a serious descent from the pass, dropping steeply down to Medicine Bow Curve, a sharp hairpin turn with an overlook. The road bends west, reaches timberline in another mile, and continues down through spruce forest and lush flower-strewn meadows into the upper Cache la Poudre River valley. Poudre Lake, the headwaters of the 75-mile-long Cache la Poudre River, sits atop the Continental Divide on 10,758-foot **Milner Pass.** A nearby trail climbs a mile up Specimen Mountain to the Crater, where bighorn sheep forage in summer. The trail is closed to hiking until after lambing season in mid-July, and the mountain is closed all year to protect a sheep mineral lick.

Lake Irene, a serene lake surrounded by spruce and fir, is nestled just down the highway. A picnic area and restrooms sit near the landslide-dammed lake. The road threads down Beaver Creek's steep canyon, passing Sheep Rock and Jackstraw Mountain to the south, and continues on down to **Farview Curve**

Overlook. This viewpoint, the last lofty overlook on the drive, gazes west into Kawuneeche Valley. During the ice ages the park's largest glacier stretched 20 miles down the valley to Grand Lake. The Colorado River, originating at the valley's head, meanders through dense willow thickets and beaver ponds in this flat glacier-carved valley. The Never Summer Range, called *Ni-chebe-chii* or "Never No Summer" by the Arapaho, lifts its craggy crest to the west.

The switchbacking road drops steeply for the next 4 miles through thick spruce, fir, and pine woods to the valley's eastern edge. The Colorado River Trailhead sits just west of the road. The trail heads north 7 miles to Poudre Pass, passing the remains of Lulu City, an 1880s mining camp. The highway runs south along the valley edge. Beaver Ponds Picnic Area, the 100-site Timber Creek Campground, and several trailheads sit along the drive. **Holzwarth Trout Lodge Historic Site,** just past the campground, makes a good stop. The historic site began as the Holzwarth Homestead in 1916 and later became a dude ranch after the Fall River Road was built, which ran until 1972. The site, reached by a 0.5-mile trail, is seen on a self-guided tour or tours led by volunteers in summer.

The highway continues south through lodgepole pine forest and open grasslands. Deer, elk, and moose frequently graze in the wide roadside meadows along the road. The **Kawuneeche Visitor Center,** sitting at 8,720 feet, is the drive's last point of interest. The center offers displays on the park's history, geology, and natural history, gives free park information and permits, and sells books. Trail Ridge Road scenic drive ends almost a mile past the visitor center on the park boundary. **Grand Lake** sits another mile farther south. US 34 continues past Arapaho National Recreation Area to Granby.

18

Cache la Poudre– North Park Scenic Byway

Fort Collins to Walden

General description: This 101-mile-long scenic drive follows CO 14 from Fort Collins on the eastern edge of the Front Range to Walden in North Park. The road runs through Poudre Canyon and climbs over Cameron Pass to North Park.

Special attractions: Poudre Canyon, Cache la Poudre Wild and Scenic River, Roosevelt National Forest, Cache la Poudre Wilderness Area, Comanche Peak Wilderness Area, Cameron Pass, Rawah Wilderness Area, Colorado State Forest, North Park, Arapaho National Wildlife Refuge, hiking, camping, backpacking, fishing, rock climbing, kayaking, cross-country skiing.

Location: North-central Colorado. The drive begins in Fort Collins just off I-25 and ends in Walden.

Drive route name and number: Cache la Poudre–North Park Scenic Byway, CO 14.

Travel season: Year-round. Chains or adequate snow tires might be needed in winter.

Camping: Several national forest campgrounds line the drive, including Ansel Watrous, Stove Prairie Landing, Narrows, Mountain Park, Kelly Flats, Big Bend, Sleeping Elephant, Big South, Aspen Glen, and Chambers Lake. Three state park campgrounds sit along the Michigan River on the west side of Cameron Pass.

Services: All services are found in Fort Collins and Walden. Limited services are along the drive.

Nearby attractions: Rocky Mountain National Park, Trail Ridge Road (see Drive 17), Pawnee National Grassland, Lory State Park, Horsetooth Reservoir, Mount Zirkel Wilderness Area, Rabbit Ears Pass, Arapaho National Forest, Routt National Forest, Never Summer Wilderness Area, Estes Park.

The Drive

The 101-mile-long Cache la Poudre–North Park Scenic Byway weaves through the Cache la Poudre River's deep canyon from Fort Collins to the 10,276-foot summit of Cameron Pass before plunging into North Park, a broad intermontane basin ringed by snowcapped mountains. The highway traverses a solid landscape seamed by canyons, excavated by glaciers, and studded with granite cliffs. It climbs over the Medicine Bow Mountains, a windswept gallery of towering peaks, and threads along the Cache la Poudre River. Four wilderness areas—the Cache la Poudre, Comanche Peak, Neota, and Rawah wildernesses—in Roosevelt National Forest and the Colorado State Forest abut the drive.

The drive, open year-round, is best in summer and fall. Elevations vary from 5,000 feet to more than 10,000 feet, offering a diverse range of temperatures and

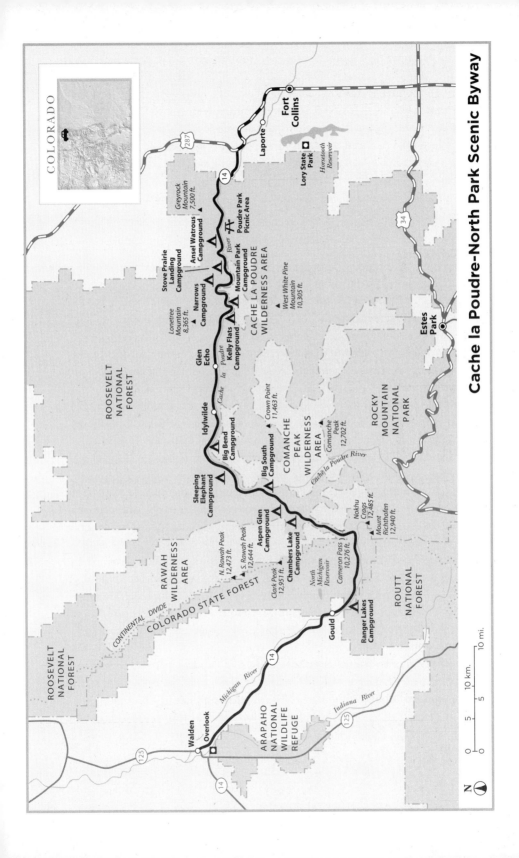

Cache la Poudre–North Park Scenic Byway

climates. Summer high temperatures vary from the eighties at Fort Collins to the fifties atop the Cameron Pass. Nights in the higher elevations can be cold. Afternoon thunderstorms frequently build over the mountains, bringing localized heavy rain. Autumn yields brisk but mild weather, with colorful aspens lining the highway. Winter days are cold with highs between ten and forty degrees. Heavy snow falls on the pass and the drive's western slope. Be prepared for icy roads, particularly on shaded corners, and carry chains or have adequate snow tires. Spring creeps slowly up the drive from the prairie beginning in April. The roadside snowpack is mostly melted by late May. Expect cool, breezy days and cold nights.

Fort Collins

The drive begins at **Fort Collins** on CO 14/U.S. Highway 287. Fort Collins, sitting 2 miles west of Interstate 25, sprawls along the Cache la Poudre River at the foot of the Front Range escarpment. The city, poised on the edge of the Great Plains and the Rocky Mountains, relies on an economic base of agriculture, high-tech industry, and Colorado State University. Started in 1862 as an army fort by two companies of the Kansas Volunteer Cavalry, Camp Collins's mission was to protect travelers, settlers, and the U.S. Mail on the Overland Trail. A flood erased the post in 1864 and a new camp, designated Fort Collins, was erected at today's town site. After Indian attacks abated, the fort was taken over by the Larimar County Land Improvement Company, and streets were platted for a new town in 1873. The town thrived as a farming hub, and in 1879 the Agricultural College of Colorado, now Colorado State University, opened its doors.

Points of interest include the Fort Collins Museum, the historic Avery House, and an Anheuser-Busch brewery. The town, a recreational haven, offers nearby hike and bike trails and fishing areas at Horsetooth Mountain Park and Reservoir and Lory State Park.

The drive heads north and west from Fort Collins on CO 14 across rolling farms and ranches. US 287 makes a quick bypass around **Laporte,** while CO 14 runs west through the town. Laporte, settled as a fur post by French trappers in 1858, was the area's first settlement. The name, French for "the gate," came from the natural gap in the hogbacks northwest of here, where today's highway runs. Antoine Janis, Colorado's first permanent white settler north of the Arkansas River, claimed the river bottom west of Laporte in 1844. Legend says that years earlier Janis, part of an American Fur Company supply train, stashed several hundred pounds of gunpowder and other supplies in a hole along the river one winter to lighten wagon loads, returning the next year to retrieve the goods. Afterward, trappers called the river Cache la Poudre, meaning "cache of the powder."

Lory State Park to Poudre Canyon

Just past Laporte is the turn south to **Lory State Park.** This secluded, 2,400-acre parkland is a marvelous, off-the-beaten-track natural area. The park preserves the diverse ecology of the Rockies foothills, with grasslands, upturned sandstone hogbacks, and ponderosa pine forests. Twenty-two miles of marked trails thread through the park, offering adventure to hikers, mountain bikers, and horseback riders. Climbers scale 6,780-foot Arthur's Rock, a granite crag perched above Horsetooth Reservoir. Prairie rattlesnakes are common in summer, especially around talus and on the lower grasslands.

The highway bends northwest, crossing and paralleling the hogbacks, high ridges tilted upward when the Rocky Mountains rose. Soft, easily eroded shales and mudstones form broad vales between the hogbacks. Ten miles from Fort Collins, the drive reaches Ted's Place and the intersection of US 287 and CO 14. Turn west on CO 14. Ted, or Edward Irving Herring, established his place in 1922 at the scenic entrance to Poudre Canyon.

Cache la Poudre River

CO 14 heads west up a broad valley through low, tawny hills and after a mile and a half enters **Poudre Canyon** and the Front Range. The highway threads alongside the **Cache la Poudre River** in the depths of Poudre Canyon for the next 50 miles. The 75-mile-long river, arising from Poudre Lake on Milner Pass and the Continental Divide in Rocky Mountain National Park, dashes through its craggy canyon, empties onto the plains, and ends in the South Platte River near Greeley. Throughout its length the Cache la Poudre remains a wild stream, untamed by dams. The river's marvelous scenery, excellent recreational opportunities, and wild character led to its designation as Colorado's first National Wild and Scenic River. The Poudre Canyon yields excellent fishing for brown and rainbow trout, offers serious whitewater challenges to rafters and kayakers, gives surprisingly good climbing on its cliffs, and boasts numerous national forest campgrounds and picnic areas. The river corridor, close to the urban Front Range cities, is popular, especially on summer weekends.

The drive enters 788,000-acre Roosevelt National Forest just past the canyon entrance. The forest, originally part of the 1897 Medicine Bow Forest Reserve, became Colorado National Forest in 1910 and was renamed for conservationist President Theodore Roosevelt in 1932. Past Picnic Rock River Access, the highway curves along the river. Steep, dry hillsides, covered with grass and low scrubs, border the blacktop. Greyrock Trailhead sits 7 miles up-canyon. **Greyrock National Recreation Trail,** one of the most popular hikes in the canyon, crosses the river on a footbridge and ascends 3 miles to Greyrock Mountain's 7,500-foot summit and expansive views.

The Cache la Poudre–North Park Scenic Byway follows the dashing Cache la Poudre River up Poudre Canyon.

Poudre Park, Big Narrows, and Profile Rock

The road continues west through the town of **Poudre Park** and passes Poudre Park, Diamond Rock, and Mishawaka Picnic Areas. Ansel Watrous Campground, with nineteen sites, sits among ponderosa pines in a broad canyon section. A couple of miles west the highway swings under granite cliffs, passes through a tunnel, and enters the Little Narrows. The river, making a huge bend, slices through bedrock with the road perched alongside. The canyon again broadens at the nine-site Stove Prairie Landing Campground. Stevens Gulch Picnic Area and river access sits another 0.5 mile west.

Past the picnic area the highway enters the **Big Narrows,** an impressive defile filled with soaring buttresses, cliffs, and arêtes. The frothy river churns over boulders in a mist of white spray and with a thunderous roar. Moist hanging canyons, filled with Douglas fir, grass, and ferns, climb above the river's cobbled south bank. Some of the canyon's best rock climbing is found on Ra's Buttress, Pee Wee's Playhouse, and Eve's Cave in the Big Narrows. Narrows Picnic Area and Campground sit just past the confined canyon segment.

The winding canyon, making an immense horseshoe bend, briefly opens at Big George Flat. The **Mount McConnell National Recreation Trail** begins near Mountain Park Campground. This 5-mile loop trail twists up through fir and pine forest to Mount McConnell's summit on the northern edge of 9,258-acre **Cache la Poudre Wilderness Area.** This small wilderness, traversed by the river's South Fork, protects a sparsely visited region of rugged mountains and canyons to the south. The Poudre Canyon again constricts down to a rocky, confined gorge. Kelly Flats Campground, with twenty-three campsites spread along the river bank, is nearby.

As the drive heads west the canyon walls are taller and the floor alternately widens and narrows. Mountain mahogany and sagebrush cover the dry south-facing slopes above the highway, while ponderosa pine and Douglas fir populate the moister north-facing slopes. Open grasslands blanket the wider valley floor at Indian Meadows. Anglers should check signage marking fishing areas restricted to fly and lower catch limits. Rustic and **Glen Echo,** small resort villages with summer cabins, straddle the broad valley further west. Willows and cottonwoods shade the river banks. **Profile Rock,** the craggy silhouette of a face, towers south of the river almost 3 miles past Glen Echo. A small visitor center with national forest information sits 0.5 mile upriver.

Poudre Canyon assumes a different complexion 3 miles past Profile Rock. The roadside Home Moraine Geologic Site, an interpretive pullout, marks the easternmost advance of a great valley glacier that excavated the U-shaped canyon to the west. Time and the flow of the river chiseled the confined, V-shaped canyon the drive has followed thus far. The pullout gives a view of the terminal moraine, a jumble of boulders and cobbles, that marked the glacier's farthest advance eastward.

The highway runs up the broad valley, its flanks stair-stepping up to forested summits. A state fish hatchery, the nine-site Big Bend Campground, and Roaring Creek Trailhead sit along the road. At Kinikinik's summer cottages, the Poudre River and canyon make a big bend southwest. The canyon's southern rim forms the northern boundary of 66,791-acre Comanche Peak Wilderness Area, a large swath of high mountains topped by 12,702-foot Comanche Peak in the Mummy Range. The highway heads southwest up the wide canyon. Sheer crags etched by glaciers perch on steep canyon slopes. Sleeping Elephant Campground, with fifteen aspen-shaded sites, sits along the river, and rocky Sleeping Elephant Mountain looms overhead. Tunnel Picnic Area sits along the river by Tunnel Creek. Poudre Falls, a spectacular whitewater cascade, spills over boulders just after the highway crosses from the river's west to east bank. At the four-site Big South Campground, the highway takes leave of the Cache la Poudre River and Poudre Canyon and begins steeply climbing up Joe Wright Creek's side canyon.

The Rawah Range and Cameron Pass

The road passes Aspen Glen Campground and a Roosevelt National Forest information kiosk. A string of popular fishing lakes and reservoirs is scattered throughout the lodgepole pine forest off the highway. Barnes Meadow Reservoir sits south of the drive and Chambers Lake, named for early trapper Robert Chambers, spreads to the north. The Laramie River, running north to Wyoming and the North Platte River, begins here.

The 76,394-acre **Rawah Wilderness Area** stretches north from the highway, encompassing almost the entire east flank of the Rawah range, a southern extension of Wyoming's Medicine Bow Mountains. The Arapaho Indians used their word for "wilderness," *rawah*, to describe this pristine sierra of high peaks and crystal lakes. The drive continues climbing above the shallow creek valley, edges past Joe Wright Reservoir, and reaches the broad summit of 10,276-foot **Cameron Pass.** The col, named for pioneer railroad builder General Robert Cameron, is flanked by white fir forest that climbs to timberline on snow-capped 12,951-foot Clark Peak. Small 9,924-acre Neota Wilderness Area protects an above-timberline region of flattened ridges fringed by fir and spruce.

Colorado State Forest

The drive heads down the pass's west slope and after a mile bends west above the Michigan River valley. The highway edges past a scenic overlook that offers a superlative view south of ragged 12,485-foot Nokhu Crags and 12,940-foot Mount Richthofen on Rocky Mountain National Park's northwest corner. The road continues to descend and passes a turnoff that leads south to the Lake Agnes trailhead.

The 0.5-mile trail climbs over glacial moraines to Lake Agnes, a timberline lake cupped in a deep basin below the Nokhu Crags. Nokhu is an abbreviated name derived from *Nea ha-no-Xhu,* or "Eagle's nest" in Arapaho. Crags Campground, administered by the Colorado State Forest, is scattered throughout spruce forest along the side road.

The byway drops into the Michigan River's broad, willow-covered valley. This area, along with the western flank of the Rawah Range, is part of the **Colorado State Forest State Park.** This 71,000-acre parkland, Colorado's largest state park, is administered by the Colorado Division of Parks as a trust land, funding the state's public school system. Besides recreational uses, grazing, logging, and hunting are permitted. The park offers four campgrounds with 158 sites, almost 20 miles of trails, and fishable lakes and streams. Kelly Lake, just below the range crest, is one of the few places in Colorado that holds the rare golden trout, an introduced California species. The park's diverse habitat also shelters more than 125 bird species, as well as mammals including marmot, marten, beaver, red fox, coyote, mink, bighorn sheep, and moose. The park's small moose population usually shelters among the willows along the upper Michigan River on the drive.

Past the campground at Ranger Lakes, the highway and river swing northwest around 10,390-foot Gould Mountain. A dense lodgepole pine forest, broken by scattered aspen groves, borders the asphalt. The small town of **Gould** offers gas and groceries. The state park headquarters and the turnoff to North Michigan Reservoir and Campground sits a couple miles farther.

The drive bends west and crosses the Michigan River valley. The ragged crest of the Rawah Range forms an immense wall to the east, while low-browed hills stretch along the valley's western rim. Wide grasslands, sprinkled with grazing cattle, spread out from the river. The highway, running northwest along rolling hills, passes open lodgepole pine and aspen woodlands before leaving the river valley and the mountains behind.

North Park

North Park, a huge glacial basin hemmed in by mountains, lies ahead. The basin, 35 miles wide and 45 miles long, is characterized by sagebrush rangelands and slow rivers. The Ute Indians, who frequently hunted the park's bison in summer, called it "Cow Lodge" and "Bull Pen." Lieutenant John C. Fremont, one of its first Anglo explorers, noted in his 1844 journal " . . . a beautiful circular valley of thirty miles in diameter, walled in all around with snowy mountains, rich with water and grass, fringed with pine on the mountain sides below the snow, and a paradise to all grazing animals." The road crosses low, sagebrush-covered bluffs and dips across Owl Creek's shallow valley. Seven miles after leaving the Michigan River the highway reaches Brocker Overlook above **Arapaho National Wildlife Refuge.**

The Rawah Range lifts its rounded crest above Michigan Creek Reservoir in Colorado State Forest State Park.

The 24,804-acre refuge, established in 1967, provides important nesting habitat for migratory waterfowl along the Illinois River. Water diverted from the river irrigates meadows and fills shallow ponds. After the ice melts in the refuge in late May, thousands of ducks, including pintail, mallard, gadwall, and American wigeon, as well as Canada geese, begin arriving to nest and raise their broods. Other shore and water birds seen are Virginia rails, Wilson's phalaropes, avocets, sandpipers, great blue heron, bitterns, and grebes. Numerous raptors—eagles, hawks, and prairie falcons—wheel across the sky in search of prey. Moose, elk, and mule deer range across the refuge, particularly during winter. A 6-mile self-guided auto tour, beginning 3 miles south of Walden on CO 125, explores the wildlife area.

The byway continues northwest along a bluff above the river and 3 miles later enters Walden and the scenic drive's end. Walden, North Park's largest town and a ranching center, is named for Mark Walden, the former postmaster of the nearby ghost town of Sage Hen Springs. The town, founded in 1889, was originally called Sagebrush for the ubiquitous stands of gray *Artemisia tridentata* that blanket North Park. Walden offers all visitor services, including gas, restaurants, and lodging.

19

Independence Pass Scenic Drive

Twin Lakes to Aspen

General description: This 44-mile-long drive climbs over 12,095-foot Independence Pass, Colorado's highest paved pass, and the Continental Divide between the upper Arkansas River valley and Aspen.

Special attractions: Twin Lakes, Mount Elbert, Colorado Trail, La Plata Peak, Independence Pass, Independence ghost town, Hunter-Fryingpan Wilderness Area, Collegiate Peaks Wilderness Area, Continental Divide, Braille Nature Trail, San Isabel National Forest, White River National Forest, camping, mountaineering, rock climbing, fishing, hiking, backpacking, scenic views.

Location: Central Colorado. The drive runs from US 24 20 miles north of Buena Vista to Aspen.

Drive route name and number: Independence Pass Road, CO 82.

Travel season: Spring through fall. The highway usually opens sometime in May and closes after the first major autumn snows, in late October or early November. Vehicles over 35 feet long are prohibited from crossing Independence Pass.

Camping: Several national forest campgrounds are along the drive. Lakeview, Parry Peak, and Twin Peaks Campgrounds sit on the east side of the pass. Lost Man, Lincoln Gulch, Weller, and Difficult Creek Campgrounds lie on the west side.

Services: All services are found in Aspen, Buena Vista, and Leadville. Limited services are at Granite and Twin Lakes.

Nearby attractions: Leadville National Historic District, National Mining Hall of Fame, Leadville National Fish Hatchery, Arkansas River, Mosquito Pass, Turquoise Lake, Holy Cross Wilderness Area, Clear Creek Canyon, Cottonwood Pass, Buena Vista, Mount Massive Wilderness Area, Ashcroft, Pearl Pass, Maroon Bells–Snowmass Wilderness Area, Maroon Lake, Buttermilk Mountain and Snowmass ski areas, Roaring Fork River.

The Drive

This 44-mile scenic drive crosses 12,095-foot Independence Pass, Colorado's highest paved pass, perched atop the Sawatch Range in central Colorado. The Sawatch Range, crested by the twisting Continental Divide, is one of the state's main mountain ranges. It stretches more than 100 miles from the Eagle River and Interstate 70 south to Marshall Pass and the Cochetopa Hills above the San Luis Valley. Sawatch, a Ute word meaning "water of the blue earth," describes an ancient lake that once filled the San Luis Valley. Later explorers, including Captain John Gunnison in 1853, applied the name to the mountain chain. The spelling of Sawatch was also changed from Saguache, which one wag said could only be pronounced by sneezing.

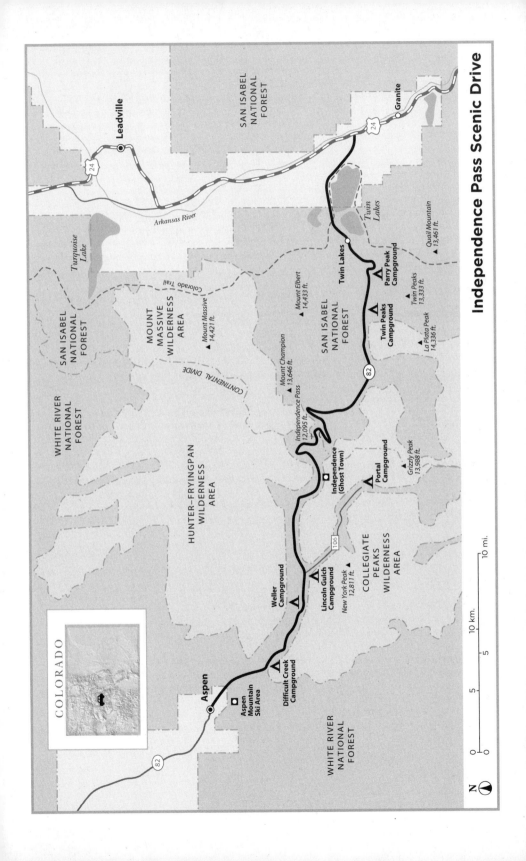

Independence Pass Scenic Drive

COLORADO

SAN ISABEL NATIONAL FOREST

Leadville

24

Arkansas River

Turquoise Lake

SAN ISABEL NATIONAL FOREST

WHITE RIVER NATIONAL FOREST

Colorado Trail

MOUNT MASSIVE WILDERNESS AREA

▲ Mount Massive 14,421 ft.

Granite

24

Twin Lakes

▲ Mount Elbert 14,433 ft.

Twin Lakes

Parry Peak Campground

▲ Quail Mountain 13,461 ft.

CONTINENTAL DIVIDE

HUNTER–FRYINGPAN WILDERNESS AREA

▲ Mount Champion 13,646 ft.

Independence Pass 12,095 ft.

SAN ISABEL NATIONAL FOREST

Twin Peaks Campground

▲ Twin Peaks 13,333 ft.

▲ La Plata Peak 14,336 ft.

82

Independence (Ghost Town)

Portal Campground

▲ Grizzly Peak 13,988 ft.

Weller Campground

106

Lincoln Gulch Campground

New York Peak 12,811 ft. ▲

COLLEGIATE PEAKS WILDERNESS AREA

Aspen

82

Difficult Creek Campground

Aspen Mountain Ski Area

WHITE RIVER NATIONAL FOREST

N

0   5   10 km.

0   5   10 mi.

The Sawatch Range, lying within the San Isabel and White River National Forests, contains fifteen of Colorado's fifty-four 14,000-foot peaks, including four of the five highest. Mount Elbert, the state's highest point at 14,433 feet, tops the list, followed by 14,421-foot Mount Massive, 14,420-foot Mount Harvard, and 14,336-foot La Plata Peak. Large tracts of wild lands—the Holy Cross, Mount Massive, and Collegiate Peaks Wilderness Areas—straddle the range and preserve large areas of pristine, roadless mountains. The range's snowy crest also gives birth to numerous rivers, including the Arkansas, Taylor, Roaring Fork, Fryingpan, and Eagle Rivers. On the east the Independence Pass scenic drive follows Lake Creek's deep, glaciated valley between Mount Elbert and La Plata Peak, while on the west the drive plunges down the Roaring Fork River corridor surrounded by the Hunter-Fryingpan and Collegiate Peaks Wilderness Areas.

Heavy snow shuts down the highway in winter. The road opens, usually in May, when deep drifts on the upper section melt back enough for snowplows to scour the roadway clean. It closes again when snow flies, usually in late October. Expect cool temperatures atop the pass from May through October, with possible afternoon thunderstorms and even summer snow. Summer temperatures can reach into the seventies, but breezes usually cool the air. If hiking on ridges atop the pass, watch for lightning on summer afternoons. Also use caution when crossing snowfields—they are deceptively dangerous. Carry and know how to use an ice axe and wear proper footwear. As a rule of thumb, air temperatures decrease three degrees for every 1,000 feet of elevation ascended. Consequently, the lower elevations, including Aspen and Twin Lakes, are warmer than the pass summit, with temperatures reaching eighty degrees.

Twin Lakes

The drive begins at the intersection of U.S. Highway 24 and CO 82, 20 miles north of Buena Vista and 15 miles south of Leadville in the Arkansas River valley. Granite, almost 3 miles south of the intersection, was the site of the area's first gold discovery in 1859. The camp was short lived as richer deposits were found upstream at California Gulch near today's Leadville. Turn west on CO 82, the Independence Pass Road. **Vehicles over 35 feet long are prohibited from crossing Independence Pass.**

The highway runs east alongside turbulent Lake Creek as it rushes across a huge boulder-strewn moraine left by the ancient Lake Creek Glacier, an immense glacier that scoured out the deep valley to the west. The moraine forms **Twin Lakes,** two large lakes that have been enlarged for water storage as part of the Fryingpan-Arkansas Project. This huge water project, supplying water primarily to Colorado Springs and Aurora on the Front Range, pumps water from the western slope of the Continental Divide to Turquoise Lake west of Leadville. The water is piped south to Twin Lakes, where it is used to generate electrical power before being sent to thirsty Front Range cities.

The highway reaches the north side of Twin Lakes and Mountain View Overlook after 1.5 miles. The drive continues west across sagebrush-covered slopes above the lake. At 2.4 miles the road passes Dexter Point Campground and a boat ramp, both part of Twin Lakes Recreation Area. Farther west a side road leads north to the fifty-nine-site Lakeview Campground and Mount Elbert Picnic Ground. The Fryingpan-Arkansas Project Visitor Center is reached at 4.5 miles. The center explains the history and hydraulics of the project. The lakes offer excellent fishing, with lake trout exceeding thirty pounds as well as rainbow and cutthroat trout. Beyond the center the highway bends southwest through piney hills, passes White Star Campground on the lakeshore, and enters the town of Twin Lakes.

This picturesque community, set at 9,015 feet at the foot of **Mount Elbert,** was settled around 1880 after the initial silver rush to nearby Leadville. The valley yielded a few prosperous lodes, such as the Little Joe, Bartlett, and Fidelity mines, but it was the natural beauty that attracted newcomers then and now. The town, offering few services, lies near a major avalanche chute that erased the western part of town. Look for some overgrown cabin foundations in the meadows below 12,682-foot Parry Peak, a spur of Mount Elbert. The town hosts an infamous tomato war every September. While driving through keep an eye out for the uniformed police officer mannequin in his roadside patrol car.

Lake Creek Valley

Past Twin Lakes the highway bends southeast for a mile, skirting marsh and willow thickets on the west edge of the lake before swinging into Lake Creek's narrowing valley. The creek rushes over worn cobbles and boulders in a shallow canyon below the road. Dense forests of lodgepole pine and aspen line the way and blanket steep mountainsides. Parry Peak Campground, with twenty-six sites, lies near the valley entrance. Thirty-nine-site Twin Peaks Campground spreads alongside the highway a mile farther west. Monitor Rock, a bold white cliff, looms over the drive on the southern flank of Mount Elbert. Glacial striations, scratched by boulders embedded in a deep glacier as it crept down the valley, scar the massive rock. A short walk to the cliff's rounded southern buttress reveals deep, parallel grooves in the smoothed rock surface. Over the last few million years, glaciers periodically excavated this valley and the rest of the Sawatch Range. The scenic drive travels through U-shaped valleys on both sides of the pass. The glaciers that once rested here were several thousand feet thick, with only the high peaks poking above the whiteness. The glaciers sculpted today's mountain scenery, leaving cirques, arêtes, hanging valleys, and moraines as evidence of their passage.

The valley broadens past Monitor Rock and the creek swings between willow-lined banks. Thick stands of aspen border the drive and offer spectacular color in late September. **La Plata Peak** dominates the valley. Its long ridges, corniced with winter snow and studded with rock pinnacles and crags, sweep south to the peak's 14,336-foot apex. La Plata Peak, one of the range's most satisfying climbs, was named by pioneer surveyor Ferdinand Hayden in 1874 with the Spanish word for silver. The summit is best reached via the La Plata Trail. Park alongside the highway at the turnoff for Forest Road 391, the South Fork of Lake Creek Road, almost 15 miles from the drive's start. The trail drops down and crosses Lake Creek, wanders through thick spruce forest into La Plata Gulch, and then ascends east up a grassy, above-timberline spur to the summit ridge.

At 15 miles the highway heads northwest up Lake Creek's North Fork into a wide, flat-bottomed valley. Dense willows carpet the damp valley floor and hem in the creek. Beaver ponds still the tumbling stream and make good fishing holes. A few miles later the highway makes a sharp switchback and begins climbing steeply up a shelf road chiseled into the mountain slope. Watch for fallen boulders on this road section. Just over 1 mile later the highway exits the shelf into Mountain Boy Gulch, a hanging valley with verdant meadows and dense forest. A waterfall sweeps over a cliff band at timberline west of the drive and thick snow cornices line the Continental Divide's ridgeline above. The road switchbacks up the valley's north slope, twisting through stunted, windswept trees at timberline. Just past tree line the drive bends sharply west and begins the final ascent to the pass summit.

Independence Pass

Americans have long been a pass-loving people. A sense of freedom is found in crossing a wild sierra. Out there, beyond the summits, stretches a whole new world, waiting patiently to be discovered and explored. On surmounting a pass, the first instinct is to continue, to plunge down into the unknown valleys below. But here, atop 12,095-foot **Independence Pass,** stop and linger. Breathe in this moment and this majestic panorama.

A parking area and sign mark the lofty summit. A short trail wends south to a lookout point above Mountain Boy Gulch. Mountains surround this overlook—La Plata Peak to the south; Mount Elbert and its high satellites dominate the eastern skyline; and rows of peaks and ridges march westward to the Maroon Bells, Snowmass Mountain, and Capitol Peak. The pass summit introduces the world above the trees, a world more similar in climate and flora to the lands beyond the Arctic Circle thousands of miles to the north than to the nearby lowland valleys. Mats of

Opposite: Lake Creek, filled with spring snowmelt, pours into a narrow slot canyon along the Independence Pass scenic drive.

wiry grass sprinkled with delicate wildflowers brighten the broad crest. Deep snow-drifts, persisting well into August, cling to leeward edges and deep ravines. Frigid tarns of snowmelt fill shallow depressions with sky and cloud reflections. Beyond the pass, rounded ridges clad in tundra plants sweep up to boulder fields, rocky buttresses, and windy summits.

Independence to Aspen

The highway falls abruptly west, edging north down a steep shelf road for over a mile. Watch for fallen boulders. No guardrail or shoulder comforts the nervous driver here. On reaching the valley floor and timberline, the drive bends south above the Roaring Fork River and heads downhill through subalpine fir forest and open meadows. The ghost town of Independence sits 2 miles from the pass. Gold was discovered on Independence Day, 1879, in this alpine valley, bringing a stampede of prospectors to the new town dubbed Independence. By 1880 the path over what was then called Hunter's Pass and later Independence Pass became a horse trail operated by the Twin Lakes and Roaring Fork Toll Company. On November 6 the following year, the company opened a frightful wagon road that climbed the lofty pass between Leadville and the burgeoning silver town of Aspen. The road was an instant success, with freight traffic swarming over the divide. Hefty tolls ensured temporary prosperity. For five winters, an army of snow shovelers labored to keep the road open—a feat today's highway department will not undertake with the area's high avalanche danger. The stagecoach trek over the pass took twenty-four hours, five changes of horses, and three toll gates. In 1888 the railroad reached Aspen and the trail closed down until resurrected as an automobile road in the 1920s.

The town of Independence, at its peak in the early 1880s, boasted a population of 2,000 and ten saloons. By the turn of the twentieth century, the last prospector had pulled up stakes, leaving the town for the owls and mice. Weather-beaten cabins and a few crumbling buildings are all that remain of Independence today. The ghost town, preserved through the efforts of the Aspen Historical Society, makes a good stop. Walk through the grassy streets today and imagine the daily rigors and trials faced by the nineteenth-century miners.

The highway passes Lost Man Trailhead, the jumping-off point for a popular hike into the 82,729-acre **Hunter-Fryingpan Wilderness Area,** and ten-site Lost Man Campground 2 miles past Independence. A dense forest of lodgepole pine, spruce, and fir shades this pleasant 10,700-foot-high campground. The Braille Nature Trail, a barrier-free pathway, explores the forest farther down the road. Past the trail the highway narrows and winds down a steep canyon above the Roaring Fork River. Numerous granite crags nestle in the woods between here and Aspen, offering a diverse selection of routes for rock climbers. Some of the best

The now placid ghost town of Independence on the west side of Independence Pass bustled with mining fever some 120 years ago.

cliffs include the Grotto Walls, Whirlpool Rock, and Weller Slab. More information can be found at the climbing shop in Aspen.

The Lincoln Creek Road, Forest Road 106, starts 10 miles west of Lost Man. This road, rapidly turning to rough four-wheel drive, leads southeast up Lincoln Creek to Grizzly Reservoir and Portal Campground. Past the turn the road narrows and twists underneath the looming **Grotto Walls.** Look for another pullout just past the bends. A trail begins at the road's end, crosses the river on a footbridge, and heads east across glacier-polished granite a hundred yards to the Grottos. The Grottos are a series of caverns chiseled by the Roaring Fork River before it cut its present channel. The caverns, roofed by a slit of light, are best accessed via their west end. They are generally dry, although snow and ice linger inside the Grottos through the early summer.

The drive continues west to eleven-site Weller Campground, its sites surrounded by a lush aspen grove. Aspens sprinkle among fir and spruce forests along the road or form moist glades with a thick understory of grass, columbines, and ferns. In late September, the aspens drape sheer mountainsides with their rippling gold color. Past the campground, the highway abruptly narrows to one and a half lanes and creeps shelf-like above a granite slab. After 0.25 mile the highway widens and drops onto a broad glaciated valley. The road stairsteps down to a lower valley. Difficult Campground, with forty-seven sites, sits along the river among dense willow thickets and beaver ponds. Heading west the highway crosses wide meadows below steep aspen-covered hillsides. North Star Wildlife Preserve, threaded by a footpath, protects critical elk habitat along the valley floor. The highway reaches 7,908-foot-high **Aspen** and the drive's end a mile farther downstream.

Aspen, Colorado's famed ski resort, began as a silver mining camp in 1879. Prosperity poured from its wealthy lodes, including the Smuggler, Montezuma, Midnight, and Molly Gibson mines, until the great silver crash of 1893. At that time, Aspen, with a population of 12,000, was the state's third-largest city. The town, one of the first to run on electricity, boasted six newspapers, two banks, the Wheeler Opera House, and the fabulous Hotel Jerome. Victorian homes and buildings from that era still line the streets. Skiers began sampling Aspen's deep snow in 1936, and by the late 1940s the town stood poised to become one of America's great ski resorts. Aspen, besides its four ski areas, offers all visitor services as well as numerous festivals and events.

Cottonwood Pass Scenic Drive

Buena Vista to Almont

General description: This 60-mile-long paved and gravel road crosses 12,126-foot Cottonwood Pass on the Continental Divide and follows the Taylor River to Almont.

Special attractions: Collegiate Peaks Wilderness Area, Mount Yale, Cottonwood Pass, Taylor Reservoir, Taylor Canyon, Continental Divide, Colorado Trail, camping, hiking, backpacking, rock climbing, fishing, fly-fishing.

Location: Central Colorado. The drive runs from Buena Vista in the Arkansas River valley to Almont, 11 miles north of Gunnison.

Drive route name and numbers: Cottonwood Pass Road; Chaffee County Road 306; Forest Roads 306, 209, and 742.

Travel season: Late spring through autumn. The drive closes in winter after the first big snowfall and opens in late spring after snowmelt. Check with the national forest offices for opening and closure dates.

Camping: Nine national forest campgrounds lie along the drive.

Services: All services are in Buena Vista. Limited services are in Almont, with complete services nearby in Gunnison and Crested Butte.

Nearby attractions: Elk Mountains, Crested Butte, West Elk Scenic Byway, Gunnison, Curecanti National Recreation Area, West Elk Wilderness Area, Tincup, Cumberland Pass, Alpine Tunnel, St. Elmo, Mount Princeton Hot Springs, Arkansas Headwaters State Recreation Area, Buffalo Peaks Wilderness Area.

The Drive

The Sawatch Range lines the west side of the Arkansas River Valley, its high peaks soaring to meet the clouds and sky. This long range, stretching more than 100 miles from the Eagle River to Marshall Pass, is studded by fifteen 14,000-foot peaks, including 14,433-foot Mount Elbert, Colorado's highest point. Only two highways—Independence and Monarch Passes—and a handful of gravel roads cross the range. The Cottonwood Pass Road, surmounting the Continental Divide at 12,126 feet, is the only one of the gravel roads passable in a standard two-wheel-drive passenger car. The road makes a spectacular backcountry tour that is easily accessible from the Front Range cities. It threads up Cottonwood Creek past beaver ponds and the Collegiate Peaks Wilderness Area, loops above timberline to the pass summit, and drops down through Taylor Park and the Taylor River Canyon to Almont and the Gunnison River.

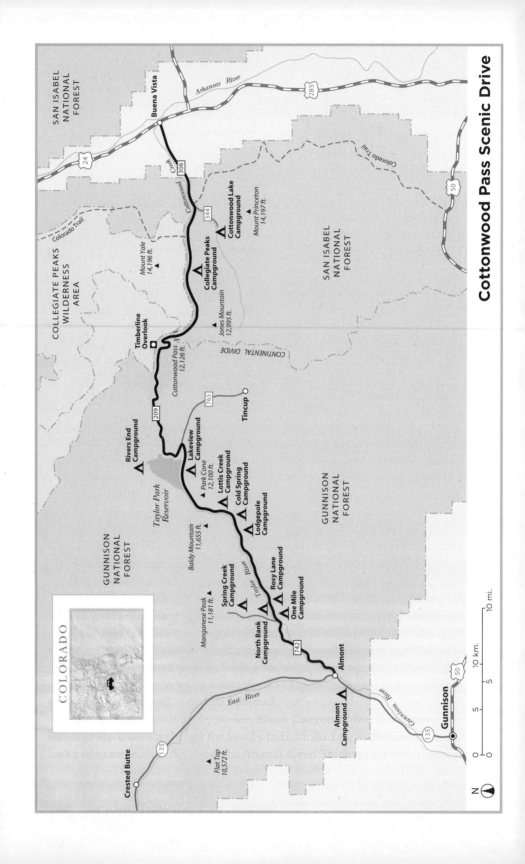

Cottonwood Pass Scenic Drive

COLORADO

SAN ISABEL NATIONAL FOREST

Arkansas River

Buena Vista

24

306

Cottonwood Creek

285

50

344

Cottonwood Lake Campground

Mount Princeton 14,197 ft.

SAN ISABEL NATIONAL FOREST

Collegiate Peaks Campground

Mount Yale 14,196 ft.

COLLEGIATE PEAKS WILDERNESS AREA

Colorado Trail

Timberline Overlook

Jones Mountain 12,995 ft.

CONTINENTAL DIVIDE

Cottonwood Pass 12,126 ft.

Colorado Trail

209

765

Tincup

Rivers End Campground

Lakeview Campground

Park Cone 12,100 ft.

Lottis Creek Campground

Cold Spring Campground

Lodgepole Campground

Taylor Park Reservoir

Baldy Mountain 11,655 ft.

GUNNISON NATIONAL FOREST

GUNNISON NATIONAL FOREST

Manganese Peak 11,181 ft.

Spring Creek Campground

Taylor River

Rosy Lane Campground

One Mile Campground

North Bank Campground

742

East River

Crested Butte

135

Flat Top 10,572 ft.

Almont

Almont Campground

Gunnison River

Gunnison

50

135

N

10 mi.

10 km.

0   5   10

0   5

Cottonwood Pass opens in May or June, depending on snowfall amounts, and closes after the first major snow, usually in November. Check with the forest office for closure dates and road conditions. Temperatures vary greatly on the drive, depending on elevation. Summer days are pleasant, with highs ranging from sixty to eighty in the lower elevations and the fifties and sixties atop the pass. Expect afternoon thunderstorms. Watch for lightning if hiking on ridges. Temperatures begin declining in early September, with the difference between day and night temperatures differing as much as forty degrees. Highs are in the sixties and low seventies with nighttime lows dipping below freezing. September and October are generally dry, although cold fronts often bring rain and snow to the high country. The drive offers one of Colorado's best foliage tours in late September.

Buena Vista

The Cottonwood Pass scenic drive begins at the traffic light marking the intersection of U.S. Highway 24 and Chaffee County Road 306 in **Buena Vista.** The town, at an elevation of 7,954 feet, was settled by silver miners in 1879. The Denver & Rio Grande Railroad arrived in 1880 en route to the upstream Leadville mines. The town grew as a supply and transportation center for towns and mines in outlying canyons, including Clear Creek and Chalk Creek Canyons. A mill and smelter built in 1881 brought additional prosperity. Buena Vista quickly outgrew Granite, the county seat, 20 miles upriver, and the town was voted the new county seat. When Granite refused to yield the county records, Buena Vista locals broke into the courthouse at night and claimed the papers and county business. Buena Vista was a rowdy town, and thirty-six bars did their best to fuel the brashness.

Today Buena Vista thrives on tourism and bills itself as the "Whitewater Capital of Colorado." The nickname is no lie—the nearby Arkansas River offers some of the nation's best kayaking and rafting adventures. The Numbers rapid, just upstream from town, offers a technical and treacherous run for kayakers. Brown's Canyon, the most popular river run in Colorado, lies a few miles downstream. The river plunges through a series of demanding rapids with names like Widowmaker, Big Drop, and Zoom Flume. Numerous outfitters offer guided river trips. The Arkansas River here is part of the 148-mile-long **Arkansas Headwaters Recreation Area.**

Buena Vista, meaning "good view" in Spanish, sits in a superlative location at the confluence of Cottonwood Creek and the Arkansas River. Towering mountains, flanking the broad river valley, form a staggering presence. Low peaks, covered with brushy pines, climb eastward to the Buffalo Peaks at the southern end of the Mosquito Range. Westward looms the Collegiate Peaks section of the Sawatch Range, rising 6,000 feet from the valley floor. Bulky 14,197-foot Mount Princeton, with long, sweeping ridges, dominates the view. Another "fourteener," Mount Yale, lies half-hidden by lower mountains to the north.

Cottonwood Creek

The drive heads west from Buena Vista toward the deep cleft chiseled by Cottonwood Peak between the two massive peaks. The road leaves Buena Vista behind after a mile, running over a gravel bench past scattered homes. **Cottonwood Creek** hides beneath tall cottonwoods north of the road, while Mount Princeton looms to the southwest. After 4.5 miles the road enters San Isabel National Forest, a 2.5-million-acre forest that stretches across central and southern Colorado. The road enters the mountain rampart and Cottonwood Creek's canyon 0.25 mile farther up. The drive twists along the tumbling stream, its banks a tangle of cottonwoods and willows. Abrupt slopes climb north of the road, broken by white cliffs, scree, and ponderosa and piñon pines. A couple of miles past private Cottonwood Hot Springs, the road, now Forest Road 306, bends up the creek's main fork. A left turn on Forest Road 344 runs southwest to Cottonwood Lake. This small lake nestled in woods offers good rainbow trout fishing from its banks. Twenty-eight-site Cottonwood Lake Campground sits on the south shore.

The paved drive ascends the broad, glaciated valley for 8 miles before steeply switchbacking for 5 miles through spruce forest and open meadows to reach timberline and the cloud-scraping pass summit. The rugged country abutting the drive on the north lies within 167,414-acre **Collegiate Peaks Wilderness Area,** an untrampled swath of peaks and valleys spreading north to the Independence Pass highway. Several roadside trailheads offer access to the area. The Avalanche Trailhead, at 9 miles, climbs Avalanche Gulch via the Colorado Trail. Denny Creek Trailhead, at 12 miles, scales scenic Denny Creek to Brown's Pass. The fifty-six-site Collegiate Peaks Campground, a mile east of Denny Creek, is the jumping-off point for walkers to climb 14,196-foot **Mount Yale.** The hike begins just west of the campground on an old, unmarked jeep road that zigzags up Denny Gulch before turning into a well-traveled trail that scrambles up ridges above timberline to the summit. Ptarmigan Trail, in the upper valley, wends south to Ptarmigan Lake nestled below **Jones Mountain.**

Jones Mountain, a round-shouldered, 12,995-foot peak, dominates the upper valley. Good views of the mountain are found at **Holy Water Beaver Ponds** at mile 13. A paved parking lot allows travelers to stop and perhaps catch a glimpse of an elusive beaver swimming across a still pond densely lined with willows, a favorite beaver food. The beaver, North America's largest rodent, builds numerous dams that stairstep up most of Colorado's high mountain valleys. The chains of lakes constructed by these small conservationists combat erosion, provide flood control, and create habitat for birds and fish. Their ponds silt up over time,

Opposite: Mount Yale in the Collegiate Peaks Wilderness Area soars high above the Cottonwood Pass drive.

creating rich soil for mountain meadows. Forests of spruce, set off with glades of quaking aspen, cover the mountain slopes above the beaver ponds.

Cottonwood Pass Summit

Just before the pass summit the road curves across an above-timberline cirque etched by ancient glaciers. Low willows clot the roadside. The climbing road makes a last hairpin turn, and edges along a shelf road for 0.5 mile to the 12,126-foot summit of **Cottonwood Pass.** This saddle lies on the Continental Divide, the twisting mountain backbone that separates the Atlantic and Pacific watersheds.

Cottonwood Pass has long been an important mountain crossing. An early wagon track, roughly following today's pass road, served as the main route into Aspen until the Independence Pass trail opened in 1881. The road, although serving Tincup and Taylor Park, fell into relative disuse until the Forest Service reconstructed the road in 1960. The summit allows a great panoramic view that encompasses Taylor Park and Castle Peak to the west and the Sawatch Range to the north. A short hike climbs south up the divide ridge to a higher viewpoint. The pavement ends atop the pass. The west side is gravel for the 14 downhill miles to Taylor Park Reservoir.

Taylor Park

The drive, now Forest Road 209, drops northwest above a high cirque and reaches Timberline Overlook, a roadside pullout, after a mile. Here the road begins lacing down toward the cirque floor and timberline. Spiraling down, the road parallels Pass Creek, running through spruce forest and below open slopes. Numerous beaver ponds step down the valley floor. As the road descends, the forest is mixed lodgepole pine and aspen. After 8 miles the road reaches the edge of **Taylor Park,** a high intermontane basin covered with forest and sagebrush meadows. The park is named for James Taylor, leader of a group of 1860 prospectors. The drive gently descends over ridges and through shallow valleys. Taylor Park Ranger Station sits 12 miles from the pass summit at 9,524 feet. A mile and a half later the drive merges with paved Forest Road 742 and turns southward. An overlook with picnic tables sits at the junction.

Taylor Park Reservoir, with 2,033 surface acres, spreads across the valley floor west of the road. The drive twists south on gravel benches above the lake. Forest Road 765 heads east a couple of miles down the drive, leading to the picturesque mining town of Tincup. The road climbs over Cumberland Pass from Tincup and provides access to several excellent jeep trails.

Past the junction with Forest Road 765, the drive crosses Willow Creek and turns west above the lake. A viewpoint offers excellent views of the wind-tossed lake and a long row of peaks perched on the Continental Divide. Lakeview Campground, with forty-six sites, sits south of the drive, while another road offers lake access at the Taylor Lake Boathouse. The regularly stocked lake yields excellent fishing for large lake trout, pike, Kokanee salmon, and rainbow, brown, and Snake River cutthroat trout.

Taylor Canyon to Almont

The road continues along the lake's southern shore, winding through lodgepole pines and blue spruces. After 2 miles the drive reaches the large earthen dam that forms the reservoir and drops into **Taylor Canyon.** Taylor Dam Vista Point overlooks the dam. The 206-foot-high dam, finished in 1937, backs up 106,200-acre feet of snowmelt used for summer irrigation water.

The drive, paved FR 742, follows the Taylor River for 21 miles through Taylor Canyon to **Almont** and the Taylor River's confluence with the East River. Steep walls, blanketed with spruce, pine, and aspen and broken by ragged cliffs, climb above the river to 12,100-foot Park Cone and 11,655-foot Baldy Mountain in the upper gorge. The large river rushes through cobbled rapids and pools in deep ponds by dark boulders. The Taylor River offers great fly-fishing for rainbow and brown trout. Be aware that private property borders much of the river. Look for public access areas. A trio of forest campgrounds—twenty-nine-site Lottis Creek, six-site Cold Spring, and seventeen-site Lodgepole—scatter above the river in the central canyon. Farther west are nineteen-site Rosy Lane, twenty-five-site One Mile, and seventeen-site North Bank campgrounds. Decent rock climbing is found on the towering granite cliffs near North Bank. More broken cliffs scatter along the canyon flank.

The canyon widens past the campgrounds and leaves Gunnison National Forest. Dry, rolling hills colored gray with sagebrush surround the canyon, with groves of spruce and fir tucked into moist side ravines. Hay fields and cattle spread across the wide canyon floor, before the river again plunges into a cliff-lined gorge. Gunnison Mountain Park, with picnic facilities and a nature trail, lies below cliff bands in this lower canyon. Cottonwoods and willows border the Taylor River. At Almont, a small resort town, the road and drive dead-ends on CO 135. The East and Taylor Rivers join here in this shallow valley to form the Gunnison River. Almont, established in 1881 as a railroad stop, was named for a famed Kentucky racehorse. A turn north on CO 135 leads 17 miles to Crested Butte, while a south turn heads 11 miles to Gunnison and U.S. Highway 50.

21

West Elk Loop Scenic Byway

Gunnison to Crested Butte

General description: This 164-mile-long loop drive encircles the West Elk Mountains, passing numerous geologic features, dense aspen woodlands, and spacious valleys.

Special attractions: Curecanti National Recreation Area, Dillon Pinnacles, Blue Mesa Reservoir, Morrow Point Reservoir, Gunnison National Forest, West Elk Wilderness Area, Crawford State Park, Paonia State Park, Raggeds Wilderness Area, Lost Lake, Kebler Pass, Crested Butte National Historic District, Crested Butte Mountain Resort, hiking, camping, backpacking, sailboarding, skiing, scenic views, fall colors, fishing.

Location: West-central Colorado. The drive makes a huge loop around the West Elk Mountains to the north and west of Gunnison.

Drive route name and numbers: West Elk Loop Scenic Byway; US 50; CO 92, 133, and 135; Gunnison County Road 12.

Travel season: The paved highway portions are open year-round, although snow may temporarily close the highways. Adequate snow tires or chains are advised. The gravel road over Kebler Pass closes in winter and opens in late spring when the snow melts away.

Camping: Numerous campgrounds lie along or just off the drive.

Services: All services in Gunnison, Crawford, Hotchkiss, Paonia, and Crested Butte.

Nearby attractions: Black Canyon of the Gunnison National Park, Grand Mesa, Lake City, McClure Pass, Maroon Bells–Snowmass Wilderness Area, Glenwood Springs, Marble, Cottonwood Pass, Taylor River Canyon, Tincup, Uncompahgre National Forest.

The Drive

The 164-mile-long West Elk Loop Scenic Byway loops around the rugged West Elk Mountains in western Colorado. The drive explores a diverse landscape. Precipitous peaks lift snowcapped summits into the turquoise sky. Aspens spread golden tapestries across rolling hillsides. Granite cliffs stud sharp canyons, their walls chiseled by time and the river. It's a land of majestic grandeur, but it's also a land of details waiting to be discovered. It's in those close-up vignettes that the world comes more alive—the clarity of a jewel-like dewdrop on a shaft of grama grass; the rustle of scrub oak leaves from a rufous-sided towhee; the cold smoothness of a river-worn cobble; ridgeline trees silhouetted against an evening thunderstorm.

Traffic along the drive's 132 paved miles and 32 gravel miles is generally light, although the U.S. Highway 50 section west of Gunnison can be heavy in summer.

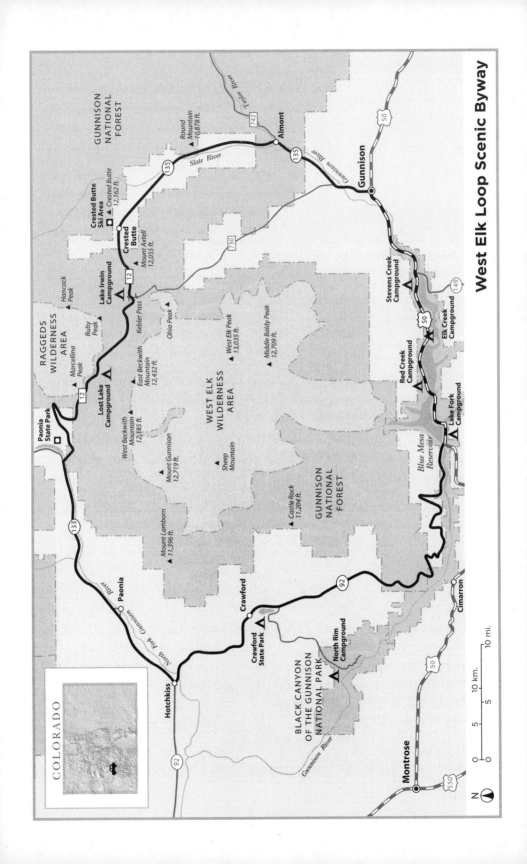

West Elk Loop Scenic Byway

COLORADO

GUNNISON NATIONAL FOREST

RAGGEDS WILDERNESS AREA

WEST ELK WILDERNESS AREA

GUNNISON NATIONAL FOREST

BLACK CANYON OF THE GUNNISON NATIONAL PARK

Round Mountain 10,878 ft.

Crested Butte 12,162 ft.

Crested Butte Ski Area

Mount Axtell 12,055 ft.

Hancock Peak

Ruby Peak

Marcellina Peak

Kebler Pass

Ohio Peak

East Beckwith Mountain 12,432 ft.

West Beckwith Mountain 12,185 ft.

West Elk Peak 13,035 ft.

Middle Baldy Peak 12,709 ft.

Mount Gunnison 12,719 ft.

Sheep Mountain

Mount Lamborn 11,396 ft.

Castle Rock 11,204 ft.

Blue Mesa Reservoir

Lake Irwin Campground

Lost Lake Campground

Stevens Creek Campground

Red Creek Campground

Elk Creek Campground

Lake Fork Campground

North Rim Campground

Crawford State Park

Paonia State Park

Almont

Gunnison

Crested Butte

Paonia

Hotchkiss

Crawford

Cimarron

Montrose

Taylor River

Slate River

Gunnison River

North Fork Gunnison River

Gunnison River

742

135

135

12

12

730

50

149

50

92

133

92

50

550

N

0   5   10 mi.

0   5   10 km.

The mountain roads are winding and narrow, with occasional turnoffs. Watch for blind corners. The gravel segment is easily driven in summer and fall by passenger cars. Muddy and slick patches linger after heavy rain. Winter snow closes Kebler Pass, although the rest of the route remains open.

Summer and autumn are the best times to drive the roads, with pleasant daily high temperatures between sixty and eighty degrees, depending on the elevation. A wide range of elevations, from 5,351 feet at Hotchkiss to the 9,980-foot summit of Kebler Pass, and the diverse topography make for a variety of climates and ecosystems on the drive. Expect regular afternoon thunderstorms in summer, with localized heavy rain on the mountains. Occasional cool, rainy periods occur in September, and by late October snow begins falling on the high country. Winters are frigid. Every winter Gunnison, lying in a valley, records a number of national lows with below-zero temperatures. Daily highs climb into the twenties. Crested Butte tends to be a little warmer, but an annual average of 230 inches of snow falls on its ski slopes. Warmer winter weather and less snow is found in the North Fork Valley at Paonia and Hotchkiss. Spring begins in April at the lower elevations and slowly creeps up the slopes until early June, when most of the snow is melted. Spring brings unpredictable weather with warm, breezy days and unsettled periods with rain and sleet.

Gunnison to Crawford

The drive begins in **Gunnison** on US 50. Gunnison, at 7,703 feet, sits in the broad Gunnison Valley at the confluence of the Gunnison River and Tomichi Creek. Gunnison has strong farming and ranching roots, although it was established in 1880 as a railroad stop and supply center for nearby mining areas. Originally called Richardson's Colony for local town organizer Dr. Sylvester Richardson, the community was renamed for ill-fated railroad surveyor Captain John Gunnison. Gunnison and his party, surveying a possible transcontinental railroad route, camped here on September 6, 1853. The group explored westward along today's US 50, before being killed by Indians in Utah's Sevier Valley in late October. Gunnison, home of Western State College, thrives as a ranching and tourism hub.

The drive's 28-mile first segment goes west on US 50. The highway runs through a broad valley lush with cattle paddocks and hayfields. Narrow-leaf cottonwoods densely line the Gunnison River's banks. After a few miles the highway and river enter **Curecanti National Recreation Area,** a 41,972-acre site managed by the National Park Service. Blue Mesa, Morrow Point, and Crystal Lakes, part of the Bureau of Reclamation's Colorado River Storage Project, offer fishing, camping, and boating recreation and provide water for irrigation and hydroelectric power. The two lower reservoirs fill the narrow floor of the Gunnison River's

Sailboarders skim across the Bay of Chickens on Blue Mesa Lake at Curecanti National Recreation Area.

upper Black Canyon, forming long, fjord-like lakes, while **Blue Mesa Lake,** the upper reservoir, drowns a wide valley.

The highway enters a shallow canyon and passes Neversink, Crystal Ranch, and Beaver Creek picnic areas. All three offer Gunnison River fishing access. Past Beaver Creek the highway winds alongside upper Blue Mesa Lake, a narrow lake amid granite bluffs and sagebrushed hillsides. At the Lake City Bridge and the junction with CO 149, the lake opens into broad Iola Basin.

The highway borders Blue Mesa Lake for the next 19 miles to its dam. Blue Mesa Lake, Colorado's largest lake, stretches 20 miles from dam to inlet, covers 9,000 surface acres when full, boasts 96 miles of shoreline, and reaches 330 feet in depth near its dam. Blue Mesa is Curecanti's most accessible and most popular recreation site. The lake offers excellent fishing, particularly for big mackinaw lake trout. The largest "macs," preferring deep, cold water, reach weights exceeding thirty pounds. Kokanee salmon and brown and rainbow trout also flourish in Blue Mesa Lake. The lake also offers great winter ice fishing.

High, flat-topped mesas, capped with a layer of volcanic West Elk breccia, surround Blue Mesa Lake. The breccia, a mixture of ejected rock fragments and ash, exploded from immense volcanoes in today's West Elk and San Juan Mountains. Below the mesa rims, erosion chisels strange shapes from the volcanic palisades. The **Dillon Pinnacles,** a bizarre collection of spires, buttresses, gargoyles, fins, and hoodoos, sits prominently above the drive near the lake's west end. A 2-mile trail climbs to a bench below the pinnacles. Sagebrush colors the rounded mesa slopes above the lake a dull gray, while green cottonwoods and scrub oak tint side canyons and ravines.

Several picnic areas and campgrounds are scattered along the lake and highway. Stevens Creek Campground, 12 miles west of Gunnison, offers fifty-three lakeside sites. Elk Creek Campground spreads 160 sites across a dry vale. Nearby is the park visitor center with informative displays on area natural history, history, geology, and recreational opportunities. The Bay of Chickens, a mile past Elk Creek, is the lake's best sailboarding area. Nine-site Dry Gulch and three-site Red Creek Campgrounds are located just off the drive in their respective side canyons. The Dillon Pinnacles Trail and Picnic Area begins on the north side of the Middle Bridge between the lake's Sapinero and Cebolla basins. The drive crosses the bridge, passes a scenic overlook above the south shore, and loops around Sapinero Mesa's broad north flank to the Lake Fork Bridge over the Lake Fork Arm. Lake Fork Campground, with ninety sites, is on the right just past the bridge. US 50 climbs a hill and intersects CO 92, the second leg of the byway journey.

Turn north on CO 92. The drive's second segment travels 52 miles to Hotchkiss in North Fork Valley. The two-lane highway drops past eighty-seven-site Lake Fork Campground, a pull-through RV camping area, and crosses Blue Mesa Lake's 342-foot-high earth and concrete dam. The dam, completed in 1965, plugs the narrow river channel with over three million cubic yards of fill. The highway creeps over the 800-foot-long dam and twists onto a bench above Morrow Point Lake and the precipitous upper **Black Canyon of the Gunnison River.**

The Black Canyon, one of Colorado's most startling earth features, stretches 50 miles through the Gunnison Uplift. The Gunnison River, the state's fourth-largest river, sliced into ancient two-billion-year-old bedrock over the last three million years to create this marvelous chasm. The river cuts downward about one inch per century. The lower canyon is protected in Black Canyon of the Gunnison National Park, while the upper canyon hides two fingering reservoirs beneath somber canyon walls.

The highway winds along a granite bench above the canyon. Geologists say the bench is the erosional remnant of a gentle highland that rose here over two billion years ago. Above the bench lie multicolored layers of the Morrison Formation and Dakota sandstone, and rimming the mesas above is West Elk breccia. The road passes several scenic viewpoints before reaching **Pioneer Point.** This spectacular overlook views the inner gorge. Curecanti Needle, one of the canyon's prominent landmarks, juts into Morrow Point Lake far below. The 700-foot-high pyramid-shaped Needle once was the emblem of the Denver & Rio Grande Railroad, which traversed the canyon in the 1880s. Trains often stopped for travelers to admire Curecanti Needle. The excellent **Curecanti Creek Trail** drops 2 miles down from the overlook to the lake via a steep rock canyon.

The drive bends away from the gorge at Pioneer Point and runs north up Curecanti Creek's valley before crossing the creek and climbing southward through thick aspen forest. The road clings to steep slopes above Morrow Point Lake. The southern edge of Black Mesa forms a cliffed palisade above the road. Aspens and scrub oaks blanket the roadside. **Hermits Rest,** the next stop, is a lofty viewpoint poised almost 2,000 feet above the lake. Steep slopes loom above the green water, breaking to crags and forested ridges. Beyond tower the San Juan Mountains, including bulky 14,309-foot Uncompahgre Peak and pointed 14,017-foot Wetterhorn Peak. Restrooms, picnic tables, and interpretive signs are at the point. Three-mile-long Hermits Rest Trail descends sharply to the lake and a primitive campground.

The highway bends away from the canyon brink, doglegs through a couple of moist ravines filled with trickling creeks and aspen groves, and emerges on the rounded rim above Crystal Lake. Crystal Creek Trail leads 2.5 miles west to a sweeping 8,900-foot overlook above the lake. A picnic area sits by the pullout. The road descends north through Gambel oak thickets into Crystal Creek's shallow valley. Past Big Hill, the highway skirts Crystal Valley and drops into Onion Valley. Low hills covered with piñon pine and juniper flank this valley. The road passes Gould Reservoir and numerous ranches before reaching **Crawford State Park** and its 400-acre reservoir. This remote state parkland offers excellent perch fishing, boating, swimming, and two campgrounds with sixty-six sites. A turn here leads 11 miles south to the North Rim of the Black Canyon of the Gunnison National Park. The monument holds great views into the abyss, a scenic drive, and a primitive campground.

Crawford to Paonia

The highway crosses the Smith Fork River and enters **Crawford.** This pleasant ranching town, named for Indian scout and former Kansas governor Captain George Crawford, began as a layover on the arduous Hartman Cattle Trail between Gunnison and the North Fork Valley. By 1881 ranchers had settled the area, bringing cattle herds to graze the upland meadows, and the town was established in 1883.

Crawford sits in a spectacular setting. Grand Mesa rims the northern skyline and the spiked peaks of the West Elk Range fill the eastern horizon. Most of the West Elks are protected in the 176,412-acre West Elk Wilderness Area, one of

Colorado's largest wildernesses. The range boasts numerous high peaks, including the high point, 13,035-foot West Elk Peak. Needle Rock, sitting just east of Crawford, is a volcanic plug. The rock, once the inner conduit of an extinct volcano, is solidified lava that remained after the volcano's softer outer layers eroded away.

The drive turns northwest from Crawford onto fertile Crawford Mesa and drops 11 miles through barren Mancos shale hills to 5,351-foot-high Hotchkiss in the North Fork Valley. Hotchkiss, nicknamed "The Friendliest Town Around," was the first hamlet established in the fertile North Fork Valley along the North Fork of the Gunnison River. Enos T. Hotchkiss wandered into the valley, a popular Ute Indian wintering site, in 1879 and returned with others in 1881 after the Utes were removed to reservations. Hotchkiss homesteaded the area and planted an orchard. A small community of homesteaders, ranchers, and farmers sprang up, and the town incorporated in 1901. The town's first commercial building, listed on the National Register of Historical Places, was an old hotel that now houses several shops. The railroad, en route to the up-valley coal mines, came through in 1902. Hotchkiss continues its rural tradition with an economy based, as it was more than a century ago, on cattle, sheep, fruit, logging, and the annual Delta County Fair each August.

CO 92 intersects CO 133 in Hotchkiss. Turn east on CO 133 for the drive's 24-mile third leg. The highway crosses cornfields and climbs onto a shale bluff north of the river. A couple of pullouts overlook the broad valley. The river riffles below over gravel bars. Thick cottonwoods broken by pastures cover its floodplain. The **West Elk Range,** including 11,396-foot Mount Lamborn and 10,906-foot Landsend Peak, dominate the valley view. The highway descends onto the valley's north edge and runs through a pastoral countryside with hay fields and grazing cattle and horses. Paonia is reached after 9 miles.

While the drive and highway bypass Paonia on its north side, it's worth a turn on CO 187 to visit the town. Paonia, situated on the south bank of the North Fork of the Gunnison, lies at the upper end of North Fork Valley, with mountains and mesas looming above. The town, established in 1881 by rancher Samuel Wade, was named Paonia, a misspelling of the Latin name for peonia, a common area flower. In 1882 Wade brought a trunk of young fruit saplings from Gunnison on a difficult, cold two-week trek, giving the town its main business for the next century. The orchards flourished in the valley's mild climate, with its more than 300 sunny days a year and cool nights. Paonia, with more than 3,000 residents, thrives with its orchards, nearby coal mining, sheep and cattle ranching, and its many artists and artisans. The town once made *Ripley's Believe It or Not* with its record twenty churches per capita. A chamber of commerce visitor center sits along the drive just north of Paonia.

Mount Lamborn and Landsend Peak rise beyond fertile pastures in the North Fork Valley along the West Elk Loop Scenic Byway.

Paonia to Kebler Pass

Past Paonia the valley begins to narrow, with steep shale hillsides covered with piñon pine, juniper, and scrub oak climbing away from the river. Orchards, including apple, pear, peach, and cherry, line the highway and perch on river terraces. Delta County, with over 450,000 apple trees, produces two-thirds of Colorado's apples. The narrow, 15-mile canyon between Paonia and Paonia Reservoir boasts a long history of coal mining. The highway runs past several working mines and mining towns including Somerset. Coal, first discovered here in 1883, boomed during World War I and again in the 1970s. Four working mines—Somerset, Bear, West Elk, and Cyprus—now produce over three million tons of coal annually. The coal silos along the highway allow for rapid loading of railroad cars. The canyon narrows past Somerset and the road winds above the river. Below Paonia Dam the drive intersects Gunnison County Road 12, the 32-mile fourth segment of the drive. CO 133 continues north past Paonia State Park, and over McClure Pass to Carbondale.

Turn east on County Road 12 and head up Anthracite Creek's canyon. This gravel road section to Crested Butte offers some of Colorado's best backroad scenery and spectacular aspen foliage in late September. The road runs up the canyon for 6 miles, its south-facing flank coated with scrub oak and mountain mahogany and its cross-river north-facing flank dense with aspen, spruce, and fir trees. Erickson Springs Recreation Area, with eighteen campsites, restrooms, tent pads, and a well, nestles below the Raggeds Wilderness Area. The road crosses the creek here and begins steeply switchbacking up the valley's south slope. After a couple of miles of climbing the angle eases and the road bends across Watson Flats through oak thickets and open meadows. The drive bends east and heads toward 11,348-foot Marcellina Mountain, an immense rocky peak seamed with snow gullies and serrated ridges. The West Elk Range looms to the south across a broad aspen-filled valley, including 12,185-foot West Beckwith Mountain and 12,432-foot East Beckwith Mountain.

The road, following an old Ute trail, runs across a rolling bench below Marcellina Peak through lovely aspen groves. Two wilderness areas flank the drive. The 64,992-acre Raggeds Wilderness Area protects a magnificent swath of high peaks, including Marcellina Mountain, north of the byway. The West Elk Wilderness encompasses the volcanic West Elk Range to the south. Both Beckwith peaks as well as the Anthracite Range south of Kebler Pass lie in the area. The road scales a rounded ridge below Marcellina Mountain, passes the Ruby/Anthracite Trail, and 1.5 miles later reaches the turn to **Lost Lake Slough.** This rough national forest road climbs 2 miles south to the lake, a tranquil pond cradled in a glacier-carved basin beneath East Beckwith Mountain. The peak soars above aspen and spruce forest and cliffed ridges. This idyllic spot, with an eleven-site campground and good fishing, makes a wonderful overnight stay.

The drive continues over aspen-covered hills and twists down to Anthracite Creek and Horse Ranch Park, a spacious valley filled with low willows. The road bends east along the creek and skirts The Dyke, a sawtoothed wall of pinnacles that climbs the southern end of the Ruby Range. The Ruby Range is a small sierra that connects the Elk Range on the north to the West Elk Range. It's a long ridge decorated with numerous sharp peaks. Ruby Peak and Mount Owen, the 13,058-foot range high point, tower north of The Dyke.

The road gently climbs out of the valley through a thick spruce woodland and tops out on the wide 9,980-foot summit of **Kebler Pass.** A few lonely gravestones sit in the old Irwin Cemetery atop the pass. The silver mining town of Irwin once thrived near here, with over 5,000 residents in 1879 despite the town's location on Ute Indian territory. The town once boasted a bank, the Pilot newspaper, hotels, three churches, six sawmills, twenty-three saloons, and the exclusive Irwin Club, which hosted ex-president Ulysses S. Grant in 1880. Irwin quietly faded away after the great silver crash of 1893.

Kebler Pass to Gunnison

Forest Road 730 begins immediately below the Kebler Pass summit and heads south to 10,033-foot Ohio Pass and down Ohio Creek to Gunnison. The scenic drive continues on County Road 12, swinging north from the pass and descending into Coal Creek's glaciated valley. The road bends east almost a mile from the pass. A left turn here bumps north to Lake Irwin, a picturesque lake tucked into the east flank of the Ruby Range. A thirty-two-site campground sits alongside the popular lake. The drive drops down Coal Creek's narrow canyon 7 miles to Crested Butte along a wide road that follows the abandoned Crested Butte branch of the Denver & Rio Grande Railroad.

Crested Butte, a charming, unpretentious Victorian town, offers superb powder skiing in winter and is reputed to be Colorado's mountain bike capital in summer. The town, hiding in the morning shadow of 12,162-foot Crested Butte, sits at 8,885 feet in a wide basin surrounded on three sides by lofty peaks.

Crested Butte began as a gold camp and supply center in the early 1880s. As the gold and silver boom abated, discoveries of nearby high-grade coal deposits turned Crested Butte into a Colorado Fuel & Iron company town until the mine closed in 1952. The opening of the ski area and the spectacular mountain scenery ringing the town now fuel the economy. Much of old Crested Butte, a National Historic District, retains its nineteenth-century ambience. A walking tour explores historic Crested Butte. The ski resort boasts more than 20 feet of winter snow, 121 trails spread over 1,125 ski-acres, and 550 acres of double black-diamond terrain. Excellent cross-country ski trails thread through surrounding Gunnison National Forest. The area also offers some of the Rockies' best mountain biking, with numerous trails and jeep roads lacing the backcountry. Crested Butte has all visitor services, with fine hotels and excellent restaurants.

After entering Crested Butte, follow Whiterock Avenue for 0.5 mile to Sixth Street and CO 135. Turn south on CO 135. This last part of the journey travels 28 miles south to Gunnison and the drive's endpoint. The highway runs along the Slate River in a broad, grassy valley. Whetstone and Red Mountains, their lower slopes cloaked in aspens and evergreens, loom to the west. After a few miles the Slate joins the East River. The road continues along East River and passes through a narrow canyon below humpbacked 10,878-foot Round Mountain. Low sagebrush-covered hills border the valley and highway. At Almont the East and Taylor Rivers combine to form the Gunnison River. The highway runs through low bluffs along the Gunnison, passes ten-site Almont Campground, and emerges into a broad valley. The last 11 miles traverse the Gunnison River's cottonwood-lined banks. Small ranches and fields full of grazing cattle and horses abut the asphalt. The highway passes the Ohio Pass turnoff and bends south to Gunnison and US 50.

22

Silver Thread Scenic Byway

South Fork to Lake City

General description: This 75-mile route follows the Rio Grande, climbs over Spring Creek Pass and the Continental Divide, and ends in Lake City in the heart of the San Juan Mountains.

Special attractions: Wagon Wheel Gap, Creede National Historic District, Rio Grande, Clear Creek Falls, Spring Creek Pass, Slumgullion Earthflow, Rio Grande National Forest, Colorado Trail, La Garita Wilderness Area, Weminuche Wilderness Area, Gunnison National Forest, Lake San Cristobal, Lake City National Historic District, hiking, camping, fishing, backpacking, scenic views.

Location: South-central Colorado. The highway runs between South Fork on the west edge of the San Luis Valley to Lake City, 55 miles southwest of Gunnison.

Drive route name and number: Silver Thread Scenic Byway, CO 149.

Travel season: Year-round. The drive may occasionally be closed in winter due to heavy snow. Carry chains and be prepared for bad weather if you drive it in winter.

Camping: Seven national forest campgrounds—Palisade, Marshall Park, Rio Grande, Bristol View, Silver Thread, North Clear Creek, and Slumgullion Pass—lie along the drive.

Services: All services are found in South Fork, Creede, and Lake City.

Nearby attractions: San Luis Valley, Los Caminos Antiguos Scenic Byway (see Drive 6), Wheeler Geologic Area, San Luis Peak, San Juan National Forest, Alpine Loop Back Country Byway, Handies Peak, Big Blue Wilderness Area, Uncompahgre Peak, Curecanti National Recreation Area.

The Drive

The Silver Thread Scenic Byway, following CO 149 between South Fork and Lake City, traverses a spectacular, off-the-beaten-track part of Colorado. The drive parallels the Rio Grande below cliffed palisades, passes through historic Creede, climbs over lofty Spring Creek and Slumgullion Passes, crosses an active earthflow, and ends in Lake City in the heart of the rugged San Juan Mountains. The San Juans, Colorado's largest mountain range, are a tumble of peaks and canyons that spread across 10,000 square miles, an area the size of Vermont. The range encompasses almost all of southwestern Colorado south of the Gunnison River and west of the San Luis Valley and includes nine subranges—Sneffels Range, San Miguel Range, La Plata Mountains, La Garita Mountains, Needles Range, West Needles Range, Rico Mountains, Grenadier Range, and Piedra Mountains. The San Juans also boast ten 14,000-foot peaks and a million acres preserved in wilderness areas; they also hold the headwaters

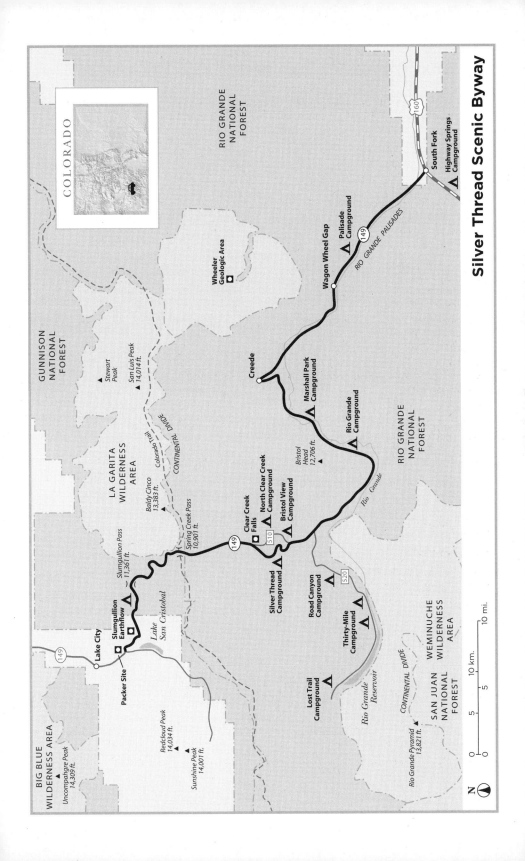

Silver Thread Scenic Byway

of numerous rivers, including the Rio Grande, and the Dolores, Animas, and Uncompahgre Rivers.

Climate changes dramatically along the byway because of a wide range of elevations from 8,180 feet at South Fork to 11,361 feet atop Slumgullion Pass, the drive's high point. Summer days along the Rio Grande range into the eighties, but are usually cooler at the upper elevations. Expect afternoon thunderstorms, particularly in July and August, with locally heavy rain. Nights at the campgrounds are cool. Autumn offers warm weather, with generally clear skies and golden aspens. Cold fronts sweeping out of the north often bring snow in October. Winter arrives by late October and locks the land in a blanket of white until March or April. The road will occasionally be closed by heavy snow. Carry chains, a shovel, and extra clothes in winter. Snow lingers on the higher elevations well into early summer. The San Juan Mountains, the wettest part of Colorado, receive as much as fifty inches of annual precipitation and 350 inches of snow. Spring weather is unpredictable, with rain, snow, sleet, sun, and wind possible—all on the same day.

South Fork to Creede

The Silver Thread Scenic Byway, a designated National Forest Byway, begins at the junction of U.S. Highway 160 and CO 149 in **South Fork,** 48 miles west of Alamosa on the western edge of the San Luis Valley. South Fork, a small resort and lumber town, sits at the confluence of the Rio Grande and the South Fork of the Rio Grande. Head northwest on CO 149.

The road leaves South Fork and crosses the Rio Grande after 0.5 mile and enters 1.8-million-acre Rio Grande National Forest almost 5 miles up. Collier State Wildlife Area, providing crucial winter habitat for deer and elk, spreads along the river bottomlands here. The highway parallels the river in the bottom of a deep, broad canyon. Long cliff bands, composed of welded volcanic tuff, stair-step upward, forming the **Rio Grande Palisades.** Open ponderosa pine forest scatters across the warm south-facing slopes, while glades of aspen mix with spruce and fir woodlands on the cooler north-facing mountainsides. Tall cottonwoods and dense willow thickets line the rushing Rio Grande. At 6 miles the wildlife area offers picnic tables and rest rooms for picnickers and anglers.

Farther up, the canyon narrows and its cliffs steepen. Palisade Campground, with thirteen pine-shaded sites, sits alongside the river at 10 miles. The campground, lying in the shadow of the looming Palisades, is a popular put-in point for river rafters. The river section from here to South Fork offers an easy and scenic half-day run. The Rio Grande from South Fork to Wagon Wheel Gap is

Opposite: The volcanic Rio Grande Palisades rim the skyline above the Silver Thread Scenic Byway at Wagon Wheel Gap.

also designated Gold Medal fishing waters, with anglers catching rainbow and brown trout.

After 11 miles the highway swings under an abrupt escarpment of tall cliffs broken into flying buttresses, arêtes, gargoyles, and castles. Immense talus slopes cascade down to the highway. These volcanic cliffs form **Wagon Wheel Gap,** a narrow gorge named for an abandoned wagon wheel found here in 1873. The wheel was supposedly left by the 1861 Baker prospecting party after being ordered by Utes to vacate their upstream camp. The party left so quickly that equipment and supplies were scattered along their retreating trail.

Forest Road 600 begins just past the gap and winds 12 miles north to Hansons Mill, the site of a former lumber mill. Road's end, in a high grassy park below Pool Table Mountain, is the jumping-off point for visitors who either walk or jeep 7 miles to **Wheeler Geologic Area.** The 640-acre area, tucked into a shallow canyon below Halfmoon Pass and the crest of the La Garita Mountains, is a rough landscape of fantastic rock formations. Erosion sculpted the soft volcanic rock into a fairyland of spires, minarets, goblins, fluted cliffs, and jumbled badlands. The area, now part of La Garita Wilderness Area, was designated the nation's first National Monument in 1906. Its isolation and low volume of visitors, however, prompted the tract's removal from the national park system in 1950.

The scenery changes dramatically past Wagon Wheel Gap. The canyon opens into a broad, grassy valley, flanked by sagebrush slopes on the north and spruce and fir forest on the rounded ridges to the south. The drive runs up the south side of the widening valley for 5 miles, crosses the Rio Grande at the abandoned site of Wason, now the Wason Ranch, and bends northwest up Willow Creek to **Creede.**

Creede

This historic mining town, nestled at the foot of a cliffed canyon, got its start in 1889, after prospector Nicholas Creede stumbled onto a rich silver lode at a lunch stop. He supposedly exclaimed, "Holy Moses, I've struck it rich." His wealthy Holy Moses Mine attracted thousands of fortune seekers.

Almost overnight the camp erupted into a tent city. The boom town grew by 300 people a day in the frenzied summer of 1890. By 1892 more than 10,000 lived in Creede. The town just as quickly developed a boisterous, hell-raising reputation. Writer Cy Warman, who founded the town's first newspaper, immortalized Creede in a popular poem that read, "It's day all day in the daytime, And there is no night in Creede." Another writer noted, "At night there are no policemen to interfere with the vested right of each citizen to raise as much Cain as he sees fit and . . . three-fourths of the population are of the kind that does see fit." The infamous town attracted numerous outlaws, gamblers, gunslingers, madams, murderers, and preachers. Its cast of characters included con man Soapy Smith, quick-draw artist Calamity Jane Canary, cigar-smoking card shark Poker Alice, lawman Bat Masterson, and Bob Ford, killer of Jesse James. Saloon keeper Ford got his due when Ed O'Kelly, a Missouri friend of James, murdered him with a double-barreled shotgun in 1892.

In 1892 Creede, nicknamed "Colorado's Silver Ribbed Treasure Trove," yielded $1 million of silver ore a month. The following year Congress enacted the Silver Act and the price of silver plummeted from $1.29 an ounce to 50 cents; Creede almost shut down. Catastrophic fires and floods destroyed the town several times, but townspeople, overcoming adversity, rebuilt. The mines, far from exhausted, continued to work well into the twentieth century. In 1939 some 500,000 ounces of silver were shipped every week, and in 1966 Mineral County produced almost 150,000 ounces of silver.

Creede, now a National Historic District, makes a delightful stop on the scenic drive. The picturesque town boasts numerous visitor attractions, including an underground fire station and the renowned Creede Repertory Theater, which rotates plays and dramas nightly through summer in the old Creede Opera House. The town makes a good base camp for exploring the surrounding high country and enjoying the myriad fishing, hiking, and mountain biking possibilities. A 17-mile-long auto trip, the Bachelor Historic Tour, begins on Creede's south side and climbs to the Equity Mine before returning on Bachelor Road. The tour offers sixteen interpretive stops, including ghost towns, old mines, and the Sunnyside Cemetery, as well as several scenic overlooks.

Creede to Slumgullion Pass

The highway runs south from Creede and after a mile bends into the Rio Grande valley. The road heads southwest across terraced benches deposited on old river floodplains. Marshall Park Campground, with sixteen sites, spreads along the river west of Seven-Mile Bridge. Forest Roads 523 and 528 head south from here to Spar City, a ghost town that was contemporary with Creede. Four-site Rio Grande Campground sits a few miles farther upstream along the river and provides good fishing access.

At mile 35 the highway and Rio Grande swing northwest up a broad valley flanked by rounded mountains. The river, its headwaters on Stony Pass atop the Continental Divide west of here, uncoils in long, lazy loops across the flat valley meadows. The valley here was not actually carved by the river, but is a down-dropped block with faults on either side. A roadside overlook near the valley head offers views west toward the Rio Grande headwaters and the remote backcountry of the 488,210-acre **Weminuche Wilderness Area.** Rocky 12,706-foot Bristol Head's high volcanic cliffs hem in the eastern skyline and form, along with its long northern ridge, the uplifted border of the valley. Jim Stewart's hidden treasure still resides somewhere on Bristol Head's western flank. In 1852 Stewart, an army mail courier, detoured through these mountains to avoid Indian trouble. While crossing a creek, he accidentally dropped his mailbag into the water. While drying out the mail he panned the stream and found gold nuggets. Noting the location, Stewart later returned but was never able to find his placer gold stash.

Forest Road 520 leaves the drive at the valley's northern end and heads west 9 miles up a narrow canyon to Rio Grande Reservoir, a long fingerlike lake that offers excellent fishing and camping opportunities. Road Canyon Reservoir, off FR 520, yields rainbow trout up to six pounds, while numerous backcountry lakes and streams in the Weminuche Wilderness south of Rio Grande Reservoir give excellent fishing. The road, continuing west from the reservoir as a four-wheel-drive track, climbs another 20 miles to the 12,594-foot summit of Stony Pass along a historic wagon route before dropping steeply to Silverton.

The scenic drive, leaving the Rio Grande's valley, heads north up Spring Creek's shallow valley and passes Spring Creek Reservoir Rest Site. This national forest area offers fishing in a small lake and picnicking. The road twists up rolling ridges coated with stands of spruce, fir, and quaking aspen and grassy meadows. Several campgrounds—Bristol View, Silver Thread, and North Clear Creek—lie on the drive or just off, on Forest Road 510, North Clear Creek Road. Silver Thread Campground, with eleven sites, lies on a highway hairpin turn. A short trail leads east to South Clear Creek Falls from the campground. A couple of miles higher sits a scenic overlook on the edge of an aspen-fringed meadow. The marvelous view west looks up the glaciated valley of South Clear Creek. Brown and Hermit Lakes glimmer on the valley floor, while 13,821-foot Rio Grande Pyramid dominates the Continental Divide above. The 1874 Wheeler Survey called the pyramid "one of the handsomest and most symmetrical cones in Colorado."

The drive crosses a low divide and drops northeast into North Clear Creek's broad drainage. Forest Road R 510 heads east for 0.5 mile from the drive to **Clear Creek Falls,** one of Colorado's most spectacular waterfalls. North Clear Creek meanders across its broad valley, through willow-lined banks before plunging almost 100 feet over a cliff of hard basalt in a craggy chasm. The frothy creek continues down the steep, rocky canyon to the Rio Grande. The falls observation area offers a fenced overlook, picnic tables, and restrooms.

From the falls the highway runs north up Spring Creek's brushy valley, past aspen groves and grasslands. After 7 miles the drive reaches the crest of 10,901-foot Spring Creek Pass atop the Continental Divide. East of here towers Baldy Cinco, a 13,383-foot peak in the La Garita Wilderness Area. The **Colorado Trail,** a 469-mile-long footpath from Denver to Durango, crosses the highway here while following the divide westward. A kiosk on the pass gives information on local geology, recreation, and hiking.

Clear Creek Falls plunges spectacularly over basalt cliffs along the Silver Thread Scenic Byway.

Slumgullion Pass to Lake City

The byway drops down across the headwaters of Cebolla Creek and winds west through moist spruce forest for 6 miles to 11,361-foot **Slumgullion Pass.** This high point, not a true pass, divides Cebolla Creek from the Lake Fork of the Gunnison River. Slumgullion Campground, with twenty-one sites, sits just north of the highway on the west side of the pass. The drive begins steeply descending on 7 percent grades through dense spruce and aspen woodlands. Windy Point Overlook yields great views west into the San Juans. To the southwest towers the Continental Divide ridgeline and 14,001-foot Sunshine Peak, 14,034-foot Redcloud Peak, and 14,048-foot Handies Peak; to the northeast looms pointed 14,017-foot Wetterhorn Peak and bulky 14,309-foot Uncompahgre Peak, the San Juans' highest mountain. Steep hillsides fall away below to the river's deep canyon. A sign identifies the peaks and other notable features.

Below the overlook the highway passes the **Slumgullion Earthflow,** one of Colorado's most unique natural wonders. The earthflow, or mudslide, occurred some 700 years ago on the southern flank of Mesa Seco to the north, when weak volcanic tuff and breccia, lubricated by heavy rains, slumped 5 miles down the steep mountainside to the valley floor. The 2,700-foot-high flow blocked the river and formed narrow Lake San Cristobal, Colorado's second-largest natural lake. A second flow some 350 years ago overlies the upper part of the flow. This active new slide sporadically lurches as much as 20 feet downhill every year. The trees studding the active flow are readily apparent by their drunken angles. The pass and earthflow were named for slumgullion, a yellowish stew concocted by hungry miners who tossed whatever ingredients they might have on hand into a single pot, usually some combination of game, potatoes, bacon, and beans.

Lake San Cristobal Overlook, with views of the lake and glaciated valley, sits on the slide's south side. The highway runs a mile across the slide and bends northwest down steep slopes to the valley floor. A historic marker commemorating Alferd Packer and his grisly deeds lies just north of the highway before crossing the Lake Fork. Packer, guiding a group of prospectors into the San Juans in the winter of 1873, murdered and ate his five clients. Packer escaped the clutches of the law for nine years before being apprehended in Wyoming under the assumed name of John Schwartze. The cannibal, sentenced to hang in 1883, spent seventeen years in the state prison for his deed before being paroled. Legend says presiding judge Melville Gerry cursed, "Packer, you man-eating son-of-a-bitch, there were seven Democrats in Hinsdale County and you ate five of them." The salty story, made up by local Irish barkeep Larry Dolan to entertain his customers, was embellished over the years to its current mythological status.

The Alpine Loop Back Country Byway, a Bureau of Land Management drive that climbs over Cinnamon and Engineer passes via jeep roads, begins 0.5 mile past the Lake Fork crossing. The highway continues north above the river, winding through aspen and pine forests to 8,663-foot **Lake City** and the drive's end.

Lake City, a National Historic District, is a picturesque resort and mining community nestled in the valley bottom. The small town is the seat of Hinsdale County, a county of peaks and valleys as big as Rhode Island. Locals boast that if the land were flattened out the county would be as large as west Texas. Hinsdale County is the most sparsely populated county in the United States, with Lake City as its only town.

Lake City started, like most Colorado mountain towns, as a mining settlement, after Enos Hotchkiss found gold in 1874. The town, a stage and freight hub for surrounding towns, flourished through the 1880s with two banks, seven saloons, two breweries, and the first newspaper and first church on Colorado's western slope. After the boom, Lake City carried on as a mining and ranching center, but today relies on its gorgeous scenery to attract tourist dollars. The town is a great base to explore the natural history of the San Juan Mountains and the area's rich historical legacy. Numerous ghost towns scatter across the mountains, with trails that climb the peaks and traverse nearby wilderness areas. CO 149 continues north for 55 miles from Lake City to Gunnison, heading up the Lake Fork before turning inland to Blue Mesa Lake.

23

San Juan Skyway All-American Byway

Durango to Dolores

General description: This 236-mile scenic drive makes a spectacular loop drive through the rugged San Juan Mountains, crossing several high passes, twisting through deep canyons and valleys, and passing through several historic towns.

Special attractions: Durango & Silverton Narrow Gauge Railroad, Durango National Historic District, Purgatory Ski Resort, San Juan National Forest, Animas River Canyon, Weminuche Wilderness Area, Molas Pass, Molas Lake, Silverton National Historic District, Red Mountain Pass, Box Canyon Falls, Ouray National Historic District, Dallas Divide, Telluride, Telluride Ski Area, Lizard Head Pass, Lizard Head Wilderness Area, Ophir, Dolores River Canyon, Galloping Goose, Escalante Ruins and Anasazi Heritage Center, McPhee Reservoir, Mancos State Park, scenic views, camping, backpacking, mountaineering, fishing, hiking, mountain biking, historic sites, fall colors.

Location: Southwestern Colorado. The loop drive follows US 550 from Durango to Ridgway, then goes west to Placerville, south to Telluride, and over Lizard Head Pass to Dolores. The drive finishes by heading east on US 160 back to Durango.

Drive route name and numbers: San Juan Skyway; US 550 and 160; CO 62 and 145.

Travel season: Year-round. The drive is closed occasionally in winter due to heavy snow and avalanche danger. Chains often are required to drive the highway in winter. Check with the Colorado State Patrol for current road conditions.

Camping: Many national forest campgrounds lie on or just off the drive. Camping also is available at Mesa Verde National Park, Mancos State Park, and Ridgway State Park. Dispersed, primitive camping is permitted on both Bureau of Land Management and National Forest public lands along the drive.

Services: All services are found in Durango, Silverton, Ouray, Ridgway, Telluride, Dolores, Cortez, and Mancos. Limited services are found in various other towns along the drive.

Nearby attractions: Alpine Loop Back Country Byway, Mount Sneffels Wilderness Area, Unaweep-Tabeguache Scenic and Historic Byway (see Drive 27), Uncompahgre Plateau, Owl Creek Pass, Lake City, Mesa Verde National Park, Black Canyon of the Gunnison National Park, Hovenweep National Monument, Four Corners, Ute Mountain Indian Reservation, and Ute Tribal Park.

The Drive

The San Juan Mountains, a 12,000-square-mile block of high country, encompasses almost all of southwestern Colorado. The San Juan Range, with a mean elevation of 10,000 feet, boasts more than 100 peaks topping 13,000 feet and fourteen of Colorado's fifty-four 14,000-foot peaks. This huge range, dissected

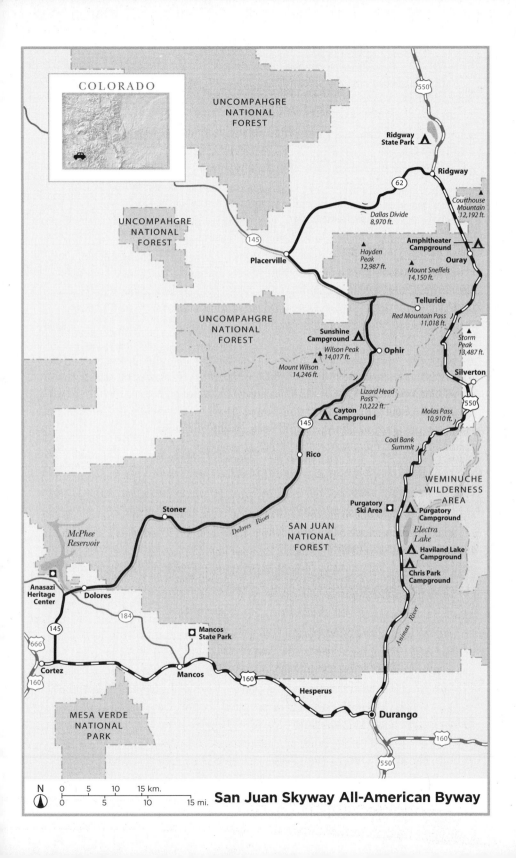

COLORADO

UNCOMPAHGRE
NATIONAL
FOREST

Ridgway
State Park

550

Ridgway

62

Courthouse
Mountain
12,192 ft.

UNCOMPAHGRE
NATIONAL
FOREST

145

Placerville

Dallas Divide
8,970 ft.

Hayden
Peak
12,987 ft.

Amphitheater
Campground

Ouray

Mount Sneffels
14,150 ft.

Telluride

UNCOMPAHGRE
NATIONAL
FOREST

Sunshine
Campground

Red Mountain Pass
11,018 ft.

Storm
Peak
13,487 ft.

Ophir

Wilson Peak
14,017 ft.

Mount Wilson
14,246 ft.

Silverton

550

Lizard Head
Pass
10,222 ft.

Molas Pass
10,910 ft.

145

Cayton
Campground

Rico

Coal Bank
Summit

WEMINUCHE
WILDERNESS
AREA

Purgatory
Ski Area

Purgatory
Campground

Stoner

Dolores River

SAN JUAN
NATIONAL
FOREST

Electra
Lake

Haviland Lake
Campground

McPhee
Reservoir

Chris Park
Campground

Anasazi
Heritage
Center

Dolores

184

Animas River

145

Mancos
State Park

666

Cortez

160

Mancos

160

Hesperus

MESA VERDE
NATIONAL
PARK

Durango

550

160

N

0   5   10   15 km.

0   5   10   15 mi.

San Juan Skyway All-American Byway

by sharp canyons and spiked with skyscraping peaks, is divided into numerous subranges, including the San Miguel Range, Rico Mountains, La Plata Mountains, Sneffels Range, West Needle and Needle Mountains, Grenadier Range, La Garita Mountains, and Cochetopa Hills. The heart of the San Juans, however, is the San Juan Range itself, towering above the historic mining towns of Ouray, Silverton, and Telluride.

The San Juans formed some 35 million years ago, when immense volcanic eruptions spewed some 8,000 cubic miles of lava and thousands of feet of ash across the region. Precious minerals, including gold, silver, lead, copper, and zinc, percolated in underground fissures inside volcanic calderas. At today's prices the San Juans yielded billions of dollars of riches, and prospectors believe still more lies buried beneath the mountain flanks in the region's fifty mining districts. Periodic glaciation over the last two million years sculpted the mountains with precipitous gorges, wide valleys, and serrated peaks and ridges. The range is also the headwaters of numerous rivers, including the Rio Grande, San Juan, Uncompahgre, Dolores, Animas, and La Plata Rivers.

The San Juan Skyway, a designated National Forest All-American Byway, traverses this rugged mountain heartland for 236 miles. The drive, making a huge loop, is one of America's most beautiful and most spectacular scenic drives. The drive described here begins and ends in Durango, although it can easily be started in Cortez or Ridgway as well as other points. Allow at least eight hours to drive the route, but remember it could easily take eight days to explore the wealth of scenery and points of interest along the skyway.

The highway, open year-round, is best driven in summer and fall. The wide variation in elevation along the drive, from 6,512 feet at Durango to 11,018 feet atop Red Mountain Pass, gives a wide diversity of both temperature and precipitation. Summer temperatures in the lower elevations at both ends of the road are typically warm, with highs ranging from seventy to ninety degrees. The mountain heights are as much as twenty degrees cooler. Afternoon thunderstorms are an almost daily occurrence somewhere along the highway; watch for slippery roads. Autumn is delightful, with cool, crisp days and spectacular aspen colors.

The first snow falls sometime in October on the high peaks, and winter begins in November with heavy snowfall. As much as 4 feet of snow can fall in a day, leading to extreme avalanche danger. The highway regularly closes due to avalanches. The steep Uncompahgre Gorge highway section between Ironton Park and Ouray is the most dangerous, with the Riverside and Mother Cline Slides. The Riverside Slide, dropping 3,200 vertical feet down abrupt chutes, makes this highway Colorado's deadliest avalanche crossing. Today a snowshed protects the road from the slide's wrath, but not before five highway travelers perished in avalanches. Chains often are required to drive the highway in winter. Watch for the omnipresent snowplows clearing the highway and bring extra clothes and sleep-

The rugged Sneffels Range looms above aspen forests and CO 145 west of Telluride.

ing bags in case of a breakdown. Spring comes slowly to the high country, with the snow cover slowly retreating in warm April and May days. Expect cool, breezy days with occasional snow and rainstorms.

Durango

The drive begins in **Durango** at the junction of U.S. Highway 160 and U.S. Highway 550. Turn north on US 550, nicknamed the Million Dollar Highway, on the town's south side. The road bypasses downtown Durango and heads up Main Avenue. Durango, straddling the Animas Valley, was established in 1880 as a Denver & Rio Grande Railroad town. Animas City, the area's first town, started just north of Durango in 1861 as a supply center for San Juan miners. The railroad, wanting to capitalize on the San Juan's rich mines, pushed its narrow gauge tracks west from Alamosa to the Animas River valley. Animas City seemed the logical choice for the new railroad center, but the town and the railroad couldn't come to terms. Investors then set up the Durango Land and Coal Company and surveyed a new town site 2 miles south of Animas City, calling it Durango because of the area's similarity to Durango, Mexico. The town thrived as a railroad hub, hauling valuable ore from mountain mines to Durango's smelter.

Long after the San Juan mines shut down, Durango is still a railroad town. The **Durango & Silverton Narrow Gauge Railroad,** a National Historic and National Engineering Landmark, begins at the train station on the town's south side and runs north up the old Denver & Rio Grande rail bed 45 miles to Silverton. This spectacular train ride, threading through the steep Animas River gorge, is a living-history exhibit that takes travelers back in time to mining's heyday. Reservations and advance ticket purchases are advised, particularly during the busy summer months. Durango also is a wonderful outdoor sports town, with nearby mountain bike trails, excellent fly-fishing streams, numerous four-wheel-drive tracks, kayaking and rafting on the Animas River, rock climbing on many cliffs, and a wealth of hiking paths, including the terminus of the 469-mile **Colorado Trail** that runs from Durango to Denver. Durango also offers all visitor services, including hotels, dining, groceries, and service stations.

The Animas Valley

The highway leaves Durango after 3 miles and runs north on the western edge of the **Animas Valley** for 15 miles. The Animas River, a 110-mile-long river originally called *Rio de las Animas Perdidas,* or "River of Lost Souls," by early Spanish explorers, meanders in long, graceful loops across the wide-bottomed valley past green pastures grazed by horses and cattle. Dense willows and tall narrow-leafed cottonwoods hug the river's rocky banks. The river did little to excavate this deep valley. Thick glaciers, spilling down from the high mountains, scoured the valley floor, chiseled its steep sidewalls, and left a characteristic U-shaped glacial valley behind. Sandstone cliffs abruptly lift from the valley, striping the slopes with diagonal bands.

Durango straddles the edge of the San Juan Mountains and the Colorado Plateau, a vast geographic province that spreads across the Four Corners region. As the highway runs north, it slowly leaves the plateau by traversing upturned sedimentary rock formations—gray Mancos shale; Dakota sandstone; the dinosaur-bearing Morrison Formation; Entrada, Navajo, and Wingate sandstones; and finally old Permian redbeds at Hermosa. Still older formations, including the 300-million-year-old Hermosa Formation, lie farther north. The 2,000-foot-thick Hermosa Formation, laid down as marine sediments in basins offshore from the Ancestral Rockies, forms lofty gray ramparts above the highway north from Hermosa to Engineer Mountain.

As the highway runs north from Durango, it passes **Trimble Springs** at 6 miles. These hot springs, located just west of the road, were named for 1874 settler Frank Trimble. He developed two springs, spewing water as hot as 126 degrees, and built a hotel for visitors wanting to sample the springs' "curative value." A forty-room brick hotel, the Hermosa House, was erected in the late 1890s and offered stables, a gym, a bowling alley, a golf course, and a saloon. After fire destroyed the hotel in 1938, it was replaced by another hotel that burned in 1957. The springs now offers a bathhouse, an Olympic-size outdoor pool, and a smaller hot pool. **Hermosa,** an old stage and railroad stop, sits just north of Trimble. The town, settled in 1873 as a ranching center for the Animas Valley, now serves as a Durango bedroom community.

The highway continues north, skirting the valley's steep wall, and reaches another historic site near the valley head. **Baker's Bridge,** designated by a State Historical Society bronze marker, crossed the Animas River here. Charles Baker and several men prospected through the San Juans in 1860, and, after working their way down from Baker's Park at today's Silverton, resolved to spend the winter in the northern Animas Valley. The party laid out a town site, built rustic log cabins, and suffered through the cold winter. With news of the Civil War, they abandoned the site and returned east. Baker fought in the Confederate Army before Indians killed him while prospecting in 1868.

The flat valley abruptly ends, replaced by forested hills. The Animas River takes leave of the valley and bends northeast into a steep, cliffed gorge. The drive also leaves the valley, bumping across the narrow gauge railroad tracks and climbing onto wooded slopes below the Hermosa Cliffs. A turnoff sits just past the tracks and makes a good stop to watch the train pass by. A side road, La Plata County Road 75, drops east to a secluded glen and the remains of the old town of Rockwood. This town served as the jumping-off point for miners and freighters heading north to Silverton and Rico. An old wagon toll road, now a National Historic Landmark, twisted north from here, with one branch following today's highway up to Purgatory and over Scotch Creek Pass to Rico and the other branch to Silverton.

The highway runs north below the cliffed escarpment and enters **San Juan National Forest.** Dense scrub oak thickets line the asphalt, and beyond tower ponderosa pines and Douglas firs. Tamarron, a year-round resort, offers golf on a stunning 18-hole course, as well as tennis, swimming, and night skiing on a beginner hill. The road swings past Haviland Lake, a small lake tucked below in thick forest. Haviland Lake Campground, with forty-five sites, sits on its east shore. Electra Lake, a 3-mile-long reservoir created for electric power, lies to the north. The highway sweeps across a high bench through dense aspen groves. Engineer Mountain, its talus flanks broken by cliff bands, looms to the north, and the West Needle Mountains rise to the northeast. Castle Rock, a castellated promontory, juts from the Hermosa Cliffs at 25 miles. The road becomes four lanes and reaches **Durango Mountain Resort.** This popular destination ski resort boasts over 300 inches of dry powder and 85 trails spread over 1,200 acres. Groomed cross-country ski trails thread across the surrounding woodlands for 40 miles. Purgatory Campground, with fourteen sites, sits just east of the drive.

Coal Bank Summit and Molas Pass

The highway squeezes back to two lanes, crosses Cascade Creek below 12,968-foot Engineer Mountain, and begins steeply ascending above Mill Creek. The blacktop switchbacks through a spruce forest sprinkled with aspen. Potato Hill rises to the east, and beyond towers 13,158-foot Twilight Peak in the West Needle Mountains, its rocky flanks chiseled by glaciers into deep cirques, sharp arêtes, and flying buttresses. After 8 miles the highway emerges on **Coal Bank Summit,** a 10,640-foot saddle between Engineer Mountain and Potato Hill.

The drive winds down from the summit, crosses Deer Creek, and swings up aspen-covered slopes. Most of the rolling countryside adjoining the highway was consumed in a 26,000-acre forest fire in 1879. Civic groups later replanted much of the Lime Creek Burn. After bending over West Lime Creek, the highway turns east and climbs alongside East Lime Creek. The creek trickles in a shallow valley, with aspens coating the warm south-facing slopes and dense spruce woods blanketing the cooler north-facing hillsides. East Lime Creek Rest Site sits on the east side of the highway. Park here to hike south to Andrews Lake, a popular trout lake.

The road continues up East Lime Creek and a mile and a half later reaches 10,910-foot **Molas Pass,** which offers one of Colorado's most stunning mountain panoramas. Sharp peaks spike the horizon in a wide circle from the summit. The Needle and Grenadier Mountains tower to the east, their ragged flanks strewn with glacier-carved buttresses and cirques. The Animas River gorge, an abrupt forested chasm, hides between the pass and the peaks. Molas Lake, its placid waters reflecting the sky, tucks into a hollow on a broad bench above the canyon. Spruce forest and open willow meadows surround the lake. Snowdon Peak, the 13,077-foot northern outpost of the West Needle Range, looms to the south. Rounded ridges, green with above-timberline tundra grass and broken by rocky crags on the skyline, stair-step up west from the pass. Molas Lake, owned by Silverton and operated by a private concessionaire, offers camping, picnicking, and fishing. Good day hikes are found on the Colorado Trail at Molas Pass.

Silverton

The highway descends sharply for 5 miles from Molas Lake to **Silverton,** clinging to steep mountainsides above the Animas River. Thick spruce forest hems in the road, with open slopes offering glimpses north into Baker's Park. Finally the road makes a couple of hairpin turns, reaches the valley floor, and bends west up Mineral Creek. A right turn here leads to Silverton. A visitor center, housed in an ornate building, sits on the south edge of town.

Silverton, at an elevation of 9,320 feet, lies along the Animas River in Baker's Park, a flat, 2,000-acre glacial valley encircled by a wall of mountains. Winter blankets the town, one of Colorado's most isolated settlements, with over 300 inches of annual snowfall. Before modern snow-removal equipment, Silverton often was cut off from the outside world for weeks at a time; even now the highway shuts down for a few days each winter. The town is undeniably a tough place to live—the year-round average temperature is about thirty-five degrees and summer's growing season is but twelve days. Towering peaks ring Baker's Park, with 13,370-foot Sultan Mountain to the south, 13,068-foot Kendall Mountain on the east, and 13,487-foot Storm Peak to the north.

These mountains, fringed with forest, capped by snow, and filled with mineral riches, attracted the remote valley's first visitors in 1860. Charles Baker and six fellow prospectors trekked over Cinnamon Pass and wandered south down the Animas River to the broad park. These early miners panned the streams for the next couple of years, but found little gold to hold their interest. Not until 1870 did miners find promising color and stake their claims on the steep mountainsides. The Little Giant Lode up Arrastra Creek was the first producing mine in the area. The San Juans, however, still remained under Ute Indian control. The Utes protested the miner incursions, and federal troops were dispatched to keep the Anglos off Indian land. The Brunot Treaty in 1873, however, removed the Utes from the mountains and opened the San Juans for prospecting.

Miners flocked into the area, and by 1873 more than 1,500 mining claims were filed. Silverton, established in June 1874, was deemed the county seat. The new town was dubbed Silverton after a miner remarked, "We may not have gold here, but we have silver by the ton." Wagon routes over Stony and Cinnamon Passes connected Silverton to the outside world until July 8, 1882, when the Denver & Rio Grande Railroad completed its narrow gauge track from Durango to Silverton. The town boomed through the 1880s, with millions of dollars worth of gold and silver mined from the hills, but the 1893 silver crash slowed the growth. At its peak Silverton boasted more than thirty mills, two smelters, thirty-seven saloons, and numerous card houses, opium dens, and "pleasure palaces" on its infamous Blair Street.

Silverton today wears its colorful history well. Most of the town, preserved as a National Historic District, still reflects the mining heyday of more than a century ago. It appears at first glance like a movie set, with false-fronted buildings, opulent Victorian homes, the gold-domed county courthouse, the 1903 brick jail that houses the San Juan County Historical Society Museum, and rustic miner's cabins.

Silverton boasts three of Colorado's twenty designated National Historic Landmarks. The town is also the northern terminus of the Durango & Silverton Narrow Gauge Railroad, the last vestige of Silverton's railway glories. Several hotels dot the town, including the landmark Grand Imperial Hotel. Hillside Cemetery, perched northeast of town, makes an interesting stop. Markers reading killed in mine accident testify to the dangers found underground. Visit the San Juan County Historical Museum to understand more of the town's colorful history. Silverton also offers a host of festivals, including the Silverton Jubilee Folk Music Festival, the International Rhubarb Festival, the Hardrock 100-Mile Endurance Run, and the Mountain Man Softball Tournament.

Mineral Creek to Red Mountain Pass

The drive bends west from Silverton on US 550 and heads up Mineral Creek valley. The North Star Mine and Mill, surrounded by quaking aspens, sits across the creek just west of town. Forest Road 585 turns off the highway and heads west up Mineral Creek's South Fork in a broad, glaciated valley for 5 miles to the twenty-six-site South Mineral Campground. This 9,800-foot campground makes a good base camp for exploring the surrounding peaks and basins. Ice Lake Basin, 3 miles to the west, sits amid sheer cliffed peaks including 13,894-foot Vermillion Peak and 13,738-foot Pilot Knob. The highway scales the valley's north flank through mixed aspen and spruce forest and after a couple of miles swerves into a valley carved by glaciers and the Middle Fork of Mineral Creek. Numerous avalanche chutes slice through the forest on the steep valley sides.

The Ophir Pass Road, beginning about 5 miles west of Silverton, takes off from US 550, crosses Burro Bridge, and climbs for 4 miles to a 11,750-foot summit. The track, one of the area's easier four-wheel-drive routes, continues down the old stage and wagon road 6 miles to Ophir and CO 145. US 550 heads up the valley to the foot of Red Mountain Pass and the old 1883 town site of Chattanooga. While almost nothing remains now, the town once held 300 residents and seventy-five buildings. A fire and disastrous snow slides wiped out the town. Reverend J. Gibbons noted in 1898 that "the ruins of roofs and houses were strewn for half a mile over the valley and the population of this once-flourishing hamlet dwindled down to two."

The highway, traversing the old Silverton Railway's right-of-way, turns west onto the Chattanooga Loop and begins the final 3-mile ascent to the summit of **Red Mountain Pass.** The blacktop, with no guardrail, edges along precipitous slopes. Look down the valley for great views of Bear Mountain. Note the forest shape on its flank; it appears to be a giant bear licking a honeycomb. The highway bends into a steep gorge, passes the remains of the Silver Ledge Mine, and climbs up to 11,018-foot Red Mountain Pass. Abandoned buildings of the Longfellow

Mine and a small, willow-lined tarn sit on the summit. The dangerous, one-way Black Bear Road, one of Colorado's toughest jeep tracks, climbs west from here to Ingram Pass and down to Telluride.

The Uncompahgre Gorge to Ouray

The Million Dollar Highway between Silverton and Ouray follows an old toll road that was started in 1880 and finished in 1884 by road builder and transportation magnate Otto Mears. The road operated as a mail, stage, and freight line until Mears opened his Rainbow Route railway from Silverton to the rich mines at the summit of Red Mountain Pass. The Million Dollar Highway, traversing the old rail and wagon route, was completed in 1924. The road section from Ouray to Red Mountain Pass cost about a $1 million and gave the highway its name.

The highway descends from the pass summit 12 miles to Ouray. The first section, a maze of switchbacks and hairpin turns, twists down steep slopes to Ironton Park. Just north of the summit the highway passes the mostly abandoned Idarado Mine, one of the twentieth century's largest ore producers. The mine, nicknamed "Treasury Tunnel," yielded gold, silver, copper, lead, and zinc. Its tunnels bore through the mountains to the Smuggler Mine above Telluride. The surrounding mineralized peaks, including Red Mountain on the east, are tinted yellow and orange with iron oxides and are pockmarked by old mines, weathered buildings, and ore dumps. Several towns once scattered across the slopes here, including Red Mountain and Guston. Millions of dollars' worth of gold and silver streamed from the area mines. Wealthy producers were the Guston, Yankee Girl, and Robinson Mines.

Red Mountain Creek runs through Ironton Park. Aspens blanket the mountainsides above, creating a stunning display of color in late September. The old mining town of Ironton sat near the valley head. After a couple of miles, the highway leaves the valley and drops into the **Uncompahgre Gorge,** a deep canyon sliced by the Uncompahgre River. The road angles across steeply tilted cliffs of quartzite, slate, and schist, and scree slopes. Three crosses and a roadside memorial honor Reverend Marvin Hudson and his daughters Amelia and Pauline, and snowplow drivers Terry Kishbaugh and Bob Miller. The deadly Riverside Slide, an avalanche chute now covered with a snowshed, killed the five in separate winter accidents. The Hudsons died in 1963 after stopping to put on tire chains.

The highway edges north and passes Forest Road 878, the start of the four-wheel-drive **Alpine Loop Back Country Byway.** Farther north the road, clinging to cliffs, crosses Bear Creek Falls. The creek cascades 227 feet down to the river below. The tollgate for Otto Mears's road sat at this narrow site so wagon trains couldn't avoid paying the $3.75 toll for a vehicle with two animals. A nearby monument remembers Mears and his contribution to Colorado history. The drive runs through a short tunnel and emerges at Lookout Point above Ouray. A vast amphitheater of cliffs, formed by volcanic San Juan Tuff, soars above the town to lofty peaks and sharp ridges. Amphitheater Campground, with thirty sites, is reached from a side road past the viewpoint. The highway snakes down into **Ouray.**

Mountains dominate 7,760-foot-high Ouray. The town, named for a Ute chief, sits cupped in a deep canyon. Three waterfalls thunder within shouting distance of Ouray, and five creeks dash through town to the Uncompahgre River. Box Canyon, on the southwest edge, is most impressive, with Canyon Creek roaring through a narrow gorge. Geothermal hot springs dot Ouray, filling pools and bathhouses. The springs, named Uncompahgre, or "hot water springs," by the Utes, still attract visitors to the town.

Ouray began with rich gold and silver strikes in late 1875. The following year the town was surveyed and quickly boomed. The first building was supposedly a saloon, but by the end of 1876 a school, 214 cabins, two hotels, and a post office also lined the streets. The 1893 silver crash brought Ouray to its financial knees, but Tom Walsh's Camp Bird Mine in Yankee Boy Basin west of town brought new prosperity in 1895. The fabulous lode yielded over $20 million in gold before Walsh sold the mine in 1902 to an English consortium. Through the twentieth century Ouray relied on an economy based on mining and tourism.

 Now Ouray makes a fabulous base camp to explore what locals call the "Switzerland of America." A legacy of old mining roads lace the mountains and canyons, making Ouray the jeep capital of America. Some of the best roads are the Corkscrew Road, Poughkeepsie Gulch, Engineer Pass, Yankee Boy Basin, and Imogene Pass. Jeep rentals are available in town. Numerous trails also thread the backcountry, climbing to waterfalls, alpine basins, and sheer peaks. The **Ouray Hot Springs Pool,** on the north end of town, gives a relaxing soak at day's end. The 9-block-long town, a National Historic District, offers neat streets lined with restored Victorian homes, brick buildings, the haunted Beaumont Hotel, the Ouray County Historical Museum, and a designated walking tour. Also of interest is the Ouray Ice Park, which opened in 1995 as the world's first park devoted exclusively to ice climbing. Every January the town hosts an ice festival that attracts climbers from across the United States and Canada.

Ridgway

The drive's next 10 miles connect Ouray to **Ridgway,** an old railroad hub. The highway runs through a narrow gap lined with towering sandstone walls and takes leave of the San Juan Mountains. The valley ahead, flanked by forested slopes, is lush with green pastures, grazing cattle, and narrow-leaf cottonwoods. Herds of elk and deer graze in roadside meadows, particularly from late fall to spring. The drive yields great vistas of the ragged Sneffels Range to the west, low-browed

Grand Mesa to the north, and Chimney and Courthouse Peaks to the east. This drive segment ends in Ridgway at the intersection of US 550 and CO 62.

Ridgway, at an elevation of 7,003 feet, straddles the Uncompahgre River. Ridgway got its start as a railroad junction and transportation hub in 1890 by road builder Otto Mears and his Rio Grande Southern Railroad. The railroad, which ran 172 miles from Ridgway to Durango via Dolores, linked the isolated mines at Telluride, Ophir, and Rico with the Denver & Rio Grande Railroad's main line in Montrose. The town, earlier known as Dallasville, was renamed by the railroaders for R. M. Ridgway, the superintendent of the Denver & Rio Grande's mountain division. During its heyday the town boasted a huge railroad yard, stockyards, the fifty-five-room Mentone Hotel, and a depot that still stands. Today Ridgway thrives as a crossroads for travelers as well as local ranchers. The town serves as a gateway to the San Juan Mountains to the south and 3,260-acre **Ridgway State Park** 4 miles to the north. The park, dominated by Ridgway Reservoir, offers fishing, boating, hiking, and a 258 campsites in three campgrounds.

The Dallas Divide

From Ridgway, head west on CO 62. The road crosses the river and passes through town. A large park, with tables shaded by tall cottonwoods, makes a good picnic site. The highway bends north out of Ridgway, climbing a scrubby slope of gray shale into Dallas Creek's broad, lush valley, aptly named Pleasant Valley. Bales of fresh hay, drying in the autumn sun, and cattle scatter across green, fenced paddocks. Loghill Mesa walls in the valley on the north, while Miller Mesa hems it in on the south. Round Top, a shale knob, guards the valley's eastern entrance north of the highway. The drive rushes southwest past neat ranch homes, crosses cottonwood-lined Dallas Creek, and stumbles onto a magnificent panorama. **Mount Sneffels** and a long ridge of ragged peaks pierce the southern horizon, forming one of Colorado's most scenic mountain escarpments.

Pastoral ranchland, mostly part of fashion designer Ralph Lauren's Double RL Ranch, spreads across Dallas Creek's valley south of the highway. Humped ridges, thick with scrub oak and aspen, climb to spruce-coated hills, rounded by ancient glaciers, along the foot of the Sneffels Range. Above, the mountain wall is marked by sheer cliffs, snowfields tucked under north walls, gullies of ice, sharp summits, and aiguille-studded ridges. A series of high peaks—13,686-foot Cirque Mountain, 13,786-foot Potosi Peak, and 13,819-foot Teakettle Mountain—sit east of Mount Sneffels, an imposing 14,150-foot peak barricaded by immense cliffs. The long ridge to the west is topped by 13,809-foot Dallas Peak, 13,496-foot Mears Peak, and anchored on the west by pointed 12,987-foot Hayden Peak. The Sneffels Range, protected in the 16,200-acre Mount Sneffels Wilderness Area, is mostly composed of volcanic rocks. Mount Sneffels was named in 1874 by the

Deep winter snow blankets rocky Mount Sneffels and Dallas Divide along the San Juan Skyway.

Hayden Survey for a mountain in Jules Verne's novel *Journey to the Center of the Earth.* Dallas Peak was named for U.S. Vice President George Dallas, Mears Peak commemorates road and railroad builder Otto Mears, and Hayden Peak honors Ferdinand Hayden. Hayden's indefatigable survey team, including pioneer photographer William Henry Jackson and painter Thomas Moran, intensively studied western Colorado from 1873 through 1876. The survey climbed, measured, and named the major mountains and ranges; followed the rivers and traversed the high passes; and gathered data on climate, plants, animals, and future mining and agricultural possibilities. The East Dallas and West Dallas Roads head south from the drive to high valleys below the range crest.

Past the Double RL Ranch, the highway ascends the broad flank of a plateau, gaining 1,500 feet in 4 miles to the 8,970-foot summit of **Dallas Divide.** Scenic mountain scenes unfold as the road climbs. A couple of overlooks, one just below the top, and the other at the summit yield great views of the mountainous wall to the south. Eastward tower Uncompahgre and Wetterhorn Peaks, both over 14,000 feet, and blocky Chimney Peak and Courthouse Mountain. The divide's summit, surrounded by aspen-covered hills, was the site of a railroad station, post office, and stock-loading chutes. The dense aspen forests atop Dallas Divide are spectacular in late September, when their gold flush brightens the hillsides.

The San Miguel River

The highway runs west from the summit down a shallow draw. Stands of aspen flutter on rolling hills among meadows of sagebrush and grass. Low willows huddle along Leopard Creek. The Last Dollar Road, a rough dirt track connecting Dallas Divide and Telluride, heads south across Hastings Mesa a mile west of the divide summit. The highway, following the old rail bed, begins dropping down Leopard Canyon toward the **San Miguel River.** The canyon deepens as it descends. The remains of a carnotite claim, the Omega Mine, perch on the south slope above the highway near the canyon mouth.

The drive reaches the junction of CO 62 and 145 at **Placerville** in the San Miguel River Canyon, 24 miles from Ridgway. Turn south on Colorado 145 toward Telluride.

Placerville, at 7,321 feet, spreads along the highway on the narrow floor of the San Miguel River Canyon. Although its origins are uncertain, the town sprang up sometime in the 1870s after prospectors discovered color in gravel deposits along the river floodplain. By 1878 a post office was established, and large placer operations lent the name Placerville to the new community. In autumn of 1890, about the time the placer deposits played out, the Rio Grande Southern Railway reached Placerville. The town formed a good railroad junction, with the main line steaming upriver to Telluride, and another line heading down-canyon to other towns. Placerville quickly became a major shipping center for thousands of cattle in western Colorado. Even as late as 1949, more than 1,000 carloads of sheep embarked to market from here.

The drive heads south through Placerville on CO 145 and up the canyon. The San Miguel River, beginning in the mountains above Telluride, riffles over cobbles and worn boulders below the highway. Tall narrow-leaf cottonwoods and thick willows line its banks. The river, a favorite of fly fishers and kayakers, offers excellent trout fishing. Red sandstone layers form cliff bands on the steep canyon walls. The road, following the old railroad grade, winds through a series of small towns that once served as mining centers and railroad stops. At Fall Creek the Fall Creek Road climbs south to Woods Lake, a pretty lake nestled in a high cirque below Dolores Peak. The town of **Sawpit** boomed as an 1890s mining town after the Champion Belle Mine yielded $1,800 in silver with its first three carloads. The mill foundations are all that remain of **Vanadium,** another mining town that dug and milled vanadium, an alloy used in hardening steel. Uranium, used in World War II, also was extracted here. The Silver Pick Road, at Vanadium, heads south up Big Bear Creek to Silver Pick Basin, the base camp for climbers that scale the three "fourteeners"—Wilson Peak, Mount Wilson, and El Diente Peak—in the San Miguel Range.

The road begins climbing Keystone Hill 10 miles from Placerville. The South Fork Road, leading to Ilium and Ames, turns south from the drive up the San Miguel's South Fork just after the ascent begins. The highway clings to the steep mountainside under a palisade of sandstone bluffs. Good views of Sunshine Peak and the South Fork valley lie south of the highway. After 3 miles the drive emerges in a flat-bottomed glaciated valley ringed by towering mountains. **Telluride,** a picturesque ski community, straddles the valley's eastern head. The scenic drive crosses the valley mouth, but a highway spur leads 3 miles east to Telluride.

Telluride

Telluride boasts perhaps the most spectacular setting of any American town. Mountains rise almost a vertical mile out of Telluride's valley. Cliff bands, seamed by frothy waterfalls, punctuate the mountain flanks, and spruce and fir forests, broken by glades of quaking aspen, spill down the steep slopes. Snowfields whiten the upper alpine cirques and rocky ridges, and arêtes form bold outlines against the azure sky. This town is a place to savor, to stop and stretch, and to gaze in awe at nature's stunning artistry. It also offers some of North America's most magnificent skiing terrain.

The town, like most San Juan communities, began as a support center for local mines. Gold was first discovered here in 1875, and the following year J. B. Ingram located the fabulously wealthy Smuggler Mine. The strike produced eighteen ounces of gold and 800 ounces of silver per ton. The town, established in 1878, was named for tellurium, a rare element found in association with gold and silver. Colorful locals, however, said the name derived from "To hell you ride," a reference to the town's winter isolation and rowdy reputation.

Telluride thrived on its earth riches, eventually yielding almost $400 million from its mines, including the Black Bear, Liberty Bell, Cimarron, Japan, Champion, and Snow Drift Mines. Almost 300 miles of tunnels puncture the surrounding mountains. With the 1890 arrival of the railroad, Telluride boomed and reached a population of 5,000. All the excitement also brought ruffians and outlaws. On June 24, 1889, a small-time robber and two of his gang helped themselves to $10,000 at the San Miguel Valley Bank and fled north to Brown's Park near Wyoming. Butch Cassidy had pulled off his first holdup and set off down history's path of infamy.

The 1893 silver panic closed Telluride's silver mines and almost bankrupted the new railway, but valuable gold strikes brought new prosperity to Telluride in the late 1890s. With them came trouble between new unions and mine owners.

Telluride, proclaimed a National Historic District in 1961, preserves its rich past. The New Sheridan Hotel, built in 1895, still beds visitors and next door stands the 200-seat Sheridan Opera House, now a movie theater. The town, despite soaring land prices and encroaching condominium developments, maintains a Victorian charm and is trying to avoid becoming another Aspen or Vail. A parade of festivals brings visitors to Telluride, including the premier Telluride Bluegrass Festival in June and September's renowned film festival. The town makes a super base camp for backcountry explorers. Nearby Imogene and Black Bear Passes beckon backroad enthusiasts. Numerous hiking trails lace the canyons and climb the mountains. And Telluride Ski Area, with over 3,000 feet of vertical drop, offers the expert skier superb bump runs that include the infamous Plunge. The southern backside hides good beginner and intermediate runs.

Ophir and Lizard Head Pass

The drive crosses the valley mouth west of Telluride and swings up a mountain flank. The highway quickly reaches a rolling bench high above the San Miguel River's South Fork valley. The road rolls across this high plateau over open grasslands and through aspen groves. Marvelous views unfold from every highway bend. Wilson Peak, a sharp, 14,017-foot mountain, and 12,930-foot Sunshine Mountain tower to the southwest, while peaks loom across the northern and eastern skylines. The Ophir Needles lift a ridge of pinnacles and buttresses above the asphalt.

Past Cushman Lake and the fifteen-site Sunshine Campground, a side road climbs to the ghost town of Alta and Alta Lakes. Past that turn the highway steeply drops toward the narrow canyon mouth of the Howard Fork and **Ophir.**

Wilson Peak rises beyond a carpet of wildflowers near Ophir on the San Juan Skyway.

Ophir started as an 1870s silver camp and flourished as a railroad stop in the 1890s. One of the first roads to Telluride came over 11,750-foot Ophir Pass from Silverton; today that road makes a relatively easy but scenic four-wheel-drive tour from Red Mountain Pass on US 550. Old Ophir, a collection of rustic cabins, sits just east of the drive in a U-shaped hanging valley. The railroad's famed Ophir Loop traversed the canyon entrance, where today's highway runs. The great loop spiraled up on wooden trestles to gain elevation to put the train into the upper valley below the final pull up Lizard Head Pass. The Ophir Wall, popular with local rock climbers, is the huge cliff on the left side of the valley just left of the scenic drive.

Past Ophir, the highway edges above the South Fork valley and bends into a broad, glaciated basin. Matterhorn Campground, with twenty-nine sites, sits just off the highway. The basin, floored by the San Miguel's Lake Fork, is surrounded by alpine peaks. After crossing the river the drive begins climbing slopes north of the basin. Trout Lake sits in the valley below at 9,714 feet. The road steadily ascends through spruce forest, wide meadows, and willow thickets to the summit of 10,222-foot **Lizard Head Pass,** the drive's high point. A small picnic area, parking lot, and overlook lie on the summit. Several interpretative displays explain the area's history, geology, and natural history. The old Rio Grande Southern Railway climbed over the pass here, its bed sitting south of the highway in the meadow. The railroad, built by Otto Mears for $9 million, ran from Ridgway to Durango from 1890 until 1951. Indians used the pass for 7,000 years before that. The first known white men in the area were sixty St. Louis Fur Company trappers who spent a summer trapping beaver around Trout Lake in 1833.

The pass is named for **Lizard Head,** a 13,113-foot tower with a reputation as Colorado's most difficult mountain summit to reach. The crumbling 400-foot-high volcanic peak was first ascended by pioneer climbers Albert Ellingwood and Barton Hoag in 1920. It was probably the most difficult rock climb in America at the time. Lizard Head sits, along with neighboring Wilson Peak, Mount Wilson, and El Diente Peak, in the 41,193-acre Lizard Head Wilderness Area north of the highway. The wilderness can be accessed via the Lizard Head Trail at the trailhead on the pass summit. Sheep Mountain, a 13,188-foot peak, looms south of the drive. Silverton sits a mere 9 miles from the pass over Vermillion Peak to the east.

The Dolores River Valley

The highway heads southwest from the pass summit, gently descending along Snow Spur Creek. As the road and creek drop, the valley narrows into a short, steep canyon. The Rico Mountains stud the western horizon and Mount Wilson and Lizard Head lift above rounded, spruce-covered ridges to the north. After a couple of miles the drive reaches the **Dolores River** in a glaciated valley. Beaver ponds block the twisting river. Thick spruce forest blankets the southern hillsides, while aspen groves broken by wide meadows coat the steep northern slopes. Cayton Campground, with twenty-seven sites, lines the riverbank a couple of miles down. Forest Road 535 climbs out of the valley here and leads to Dunton and the West Dolores River. As the highway drops down the river valley, it passes through a succession of tilted sandstone formations, including Dakota and Entrada sandstones and Triassic and Permian redbeds deposited on floodplains over 200 million years ago.

After almost 10 miles the valley squeezes into a canyon. The drive passes a San Juan National Forest Information Station, crosses the Dolores River, and enters the old mining town of **Rico.** This charming town, at 8,827 feet, spreads along a hillside above the river. The road is lined with old stone and brick buildings and Victorian homes. Gold was discovered here as early as 1866, but Indians drove away the intruding prospectors. Mining, however, began in earnest after the Utes ceded the San Juans in 1873. Rico boomed with silver mining after 1879. Later mines extracted lead, zinc, and gold from the area's volcanic rocks.

The highway follows the Dolores River for the next 37 miles. As the road heads west, the canyon widens and its slopes step back to rocky rims. Bands of sandstone cliffs, first a wave of salmon-colored Entrada sandstone and then blocky Dakota sandstone, form the canyon sides. The climate dries as the river and highway run west, with scrub oak and ponderosa pine covering the lower canyon slopes. Stoner sits at the confluence of the Dolores and West Dolores Rivers partway down-canyon.

The 230-mile-long Dolores River originates south of Lizard Head Pass, runs southwest to Dolores, pools in McPhee Reservoir, and twists through sandstone canyons before emptying into the Colorado River above Moab, Utah. The river's name, given by seventeenth-century Spanish explorers, was shortened from the original *El Rio de Nuestra Señora de los Dolores,* or "The River of Our Lady of Sorrows," to simply the Dolores River. Franciscan priests Silvestre Escalante and Atanasio Dominguez crossed the Dolores River during their epic 1776 exploration of the American Southwest.

Dolores and the Anasazi Heritage Center

Dolores, a pleasant town spread across the shallow valley at 6,936 feet, sits just above McPhee Reservoir and the Dolores River's northward bend. McPhee Reservoir, formed by the only dam on the otherwise free-flowing Dolores River, supplies irrigation water to the nearby Montezuma Valley for crops, including pinto beans. The 4,470-acre lake, Colorado's second-largest when full, is stocked with rainbow trout, bass, bluegill, and crappie.

Established in 1891 along the Rio Grande Southern Railroad, Dolores serves as the southwestern gateway to the San Juan Mountains. The **Galloping Goose,** alongside the highway in Flanders Park in Dolores, makes an interesting stop. As rail traffic decreased on the railroad, train mechanics devised this ingenious gasoline-powered railcar to continue mail and passenger service. Seven of these silver "railroad buses," made by grafting automobile bodies to railcars, traversed the tracks between Ridgway and Durango from 1931 until the railroad closed down in 1952. The Goose, without breakdowns or snow slides, could travel the route's 175 miles in nine hours.

The drive climbs south out of the Dolores River Canyon just past the town. A right turn on CO 184 leads to Escalante Ruin and the **Anasazi Heritage Center.** The Anasazi ruin, a twenty-five-room pueblo occupied from the late 1000s to about 1300, perches atop a bluff overlooking the Montezuma Valley. The site, excavated in the 1970s as part of the Dolores Archeological Project, is named for its discoverer, Padre Escalante. He wrote in his 1776 journal, "Upon an elevation of the river's south side, there was in ancient times a small settlement of the same type as those of the Indians of New Mexico." Dominguez Ruin, named for

Escalante's partner, sits nearby. The Anasazi Heritage Center, run by the Bureau of Land Management, houses artifacts from the ruin and offers information about the Anasazi.

Cortez to Durango

The drive heads south on CO 145 for 10 miles, running past small ranches and farms shaded by tall cottonwoods. The highway ends at its junction with US 160 on the east side of **Cortez.** Turn left onto US 160 for the last 46 miles of the San Juan Skyway. Mesa Verde stretches its high escarpment to the south. Its entrance and a scenic drive begin 10 miles east of here on US 160.

Below the La Plata Mountains, a fisherman angles for trout in Jackson Gulch Reservoir at Mancos State Park.

Cortez, the seat of Montezuma County, still thrives as an agricultural and ranching town and offers all traveler amenities. Cortez, considered to be the archaeological center of the United States, was originally called *Tsaya-toh* ("rock water") by the Navajos for its nearby springs. Since its founding in 1886, Cortez has been the ranching and agricultural center for the Montezuma Valley. Navajos live on a sprawling reservation to the southwest of town, and Utes from the adjoining Ute Mountain Indian Reservation come into town. Their arts and crafts are displayed at many area galleries and trading posts, and Indian dances and cultural programs are held at the Cortez Cultural Center through the summer.

The skyway runs east from Cortez, passing the entrance to **Mesa Verde National Park.** This marvelous parkland, one of America's premier archaeological areas and a United Nations World Heritage Site, is explored by the Mesa Verde scenic drive (see Drive 28). It's worth at least a day to visit the park and its best sites. *National Geographic* calls it one of the world's fifty must-see attractions.

The drive continues east from the park's entrance on US 160 and drops into the valley of the Mancos River. The town of **Mancos,** at 7,035 feet, is a ranching and agricultural center nestled in the valley below the rugged La Plata Range, the westernmost extension of the Rocky Mountains in Colorado. The river was named *Rio de los Mancos* ("River of the Cripple") by Escalante and Dominguez on their 1776 expedition, for one of their injured members. The town was laid out in 1881. One of the first families to settle here was the Wetherills at their Alamo Ranch. The Wetherill brothers were among the first Anglos to discover the cliff dwellings in nearby Mesa Verde, including Cliff Palace in 1888.

A turn north on CO 184 in Mancos leads a few miles north to **Mancos State Park.** The centerpiece of this 338-acre park is Jackson Gulch Reservoir, a 216-acre lake that supplies drinking water to Mancos and Mesa Verde National Park. This pretty recreation area offers dramatic views of the La Plata Range, 32 campsites in two campgrounds that are shaded by ponderosa pines, wakeless boating, and good trout fishing. A 3.5-mile-long trail circles the lake for hikers.

From Mancos the highway climbs eastward to the crest of a divide between the Mancos River and Animas River watersheds before descending along the East Fork of the La Plata River. The La Plata Mountains tower to the north. At Hesperus a forest road heads north into the heart of the range. The highway continues to descend eastward through a steep canyon before completing the San Juan Skyway loop drive at Durango.

24

Flat Tops Trail Scenic Byway

Meeker to Yampa

General description: The 82-mile-long Flat Tops Trail, a National Forest Scenic Byway, traverses the upper White River valley and crosses Ripple Creek and Dunckley Passes on the White River Plateau.

Special attractions: Meeker, White River, White River National Forest, Routt National Forest, Flat Tops Wilderness Area, Trappers Lake, Ripple Creek Pass, autumn colors, fly fishing, hiking, camping, backpacking, scenic views.

Location: Northwestern Colorado. The drive begins in Meeker, 41 miles north of I-70 and Rifle, and ends in Yampa, 31 miles south of Steamboat Springs.

Drive route name and numbers: Flat Tops Trail Scenic Byway, Rio Blanco County Road 8, Routt National Forest Road 16, Routt County Road 17.

Travel season: Only the lower road section outside Meeker is open year-round; other-

wise the drive closes after the first heavy snow and opens after the spring thaw. Check with the national forest office for road conditions and closures.

Camping: Campgrounds along the drive are North Fork and Vaughn Lake. Himes Peak Campground sits on Forest Road 205 to Trappers Lake and Trapline, Bucks, Cutthroat, and Shepherds Rim Campgrounds cluster near Trappers Lake. Other forest campgrounds lie on side roads off the drive.

Services: All services are found in Meeker and Yampa at either end of the drive. Limited services in Buford.

Nearby attractions: Rifle Falls State Park, Rifle Mountain Park, Grand Hogback, Stagecoach State Park, Steamboat Springs, Gore Pass, Finger Rock, Upper Yampa River, Craig, Dinosaur National Monument.

The Drive

The White River Plateau, part of Colorado's plateau geographic province, lies just west of the main bulk of the Rocky Mountains between the Yampa and Colorado Rivers. Deep canyons and valleys excavated by rivers and streams dissect this upland of raised sandstone layers. Ancient lava flows top the plateau's central section, forming the magnificent Flat Tops Wilderness Area.

The eighty-two-mile-long Flat Tops Trail Scenic Byway begins in Meeker west of the plateau and follows the White River's deep gash eastward almost to the heart of the Flat Tops before swerving northeast over Ripple Creek and Dunckley Passes to the Yampa River's upper valley. The road crosses the ancestral homeland of the Ute Indians, the second-oldest national forest in the United

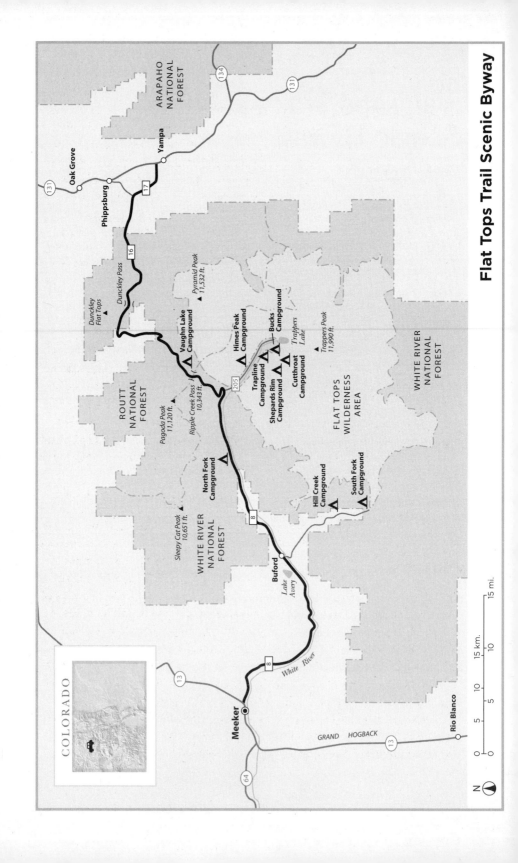

Flat Tops Trail Scenic Byway

States, and some of Colorado's best aspen colors and most dramatic scenic views.

Temperatures along the drive, open spring through fall, vary according to elevation. Summer highs in the lowlands near Meeker climb into the low nineties, while 4,000 feet higher atop the passes the temperatures range in the sixties or seventies. Expect chilly nights at the higher elevations, particularly near Trappers Lake, with lows dipping to the thirties and forties. Insect repellent checks ubiquitous mosquitoes along the drive's moist creeks, beaver ponds, and lakes. Expect thunderstorms almost every afternoon, some locally heavy. Drive carefully during and after rain— the gravel roads can be slippery. Side roads are often muddy. September and early October brings cool, crisp days with generally clear skies. The first snow falls on the higher mountains by late October, and the road closes in early November until spring thaw. Check with the forest office in either Meeker or Yampa for road closing and opening dates. The drive's upper reaches accumulate as much as 10 feet of snow, allowing excellent snowmobiling and cross-country skiing conditions.

Meeker

Meeker, a pleasant off-the-beaten-track town, nestles in the White River valley. The fertile bottomland along the river has long attracted settlers. The earliest residents were Ute Indians who camped among cottonwoods along the river and grazed their horses in the lush pastures. The Utes, Colorado's mountain tribe, ranged across the Rocky Mountains gathering edible plants and hunting plentiful game. Summer camps in the high mountains offered superb hunting, while winter camps were made in mild valleys.

After gold was discovered in Colorado's high country in the 1860s, a collision between the Utes and incoming prospectors and settlers became inevitable. A series of treaties drove the Utes from their ancestral mountain homeland. An 1868 treaty ceded central Colorado from the San Luis Valley to North Park to incoming Anglo settlers. Western Colorado remained reserved for the Utes. Rich mineral discoveries in the San Juan Mountains, however, precipitated another pact, and the Utes were relocated to southwestern and northwestern Colorado. Settlers still chafed that almost a third of Colorado remained in Ute hands, and by 1876 the state legislature asked Congress to relocate the Utes to an Oklahoma reservation. In 1879 Colorado Governor Frederick Pitkin wrote, "if this reservation could be extinguished, and the land thrown open to settlers, it will furnish homes to thousands of the people of our State who desire homes." The beginning of the end of the Ute presence in western Colorado came near Meeker in 1879.

The green river bottom just west of Meeker, originally known as Powell Park for Major John Wesley Powell who explored here in 1868, was the site of the White River Indian Agency. The agency, established in 1869, had a succession of agents until Nathaniel C. Meeker came in 1878. Meeker, who established the town of Greeley as an agricultural utopia in the early 1870s, arrived with the idea of domesticating the Utes, changing them from a nomadic people to sedentary Christian agriculturists. Conflict became inevitable after Meeker forbade hunting, fishing, gambling, and the pursuit of other traditional activities. Meeker angered the Utes further by digging an irrigation trench across their racetrack and plowing under a prime winter horse pasture. On September 29, 1879, the Utes rebelled by killing Meeker and eleven white men at the agency, taking Meeker's wife and daughter and three others as captives. A military force led by Captain Thomas Thorburgh was also defeated by the Utes. After the hostages were released, a new agreement was signed in 1880 that pushed the White River Utes onto today's reservation in Utah. The Meeker Massacre site lies 4 miles west of Meeker on CO 64.

Today Meeker, the 6,180-foot-high seat of Rio Blanco County, serves as a supply center for area sheep and cattle ranches. The town, established in 1883, bills itself as the "Gateway to the Flat Tops." The town thrives on hunters who flock here in October and November and recreationists who come for the surrounding wilderness and spectacular mountain scenery. Meeker's **White River Museum,** housed in an original 1879 log cabin built by U.S. cavalry troops, offers displays of pioneer and Indian artifacts and historical photos. Annual events include the 55-mile-long Almost Meeker to Rangely Canoe Race in May and the July 4th Range Call Celebration, Colorado's oldest continuous rodeo.

Meeker to Ripple Creek Pass

The drive heads east from Meeker along Rio Blanco County Road 8 on the northern edge of Agency Park. The White River meanders gracefully across the grassy valley, past hay fields and grazing cattle. Low hills, coated with juniper and sagebrush, flank the flat-bottomed valley. After 6 miles the road passes 8,000-acre **Oak Ridge State Wildlife Area,** and the valley narrows into a canyon. The White River Agency Monument, marking the original agency site, sits alongside the road 7 miles from Meeker. Meeker floated the buildings downstream to Powell Park in 1878, thinking it a better farming area. Ranches spread across the canyon floor, with thick stands of cottonwoods and willows lining the river bank. Spruce and fir darken the moist north-facing slopes above the river while juniper stud the dry south-facing hillsides.

The drive passes **Lake Avery State Wildlife Area** at 20 miles. This large reservoir offers great fishing year-round, as well as camping and picnicking facilities. The drive enters 7,009-foot **Buford** a mile later. A store offers supplies and gasoline, the last services until Yampa. The New Castle/Buford Road, Forest Road 244, begins here and twists south across the White River Plateau's western edge to New Castle on the Colorado River.

A cowboy traffic jam, Colorado style, stops a couple of trucks along the Flat Tops Trail.

The drive continues northeast, following the north bank of the White River. Large aspen groves spill down the south canyon slopes, and dense scrub oak thickets blanket the north hillside. The paved road ends at 31 miles and becomes gravel for the next 47 miles. **White River National Forest,** a 2-million-acre plot of public land, borders the river north of the road. The drive enters the forest 11 miles east of Buford and becomes Forest Road 8. North Fork Campground, with forty sites at 7,750 feet, spreads across grassy meadows among towering aspens 0.5 mile into the forest. The canyon narrows as the road runs east. After a few miles the road climbs away from the river up a shallow valley, swings across wooded slopes to Ripple Creek, and reaches a junction with Forest Road 205 40 miles from Meeker.

Forest Road 205 leads south above the North Fork of the White River 8 miles to **Trappers Lake Recreation Area,** passing eleven-site Himes Peak Campground on the way. Trappers Lake, the headwaters of the White River, glistens like a shiny jewel cupped in a high basin surrounded by flat-topped mountain peaks.

Trappers Lake, sometimes called the "Cradle of Wilderness," figures prominently in the preservation of public lands as wilderness. The area was first protected by President Benjamin Harrison in 1891 as the 1.2-million-acre White

River Plateau Timberland Reserve, the nation's second national forest. In 1919 the USDA Forest Service decided to develop the recreational potential of Trappers Lake by building summer cabins, lodges, guest ranches, a loop road around the lake, and other amenities. A young landscape architect, Arthur Carhart, was hired to study the plan. After viewing the scenic site, Carhart made the radical assertion that the area should be preserved as untrammeled wilderness and any development should be made at least a half mile from the lake shore. The Forest Service, with Carhart's recommendation, dropped plans for the lakeside road and refused private home sites. Carhart went on, with famed naturalist Aldo Leopold from the Forest Service's Albuquerque office, to establish the nation's first wilderness area in New Mexico's Gila National Forest. In 1929 the area became the Flat Tops Primitive Area, which, after the establishment of the national wilderness system in 1964, became the 235,406-acre Flat Tops Wilderness Area in 1979.

Trappers Lake serves as a popular starting point for hikers and horseback riders venturing into the wilderness area. The wilderness includes more than thirty fishable lakes and 160 miles of trails that lace its remote backcountry. Five forest campgrounds—twenty-site Shepards Rim, fourteen-site Cutthroat, ten-site Bucks, five-site Horsethief, and twelve-site Trapline, perch on ridges north of the lake. Several trails drop down to Trappers Lake, offering scenic views and fishing access. The lake houses native cutthroat trout that reproduce naturally in its clear, cold water. Fishing is allowed only with flies or one-hook lures; native trout between 11 and 16 inches must be released; and fishing is not permitted in the lake's inlets and outlet from January 1 through July 31 to allow trout to spawn. An excellent hike climbs east from the lake on Forest Trail 1814 to the lofty Chinese Wall, an above-timberline cliffed escarpment.

Ripple Creek Pass to Yampa

The drive, continuing east on County Road 8, begins switchbacking up a broad ridge through lush aspen stands and open meadows. After 5 miles of climbing the road, now in spruce and lodgepole pine forest, reaches **Ripple Creek Overlook.** This high viewpoint yields expansive views west down the White River valley and south into the heart of the Flat Tops. Interpretive signs discuss the wilderness concept, watchable wildlife, and the area's geology. The drive crosses 10,343-foot **Ripple Creek Pass** and enters 1.2-million-acre Routt National Forest 1.5 miles later. The road drops east down spruce-clad slopes above Poose Creek and reaches Vaughn Lake almost 3 miles later. A six-site forest campground at 9,720 feet nestles under trees along the edge of the small reservoir. The drive spirals down through thick aspen and conifer forest into the upper valley of the East Fork of the Williams Fork River. Pyramid Ranger Station, built by the Civilian Conservation

Corps in 1934 near the valley head, continues to serve as a busy Forest Service center in summer.

The aspen-lined lane runs north from the station in the river valley. Tall cottonwoods and green meadows clot the river's banks, and gray sagebrush colors the dry hillsides above. The road crosses the river at the old town site of Pyramid, now a collection of summer cabins, and begins ascending steep slopes above the valley.

After twisting up for 3 miles the drive swings under the **Dunckley Flat Tops,** a long ridge broken into flat-topped summits. The road threads along steep slopes, passing through thick aspen forest, and reaches the summit of 9,763-foot **Dunckley Pass.** An overlook yields superb views southward to 11,532-foot Pyramid Peak, the Little Flat Tops, and 12,133-foot Orno Peak in the Flat Tops Wilderness Area. In midsummer wildflowers, including columbines, carpet the meadows on the pass summit.

The drive drops east from the pass, dipping through several drainages before bending northeast down Oak Creek's valley. A side road, Forest Road 959, leads 3 miles south to Sheriff Reservoir. A primitive campground and trailhead for the wilderness area sits here. The road bumps through the shallow valley for a couple of miles past beaver ponds and a thick fir and spruce woodland, before turning up a grassy side canyon. A half mile later it crosses a low divide and the turnoff to Chapman Reservoir, a popular camping and fishing site.

The last leg of the scenic drive drops east above Spronks Creek into a valley. The climate and vegetation change as the road descends, with sagebrush coating the drier slopes and aspens clinging to the moist north-facing hillsides. Rolling hills and scattered cattle ranches border the road after it leaves the creek. Keep right at the intersection with Forest Road 925 and head south on Routt County Road 17. The now-paved road dips and rolls beneath towering Rattlesnake Butte and Devils Grave Mesa. Sharp volcanic outcrops mingle with sagebrush on the steep mesa slopes. After a couple of miles the road bends east through hay fields and cattle pastures, passes the Byrd Homestead, the first recorded homestead in the Yampa Valley, and enters the small hamlet of **Yampa** perched on the banks of the Yampa River.

The 170-mile-long Yampa River, Colorado's longest free-flowing river, begins in the Flat Tops, heads north to Steamboat Springs, and flows west through valleys and canyons to its confluence with the Green River in the heart of Dinosaur National Monument. The Utes called an edible potatolike root that grew on the river's banks *yampa*, and the name was applied to the river and town. The town offers all visitor services. The Royal Hotel Visitor Center dispenses information on the Yampa Valley. The drive ends at CO 131. Steamboat Springs sits 31 miles to the north and Interstate 70 lies 39 miles to the south.

25

Grand Mesa Scenic Byway

Cedaredge to Grand Junction

General description: The 75-mile Grand Mesa Scenic Byway climbs from desert canyons and ranch lands to the subalpine summit of 11,000-foot-high Grand Mesa, the world's largest flat-topped mountain.

Special attractions: Grand Mesa National Forest, Cedaredge Pioneer Town, Crag Crest National Recreation Trail, Land's End, Powderhorn Ski Area, lakes, fishing, camping, hiking, spectacular views, excellent fall colors, cross-country skiing, snowmobiling.

Location: Western Colorado. The drive begins 4 miles east of Delta at the intersection of CO 92 and 65 and ends at the junction of CO 65 and I-70 just east of Grand Junction.

Drive route names and numbers: Grand Mesa Scenic Byway; Lands End Road; CO 65; Forest Road 100.

Travel season: Year-round. The paved drive section is open all winter and plowed

and sanded after snowstorms. Land's End Road closes in winter.

Camping: Eight National Forest campgrounds—Jumbo, Spruce Grove, Island Lake, Little Bear, Ward Lake, Kiser Creek, Eggleston Lake, and Crag Crest—sit on or just off the drive on the mesa top.

Services: All services are found in Grand Junction, Delta, and Cedaredge. Limited services at Mesa.

Nearby attractions: Colorado National Monument, Uncompahgre Plateau, Unaweep Canyon, Black Canyon of the Gunnison National Park, West Elk Loop Scenic Byway (see Drive 21), Paonia State Park, West Elk Wilderness Area, Gunnison National Forest, Grand Junction attractions, Vega State Park, White River National Forest, Debeque Canyon, Island Acres State Park.

The Drive

The Grand Mesa, lying between the Gunnison and Colorado Rivers in western Colorado, hides a remote, off-the-beaten-track landscape. It's a place studded with lakes that nestle among spruce woodlands, meadows carpeted with summer wildflowers, creeks lined with willows, and a basalt rim formed by ancient lava flows. The 75-mile-long drive traverses this massive island in the sky. The mesa, with its high point, 11,237-foot Leon Peak, boasts an average elevation of 10,000 feet. The rolling mesa top, called the world's highest flat-topped mountain, is a summer oasis of cool temperatures and plentiful rainfall that towers over surrounding desert valleys. More than 300 lakes stud the upland, and thick woodlands and broad meadows carpet the mesa's hillocks and swales. The drive yields stunning views—golden aspens that cascade over the mesa rim, the broad Grand Valley flanked by upturned cuestas and plateaus, and vistas of distant snow-capped peaks that gleam in the summer sun.

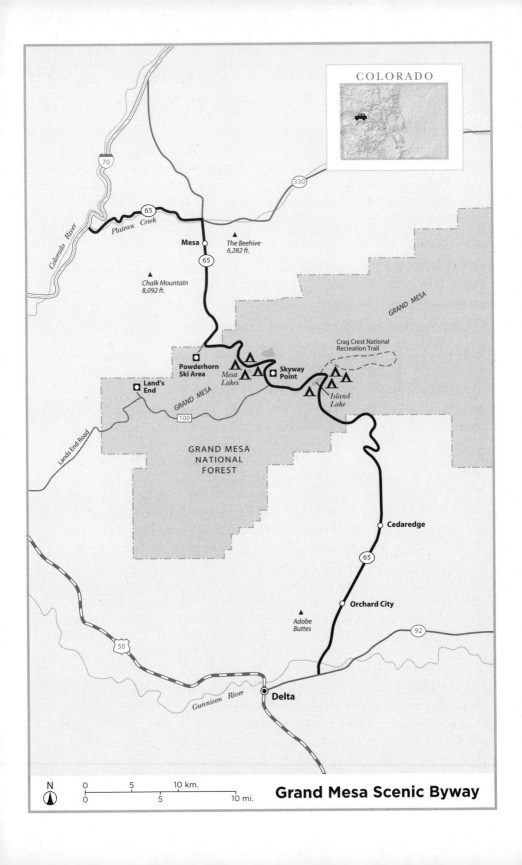

COLORADO

70

330

Colorado River

65

Plateau Creek

Mesa ○

▲ *The Beehive 6,282 ft.*

65

▲ *Chalk Mountain 8,092 ft.*

GRAND MESA

Crag Crest National Recreation Trail

□ **Powderhorn Ski Area**

Mesa Lakes

□ **Skyway Point**

Island Lake

□ **Land's End**

GRAND MESA

100

Lands End Road

GRAND MESA NATIONAL FOREST

○ **Cedaredge**

65

○ **Orchard City**

▲ *Adobe Buttes*

92

50

Gunnison River   ◉ **Delta**

N

| 0 | 5 | 10 km. |
| 0 | 5 | 10 mi. |

Grand Mesa Scenic Byway

Temperatures along the drive vary greatly from the semiarid river valleys at either end and the road's 10,839-foot summit, an almost 6,000-foot elevation difference. Precipitation varies from a scant 8 or so inches in the desert lowlands to over 30 inches atop the mesa. Summer daytime temperatures regularly climb into the nineties in the lower elevations, while temperatures atop the mesa remain in the sixties and seventies. Summer nights are cool, and occasionally drop into the thirties. Expect regular afternoon thunderstorms during the summer months, with locally heavy rain and possible hail. September brings warm days and cold nights, with infrequent showers. October begins the cooldown, with occasional dustings of snow on the higher elevations. The upper mesa road becomes locked under a mantle of snow from November through April. The Land's End Road closes in winter, but the rest of the drive remains open. Excellent cross-country skiing and snowmobiling trails thread the mesa top, while Powderhorn Ski Area offers downhill runs. Most of the snowdrifts melt away by late May.

Delta to Cedaredge

The drive begins at the intersection of CO 92 and 65 4 miles east of **Delta.** Delta, at 4,980 feet, sits at the confluence of the Gunnison and Uncompahgre Rivers. It's a pleasant Western town, with all visitor services. Points of interest include the Delta County Historical Museum, with displays of ranch and farm tools and a butterfly collection, and the Ute Council Tree, a spreading 200-year-old cottonwood on the town's north side used by Ute Indians, including Chief Ouray, as a meeting place. Grand Mesa National Forest's office sits on U.S. Highway 50 on Delta's south side and offers visitor information and maps.

The drive begins by heading east from Delta on CO 92 for 4 miles. Turn north onto CO 65 near the end of the four-lane highway stretch. The drive's first 11 miles run north from the highway intersection to **Cedaredge.** The road goes over cornfields on the valley floor and after 0.8 mile crosses the Gunnison River. Tall cottonwoods and Russian olives line the river banks. The highway climbs north into scrubby hills of gray Mancos shale, a deposit laid down on an ancient seabed some seventy million years ago. The Mancos shale stretches along the foot of Grand Mesa, forming a wide, brightly colored band of dissected badlands, broad valleys, and humpbacked ridges. The Adobe Buttes, a shale area west of the highway beyond Tongue Creek's lush valley, offer excellent backcountry hiking through austere, barren hills.

The highway ascends a low shale hill onto a broad, gently tilted mesa seamed by Surface Creek's shallow valley. **Orchard City** lies along the creek at 5,800 feet. Orchard City is not actually a town at all but rather a collection of three separate towns—Cory, Austin, and Eckert—each with its own post office. The trio incorporated in 1912 to obtain bonds to build a water system so residents could tap into Grand Mesa's spring runoff for irrigation and home water. The road runs through Orchard City, passing the small towns, old stone buildings, and grassy paddocks with grazing horses and cattle. Surface Creek parallels the blacktop, with cottonwoods, willows, and Russian olives lining its banks. After crossing the creek a couple of miles north of Eckert, the highway follows the Surface Creek valley and reaches 6,100-foot-high Cedaredge.

Cedaredge, the valley's commercial center, is a lovely backroads town. It began as the headquarters for the Bar-I Ranch in the 1890s. Sophie Kohler, the foreman's wife, called the place Cedar Edge, and when the post office was established the name became Cedaredge. All that remains of the ranch are three wooden multisided silos. These sit in **Pioneer Town,** a picturesque outdoor museum operated by the Surface Creek Valley Historical Society. The site is open during the summer, and there is no charge. Visitors enjoy a look back at western Colorado's colorful past. Pioneer Town features many historic buildings and houses, including the Lizard Head Saloon, Wells-Fargo Express, barbershop, livery stable, the Cedaredge Town Jail, an Indian museum, blacksmith shop, schoolhouse, and Chapel of the Cross. All are painstakingly furnished and outfitted with period artifacts and antiques. Cedaredge also offers numerous craft shops and hosts the Little Britches Rodeo each July. The town's annual Applefest occurs the first Saturday in October each year.

Cedaredge marks the official beginning of the Grand Mesa Scenic and Historic Byway. The highway passes downtown Cedaredge and climbs north past scattered homes and apple orchards. The Surface Creek valley, along with the North Fork valley at Paonia, is one of Colorado's renowned fruit-growing areas. Orchards were first planted in 1882 near Cory, and by the 1920s fruit farming became a major industry. Thousands of acres in the Surface Creek valley yield cherries, apricots, plums, peaches, nectarines, pears, and apples between July and October. Roadside stands sell fresh in-season fruit and vegetables at bargain prices.

Grand Mesa

The drive passes apple orchards, drops over Young's Creek, and climbs onto a rolling benchland blanketed with sagebrush and a piñon pine and juniper woodland. **Grand Mesa** towers overhead with steep aspen-covered slopes spilling over its cliffed rim and down abrupt ravines. The drive climbs through four distinct biological life zones that represent a telescoped journey from Mexico to northern Canada's boreal forest.

The highway bends northwest and skirts the edge of a long ridge. After a few miles the road turns east, climbs onto the ridge, and begins sharply ascending hills thick with Gambel oak copses. Magnificent views unfold as the road climbs. The long snowcapped escarpment of the San Juan Mountains parades across the

A blanket of golden aspens covers mountain slopes above the Grand Mesa Scenic Byway.

southern horizon, with several 14,000-foot peaks—Uncompahgre and Wetterhorn Peaks, Mount Sneffels, Mount Wilson, and Wilson Peak—poking against the azure sky. The humped Uncompahgre Plateau spreads to the southwest above the Gunnison River valley. To the southeast towers the West Elk Range and the dark rim of the Black Canyon of the Gunnison. The highway finally leaves the oak woods behind and enters immense aspen groves. A paved overlook offers spectacular views just before the road enters 346,219-acre **Grand Mesa National Forest.**

After entering the forest the drive turns away from the aspen-clad rim up Ward Creek's shallow vale. Spruce dominates the forest atop the mesa, with only scattered patches of aspen. Willows cling to the creek's banks. The road swings past Ward Creek Reservoir and bends northeast to **Grand Mesa Recreation Area.** A series of lakes hides among the spruce forest here, including Eggleston Lake, Ward Lake, Carp Lake, Baron Lake, and Island Lake, the largest on the Grand Mesa. All offer excellent fishing for native cutthroat, rainbow, and brook trout. This popular scenic area, lying above 10,000 feet, offers campers Island Lake, Little Bear, Ward Lake, Kiser Creek, Eggleston Lake, and Crag Crest Campgrounds. Other recreation here includes hiking, four-wheeling, and boating. The national forest operates Grand Mesa Visitor Center at Cobbett Lake and three lodges near the lakes.

The drive bends west above spruce-fringed Island Lake and runs along a bench below a cliffed ridge. **Crag Crest National Recreation Trail,** a 10.3-mile circular trail, begins from a roadside 10,375-foot-high trailhead above the lake, and threads for 7 miles along the narrow, rocky Crag Crest and through quiet forests and wildflower-sprinkled meadows. The trail, climbing to over 11,000 feet, yields breathtaking views of the glistening lakes scattered across the mesa top as well as vistas of distant mountain ranges.

Grand Mesa is a huge layer-cake of horizontal rock layers. Late Cretaceous rocks—the Mancos shale and above-lying Mesa Verde Formation—form the bottom layers at Cedaredge, while more recent sandstones and shales called the Green River and Wahsatch Formations form the upper mesa slopes. The mesa top is capped by a thick layer of erosion-resistant basalt laid down as lava flows in ancient river valleys ten million years ago. The lava spewed from vents on the mesa's east side, forming twenty-five separate flows between 10 and 70 feet thick. Grand Mesa's lava cap varies between 200 and 600 feet thick. Later erosion swept away the softer hills that surrounded the lava-filled valleys, leaving them as a high, isolated plateau. Glaciers also blanketed the mesa top and the mesa's northern slopes, leaving piles of boulders and etching depressions that later formed lakes.

The drive runs west below broken cliffs and tumbled boulder fields before climbing higher onto the flattened mesa. A rest area sits at the 10,839-foot drive high point on the Mesa-Delta County line. The road rolls through open meadows with willow-lined tarns tucked amid boulders and Engelmann spruce woods.

Land's End

At just over 32 miles the highway intersects the Land's End Road, Forest Road 100. This 12-mile-long gravel road travels west to **Land's End,** one of Colorado's most stunning viewpoints. The road heads southwest across the mesa, traversing the west rim of Kanah Creek's canyon for a few miles before bending west along the edge of a gigantic amphitheater. Wide meadows broken by sparse spruce woodlands and small aspen groves characterize the mesa top. A dense aspen forest spills down steep slopes below the cliffs along the rim and road.

As the road runs west the mesa's climate becomes more temperate, moderated by warm winds that sweep up from the Grand Valley to the west. Sagebrush replaces the thick grasses and the forest disappears altogether. After 10 miles the road bends northwest, dipping through shallow ravines and crossing hillocks. A short spur leads to Coal Creek Overlook, a spectacular point perched atop black basalt cliffs. Small waterfalls drop over nearby cliffs. A couple of miles later the road reaches Land's End.

A magnificent panorama stretches away from the point. Steep slopes, colored brilliant yellow with changing aspen in September, cascade down to barren hills. The Grand Valley, seamed with the Colorado River and divided into green fields, reaches west to Utah. The Book Cliffs and a host of broken ridges march north from the valley, while the Uncompahgre Plateau, its northern edge eroded into Colorado National Monument's red rock canyons, looms to the southwest. The La Sal Mountains in Utah pierce the sky above the plateau. The National Forest Service's Land's End Visitor Center, open in summer, sits at the overlook. To continue the drive, head 12 miles back to the road's junction with CO 65. Land's End Road, however, continues west and twists downward for more than 5,000 feet to US 50.

Skyway Point to the Colorado River

The scenic drive continues north from Land's End Road over the rolling mesa top. After about a mile the highway reaches **Skyway Point** and the northern edge of Grand Mesa. The road descends east in the shadow of tall basalt cliffs and boulder fields to a broad bench before making a U-turn westward. A thick spruce forest borders the asphalt. The road passes fifteen-site Spruce Grove Campground and drops down to **Mesa Lakes Recreation Area.** The Mesa Lakes, scattered through the forest, are a popular overnight and fishing destination. Another campground, twenty-six-site Jumbo, two picnic areas, and Mesa Lakes Resort surround the lakes.

The highway drops past a small reservoir and turns onto the northern flank of Grand Mesa. A couple of paved turnoffs give great views north down the aspen-covered slopes to the Colorado River's salmon-colored Debeque Canyon. The road descends steep slopes for the next 4 miles, running through a spectacular aspen forest. Drive this road section in late September when the colors run from orange and rust to gold and yellow. At the bottom of the steepest slopes, the highway leaves Grand Mesa National Forest. The turn to **Powderhorn Resort** sits just north of the boundary. Powderhorn offers great intermediate runs, with wide views of the surrounding plateau country. It offers three lifts, 600 skiable acres, 250 inches of annual snow, and a 1,659-foot vertical drop. The area has a lodge, lessons, and ski rentals.

The highway swings into a broad tilted basin, flanked by high ridges on the east and west and the lofty rim of Grand Mesa on the south. The road curves down through a scrub oak woodland and after a few miles reaches pastures, ranchettes, and sagebrush hills. The Breaks form a ragged ridge on the east, eroded into a red rock badlands. Chalk Mountain lifts a twin-summited peak with bare white cliffs to the west. The drive descends along Coon Creek and runs down sloping pastures to the small ranching town of **Mesa.** The Beehive, a 6,282-foot butte, is a prominent landmark east of Mesa. Past Mesa the highway plunges into Mesa Creek's narrow canyon and reaches a junction with CO 330 at Plateau Creek. A right turn on CO 330 leads to Collbran and Vega State Park. The drive bends left on CO 330, crosses the creek, and heads toward Interstate 70 and Grand Junction.

The drive's last 10 miles twist down Plateau Creek's deepening canyon to its confluence with the **Colorado River.** This is dry, dusty country. Cliff bands of Mesa Verde sandstone tower above the highway, broken by erosion into bulging buttresses and tumbled boulders. Sagebrush, saltbush, dry grass clumps, and occasional piñon pines and junipers scatter over the canyon walls. The creek, lined by scraggly cottonwoods and tamarisks, riffles through cobbled rapids. The highway follows the canyon's immense curves and finally the road divides. The right branch continues on the creek's north bank to eastbound I-70 while the left branch crosses to the opposite shore and heads to the westbound interstate and Grand Junction.

26

Black Canyon South Rim Scenic Drive

Black Canyon of the Gunnison National Park

General description: This 13-mile road follows the south rim of the Black Canyon of the Gunnison National Park.

Special attractions: Black Canyon of the Gunnison, Tomichi Point, Pulpit Rock Overlook, Chasm View, Painted Wall View, High Point, Visitor Center, East Portal, camping, picnicking, hiking, wildlife, rock climbing, scenic views.

Location: West-central Colorado. The drive begins 6 miles east of Montrose off US 50.

Drive route name and number: South Rim Road, CO 347.

Travel season: Spring, summer, and fall. Heavy snow occasionally blocks the drive from Gunnison Point Overlook to High Point during winter months. Check with park headquarters in Montrose for road closure and opening.

Camping: The South Rim Campground, just inside the monument's southern boundary, offers eighty-eight campsites spread among scrub oak. It operates on a first-come, first-served basis and is closed in winter.

Services: A concessionaire operates the Rim House at Pulpit Rock Overlook in summer, offering food and souvenirs. Otherwise no services are found along the drive. Montrose offers all traveler services, including restaurants, groceries, lodging, and RV parks.

Nearby attractions: Curecanti National Recreation Area, Gunnison Gorge, Montrose, Montrose County Historical Museum, Ute Indian Museum and Ouray Memorial Park, Uncompahgre National Forest, Gunnison National Forest, Owl Creek Pass scenic drive, San Juan Scenic Skyway All-American Byway (see Drive 23), Ouray National Historic District.

The Drive

Colorado is a land of surprises. It's a land that appears at first glance to be ravishingly pure, untouched, and unchanging. But underneath that pristine veneer lies a landscape that is in constant motion and change. It's just that human life is too short to recognize geologic change. The land's shape alters over eons of time— millions of years pass in the creation of a single mountain peak or a desert canyon. The Black Canyon of the Gunnison River, lying on the edge of the Colorado Plateau in western Colorado, teaches the fundamental geologic lesson that nothing ever remains the same. There is no status quo on this dynamic earth.

The 13-mile-long South Rim Drive explores the southern edge of the Black Canyon, a deep, precipitous gorge hacked out of ancient bedrock by the Gunnison River in the Black Canyon of the Gunnison National Park. The park protects

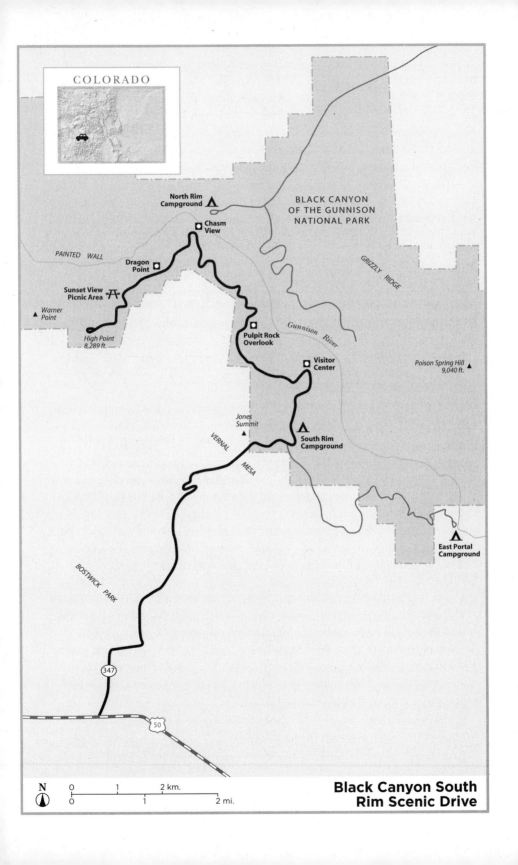

COLORADO

BLACK CANYON
OF THE GUNNISON
NATIONAL PARK

North Rim
Campground

Chasm
View

PAINTED WALL

Dragon
Point

GRIZZLY RIDGE

Sunset View
Picnic Area

Warner
Point

High Point
8,289 ft.

Pulpit Rock
Overlook

Gunnison River

Visitor
Center

Poison Spring Hill
9,040 ft.

Jones
Summit

VERNAL

South Rim
Campground

MESA

East Portal
Campground

BOSTWICK PARK

347

50

N

0   1   2 km.
0   1   2 mi.

**Black Canyon South
Rim Scenic Drive**

12 miles of the 50-mile-long canyon. The drive offers not only geologic lessons but also a wealth of scenic views, outdoor activities, and opportunities for nature study. Trails lead to observation points perched along the canyon rim. Soaring cliffs provide adventure for intrepid rock climbers and homes for raptors, swallows, and swifts. The forested canyon rim yields glimpses of life: a porcupine-gnawed piñon pine, the underbrush rustlings of rufous-sided towhees, the hoofbeats of an alarmed mule deer, and the howl of a distant coyote.

The Black Canyon slices through an uplift that reaches elevations above 8,000 feet, well over 2,000 feet higher than nearby Montrose. The canyon rim, with its higher elevation, consequently receives more precipitation than adjoining valleys, with an average of 20 inches annually. Each canyon rim season is distinct. Spring arrives in May with windy weather, rain showers, and cool nights. Summer days can be hot, occasionally reaching ninety degrees, but regular afternoon thunderstorms and breezes moderate the temperatures. Night temperatures can be very cool, dipping into the forties. Autumn brings a succession of clear, glorious days and cold nights. Winters are frigid, with snow blanketing the rim and shaded canyon walls from late November into April. The drive is open in winter to Gunnison Point Overlook only. Check with park headquarters in Montrose for information on road closures in winter.

To Gunnison Point

The drive begins 6 miles east of Montrose at the junction of U.S. Highway 50 and CO 347. Turn north on CO 347. The road climbs up dry Piñon Springs Draw, a shallow canyon carved into Mancos shale, a dark gray formation deposited in a quiet seaway some 75 million years ago during the Cretaceous period. The shale forms sharp, barren badlands on the flanks of the Uncompahgre Valley around Montrose and Delta. After 1.5 miles of climbing, the highway emerges onto a wide, level bench covered with green farm fields, before again steeply ascending slopes coated with piñon pine and juniper. Five miles from US 50 the road reaches Jones Summit on the crest of a rolling ridge between Piñon Springs and Jones Draws. The state highway ends here at the national park border and the drive becomes South Rim Road.

East Portal Road, a good side trip, begins just inside the park boundary. This 5-mile road winds east down steep slopes to **East Portal** on the canyon floor just upstream from the Black Canyon itself. East Portal, part of Curecanti National Recreation Area, offers camping, fishing, boating, picnicking, and a feel for the canyon's inner gorge. Vehicles with an overall length exceeding 22 feet are not allowed down this steep, switchbacked road.

The entrance station to 30,750-acre **Black Canyon of the Gunnison National Park** is 0.1 mile past the East Portal turn. The park, like most national park areas, is a fee area. The three-loop South Rim Campground, with eighty-

Looking down the depths of the Narrows, the narrowest part of the Black Canyon, from the North Rim.

eight campsites spread among a dense scrub oak woodland, lies just beyond the entrance at 8,320 feet. The campground, open April through October, operates on a first-come, first-served basis.

The drive heads north from the campground and after a mile reaches **Tomichi Point** and the first view of the Gunnison's stupendous chasm. Nothing prepares the first-time visitor for the inaccessibility and sheerness of the canyon. The road to this point has climbed and traversed rolling ridges, with distant peaks and low-slung mesas poking above the landscape. But here the land falls away into abrupt, sudden space. Broken side canyons, sweeps of menacing rock buttresses, and gullies and ledges mantled with fir trees fill the gorge below.

Gunnison Point Overlook and the park's visitor center are just down the road from Tomichi Point. The center displays the monument's geology, natural history, and human history, and provides information, maps, books, and daily ranger-led programs. Gunnison Point, sitting atop an erosion-resistant pegmatite dike, yields good views into the canyon's somber interior. Other pink pegmatite bands slice through the canyon walls across from Gunnison Point. Gneiss and schist, the softer metamorphic rocks that surround the pegmatite, weather more quickly and leave the resistant rock jutting into the canyon.

Black Canyon Geology

The Black Canyon's geologic story is divided into two chapters: the existing rocks and their history, and the Gunnison River's erosion of the canyon. Much of the exposed rock is gneiss and schist, metamorphic rocks originally deposited as layers of sand, silt, and mud on the floor of a primordial sea some two billion years ago. Intense heat and pressure later "metamorphosed," or transformed, the rock to its present contorted state. Molten magma, later injected into cracks and fissures in the gneiss and schist, slowly cooled into pegmatite, a coarse-grained igneous rock. Pegmatite forms the striking dikes and bands that criss-cross the canyon walls, particularly the Painted Wall. Other large magma bodies intruded into the metamorphic bedrock and form quartz monzonite, a hard, granitelike rock found on the sheer walls at Chasm View.

Time and the flowing river created the Black Canyon. The canyon, a recent topographic feature, is between two and three million years old. Its story, however, began with the uplift of the Rocky Mountains sixty million years ago. As the mountains slowly rose, erosion tackled them with glaciers, chiseling at the high peaks and snowmelt-laden rivers, including the ancestral Gunnison, carving into the uplift in western Colorado. Volcanism in the West Elk Range to the north and the San Juan Mountains to the south also affected the course of the Gunnison River by channeling it between narrow highlands. The river, cutting through layers of volcanic ash and sedimentary rock, established a course atop the buried metamorphic basement rock. By the time volcanism ceased, the Gunnison was firmly entrenched in its bedrock canyon.

The Gunnison River, Colorado's fourth-largest river, originates on the Continental Divide far to the east of the Black Canyon. West of the town of Gunnison it drops into the 50-mile-long Black Canyon before emerging in the Uncompahgre Valley near Delta. Three dams—Blue Mesa, Morrow Point, and Crystal—impound the river water in the upper canyon for flood control, water storage, recreation, and electric power. Below Crystal Lake the Gunnison plunges 12 miles through its narrow canyon in the national park, before entering Gunnison Gorge, its lower canyon. The Gunnison River has one of the nation's steepest river gradients, dropping 2,150 feet from the canyon head at Sapinero (now under Blue Mesa Reservoir) to its North Fork junction—an average fall of 43 feet per mile. By contrast the Green River drops only 12 feet a mile in Dinosaur National Monument. In the national monument below the scenic drive, the Gunnison's average gradient is 95 feet a mile. But in the 2 miles from Pulpit Rock to Chasm View it descends an astounding 480 feet. That steep gradient, combined with the abrasion of tumbling boulders on its riverbed, gives the Gunnison a sharp cutting edge. Geologists estimate the river deepens the canyon about 1 inch every century.

Pulpit Rock, Chasm View, and the Painted Wall

Past the visitor center the drive heads northeast, following the rim's contours. Dense thickets of Gambel or scrub oak line the road, with occasional open meadows. Other shrubs mix in the pygmy woodland, including serviceberry and mountain mahogany, a favorite deer food. Mule deer flourish along the canyon rim. Keen eyes can sight them in roadside meadows and near the campground. Other mammals include porcupines, marmots, rock and ground squirrels, coyotes, gray foxes, and bobcats. Mountain lion, black bear, bighorn sheep, and elk occasionally wander through.

The road reaches **Pulpit Rock Overlook** 2 miles from the visitor center. The viewpoint offers a good view of the V-shaped upper canyon and Pulpit Rock, a semidetached pinnacle. The Rim House, operated by a private concessionaire, sells snacks and souvenirs. The canyon narrows past Pulpit Rock, and a series of overlooks scattered along the drive yield excellent views. Cross Fissures View, Rock Point, and Devils Lookout all perch atop the canyon rim and are reached by short trails from the drive. **Chasm View,** the park's most spectacular and airy overlook, sits a mile past Devils Lookout. The cliffs fall abruptly away from the overlook railings to the river 1,800 feet below. North Chasm View Wall dominates the canyon here, its gray bulk seamed with cracks and fissures. The opposite North Rim stands only 1,100 feet across the abyss from the viewpoint, yet by car it's 82 miles away. Upstream lies The Narrows. Towering cliffs hem the river into a cleft only 40 feet wide, forming the most forbidding section of this canyon.

At Chasm View the road swings south and begins climbing toward High Point. Painted Wall View sits 0.1 mile past Chasm View. This point offers views of the **Painted Wall,** Colorado's highest cliff, with a 2,240-foot vertical rise from base to rim. Numerous pink pegmatite bands slash across the wall. Cedar Point and Dragon Point, the next two stops, also offer outstanding views of the Painted Wall. A short nature trail wanders out to Cedar Point, with typical rim plants identified along the path.

The Black Canyon's rims once offered the nomadic Utes cool summer camps and plentiful game and edible plants. The Utes, however, rarely entered the precipitous canyon and called the depths *Tomichi,* or "Land of cliffs and water." Captain John Gunnison first explored the canyon region and river now bearing his name on an 1853 railroad survey. Shortly afterward Gunnison was killed by Indians in western Utah. The canyon itself was first traversed in 1901 by William Torrance and A. L. Fellows on a water survey expedition. The duo endured nine days and seventy-two river crossings before climbing out of the canyon. Fellows described the trek: "Our surroundings were of the wildest possible description. The roar of the water falls was constantly in our ears, and the walls of the canyon, towering half mile in height above us, were seemingly vertical. Occasionally a rock would fall from one side or the other, with a roar and crash, exploding like a ton of dynamite when it struck bottom, making us think our last day had come."

Warner Point and High Point

The road continues ascending gentle slopes past **Dragon Point** and soon reaches **Sunset View.** This viewpoint, with a small picnic area, looks down-canyon into Gunnison Gorge. This lower canyon, composed of softer rocks, is wider and lower than the monument's narrow abyss. More erosion has widened the gorge, and the Gunnison River's gradient drops to 35 feet per mile. A mile farther lies 8,289-foot **High Point** and the drive's turnaround point. Douglas fir, mixed with piñon pine and juniper, blanket this lofty ridge and spill down the canyon side. A 0.6-mile trail heads west from here to **Warner Point.** The point, the south rim's highest spot, is named for Reverend Mark Warner, who pushed the canyon's designation as a national park. Warner Point yields great vistas of the surrounding land. Southward stretch the snow-capped San Juan Mountains and Mount Sneffels; Grand Mesa's dark bulk lingers to the northwest; and the pointed West Elk Range forms a jagged horizon to the northeast. This privileged view, reserved for those who walk out here, forms a fitting end to this short but spectacular scenic drive.

Opposite: High Point at the end of the South Rim drive yields a spectacular view into wild Gunnison Gorge.

Unaweep–Tabeguache Scenic and Historic Byway

Whitewater to Placerville

General description: This 133-mile-long drive traverses western Colorado's lonely plateau country, threading through Unaweep Canyon and following canyons along the Dolores and San Miguel Rivers.

Special attractions: Unaweep Canyon, Taylor Quarry Overlook, Driggs Mansion, Thimble Rock, Palisade Wilderness Study Area, Dolores Canyon, Sewemup Wilderness Study Area, The Hanging Flume, Norwood, San Miguel Canyon, rock climbing, camping, hiking, fishing, scenic views, historic sites, Indian rock art, rafting.

Location: Western Colorado. The drive begins at Whitewater on US 50 just south of Grand Junction and ends in Placerville 25 miles west of Ridgway.

Drive route name and numbers: Unaweep–Tabeguache Scenic and Historic Byway, CO 141 and 145.

Travel season: Year-round.

Camping: No established campgrounds lie along the drive. Primitive camping is allowed, however, on adjoining Bureau of Land Management public land. The BLM's Dominguez Campground, reached via the Divide Road from CO 141 in Unaweep Canyon, offers shaded campsites above Big Dominguez Creek. A national forest campground sits farther south on Divide Road.

Services: All services are found in Grand Junction, Naturita, Nucla, Norwood, and Placerville. Limited services in Gateway.

Nearby attractions: Colorado National Monument, Grand Mesa, Lands End Road, La Sal Mountains, Black Ridge Wilderness Study Area, Dominguez Canyon Wilderness Study Area, Uncompahgre Plateau, Divide Road, Dry Mesa Dinosaur Quarry, Canyonlands National Park (Utah), Mount Sneffels Wilderness Area, Lizard Head Wilderness Area, Telluride National Historic District, Dallas Divide, San Juan Skyway All-American Byway (see Drive 23), Ouray.

The Drive

The 133-mile-long Unaweep–Tabeguache Scenic and Historic Byway threads across the splendid Colorado Plateau country along the western fringe of the Uncompahgre Plateau. It unveils a remote, hidden landscape along a couple of off-the-beaten-track state highways, exploring wondrous Unaweep Canyon and the harshly eroded canyons of the Dolores and San Miguel Rivers. The drive passes precipitous granite cliffs and sandstone battlements, twists along dusky red rivers, and crosses a land rich in prehistoric geology.

Mild weather dominates along the drive year-round. The highways run over high desert country, characterized by sparse precipitation, hot summers, and

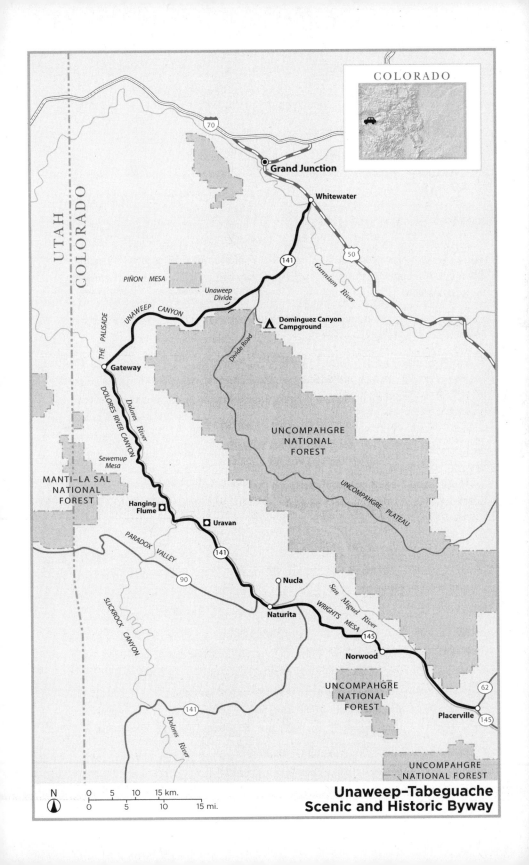

70

Grand Junction

Whitewater

141

50

PIÑON MESA

Unaweep Divide

UNAWEEP CANYON

Gunnison River

▲ **Dominguez Canyon Campground**

THE PALISADE

Divide Road

Gateway

DOLORES RIVER CANYON

Dolores River

UNCOMPAHGRE NATIONAL FOREST

Sewemup Mesa

UNCOMPAHGRE PLATEAU

MANTI–LA SAL NATIONAL FOREST

Hanging Flume

□ **Uravan**

141

PARADOX VALLEY

90

○ **Nucla**

San Miguel River

Naturita

WRIGHTS MESA

SLICKROCK CANYON

145

Norwood

62

141

UNCOMPAHGRE NATIONAL FOREST

Dolores River

Placerville

145

UNCOMPAHGRE NATIONAL FOREST

UTAH

COLORADO

N

| 0 | 5 | 10 | 15 km. |
| 0 | 5 | 10 | 15 mi. |

**Unaweep-Tabeguache
Scenic and Historic Byway**

short, chilly winters. Occasional thunderstorms rumble through in summer, with most of the rain dousing the drive's higher elevations in Unaweep Canyon and near Norwood. Expect hot summer temperatures, with daily highs in the nineties along the rivers. Higher-elevation temperatures are cooler, but can still reach into the eighties. Autumn, beginning in late September and running to early November, offers pleasant drive weather. Days are usually clear and warm with only occasional rainstorms. Winter begins in November and ends by March in the lower elevations. Snow blankets Unaweep Canyon, Wrights Mesa, and the shady slopes in the San Miguel Canyon in winter but otherwise quickly melts away under the warm sun. Days are cool with highs generally between thirty and fifty degrees, and nights are cold. Spring creeps onto the plateau in late March, with dry, windy weather punctuated by occasional rain, sleet, and snowstorms. The weather begins warming in April, and May brings wildflowers and grass to the sere lowlands.

Unaweep Canyon

The drive begins 15 miles south of Grand Junction at the intersection of U.S. Highway 50 and CO 141 at **Whitewater.** Turn west on CO 141. The drive's first leg runs 44 miles west through **Unaweep Canyon** to Gateway and the Dolores River Canyon. The paved road swings over the Gunnison River after 0.25 mile, crosses a cornfield on the river floodplain, and turns west up a shallow canyon. East Creek trickles through cottonwoods on the canyon floor. Piñon pine and junipers scatter over the dry, rocky slopes above.

East Creek, beginning on Unaweep Divide in Unaweep Canyon, cuts east through upturned rock layers on the edge of the Uncompahgre Plateau. The Uncompahgre Plateau, a broad, flattened highland crested with dense forests and meadows, stretches northwest from the San Juan Mountains to the Grand Valley and the Colorado River. The plateau reaches heights of 10,000 feet. Numerous canyons crease the 25-mile-wide uplift, slicing deeply through sandstone layers that drape over its Precambrian basement rocks. The plateau's most dramatic canyons lie in Colorado National Monument's northern end and Unaweep and Dominguez Canyons in its midsection.

Lower Unaweep Canyon slowly widens as the highway climbs west. After 3 miles the road swings away from the creek and begins ascending a tilted bench on the south canyon slope. Dakota sandstone, forming a long tawny band of cliff, rims the canyon. Immense boulders tumble down slopes above the highway. As the road climbs, the creek cuts deeply into soft shale layers, forming an abrupt canyon below. After 8 miles the highway reaches **Grand Valley Overlook,** a dramatic viewpoint that peers north to the Book Cliffs and the Grand Valley and east to imposing basalt-rimmed Grand Mesa, the largest flat-topped mountain in the

CO 141 swings through cliff-lined Unaweep Canyon, a geologic mystery on the Unaweep – Tabeguache drive.

world. Portions of the first stage and wagon route to Gateway thread along the bouldery slopes north of East Creek below the overlook.

The 6-mile highway section from the canyon's lower gate to Grand Valley Overlook ascends Ninemile Hill. The highway roughly follows an old Ute Indian trail that later became "Uranium Road," the only route that connected Grand Junction's processing mill with uranium mines along the Dolores River. In the early 1900s, teamsters used the trail up Ninemile Hill to carry mail and supplies to Gateway and several now-abandoned mining camps in Unaweep Canyon. This long hill offered vicious 18 percent grades that required doubled horse teams. When autos began using the winding shelf road, passengers usually walked ahead to lighten the load and warn the driver of oncoming traffic, as the track was too narrow for two vehicles. The road was widened and improved in the 1930s for trucks hauling uranium. It finally was paved in 1958.

The canyon widens and flattens past the overlook, with tall cottonwoods and willow thickets lining the creek. Low sandstone cliffs and slopes covered with piñon pine and juniper stairstep back to a high rim. A mile past the overlook a dirt road heads south to Cactus Park. This dry, open valley, flanked by low hogbacks, was the channel of the ancestral Gunnison River between one and five million years ago. The Gunnison Gravels Natural Research Area, 0.5 mile south of the drive, protects these ancient river deposits. As the drive runs west, the sandstone walls are replaced by cliffs of Precambrian metamorphic rock, the basement rock layer of the Uncompahgre Plateau. Unaweep Canyon's granite and metamorphic rocks, dated between 1.4 and 1.7 billion years old, are among Colorado's oldest exposed rocks. Some 300 million years ago the plateau was the site of "Uncompahgria," an ancestral Rocky Mountain range. Over ensuing millennia the range weathered down to its bedrock roots, and its eroded cobbles, gravels, and sands were deposited to the west, forming today's canyon country layers. Later sandstone was deposited on the old bedrock, forming the "Great Unconformity," with some 500 million years of geologic history missing.

Two abandoned towns sit near the drive at Nancy Hanks Gulch. Copper City and Pearl City both began in 1897 with the discovery of copper, gold, and silver in Unaweep Canyon. Both quickly flourished with populations of about 100 each. Copper City took the lead, building two schools, stores, and cabins. Pearl City, however, kept the rustic look, and in its seventeen-year existence remained a community of tents. The Pearl City Hotel offered the town's deluxe accommodations, with three tents joined together. No permanent structures were ever erected. Area fortunes sagged after a 1901 mining downturn, but the pair lingered on. Pearl City folded up its tents in 1912 and Copper City followed suit in 1914. Nothing remains of either today, save a few old photographs.

As the drive heads west the canyon deepens. Rosy sandstone caps the dark gray bedrock along the sidewalls. The creek becomes entrenched in a deep arroyo filled with reeds, cattails, tall grass, and cottonwoods. Broad ranches with grazing cattle and wide hayfields grace the flat valley floor, offering a pastoral counterpoint to the rugged walls. **Divide Road** begins just past a ranch. This gravel road twists more than 100 miles down the spine of the Uncompaghre Plateau, giving access to a vast swath of remote backcountry. Take a left turn here for a short drive up Divide Road to a stunning viewpoint above Unaweep Canyon. The gravel road climbs a couple of miles up to the site of abandoned Taylor Granite Quarry, a rock quarry that operated in 1928. Park and walk down to the cliff edge for one of western Colorado's most spectacular overlooks.

Unaweep Canyon stretches westward. The highway below uncoils like a long snake up the sagebrush valley floor. Gentle slopes, forested with scrub oak, piñon pine, and juniper, slant upward to abrupt, towering granite cliffs. Above, steep slopes lean back to the valley's sandstone rim high above the floor. Unaweep Canyon, slashing across the entire Uncompahgre Plateau, is a unique canyon. The U-shaped canyon is supposedly the only canyon in the world drained by two creeks. A divide in midcanyon separates the East Creek and West Creek drainages. (The Ute Indian name Unaweep means "Canyon with Two Mouths.") This deep canyon's formation has long been a geological enigma. Geologists agree the two small streams in today's canyon could not have chiseled the deep chasm, leading to several theories that explain its origin. Some say it was carved along a massive fault line, while others argue that glaciation alone excavated the gorge. The most credible explanation concludes that the canyon was the ancestral river bed of the Gunnison and Colorado Rivers. The Colorado River drained southward from Debeque Canyon through Unaweep Canyon and the Uncompahgre Plateau before an eroding tributary breached a divide northwest of the plateau and diverted the river flow into today's Grand Valley. This action, called stream piracy, left Unaweep Canyon high and dry.

The drive continues west up the canyon past steel gray cliffs seamed by black water streaks. The cliffs, ranging up to 500 feet high, offer excellent rock climbing on steep faces and cracks. Popular crags include the Quarry Wall just past Divide Road, and Mothers Buttress, Television Wall, and Sunday Wall farther west on the canyon's north slopes. The American Alpine Club's Access Fund owns sixty-one acres of the canyon to preserve access to the more popular crags. Otherwise, almost all the canyon floor is privately owned.

Unaweep Divide to Gateway

Unaweep Divide, a broad 7,048-foot saddle in midcanyon, separates East and West Creeks. Past the divide the highway begins gently dipping west, running through fields of grass and sagebrush. Several shallow lakes dot the canyon floor.

Look for Fall Creek Waterfall plunging off a cliff 3 miles west of the divide. The falls is on private land.

The highway drops past **Thimble Rock,** a prominent pyramid towering south of the blacktop. Ledges studded with tall trees interrupt the rock's steep cliffs. The stone ruin of Driggs Mansion sits just off the highway in the morning shadow of Thimble Rock. Lawrence K. Driggs, a wealthy New York lawyer, constructed this huge mansion between 1914 and 1918. Masons, using sandstone blocks cut from nearby Mayflower Canyon, carefully built the eight-room house, including a stone arch that mirrors an arch on Thimble Rock. The mansion boasted chandeliers and hand-carved stone mantles above the fireplaces. Despite its expensive construction, no existing record verifies the house was ever occupied. The building was acquired as a hunting lodge and named Chateau Thimblerock. It later became part of the Craig Ranch. The badly vandalized house, on private property, remains a weathered outpost of graceful opulence.

The road continues down the valley through Gill Meadows and bends through a rock portal. The canyon widens as it descends, with broken granite crags scattered on the steep mountainsides above. The southern canyon walls and the plateau beyond lies in Ute Creek Wilderness Study Area, a 44,000-acre proposed wilderness of canyons and mesas blanketed with piñon pine, juniper, aspen, fir, and spruce forest. The northern canyon walls from here west to Gateway are part of the remote 26,738-acre Palisade Wilderness Study Area. The northern slopes step almost 4,000 feet above the canyon floor to high mesa tops.

After 40 miles the canyon begins to narrow, its walls steepen, and the drive reaches **Unaweep Seep,** a collection of springs percolating from hillsides northwest of West Creek. Unaweep Seep offers an astounding diversity of plant and animal life. This unusual ecosystem, preserved as a registered Colorado Natural Area, displays numerous wildflowers as well as box elder, alder, smooth sumac, blackberry, and ground cherry. The fifty-five-acre site also protects the rare Nokomis Fritillary butterfly. This endangered butterfly, with orange 4-inch wings, is gorgeous as it flutters across the wet meadow. The Unaweep colony is seen from mid-July to early September. Other fauna inhabiting the canyon and surrounding mesas include mountain lion, black bear, elk, mule deer, and many small mammals. A roadside interpretive sign explains Unaweep Seep.

Past the seep the canyon pinches inward. The creek dashes over worn cobbles and boulders below rocky ridges and granite buttresses. The highway twists through the canyon and passes West Creek Picnic Area. This site, sitting in West Creek Narrows, offers picnic tables shaded by cottonwoods. A sign displays area riparian habitats. The road sharply curves through the canyon, and after 1.5 miles crosses the **Uncompahgre Fault.** The scenery abruptly changes after crossing the fault. The fault vertically displaces some 8,000 feet of rock, and the drive passes from the ancient bedrock to easily eroded sandstones in the Paradox Basin.

The canyon ends at the fault, and the highway runs west down a broad, shallow valley. Soft mudstone slopes climb upward to high, vertical cliffs of Wingate sandstone. The La Sal Mountains, a laccolithic mountain range in Utah, towers to the west above carved canyons and mesas. Immense old cottonwoods spread over the creek along the road.

The blacktop gently drops and enters 4,595-foot-high **Gateway,** the lowest town by altitude on Colorado's Western Slope. Gateway, established in 1890, sits at the canyon gateway on an old Ute trail. Settlers built cabins, irrigated fields with ditches full of Dolores River water, planted orchards, and ran cattle over the dry mesas. The first road reached Gateway in 1906, and the first bridge spanned the river in 1912. Electricity finally came to town in 1952, but long-distance telephone service wasn't available until 1965. Gateway boomed with uranium mining in the 1940s and 1950s. Today it's a quiet garden spot on the edge of the wilderness. The town offers a few services including a store, gasoline, and a town park with shaded picnic tables and rest rooms. The Palisade, an immense fin of salmon-colored Wingate sandstone capped with Kayenta sandstone, looms above scree and boulder slopes north of Gateway. The Palisade, part of a proposed wilderness area, also lies in the BLM's 14,000-acre Palisade Outstanding Natural Area.

Gateway to Naturita

The next drive segment runs 52 miles from Gateway to Naturita along the Dolores and San Miguel Rivers. The highway crosses the **Dolores River** and bends south in the river canyon. The 230-mile-long Dolores River begins high in the San Miguel Range near Lizard Head Pass, runs southwest to Dolores, and arcs north through a series of deep canyons along the western edge of the Uncompahgre Plateau to Gateway. Here it bends northwest, enters Utah, and empties into the Colorado River.

The highway runs south along a wide canyon floor. The river loops in broad, chocolate-colored meanders and riffles over gravel bars. Tamarisk trees, an Asian import, and occasional cottonwoods line the sandy riverbank. The canyon slopes rise above in a series of steplike benches to a castellated rampart of ruddy Wingate sandstone that forms an unbroken palisade. Ten miles south of Gateway the road passes a dirt track that bumps west up Salt Creek to Sinbad Valley, a salt basin that reminded early miners of Sinbad the Sailor's Valley of Diamonds from *A Thousand and One Nights.* Past the turn the canyon narrows, with the river and highway making great horseshoe loops beneath immense red and black cliffs. **Sewemup Mesa,** a 19,140-acre proposed wilderness area, hems in the canyon on the west. This huge mesa, isolated by towering cliff bands, preserves a pristine high desert ecosystem. The mesa acquired its unusual name from the McCarty Gang's cattle rustling operation. The outlaws brought stolen cattle here, cut off the old brands, sewed up the wounded hide, and rebranded the cattle with their own iron.

As the canyon narrows the Wingate cliffs begin dipping into the river. The highway makes graceful loops along the glassy river through this spectacular canyon section. Past Rock Creek, the southern end of Sewemup Mesa, and its fertile hayfields and cottonwoods the road makes one more grand horseshoe bend and exits the narrow gorge.

The canyon widens and the drive passes Mesa Creek and the Lone Tree Placer Gravels. The gravels, washed from ore-bearing deposits high in the San Juan Mountains, attracted prospectors with their glittering gold in 1887. These placer miners hauled the gravels by wheelbarrows, chutes, and wagons down to the river's edge, where they could be washed in machines. The highest bench held the most riches, said knowledgeable miners, but it was too far from the river to be profitable and the technology to pump water uphill did not yet exist. Engineers designed and built a 6-mile ditch and 7-mile hanging flume to carry upstream water to the placer site. The highway climbs south on a broad bench, passes a coke oven used by blacksmiths during the flume's construction, edges under a sweeping band of rosy Entrada sandstone, and reaches the Hanging Flume Overlook.

The Unaweep–Tabeguache Scenic Byway follows the Dolores River through palisades of Wingate sandstone in broad Dolores Canyon.

The Hanging Flume, a National Engineering Landmark, clings to Wingate sandstone walls in the Dolores River Canyon below. The flume, constructed from 1889 to 1891, snakes along the cliffs 100 to 150 feet above the river. The flume, 6-feet wide and 4-feet deep, used 1.8 million feet of lumber, cost over $100,000, carried eighty million gallons of water a day to the mine, and turned out to be an engineering marvel. The mine, however, turned out to be a total bust. Most of the gold was unrecoverable leaf gold, and the St. Louis–based mining company closed the mine in 1893 after turning an $80,000 profit on a $1 million investment. Area ranches stripped some of the flume, reusing the lumber for fences, cabins, and ranch buildings.

The highway continues south on a broad bench above the river canyon and after a mile swings east. A short dirt track bumps south to the confluence of the Dolores and San Miguel Rivers. The rivers merge far below in a crimson-colored gorge flanked by sandstone cliffs. The drive bends southeast and follows the edge of the San Miguel Canyon. A wave of Entrada sandstone overhangs the asphalt. The canyon broadens and the road reaches the now-abandoned town site of **Uravan.** The town, its name a contraction of uranium and vanadium, sprang up in 1936 as a company town for U.S. Vanadium Corporation, part of Union Carbide. Area mines yielded rich deposits of yellow carnotite, with radium, vanadium, and uranium ores. Vanadium, used to harden steel, was mined during both world wars, while uranium, recovered from mill tailings, went to the Manhattan Project in World War II to develop the world's first nuclear weapons. Only the mill ruins remain today on the old Club Ranch property, stair-stepping up the hillside above settling ponds. The town, its houses, stores, post office, and school have vanished. Everything was removed during environmental reclamation because of radioactive contamination.

The drive runs southeast along the San Miguel River in a broad, picturesque canyon. Steep slopes rise in steplike benches dark with piñon pine and juniper, each rimmed with sandstone strata. Dakota sandstone forms a prominent battlement atop the canyon rim, its cliffs creased with cracks. Huge boulders cascade down steep slopes above the road. Fourteen miles from Uravan the highway intersects CO 90, which heads west up the Paradox Valley to Utah. A roadside monument here commemorates the passage of Franciscan priests Francisco Dominguez and Silvestre Escalante, who explored this area in 1776 in search of an easy route to the California missions from New Mexico.

Naturita perches on terraced benches a couple of miles up the highway. Naturita Creek and this small 5,431-foot-high town, established in 1882 as a ranching and mining supply center, were named by pioneer settler "Grandma" Rockwood Blake with a Spanish word meaning "close to nature." Five miles north is **Nucla,** a utopian agricultural community founded in 1896 as a communal experiment by the Colorado Cooperative Company.

Norwood and Placerville

The highway leaves the San Miguel River just west of Naturita and bends up Naturita Creek's shallow canyon. CO 141 intersects CO 145 in the canyon. The drive continues southeast on CO 145. Past the junction the highway climbs onto **Wrights Mesa,** a long, flattened tableland between Naturita Creek and the San Miguel River Canyon.

Majestic views of the snowcapped San Juan Mountains spread away from the highway. The San Miguel Range looms to the south; Mount Sneffels studs the southeastern horizon; the Uncompahgre Plateau lifts its whiskered flanks to the east; and Utah's La Sal Mountains pierce the northwestern sky. The highway runs across the fertile mesa top, passing lush paddocks filled with grazing cattle and horses and green hay fields. The road passes Redvale, a small town founded in 1910 by an orchard company. Its high elevation coupled with a short growing season doomed the orchards.

Norwood lies 9 miles up the highway. This genuine Western community, named for a Missouri town by founder I. M. Copp in 1885, serves as a supply hub for area ranchers and farmers. The town offers all visitor services.

Past Norwood the highway crosses fields, enters a piñon woodland, and drops onto the lip of the San Miguel River's deep canyon. The road twists 2 miles down Norwood Hill to the canyon floor, passing a couple of scenic overlooks. The drive's last 12 miles wind along the river to **Placerville.** Much of the canyon's diverse riparian habitat is preserved in the 279-acre San Miguel River Canyon Preserve, one of three local preserves owned and managed by The Nature Conservancy. This lush riverside environment, one of Colorado's last undisturbed, mid-elevation riparian areas, is rich in plant and animal life.

The San Miguel River, falling over 8,000 feet in 80 miles from its mountain headwaters to the Dolores River, tumbles over cobbles and boulders. Tall cottonwoods and willow thickets clot its grassy banks. Cliff bands, punctuated by steep slopes dense with Gambel oak, piñon pine, fir, spruce, and pine, stretch along the canyon walls. The drive quietly ends at Placerville, an old placer mining town, at the junction of CO 145 and 62. CO 145, part of the San Juan Skyway, continues up the canyon 15 miles to Telluride, while CO 62 climbs east over scenic Dallas Divide to Ridgway.

28

Mesa Verde National Park Scenic Drive

Mesa Verde National Park

General description: This drive runs 21 miles across mesa tops and canyons in Mesa Verde National Park to the park museum. Ruins Road, formed by two additional 6-mile-long self-guiding loops, explores the cliffed cities and remains of the Anasazi culture on Chapin Mesa.

Special attractions: Mesa Verde National Park, Far View Visitor Center, Mesa Verde Museum, Far View Ruin, Cedar Tree Tower, Spruce Tree House, Cliff Palace, Balcony House, Long House, Step House, Badger House, pithouse and pueblo ruins, Spruce Canyon and Petroglyph Point Trails, panoramic overlooks, hiking, camping, interpretive programs, guided tours.

Location: Far southwestern Colorado. The drive begins 10 miles east of Cortez on US 160. Durango is 30 miles east on US 160.

Drive route name: Ruins Road.

Travel season: Year-round. The park and drive are open all year. Many services are curtailed from November to the end of April. The Ruins Road loop drive is open 8:00 a.m. to sunset and the museum is open 8:00 a.m. to 5:00 p.m. daily in winter. Check for times of off-season tours of Spruce Tree House and Cliff Palace. Expect hazardous road conditions during and after snowstorms. Ice lingers on shaded corners on the road's upper elevations.

Camping: Morfield Campground, operated by a private concessionaire, generally is open early May through mid-October. The 435-site campground, spread across Morfield Canyon, is 4 miles south of the park entrance. The campground offers tables, fireplaces, comfort stations, trailer dumping stations, and summer evening programs.

Services: Services, including supplies, groceries, gasoline, laundromat, and showers, are found in Morfield Campground between May and October. Far View has a gas station, restaurant, cafeteria, gift shop, and lodge. There are complete visitor services in Cortez and Mancos.

Nearby attractions: Wetherill Mesa, Ute Mountain Tribal Park, Sleeping Ute Mountain, Cortez, Four Corners Monument, Hovenweep National Monument, Anasazi Heritage Center, Escalante Ruins, McPhee Reservoir, Dolores River Canyon, Mancos State Park, La Plata Mountains, San Juan National Forest, Durango, San Juan Scenic Skyway All-American Byway (see Drive 23), Durango and Silverton Narrow Gauge Railroad.

The Drive

Anasazi, a Navajo word meaning "the ancient ones" or "enemy ancestors," describes a loose aggregate of Indian cultures that once inhabited the Colorado Plateau province in northern New Mexico and Arizona, southern Utah, and southwestern Colorado. Sharp, unfinished edges fill the plateau's distinctive

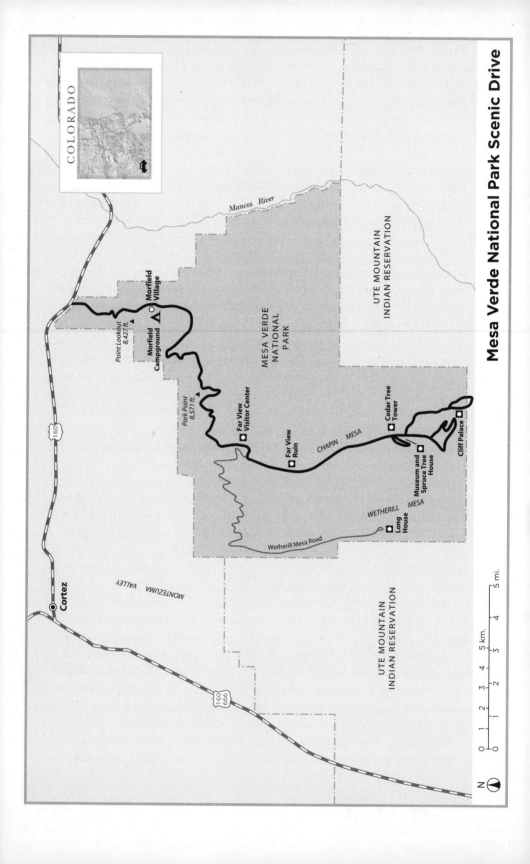

Mesa Verde National Park Scenic Drive

COLORADO

Mancos River

UTE MOUNTAIN
INDIAN RESERVATION

Morfield Village

Point Lookout
8,427 ft.

Morfield
Campground

MESA VERDE
NATIONAL
PARK

Park Point
8,571 ft.

Far View
Visitor Center

Far View
Ruin

CHAPIN   MESA

Cedar Tree
Tower

Museum and
Spruce Tree
House

Cliff Palace

WETHERILL   MESA

Long
House

Wetherill Mesa Road

MONTEZUMA   VALLEY

Cortez

UTE MOUNTAIN
INDIAN RESERVATION

160

160
666

0   1   2   3   4   5 km.

0   1   2   3   4   5 mi.

N

landscapes. It's a harsh land of sandstone sliced by deep canyons and arroyos, lorded over by towering mesas and buttes, and traversed by rivers of history and character. Sparse rainfall, a fierce temperature range, and a storm of sunlight dictate the plateau's environment and, in turn, shaped the destiny and cultures of the peoples who have lived here over the last 10,000 years.

The Anasazi, one of southwest America's three main cultural groups, developed, flourished, and vanished centuries before Columbus set foot in the New World. The hallmark trait of the Anasazi are the great stone cities built during their "classic" era almost 1,000 years ago. The Anasazi erected massive, above-ground pueblos like those seen today at their descendants' villages in Taos, Acoma, and Hopiland. They also built pueblos nestled under the protective eaves of immense caves.

Mesa Verde National Park preserves these startling cliff towns, and the 33-mile-long Mesa Verde scenic drive explores and interprets this lost world of the Anasazi. The 52,000-acre national park, established in 1906, protects more than 4,000 prehistoric sites, including almost 600 cliff dwellings.

Mesa Verde made an ideal place for human habitation. More rain falls on this highland than in surrounding lowland valleys, and its gentle tilt to the south keeps winter temperatures moderate. Rainfall on the semiarid mesa averages 18 inches a year, with the bulk of that coming in the 80 to 100 inches of annual winter snow. A long, 171-day frost-free growing season ensured good summer crops for the Anasazi farmers.

Expect cold, snowy winters and warm, dry summers when visiting the national park. Daily highs during the busy season, June through September, reach into the eighties and nineties. Thunderstorms often occur on July and August afternoons. Winters at Mesa Verde are a delight, with low visitation and clear, cold days. The road's upper elevations can be snow-packed and icy, particularly in shaded areas. Spring brings warm, breezy days and occasional rain, sleet, and snow.

Point Lookout and Morfield Canyon

The drive begins 10 miles east of Cortez on US 160. Exit south to Mesa Verde National Park. The paved road runs south up a shallow draw bordered by shale hills studded with piñon pines and junipers. A trailer parking area sits alongside the road. Because of the narrow, winding road, no trailers are permitted past Morfield Campground. Visitors not camping are required to leave their rigs here. The park entrance station is reached after a mile. Entrance fees are paid here and park information is dispensed.

The road continues south and begins switchbacking upward under 8,427-foot **Point Lookout,** an abrupt, cliff-lined promontory. This airy lookout, reached via a 2.3-mile trail from Morfield Campground, marks Mesa Verde's northernmost point. Mesa Verde, Spanish for "Green Table," lifts sharply from the Montezuma Valley in southwestern Colorado. The high plateau, bordered by sheer cliffs and precipitous shale slopes, forms a natural fortress. Only the Mancos River, following a sinuous canyon, penetrates the lofty sandstone barrier. Mesa Verde is a textbook example of what geologists call a cuesta—a tilted mesa with a steep escarpment on one side and a gently dipping slope on the other. Deep canyons, draining southward to the Mancos River, dissect Mesa Verde between long finger-like mesas laden with fertile, windblown soil deposits.

Past Point Lookout the road swings onto the mesa's east flank, edging south high above the Mancos Valley. This road section crosses gray Mancos shale, a 2,000-foot-thick layer of consolidated mud deposited sixty-five million years ago in a quiet, shallow sea. The shale weathers into the towering badlands that dominate Mesa Verde's steep edges. The formation, which swells and contracts with moisture, is prone to landslides and subsidence. The road here has been erased and closed several times by landslides. The area above the road has since been reworked and anchored to avoid future problems.

Above the Mancos shale lies the Mesa Verde Group. Three distinct formations—Point Lookout sandstone, the Menefee Formation, and Cliff House sandstone—compose this grouping of rock layers. Both the Point Lookout and Cliff House sandstones are cliff-forming units laid down as shoreline sand deposits as the Mancos Sea alternately retreated and advanced. Point Lookout sandstone forms the massive ramparts above the drive's first miles, while the Cliff House sandstone caps the mesa's interior canyons and provides the open alcoves used by the Anasazi. The easily eroded Menefee Formation, squeezed between the two sandstones, resulted from silt and sand being deposited in swampy marshes and lagoons along an ancient shoreline.

The **Mancos Valley Overlook** sits near the end of the shelf road. A great panorama spreads out beyond this lofty viewpoint. Below spreads the broad Mancos Valley, divided by ranches and green pastures. At its head sits the town of Mancos and above loom the La Plata Mountains, a small, ragged range topped by 13,232-foot Hesperus Mountain.

Past the overlook the drive bends through a saddle and enters Morfield Canyon 4 miles from the park entrance. This wide canyon, rimmed by low cliffs and fringed by scrub oak–covered slopes, houses most of the park's visitor services. **Morfield Village** offers a laundry, gas station, refreshment center, store with supplies and souvenirs, and coin-operated showers. Morfield Campground, operated by a concessionaire from May to October, boasts 435 campsites, seventeen group sites, and four handicap-accessible sites. Camping, available on a first-come, first-served basis, is limited to fourteen days. Evening campfire programs are presented nightly June through Labor Day in the Morfield Amphitheatre.

The Morfield Campground area also offers excellent hiking trails. Hiking is limited to only a few areas in Mesa Verde National Park to protect the park's unique archaeological treasures. Visitors hiking away from developed areas and off designated trails are subject to stiff penalties. Three trails roam the Morfield area. The 1.5-mile Knife Edge Trail follows the old road from the campground to the Montezuma Valley Overlook. The 2.3-mile Point Lookout Trail treks out to the point's precipitous edge and yields spectacular views. The 7.8-mile Prater Ridge Trail climbs west from the campground onto lofty Prater Ridge.

The North Rim and Park Point

The drive drops down, crosses Morfield Canyon, and enters a 0.25-mile-long tunnel through Prater Ridge. After exiting the tunnel the road climbs up upper Prater Canyon to 7,820-foot-high **Montezuma Valley Overlook.** Look for mule deer grazing on the canyon floor, particularly in early evening. The viewpoint, with picnic tables and ramadas, looks west across the Montezuma Valley. Numerous farms and ranches dot the valley around Cortez, one of southwest Colorado's largest towns. Beyond tower 9,977-foot Ute Peak and Sleeping Ute Mountain, a small laccolithic range formed when intrusive volcanic rock blistered up through the surrounding sedimentary strata.

The road winds south from the overlook, ascending steep slopes covered with scrub oaks, piñon pines, and occasional Douglas firs. For the next 9 miles the road follows the **North Rim** of Mesa Verde, climbing over high ridges, dipping across shallow canyon heads, and edging along steep slopes that plunge down to the Montezuma Valley. These upper elevations are heavily forested. Gambel or scrub oak heavily coats the hillsides, and Douglas fir, ponderosa pine, and even quaking aspen tuck into cool, moist ravines. Abundant wildlife populates Mesa Verde's diverse, wild habitats. Mule deer are abundant, while transient elk occasionally wander onto the escarpment. Mountain lion, black bear, coyote, bobcat, and gray fox roam this upland plateau, and scattered bighorn sheep inhabit the rocky canyons. The more than 160 birds species seen include turkeys, golden eagles, hawks, owls, turkey vultures, ravens, Stellers jays, chickadees, nuthatches, and hummingbirds. Rattlesnakes hide on warm, rocky canyon slopes.

After 4 miles the road reaches 8,571-foot **Park Point,** the park's highest elevation. This lookout yields a spectacular overview of the surrounding Colorado Plateau. To the northeast lie forested plateaus topped by the snow-capped San Miguel and La Plata Ranges. Utah's canyon country stretches westward beyond Ute Peak to the Abajo and La Sal Mountains. The Chuska and Lukachukai Ranges, straddling the Arizona and New Mexico border, recede to the southwestern horizon, while the immense San Juan Basin, punctuated by the volcanic peak of Shiprock, basks south of Mesa Verde in New Mexico.

Far View

The drive winds another 5 miles along the North Rim to **Far View.** Here, perched on a flattened ridge, sits the **Far View Visitor Center.** The center, open June through September, displays contemporary Indian arts and crafts and historic lifestyles. Nearby is Far View Motor Lodge and a restaurant, cafeteria, and gas station.

An excellent summer side trip begins at Far View and travels 12 miles southwest to **Wetherill Mesa** via a narrow, winding road with sharp curves and steep grades. Wetherill Mesa offers a good, uncrowded alternative to the busy Chapin Mesa ruins. Visitors can follow a self-guided tour through Step House or an hour-long ranger-led excursion into Long House, the park's second-largest ruin.

The drive bends onto upper Chapin Mesa at Far View Visitor Center, begins descending southward, and a mile later reaches **Far View Ruin.** This large mesa-top village, located just east of the road, is best visited on the return trip. Far View House, a rectangular pueblo with about fifty rooms, was a possible trading center inhabited from A.D. 1100 to 1200. A large population lived in the area surrounding Far View, with over fifty dwelling sites within the pueblo's immediate area. While this area is colder in winter than farther south on the mesa, it receives more annual rainfall—an important consideration for these early farmers.

Water became the blood of the Anasazi way of life when they became agriculturists. By controlling water, the Anasazi controlled their destiny. Without water they would remain locked into a basic hunting-and-gathering economy, following game and harvesting seasonal plants. The miracle of water, however, grew nutritious crops like corn, beans, and squash that in turn made social and religious growth possible. Water, in a sense, created Mesa Verde's vibrant Indian cities and gave their inhabitants the leisure time to develop crafts like basketry, pottery, and weaving. The Anasazi became masters of water exploitation in this semiarid land by utilizing floodwater and subsurface irrigation, planting crops near seepage springs, and building ditches and reservoirs to transport and store water.

Mummy Lake, sitting alongside the drive just north of Far View Ruin, testifies to the Anasazi reliance on water. A fan of uphill channels could have diverted runoff from rain and snow into a main ditch that drained into Mummy Lake. The stone-lined lake is possibly a reservoir 90 feet in diameter and 12 feet deep with a 500,000-gallon storage capacity. A distribution channel ran south from the reservoir to nearby fields for irrigation. The Far View Ditch, another canal, ran 5 miles down Chapin Mesa to the head of Spruce Tree Canyon. That water was probably used for irrigation, although no clear evidence indicates water ever flowed that far down the ditch. Some archaeologists also dispute that Mummy Lake was a reservoir or was used for water collection. Mummy Lake is reached via a short trail from Far View Ruin.

Mesa Verde Museum and Spruce Tree House

The road continues south on Chapin Mesa and reaches **Cedar Tree Tower** after 3 miles. This small ruin, composed of a tower connected to a "kiva," or underground ceremonial chamber, lies east of the road. Prehistoric farming terraces scatter along a short trail south of the site. A major road intersection is 0.5 mile farther south.

A mile-long loop road continues south to the **Mesa Verde Museum,** park headquarters, and **Spruce Tree House.** The museum offers an excellent introduction to the evolution of the Anasazi culture through a series of dramatic dioramas, and it displays numerous artifacts, including pottery, basketry, jewelry, and weaving. A picnic area spreads along the rim of Spruce Canyon on the west side of the loop opposite the museum.

A self-guided paved trail begins at the museum and drops east into Spruce Tree Canyon to Spruce Tree House, the park's third-largest cliff dwelling. This well-preserved ruin, protected from weathering by an immense alcove, boasts 114 rooms and eight kivas and housed as many as 150 people. The site was named by its discoverers, Richard Wetherill and Charlie Mason, after a large Douglas fir that grew in front of the village. The tree was cut down in 1891. A booklet, available at the trailhead and museum, explains Spruce Tree House's important features. Two other trails explore the park headquarters area. The 2.8-mile Petroglyph Point Trail follows Spruce Tree Canyon's eastern edge to Petroglyph Point, passing several rock art panels, before climbing onto the rim for the return walk. The 2.1-mile Spruce Canyon Trail winds into Spruce Canyon before climbing onto Chapin Mesa near the picnic area.

Ruins Road

Ruins Road, consisting of two 6-mile-long loops, begins at the intersection with the headquarters road. The drive heads down Ruins Road and goes straight on the Mesa Top Ruins drive loop. This loop explores the architectural development of the Anasazi by stopping at a succession of sites. Few places are found in the Southwest where the Anasazi's long march to civilization can be seen so clearly as along this loop. The first stop is a pithouse, a roofed semisubterranean pit, built about A.D. 575 during an era archaeologists call the Modified Basketmaker Period. The next viewpoint overlooks deep Navajo Canyon, containing over sixty cliff dwellings, including Echo House across the chasm. **Square Tower House,** one of Mesa Verde's most elegant ruins, nestles in a shallow cavern below the next stop. The seventy-room pueblo boasts Mesa Verde's tallest structure with one wall measuring 33 feet high.

The next three stops include pithouses erected before A.D. 700 and several above-ground villages dating from the Developmental Pueblo Period between

A.D. 800 and 1100. Sun Point Pueblo, at the next turnoff, dates from 1200 during the Classic Pueblo Period, a time when the Anasazi culture reached its zenith. The Anasazi began leaving the mesa tops shortly after the pueblo's construction to build their villages in caves tucked under the canyon rims. Why they retreated into the cliffs is an enduring mystery. Defense reigns as the common explanation. A village built in a protective alcove was undoubtedly easily defended, particularly with bows and arrows and stockpiles of food and water. Little evidence exists, however, that these were people at war. But whatever the reasons, the move to their cliffed aeries was the first step toward the total abandonment of the Mesa Verde by A.D. 1300.

Cliff Palace

Sun Point Overlook yields cross-canyon views of numerous ruins built during the thirteenth century. The next two viewpoints look into Fewkes Canyon and several impressive sites, including Oak Tree House, Fire Temple, and New Fire House. Sun Temple, the last stop, sits on a narrow promontory above Fewkes Canyon. This large D-shaped building, while never completed, is thought to have been a ceremonial structure. Another overlook just north of Sun Temple yields marvelous views of **Cliff Palace,** North America's largest cliff dwelling.

It was near this spot that two cowboys from the Mancos Valley stumbled upon this "magnificent city" on a cold snowy December day in 1888. Richard Wetherill and his brother-in-law, Charlie Mason, were searching this rough country for stray cattle when they happened upon the grandest cliff dwelling of all and transformed Mesa Verde from a remote plateau to America's greatest archaeological wonder. After their initial astonishment, they lashed several trees together, descended to the canyon bottom, and clambered up to the silent chamber. The ruin appeared almost undisturbed from the passage of centuries. Pots and stone tools remained hanging from the walls, awaiting the return of their owners. Parts of human skeletons scattered across the ground. The men dubbed their amazing discovery Cliff Palace.

Why the Anasazi abandoned their ancestral homeland at Mesa Verde and across the Four Corners region is an enduring mystery. While they left a rich legacy of crumbling ruins from their golden years, a time of growth, trade, and frenzied construction, they left few clues as to their disappearance. The thirteenth-century Mesa Verde Indians had built a sophisticated society with all the tools for success in this arid country, including water-control projects, solar calendars that marked the solstices and equinoxes, multistoried apartment houses, and a flourishing trade network with the rest of the Southwest and Mexico. But something

Opposite: Square Tower House hides under a sheltering alcove off Ruins Road on the Mesa Verde National Park drive.

happened, and between A.D. 1270 and 1300 the Anasazi homeland of a millennium was emptied. Archaeologists speculate a combination of factors forced the perplexing migration from the Four Corners area to New Mexico's Rio Grande Valley and Arizona's Hopi Mesas. A prolonged drought stunted crops by shifting moisture from spring and summer to autumn. The mesa's large population depleted ground cover and trees for construction and firewood, and centuries of farming robbed mesa soils of their productivity. Disease, internal bickering, social fragmentation, and raids by outside enemies also made compelling reasons to abandon the mesa for greener pastures elsewhere.

The drive continues back to the intersection with the other Ruins Road loop. Turn east. The new road drops southeast through dense piñon pine and juniper forest and reaches Cliff Palace just after turning to a one-lane road. Cliff Palace is viewed from a mesa-top overlook, and a self-guided loop trail descends into the ruin. Visitors must climb stairs and four ten-foot ladders along the trail. An excellent trail guide, available at the trailhead, details Cliff Palace and the Anasazi. Park rangers are stationed in the ruin to answer questions and ensure visitors stay on the trail.

Cliff Palace, the park's largest cliff dwelling, housed more than 200 people in its 217 rooms and twenty-three kivas. The village, built between A.D. 1209 and 1273, exhibits superb construction and masonry skills. Cliff Palace was built by accretion rather than from a grand plan—rooms were added on as they were needed. Stones, often pecked with harder hammerstones into usable shapes, were laid with a mud mortar before being carefully plastered over. Painted designs often brightened the walls.

Willa Cather aptly described Cliff Palace in her novel *The Professor's House* as "a little city of stone, asleep. It was as still as sculpture. . . . It all hung together, seemed to have a kind of composition: pale little houses of stone nestling close to one another, perched on top of each other, with flat roofs, narrow windows, straight walls, and in the middle of the group, a round tower. . . . I had come upon the city of some extinct civilization, hidden away in this inaccessible mesa for centuries, preserved in the dry air and almost perpetual sunlight like a fly in amber, guarded by the cliffs and the river and the desert."

The road continues south, skirting the sandstone rim of Cliff Canyon. Several roadside overlooks view ruins, including the House of Many Windows, tucked into shallow caves across the canyon. The road bends east across the mesa, briefly dipping into **Ute Mountain Tribal Park,** a 125,000-acre park preserving the remote canyons to the south and numerous Anasazi ruins, on the Ute Mountain Indian Reservation.

Opposite: Visitors explore Cliff Palace, the grandest cliff dwelling in Mesa Verde National Park.

The next stop atop the Soda Canyon rim offers **Balcony House,** one of the park's most popular ruin tours. This forty-five-room pueblo sits under an arching cave beneath the parking area. Regular ranger-led tours, available on a first-come, first-served basis, explore the site in summer. Line up under the ramada for a place on the tour. The hour-long tour descends a paved trail and climbs a 32-foot-high ladder into Balcony House. The exit back to the rim is via a crawl tunnel, several wooden ladders, and steps chopped into the cliff face. Visitors with health problems or fear of heights should bypass this tour. Balcony House, perched above abrupt cliffs, is the park's most defensible large ruin, with only one entry and exit path. An excellent year-round spring undoubtedly made this aerie attractive to its inhabitants.

The Soda Canyon Overlook Trailhead, the drive's last stop, sits a little farther up the road. This quiet 0.75-mile trail winds through piñon pine and juniper to a jutting promontory that yields a good view of Balcony House and Soda Canyon. The loop road continues northwest back to the main intersection. Turn north for the 21-mile journey back to the park entrance and U.S. Highway 160.

29

Rim Rock Drive

Colorado National Monument

General description: This 22-mile drive explores the sandstone rim and canyons of Colorado National Monument on the northern edge of the Uncompahgre Plateau.

Special attractions: Sandstone cliffs and spires, Monument Canyon, Alcove Nature Trail, Independence Monument, Window Rock Nature Trail, visitor center, John Otto's Trail, numerous overlooks, Coke Ovens, Ute Canyon, Cold Shivers Point, Devils Kitchen, hiking, camping, backpacking, rock climbing, wildlife, interpretive programs.

Location: West-central Colorado. The national monument and drive lie just west of Grand Junction near the Utah border.

Drive route name: Rim Rock Drive.

Travel season: Year-round. Although the road is regularly plowed in winter, snow and ice may persist on shaded road sections.

Camping: Saddlehorn Campground offers eighty sites near the visitor center on the drive's west end. The campground is open year-round, although the restrooms and water are shut off in winter.

Services: All services are found in Fruita and Grand Junction, including lodging, private campgrounds, gas, food, and medical facilities.

Nearby attractions: Grand Junction, Museum of Western Colorado, Highline Lake State Park, Island Acres State Park, Grand Mesa Scenic Byway (see Drive 25), Land's End Road, Rattlesnake Canyon and arches, Ruby and Horsethief Canyons, Colorado River, Kokopelli's Trail, Rabbit Valley Paleontology Area, Grand Mesa National Forest, Uncompahgre National Forest, Unaweep–Tabeguache Scenic and Historic Byway (see Drive 27).

The Drive

Thick sandstone layers drape across the Uncompahgre Plateau, a long humpbacked highland that stretches across western Colorado from the San Juan Mountains to the Colorado River on the eastern edge of the Colorado Plateau. Colorado National Monument, on the plateau's northern edge, protects a 20,453-acre wonderland of dipping sandstone strata chiseled by erosion into precipitous canyons, abrupt buttresses, sharp spires and buttes, and soaring cliffs. This rugged monument relates a spectacular lesson in geology. The monument's 1.5-billion-year-old basement rocks once floored a primeval ocean. The horizontal rock strata above—the Chinle, Wingate, Kayenta, Entrada, and Morrison Formations—tell more recent tales of immense dune fields, meandering rivers, and swamps alive with dinosaurs. The 22-mile Rim Rock Drive traverses the monument's canyons and airy rims, explores its geologic history, offers nineteen scenic overlooks, and passes several trails that descend into the canyons, leading to spring-fed oases of grass, birdsong, and solitude.

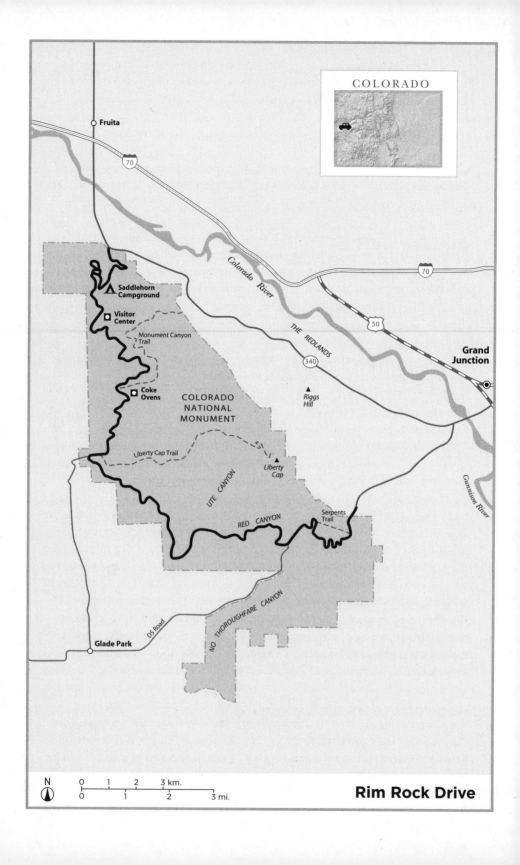

Rim Rock Drive

Colorado National Monument offers a generally pleasant year-round climate. Temperatures, however, range from below zero in winter to 100 degrees in summer. Most summer days are sunny and warm with highs in the eighties and nineties. Hikers should carry a gallon of water per day and wear a hat. Temperatures in the canyons, with heat radiating off bare rock surfaces, can be extreme. Occasional afternoon thunderstorms douse the monument's rim and canyons in July and August. Autumn brings gorgeous warm days and clear nights. Expect highs in the seventies and eighties with cool evenings. Winter days are cold and crisp, but highs often reach into the forties. Snow occasionally blankets the monument under a mantle of white. Spring offers warm weather, windy afternoons, light rain showers, and wildflowers.

Rim Rock Drive is accessed at two points—at Grand Junction on the east and at Fruita on the west. The drive description begins at Colorado National Monument's west entrance on CO 340–Redlands Road almost 3 miles south of Fruita and Interstate 70's exit 19 on the southern edge of the Grand Valley west of Grand Junction. The Colorado River, formerly called the Grand River, drifts lazily across the valley, meandering past cottonwood-lined banks, fruit orchards, and a series of towns, including Palisade, Grand Junction, and Fruita. Grand Junction, western Colorado's largest city, was named because the Gunnison River joins the Colorado River here. Mountains and cliffs hem in Grand Valley—Grand Mesa dominates the eastern horizon, the bare cliffs and eroded badlands of the Book Cliffs march across the northern edge, and the national monument's ragged cliffs and canyons mark the southern skyline.

Just before the beginning of this drive, CO 340 swings south from Fruita, a small agricultural town, passes a Colorado Welcome Center, and crosses the Colorado River's muddy channel. The road climbs away from the river through the multicolored siltstones and mudstones of the Morrison Formation. This 150-million-year-old formation preserves the skeletons of great dinosaurs that roamed the region's dense forests and swamplands, as well as some of the oldest mammal fossils found in the Western Hemisphere.

Numerous dinosaur bones are found in the Morrison rocks below the uplifted Uncompahgre Plateau between Fruita and Grand Junction. The barren hill east of the highway and above the river is the site of paleontologist Elmer Riggs's 1901 discovery of an *apatosaurus* skeleton. A bronze plaque honors the event. A short trail also loops through the area, exploring this famed dinosaur locale. Riggs Hill, another notable dinosaur quarry, lies a few miles east of here. There, in 1900, Riggs excavated the first known skeleton of the immense *Brachiosaurus*.

Wedding and Fruita Canyons

The highway bends southeast from the dinosaur site and climbs to Colorado National Monument's west entrance, almost 3 miles from Fruita. Rim Rock Drive begins here. After passing the entrance station the paved road crosses the maroon-colored Chinle Formation and quickly reaches steep Wingate sandstone cliffs. The road ascends a tight switchback on the west side of **Wedding Canyon,** with the rounded tower of the Praying Monk sitting east of the loop. Redlands View, 0.25 mile up the drive, offers a look at the Grand Valley and a fault zone below the escarpment.

Past the overlook the road bends south and enters **Fruita Canyon,** a deep box canyon sliced into the plateau rim. The road swings under towering sandstone cliffs on the canyon's east flank. A turnoff near the canyon's head yields a great view of **Balanced Rock,** a short pinnacle topped with an overhanging block of precariously balanced Wingate sandstone. The road climbs steeply past Balanced Rock, passes through two tunnels, and reaches Historic Trails View near the cliffed rim. An interpretative sign details the area's early explorations. The drive continues climbing and finally reaches the rim above Fruita Canyon and Fruita Canyon Viewpoint.

Past the canyon the drive bends south and reaches the visitor center, which details the natural history, geology, and history of Colorado National Monument. The center also offers ranger-led walks and talks in the warmer months, an introductory audiovisual program, restrooms, books, and maps. A paved, one-way side road heads north from the visitor center and loops around Saddlehorn Rock, a prominent monolith of pale Entrada sandstone. Eighty-site Saddlehorn Campground spreads along the road north of the rock. The widely spaced sites lie in a piñon and juniper woodland. The campground, open year-round on a first-come, first-served basis, offers water, restrooms, and nightly campfire programs in the warmer months.

Window Rock Trail, an excellent 0.3-mile loop trail, begins at an overlook where the campground road reaches the western lip of Wedding Canyon. The short trail winds past twisted junipers and slickrock gardens tucked in alcoves and bays above cliffs. The path leads to a magnificent viewpoint poised on the canyon rim above Window Rock, an elongated opening carved by water and ice on the cliff edge. The view encompasses Wedding Canyon and the Grand Valley. The Colorado River uncoils below. Farther north stretch the Book Cliffs, with bare shale slopes, long cliff bands, and forested summits. Evening is a great time to hike to this overlook. Silence shrouds the canyon and valley at sunset. In growing darkness, the valley below twinkles with a thousand points of light. A small pamphlet, available at the visitor center, identifies plants along the trail. The 0.5 mile Canyon Rim Trail, another good path, runs from Window Rock along the rim of Wedding Canyon to the visitor center. Hikers should beware of steep cliffs and keep children under control. A large picnic area lies just beyond the campground and Window Rock trailhead.

Rimrock Overlooks

Rim Rock Drive runs south from the visitor center and after 0.5 mile edges along a narrow bench above an overhanging cliff. At the canyon head the road bends east and continues along a broad rimrock bench. At the next pullout, **John Ottos Trail** runs 0.25 mile across a narrow promontory above Wedding Canyon to a lofty lookout perched above the Pipe Organ. John Otto, a trailblazer, promoter, patriot, and outdoorsman, worked tirelessly for the establishment of Colorado National Monument. He first settled in a canvas tent in Monument Canyon in 1906. The next year he wrote, "I came here last year and found these canyons, and they feel like the heart of the world to me. I'm going to stay and build trails and promote this place, because it should be a national park. Some folks think I'm crazy, but I want to see this scenery opened up to all people." Otto devoted himself to building trails, writing the Grand Junction Chamber of Commerce and President William H. Taft to establish a "Monument National Park" here, and guiding local citizens through the wondrous sandstone canyons of his proposed park. Otto was appointed custodian at a salary of $1.00 a month after the monument was established in 1911.

Three spectacular viewpoints—Independence, Grand View, and Monument Canyon—lie along the next few road miles. All yield spectacular views into **Monument Canyon,** a wide canyon flanked by sandstone cliffs and floored with ancient bedrock. Independence Monument View overlooks **Independence Monument,** a 450-foot-high monolith that sits atop a soft sandstone cone between Monument and Wedding canyons. Independence Monument formed after water and ice eroded walls that once connected the pinnacle to mesas on the northeast and southwest. Wingate sandstone, a buff-colored sandstone deposited as immense sand dunes 210 million years ago during the Triassic Period, forms Colorado National Monument's dramatic cliffs and spires. Atop the Wingate lies the Kayenta Formation, a thin layer deposited by rivers and streams. The Kayenta sandstone, a coarse, erosion-resistant rock, forms a capstone atop the softer underlying Wingate Formation and slows its erosion. Independence Monument, with a large, flat summit, is capped and protected by Kayenta sandstone.

By contrast, the nearby **Coke Ovens** weathered into rounded domes with small summits after they lost their Kayenta cap. Independence Monument, today a moderate rock climb, was first ascended by John Otto on July 4, 1910, to celebrate Independence Day. Otto scaled a ladder of pipes laboriously drilled into the spire. On the flat summit he hoisted Old Glory. Later Otto displayed the flag every Independence Day, giving Independence Monument its name.

Grand View Point, another 0.5 mile up the drive, offers a spectacular view of Monument Canyon, Independence Monument, and the Grand Valley from a fenced overlook. Past Grand View, the drive twists for a mile along the Kayenta

Bell Tower, also dubbed the Kissing Couple, juts into Monument Canyon below Rim Rock Drive.

sandstone rim and reaches Monument Canyon View, another scenic overlook perched atop tall sandstone cliffs. The sinuous road bends south following the rim of a spur canyon to Coke Ovens Overlook. A pullout offers views of the Coke Ovens, several domed rocks shaped like old-time coke ovens.

A quarter-mile up the drive is the Monument Canyon Trailhead. This popular 6.3-mile-long trail, built by John Otto in 1910, descends 600 feet from the rim to Monument Canyon's wide floor, traversing almost a billion years of geologic history from Entrada sandstone to ancient Precambrian gneiss and schist. The trail, a walker's delight, winds past rusty sandstone cliffs and soaring towers like the Kissing Couple and Independence Monument before dropping to a lower trailhead on CO 340. Hikers should carry plenty of water in the warmer months. The 0.25-mile Coke Ovens Trail also begins at the parking area and traverses to an overlook above the Coke Ovens.

Artist's Point sits high above Monument Canyon 0.5 mile up the road. This lofty viewpoint offers a marvelous panorama of canyons, mesas, and valleys. The drive winds upward through a pygmy forest of piñon pine and juniper, passes Highland View Overlook, and reaches the 6,593-foot-high divide between Monument and Ute Canyons on Monument Mesa. The monument's scant 11 inches of annual precipitation and an extreme temperature range limits plant and animal life on this high desert. The piñon pine and juniper woodland dominates the monument's mesas and canyons, blanketing the moist, north-facing slopes. Junipers also scatter across the desolate rimrock along the drive, sending sturdy taproots down through cracks in pursuit of water. A sparse understory of shrubs spreads over the forest's sandy floor, including mountain mahogany, a favorite deer food, and open meadows of sagebrush and saltbush. Late spring and early summer bring a colorful display of wildflowers, including Indian paintbrush, phlox, yellow mustard, evening primrose, and yucca stalks laden with bulbous white blossoms.

Common animals found in the monument include coyote, mule deer, kangaroo rat, bat, porcupine, rock squirrel, bobcat, and occasional mountain lion, black bear, and elk. Bighorn sheep, reintroduced into the monument in 1979, are sometimes sighted in the canyons. Numerous reptiles and amphibians, including the uncommon midget-faded rattlesnake, as well as 126 bird species inhabit the monument's varied habitats.

Ute Canyon

Past the divide, the road swings into upper **Ute Canyon,** a broad valley coated with sagebrush and piñon. The trailhead for 7-mile **Liberty Cap Trail** lies just before the valley floor on the road's east side. The path, a favorite cross-country ski tour in winter, threads across Monument Mesa to Liberty Cap before dropping to the lower trailhead below the monument's rocky escarpment. A side road, beginning on the south slope of Ute Canyon, heads south and west across Glade Park 5 miles to the small hamlet of Glade Park. Rough, four-wheel-drive tracks head west from here to the 75,168-acre Black Ridge Canyons Wilderness Study Area, a rough country seamed by deep canyons and studded with hidden arches.

Rim Rock Drive turns sharply east and follows Ute Canyon. The canyon's intermittent stream, flowing only after snowmelt or heavy rain, slowly sliced a V-shaped canyon into the Entrada and Kayenta sandstones. After a mile the canyon abruptly deepens at **Suction Point,** a 350-foot-high drop where the creek cut through soft Wingate sandstone. The drop makes a spectacular waterfall after a summer thunderstorm.

The drive traverses the south rim of Ute Canyon and passes two excellent rimrock viewpoints, Upper Ute Canyon and Fallen Rock Overlooks. Fallen Rock Overlook gives a great view down-canyon to Fallen Rock, a giant sandstone slab

Grand Valley spreads beyond Independence Monument, the highest rock formation at Colorado National Monument.

that fell off the sheer canyon wall above. Ute Canyon Trail, one of the monument's best hikes, begins at the parking area and descends into Upper Ute Canyon. A primitive path continues down Lower Ute Canyon to a trailhead 7 miles down-canyon. The trail, flanked by rosy cliffs, passes sagebrush meadows, tall cottonwoods that offer welcome summer shade, and cattail-lined potholes alive with spadefoot toads and singing birds.

The road swings around the east arm of Ute Canyon and climbs to 6,640 feet, the drive's highest point. A mile farther sits Lower Ute Canyon View, a fenced viewpoint that looks down the canyon to the distant Book Cliffs. The road turns away from Ute Canyon, traverses a narrow mesa, and after 0.5 mile emerges at Red Canyon Overlook. This short, deep canyon extends northeast from the viewpoint. The drive twists along Kayenta sandstone on Red and Columbus Canyons' south rims and after 2.5 miles reaches an intersection with DS Road, a county road that heads southwest above No Thoroughfare Canyon to Glade Park. No Thoroughfare Canyon offers wild terrain and primitive trails.

Cold Shivers Point and Serpents Trail

Cold Shivers Point, a barrier-free overlook, lies just north of the road junction. This aptly named overlook perches atop vertical cliffs hundreds of feet above the floor of Columbus Canyon. The drive begins descending past Cold Shivers Point, and after 0.5 mile switchbacks steeply down the uplifted escarpment of the Ladder Creek monocline. **Serpents Trail** begins above the north entrance of a long tunnel. This historic route follows the old road bed of what was nicknamed "the crookedest road in the world." The road, built by John Otto and Glade Park ranchers, was completed in 1921 and closed to vehicular travel in 1950 after the lower section of Rim Rock Drive was completed. Rim Rock Drive was built in the 1930s by work crews with the Civilian Conservation Corps, National Park Service, and Works Progress Administration. Some 23 miles of the drive were handmade, with help only from pickaxes and dynamite. Just before Christmas in 1933 a massive rock fall near Grand View killed nine workers. Serpents Trail uncoils 2.5 miles down a steep sandstone rib. It's best to hike one-way, with a driver meeting the walkers at the lower trailhead at Devils Kitchen.

The drive twists through the dark red Chinle formation below the tunnel, switchbacking across steep slopes strewn with boulders and twisted junipers. **Devils Kitchen,** a collection of tilted Wingate sandstone towers and buttes, makes a good stop. A short trail climbs 0.7 mile to the rocks. A picnic area sits down the drive from the trailhead. Nearby hides a panel of Indian petroglyphs or rock drawings carved onto a slab of Wingate sandstone. From the picnic area the drive descends to the monument's east entrance station and the park boundary. Continue northeast down the road to its junction with CO 340. Across the Colorado River lies Grand Junction, U.S. Highway 50, and I-70's business route.

Harpers Corner Road

Dinosaur National Monument

General description: This 31-mile-long drive climbs from the headquarters of Dinosaur National Monument over a high, rolling plateau to a lofty lookout atop Harpers Corner above the confluence of the Green and Yampa Rivers.

Special attractions: Dinosaur National Monument, Plug Hat Butte, Willow Creek Wilderness Study Area, Bull Canyon Wilderness Study Area, scenic overlooks, Echo Park Road, Whirlpool Canyon, Harpers Corner, Ruple Point, hiking, bicycling, picnicking.

Location: Far northwestern Colorado. The drive begins 1.5 miles east of Dinosaur on US 40.

Drive route name: Harpers Corner Road.

Travel season: Late spring through late fall. The road generally opens by late May and closes after the first heavy winter snows, usually in November. Call monument headquarters for information on road closing and opening dates.

Camping: No camping is available on the drive. Primitive camping is permitted on surrounding Bureau of Land Management lands. Dinosaur National Monument campgrounds are located at the Quarry area in Utah, almost 30 miles west of monument headquarters via US 40 and UT 149. A primitive campground is in Echo Park below the drive. Check at headquarters for road information and site availability. A park campground at Deerlodge Park lies 53 miles east of Dinosaur off US 40.

Services: All services are found in Dinosaur and Rangely.

Nearby attractions: Dinosaur National Monument Quarry (Utah), Deerlodge Park, Gates of Lodore, Cross Mountain Canyon, Skull Creek Wilderness Study Area, White River National Forest, Meeker, Flat Tops Trail Scenic Byway (see Drive 24), Uinta Mountains, Flaming Gorge National Recreation Area, Brown's Park.

The Drive

Dinosaur National Monument spreads across Colorado's empty quarter—a remote, wild land of sagebrushed valleys, sandstone canyons, and high mesas and mountains. The Green and Yampa Rivers meet in secluded Echo Park beneath soaring sandstone walls in the middle of this 326-square-mile parkland, their placid waters mingling before edging around Steamboat Rock and spinning down Whirlpool Canyon into Utah.

Two distinct natural features comprise Dinosaur National Monument—the unique deposit of dinosaur bones across the border in Utah and the wonderland of canyons incised by the mighty rivers. Most visitors come only to gaze at the extraordinary bas-relief of ancient life buried in sandstone, but out in the monument's backcountry stretches an equally spectacular natural world. The 31-mile-

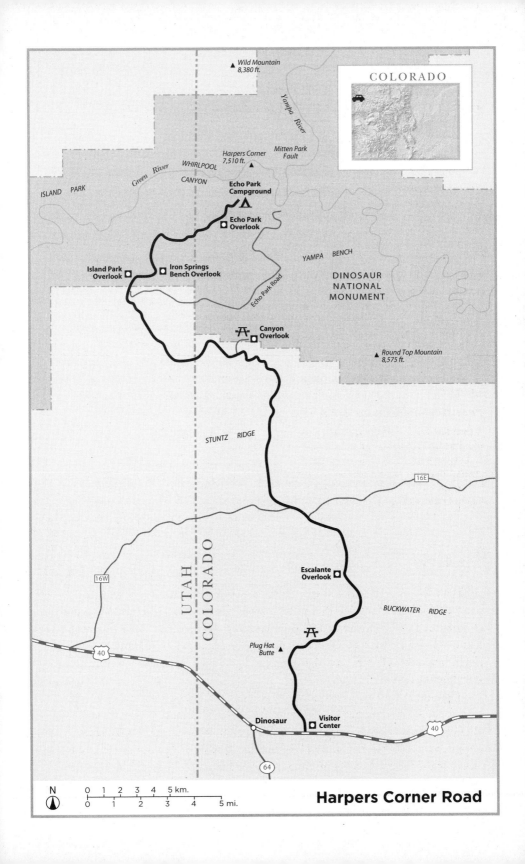

COLORADO

▲ Wild Mountain
8,380 ft.

Yampa River

Harpers Corner
7,510 ft. ▲

*Mitten Park
Fault*

Echo Park
Campground

Echo Park
Overlook

Green River

WHIRLPOOL

CANYON

ISLAND PARK

Island Park
Overlook

Iron Springs
Bench Overlook

YAMPA   BENCH

DINOSAUR
NATIONAL
MONUMENT

Echo Park Road

Canyon
Overlook

▲ *Round Top Mountain*
8,575 ft.

STUNTZ   RIDGE

16E

16W

UTAH
COLORADO

Escalante
Overlook

BUCKWATER   RIDGE

*Plug Hat
Butte* ▲

Dinosaur

Visitor
Center

40

40

64

N

0   1   2   3   4   5 km.

0   1   2   3   4   5 mi.

Harpers Corner Road

long Harpers Corner Road, beginning at monument headquarters, explores the heart of Dinosaur National Monument. It climbs onto the rounded crest of the Yampa Plateau before twisting out to Harpers Corner, an airy viewpoint perched high above Echo Park and Whirlpool Canyon.

Snow determines the drive's season. The road opens after snowdrifts melt off the higher elevations, usually sometime in May, and closes after heavy snowfall blocks the asphalt, usually in November. Check at the monument for road closing and opening dates. Expect hot temperatures in the lower elevations near the town of Dinosaur, with highs reaching into the nineties. Temperatures on the high plateau at Canyon Overlook and at Harpers Corner are cooler, ranging from sixty to eighty degrees. Heavy thunderstorms occur on summer afternoons. Watch for lightning on isolated ridges and viewpoints. Autumn offers warm days and cool nights, with occasional storms that bring rain and snow.

The small town of Dinosaur, decorated with scattered sculptures of its namesake, including a stegasaurus outside the town hall, is the gateway to northwestern Colorado and Dinosaur National Monument. The town offers visitor services, including lodging, dining, and gas. More complete services are found in Rangely 18 miles to the south. The Dinosaur Quarry section of the monument lies 30 miles west of Dinosaur near Vernal, Utah. Split Mountain and Green River Campgrounds spread along the Green River near the quarry.

The Visitor Center

The drive begins at the Dinosaur National Monument Visitor Center, 1.5 miles east of Dinosaur, at the junction of U.S. Highway 40 and the Harpers Corner Road. The center offers interpretive displays on the area's geology, archaeology, and natural history, as well as a ten-minute introductory slide show. Maps, books, brochures, and restrooms are available. A guide to Harpers Corner Road and trail are sold for a nominal fee here and at kiosks at the road's start and end. The 0.25-mile, self-guided Cold Desert Trail begins at the visitor center and explores the natural history of the cold desert community.

The drive heads north from the visitor center, passing an interpretative booth. The road corridor, while bordered by Bureau of Land Management public lands, is part of the National Monument and administered by the National Park Service. A roadside sign notes, FOSSIL BONES ARE NOT FOUND IN THIS SECTION. The road leaves the dry Mancos shale country and passes through a gateway chiseled through an upturned hogback of Dakota sandstone. The road ascends Dripping Rock Creek's shallow draw. Junipers, piñon pines, and sagebrush cover the hillsides and cottonwoods line the dry streambed below. After a half-mile the road climbs onto a broad ridge. Farther up, the drive crosses fire-ravaged hills.

Dense grass coats the ground amid blackened tree skeletons. Lightning caused this fire in 1972.

Plug Hat Butte

The road climbs across a divide and winds along the southern base of **Plug Hat Butte.** A viewpoint below the butte looks south across broad basins broken by ribbed hogbacks. Rangely and the Rangely Oil Field lie to the south and beyond stretch forested plateaus. Two distinct rock layers form the butte—the Entrada and Carmel Formations. The salmon-colored Entrada sandstone, forming the butte's hat and brim, was deposited some 200 million years ago as windswept sand dunes. Mud deposits on an ancient shallow seafloor form the butte's hatband of red Carmel mudstone.

The road climbs up through a break in the cliffs to a broad bench atop the butte. The Plug Hat Butte Picnic Area sits on the road's north edge, while the 0.25-mile-long Plug Hat Trail begins across the road. This level trail is easy to walk and offers marvelous views across the cliffed plateau edge, as well as exhibits on history, plants, and geology.

The drive bends northeast across a high, rolling benchland. Thick sagebrush and scattered junipers cover the landscape. Sagebrush coats much of western Colorado. This common plant, identified by its gray-green color and aromatic scent, withstands cold temperatures and provides important browse for mule deer in winter. Overgrazing of native grasses by cattle and sheep and the suppression of natural fires expanded the historical range of sagebrush over much of the West during the last 100 years. The piñon pine and juniper woodland also forms excellent animal habitat. Mule deer, porcupines, birds, rodents, and mice use the pygmy forest for both food and cover.

Two BLM Wilderness Study Areas—Willow Creek and Bull Canyon—abut the drive as it ascends above Plug Hat Butte. The Willow Creek area sprawls across ridges and canyons to the east, and Bull Canyon encompasses the cliff-lined drainages below the road on the west. Both offer solitude and good hiking opportunities.

After 8 miles the road swings past 7,710-foot-high **Escalante Overlook** on Buckwater Ridge. Marvelous views unfold west from this lofty point—Cliff Ridge stair-steps up from the desert to the plateau crest, and dry washes and canyons drain down to the Green River's broad shale valley. The road continues climbing past the overlook, swinging through thick sagebrush stands, onto a high upland plateau. Slight valleys, floored with ribbons of water and grass, dip east through rounded ridges. Cattle graze on these high meadows.

Moffat County Road 16E is reached after 11 miles. This dirt road twists east over the plateau and through canyons and valleys to US 40. Moffat County Road

16W begins 0.5 mile up the road. This scenic backroad drops west into Utah to US 40. The drive climbs north up a low draw that separates Stuntz Ridge and Round Top Mountain. Here the road crosses the Wolf Creek Fault, where two huge blocks of land slipped against each other. The northern block pushed higher, exposing older rocks than those found on the drive's lower elevations. The road wends north across an undulating plateau, dropping through dry washes and skirting humped hills and sagebrush-strewn plains. Groves of quaking aspen huddle in moist ravines on north-facing slopes, their golden leaves lending bright patches to the dull-colored landscape. Mule deer frequent the roadside on this highland; be watchful for them in early morning and evening.

Canyon Overlook, the Yampa Fault, and Echo Park Road

After a couple of miles the road sweeps onto a wide bench and reaches the turn-off to **Canyon Overlook.** A short road curves a mile to the overlook and the first view of the Yampa River's sinuous canyon, carved from Weber sandstone almost 3,000 feet below. The overlook perches on the edge of the Yampa Plateau, a high, rounded uplift that is an eastward extension of the Uinta Mountains. The Uintas, lifted some 65 million years ago along with the rest of the Rocky Mountains, are North America's only major east-west trending mountain range. Erosion attacked the mountains as they rose, cutting abrupt gorges and canyons into the uplift and sweeping eroded sand and gravel into surrounding basins. Geologists estimate over 25,000 feet of overlying rock washed off the rising mountains. **Zenobia Peak,** the monument high point at 9,006 feet, lies to the northeast above Yampa Canyon. A picnic area sits among firs at the overlook.

The drive crosses into Utah a couple of miles later and drops onto the broad ridge of Harpers Plateau. Shallow draws fall away from the road into steep canyons. The road passes a large corral used in spring and fall roundups, when area ranchers move cattle and sheep to and from high pastures. A parking area and lookout sit alongside the drive at 28 miles.

Two major faults are seen from here. The **Yampa Fault** forms the wide bench below Round Top in a textbook example of step-faulting. The **Mitten Park Fault** drops down and around the east side of Harpers Plateau before bending east at dramatically tilted strata north of Steamboat Rock. Faults formed some of Dinosaur's most spectacular scenery.

Echo Park Road leaves the Harpers Corner drive just past the overlook. The 13-mile-long dirt road loops over 2,000 feet down to Echo Park, a sunken hole of looming cliffs, cottonwoods poised on the crumbly river bank, and the confluence of the Green and Yampa Rivers. A park campground spreads along the bank opposite jutting Steamboat Rock. Echo Park, the lovely secret heart of Dinosaur's backcountry, was named and explored by one-armed Civil War veteran John Wesley

Powell, who, with ten men and four boats, floated down the Green and Colorado Rivers in 1869. After running disastrous rapids and making laborious portages through the Canyon of Lodore on the Green River, Powell's expedition lingered in the bucolic hollow for a few days. Repetitious echoes off Steamboat Rock gave the park its name. Powell wrote, "Standing opposite the rock, our words are repeated with startling clearness, but in a soft, mellow tone, that transforms them into magical music. Scarcely can one believe it is the echo of his own voice." Echo Park later became the home of Irishman Pat Lynch, another Civil War veteran, in the early 1880s. Lynch lived as a hermit in cabins and caves here and in the Yampa Canyon until his death in 1918. The Echo Park area still bears the name Pats Hole.

Canyon Overlooks

The drive enters Dinosaur National Monument just past the Echo Park turnoff. **Island Park Overlook** lies beyond the monument boundary. This point looks west to Island Park, a broad basin between Whirlpool Canyon and Split Mountain Gorge. The Green River threads across the emerald-colored park between numerous cottonwood-studded islands. Hills and badlands, etched with dry washes and arroyos, fringe the river's floodplain. The Ruple Point Trail, beginning at the overlook, follows an abandoned road west across Ruple Ridge 8 miles to Ruple Point, a spectacular viewpoint above Split Mountain Gorge.

The road bends east and swings past **Iron Springs Bench Overlook.** The point yields excellent views down Pool Creek and across Iron Springs Bench, the historic Chew Ranch, Pearl Park, and Red Rock Bench to Blue Mountain's rounded uplift. The road twists northeast on an ever-narrowing ridge, reenters Colorado, and reaches **Echo Park Overlook.** Echo Park and the mingling of the two great rivers lie far below the overlook.

Echo Park, now a peaceful retreat, was a battleground in the 1950s. A massive dam, creating a 107-mile-long, 43,000-acre lake, was proposed for Echo Park. The project would have flooded the river canyons, destroyed wildlife habitat, including the muddy river waters used by endangered fish species, and set a dangerous precedent that no national parkland could remain inviolate and undeveloped. A heated debate between conservationists and the Bureau of Reclamation resulted in Dinosaur National Monument and its valuable natural values being preserved for posterity.

Harpers Corner

The drive twists through gnarled junipers, becomes one-way, and reaches a parking area 1.5 miles north of Echo Park Overlook. This marks the end of the drive, but not the end of the scenery. **The Harpers Corner Trail** begins here and

The Green River twists westward into Utah through cliff-lined Whirlpool Canyon below Harpers Corner.

threads along a narrow ridge to 7,510-foot Harpers Corner, a jutting promontory high above Echo Park and the Green River. An informative brochure, found at the trail's beginning, explains the area's natural history and geology. As the trail gently descends from the road, glimpses of the canyons unfold below. Finally the path reaches a slight saddle and clambers over bedrock to a magnificent fenced overlook.

Echo Park lies to the east, with the muddy Green River making a tight horse-shoe bend around Steamboat Rock. Beyond, lost in the ivory-tinted Weber sandstone, hides the sinuous canyon of the Yampa River. The 170-mile-long Yampa River, Colorado's last major free-flowing river, arises from snow atop the Flat Tops on the White River Plateau. In Dinosaur National Monument, the Yampa winds 46 miles through a serpentine maze of pale sandstone before merging with the Green River in Echo Park.

The Green River plunges through 18-mile-long Lodore Canyon above Echo Park. This somber gorge, its stair-stepped upper walls visible northeast of Harpers Corner, possesses the monument's oldest rock formation—billion-year-old Uinta Mountain quartzite. A host of frothy rapids, with terrifying names given by Powell's 1869 expedition like Hells Half Mile and Disaster Falls, challenge river rafters.

The Green River changes character below Echo Park, as its makes a wide loop around Harpers Corner. The Mitten Park Fault's upturned rock layers are exposed in a dramatic cross-section above the river. The river enters Whirlpool Canyon at the fault, a spectacular abyss of rocks deposited on ancient seabeds. The cliff-lined river flows quickly through here, tumbling over water-worn boulders and passing secret alcoves and sand beaches. John Wesley Powell named and described the canyon: "The Green is greatly increased by the Yampa, and we now have a much larger river. All this volume of water, confined, as it is, in a narrow channel and rushing with great velocity, is set eddying and spinning in whirlpools by projecting rocks and short curves, and the waters waltz their way through the canyon, making their own rippling, rushing, roaring music." An earlier passerby, a French fur trapper, etched his name and date, "D. Julien 1836," on a rock panel below Harpers Corner.

Before starting the walk and the drive back to US 40, sit and linger atop the lofty aerie of Harpers Corner. Listen to the deep river currents far below, spinning the time-worn music heard by Major Powell. Rivers and time are alike in their relentless resolve and single-minded purpose. To be here now. To hear the flow of the river. That's important. We've left our cultural baggage back in the parking lot and begun to let the consciousness of these rivers and canyons seep in. That's the enchantment of rivers—they're disarmingly simple, yet they teach great lessons.

FOR MORE INFORMATION

General

Bureau of Land Management
Colorado State Office
2850 Youngfield Street
Lakewood, CO 80215
(303) 239-3600
www.co.blm.gov/index.htm

Colorado State Parks
Denver Administrative Office
1313 Sherman Street, No. 618
Denver, CO 80203
(303) 866-3437
www.parks.state.co.us

National Park Service
Intermountain Region
12795 Alameda Parkway
Denver, CO 80228
(303) 969-2500

USDA Forest Service
Rocky Mountain Regional Office
740 Simms Street
Golden, CO 80401
(303) 275-5350
www.fs.fed.us/r2/tcontact2_files/r2.htm

1: Santa Fe Trail Scenic Drive

Bent's Old Fort National Historic Site
35110 CO Highway 194 East
La Junta, CO 81050
(719) 383-5010
www.nps.gov/beol

Comanche National Grassland
Timpas Unit
1420 East 3rd Street
La Junta, CO 81050
(719) 384-2181
www.fs.fed.us/r2/psicc/coma/santafe
.shtml

La Junta Chamber of Commerce
110 Santa Fe Avenue
La Junta, CO 81050
(719) 384-7411
www.lajuntacochamber.com

**Trinidad-Las Animas County
Chamber of Commerce**
309 Nevada Avenue
Trinidad, CO 81082
(719) 846-9285
www.trinidadchamber.com

Trinidad Welcome Center
309 Nevada Avenue
Trinidad, CO 81082
(719) 742-3822
www.highwayoflegends.org

2: Pawnee Grasslands Scenic Drive

**Arapaho National Forest
Pawnee National Grassland**
660 "O" Street
Greeley, CO 80631
(970) 353-5004
www.fs.fed.us/r2/arnf/districts/png/
index.htm

**Arapaho National Forest
Pawnee National Grassland**
2150 Centre Avenue, Building E
Fort Collins, CO 80526
(970) 295-6600

City of Sterling
421 North 4th Street
Sterling, CO 80751
(970) 522-9700
www.sterlingcolo.com

Greeley Convention & Visitors Bureau
902 7th Avenue
Greeley, CO 80631
(970) 352-3567
(800) 449-3866
www.greeleycvb.com

3: Comanche Grasslands Scenic Drive

Comanche National Grassland
27204 US Highway 287
P.O. Box 127
Springfield, CO 81073
(719) 523-6591
www.springfieldco.info/comanche

Pike/San Isabel National Forests
2840 Kachina Drive
Pueblo, CO 81008
(719) 553-1400
www.fs.fed.us/r2/psicc/

Springfield Chamber of Commerce
948 Main Street
Springfield, CO 81073
(719) 523-4061
www.springfieldco.info

4: Highway of Legends Scenic Byway

San Isabel National Forest
San Carlos Ranger District
3170 East Main Street
Cañon City, CO 81212
(719) 269-8500

www.fs.fed.us/r2/psicc/sanc/general
.shtml

Trinidad-Las Animas County
Chamber of Commerce
309 Nevada Avenue
Trinidad, CO 81082
(719) 846-9285
www.trinidadchamber.com

Trinidad Welcome Center
309 Nevada Avenue
Trinidad, CO 81082
(719) 846-9512
www.highwayoflegends.org

5: Sangre de Cristo Scenic Drive

San Isabel National Forest
San Carlos Ranger District
3170 East Main Street
Cañon City, CO 81212
(719) 269-8500
www.fs.fed.us/r2/psicc/sanc/general
.shtml

Westcliffe Chamber of Commerce
502 Main Street
P.O. Box 81
Westcliffe, CO 81252
(719) 783-9163
(877) 793-3170
www.custercountyco.com

6: Los Caminos Antiguos Scenic Byway

Bureau of Land Management
La Jara Field Office
15571 County Road T.5
La Jara, CO 81140
(719) 274-8971

www.co.blm.gov/lajara/lajarahome
.htm

Fort Garland Museum
29477 CO Highway 159
P.O. Box 368
Fort Garland, CO 81133
(719) 378-3512
www.museumtrail.org/
FortGarlandMuseum.asp

Great Sand Dunes National Park
11500 CO Highway 150
Mosca, CO 81146
(719) 378-6399
www.nps.gov/grsa/

Rio Grande National Forest
1803 US Highway 160 West
Monte Vista, CO 81144
(719) 852-5941
www.fs.fed.us/r2/riogrande/

San Luis Lakes State Park
P.O. Box 150
Mosca, CO 81146
(719) 378-2020

7: Wet Mountains Scenic Drive

Cañon City Chamber of Commerce
403 Royal Gorge Boulevard
Cañon City, CO 81212
(719) 275-2331
(800) 876-7922
www.canoncitychamber.com

Colorado City Chamber of Commerce
P.O. Box 19042
Colorado City, CO 81019
(719) 676-3000
www.colocitychamber.org

San Isabel National Forest
San Carlos Ranger District
3170 East Main Street
Cañon City, CO 81212
(719) 269-8500
www.fs.fed.us/r2/psicc/sanc/general
.shtml

8: Phantom Canyon and Shelf Roads

Bureau of Land Management
Royal Gorge Field Office
3170 East Main Street
Cañon City, CO 81212
(719) 269-8500
www.fs.fed.us/r2/psicc/sanc/general

Cañon City Chamber of Commerce
403 Royal Gorge Boulevard
Cañon City, CO 81212
(719) 275-2331
(800) 876-7922
www.canoncitychamber.com

Cripple Creek Welcome Center
339 East Bennett Avenue
Cripple Creek, CO 80813
(719) 689-3315
(877) 858-GOLD
www.cripple-creek.co.us

9: Pikes Peak Highway

Pikes Peak Visitor Center
515 South Cascade Avenue
Colorado Springs, CO 80903
(877) 745-3773
www.experiencecoloradosprings.com

Manitou Springs Chamber of Commerce and Visitors Bureau
354 Manitou Avenue
Manitou Springs, CO 80829

(719) 685-5089
(800) 642-2567
www.manitousprings.org

Pike National Forest
Pikes Peak Ranger District
601 South Weber Avenue
Colorado Springs, CO 80903
(719) 636-1602
(719) 684-9138 (Pikes Peak Highway Tollgate)
(719) 385-7325 (Pikes Peak Highway Information)
www.fs.fed.us/r2/psicc/pp/

10: North Cheyenne Cañon and Lower Gold Camp Roads

Pikes Peak Visitor Center
515 South Cascade Avenue
Colorado Springs, CO 80903
(877) 745-3773
www.experiencecoloradosprings.com

Colorado Springs Parks, Recreation, and Cultural Services
1401 Recreation Way
Colorado Springs, CO 80905
(719) 385-5940
www.springsgov.com

Pike National Forest
Pikes Peak Ranger District
601 South Weber Avenue
Colorado Springs, CO 80903
(719) 636-1602
www.fs.fed.us/r2/psicc/pp/

Starsmore Discovery Center
2120 South Cheyenne Cañon Road
Colorado Springs, CO 80906
(719) 385-6086

11: South Platte River Roads

Pike National Forest
South Platte Ranger District
19316 Goddard Ranch Court
Morrison, CO 80465
(303) 275-5610
www.fs.fed.us/r2/psicc/spl/

Woodland Park Chamber of Commerce
210 East Midland Avenue
P.O. Box 9022
Woodland Park, CO 80866
(719) 687-9885
(800) 551-7886
www.woodlandparkchamber.org

12: Rampart Range Road

Pike National Forest
Pikes Peak Ranger District
601 South Weber Avenue
Colorado Springs, CO 80903
(719) 636-1602
www.fs.fed.us/r2/psicc/pp/

Pike National Forest
South Platte Ranger District
19316 Goddard Ranch Court
Morrison, CO 80465
(303) 275-5610
www.fs.fed.us/r2/psicc/spl/

13: South Park–Tarryall Loop Scenic Drive

Park County Tourism Office
501 Main Street
P.O. Box 1373
Fairplay, CO 80440
(719) 836-4279

Pike National Forest
South Park Ranger District
P.O. Box 219
320 US Highway 285
Fairplay, CO 80440
(719) 836-2031
www.fs.fed.us/r2/psicc/sopa/info.shtml

South Park Chamber of Commerce
P.O. Box 312
Fairplay, CO 80440
(719) 836-3410
www.southparkchamber.com

14: Mount Evans Scenic Byway

Arapaho National Forest
Clear Creek Ranger District
101 Chicago Creek Road
P.O. Box 3307
Idaho Springs, CO 80452
(303) 567-3000
www.fs.fed.us/r2/arnf/districts/ccrd/
index.htm

Clear Creek County Tourism Bureau
2060 Miner Street
P.O. Box 100
Idaho Springs, CO 80452
(303) 567-4660
(866) 674-9237
www.clearcreekcounty.org

Idaho Springs Visitor Center
2060 Miner Street
P.O. Box 1318
Idaho Springs, CO 80452
(303) 567-4382
(800) 882-5278
www.idahospringschamber.org

15: Guanella Pass Scenic and Historic Byway

Arapaho National Forest
Clear Creek Ranger District
101 Chicago Creek Road
P.O. Box 3307
Idaho Springs, CO 80452
(303) 567-3000
www.fs.fed.us/r2/arnf/districts/ccrd/
index.htm

Clear Creek County Tourism Bureau
2060 Miner Street
P.O. Box 100
Idaho Springs, CO 80452
(303) 567-4660
(866) 674-9237
www.clearcreekcounty.org

Georgetown Gateway Visitor's Center
1491 Argentine Street
P.O. Box 1037
Georgetown, CO 80444
(303) 569-2405
www.town.georgetown.co.us

The Georgetown Loop Railroad
P.O. Box 249 .
1111 Rose Street
Georgetown, CO 80444
(303) 569-2403
(888) 456-6777
www.georgetownlooprr.com

16: Peak to Peak Scenic and Historic Byway

Arapaho National Forest
Boulder Ranger District
2140 Yarmouth Avenue
Boulder, CO 80301
(303) 541-2500

www.fs.fed.us/r2/arnf/districts/brd/
index.htm

Clear Creek County Tourism Bureau
2060 Miner Street
P.O. Box 100
Idaho Springs, CO 80452
(303) 567-4660
(866) 674-9237
www.clearcreekcounty.org

Estes Park Convention and Visitors Bureau
Estes Park Visitors Center
500 Big Thompson Avenue
P.O. Box 1200
Estes Park, CO 80517
(970) 577-9900
(800) 44-ESTES
http://estesparkcvb.com

Nederland Chamber of Commerce
P.O. Box 85
Nederland, CO 80466
(303) 258-3936 (visitor center)
www.nederlandchamber.org

Rocky Mountain National Park
1000 US Highway 36
Estes Park, CO 80517
(970) 586-1206
www.nps.gov/romo

17: Trail Ridge Road All-American Byway

Estes Park Convention and Visitors Bureau
Estes Park Visitors Center
500 Big Thompson Avenue
P.O. Box 1200
Estes Park, CO 80517
(970) 577-9900

(800) 44-ESTES
http://estesparkcvb.com

Grand County Colorado Tourism Board
P.O. Box 131
Granby, CO 80446
(800) 247-2636
www.grand-county.com

Grand Lake Chamber of Commerce
P.O. Box 429
Grand Lake, CO 80447
(800) 531-1019
(970) 627-3402
www.grandlakechamber.com

Rocky Mountain National Park
1000 US Highway 36
Estes Park, CO 80517
(970) 586-1206
www.nps.gov/romo

18: Cache la Poudre–North Park Scenic Byway

Fort Collins Convention & Visitor's Bureau
19 Old Town Square, Suite 137
Fort Collins, CO 80524
(970) 232-3840
(800) 274-3678
www.ftcollins.com

North Park Chamber
491 Main Street
Walden, CO 80480
(970) 723-4600
www.northpark.org

Roosevelt National Forest
Canyon Lakes Ranger District
2150 Centre Avenue, Building E

Fort Collins, CO 80526
(970) 295-6700
www.fs.fed.us/r2/arnf/districts/clrd/
index.htm

19: Independence Pass Scenic Drive

Aspen Chamber Resort Association
425 Rio Grande Place
Aspen, CO 81611
(970) 925-1940
www.aspenchamber.org

San Isabel National Forest
Leadville Ranger District
810 Front Street
Leadville, CO 80461
(719) 486-0749
www.fs.fed.us/r2/psicc/leadvile

White River National Forest
900 Grand Avenue
P.O. Box 948
Glenwood Springs, CO 81602
(970) 945-2521
www.fs.fed.us/r2/whiteriver

White River National Forest
Aspen Ranger District
806 West Hallam Street
Aspen, CO 81611
(970) 925-3445
www.fs.fed.us/r2/whiteriver/

20: Cottonwood Pass Scenic Drive

Buena Vista Area Chamber of Commerce
343 US Highway 24 South
P.O. Box 2021
Buena Vista, CO 81211

(719) 395-6612
www.buenavistacolorado.org

Gunnison Country Chamber of Commerce
500 East Tomichi Avenue
Gunnison, CO 81230
(970) 641-1501
www.gunnison-co.com

Gunnison National Forest
2250 US Highway 50
Delta, CO 81416
(303) 874-6600
www.fs.fed.us/r2/gmug/

Gunnison National Forest
Taylor River Ranger District
216 North Colorado Street
Gunnison, CO 81230
(970) 641-0471

Pike/San Isabel National Forests
2840 Kachina Drive
Pueblo, CO 81008
(719) 553-1400
www.fs.fed.us/r2/psicc/

San Isabel National Forest
Salida Ranger District
325 West Rainbow Boulevard
Salida, CO 81201
(719) 539-3591
www.fs.fed.us/r2/psicc/sal/

21: West Elk Loop Scenic Byway

Crested Butte Chamber of Commerce
P.O. Box 1288
Crested Butte, CO 81224
(970) 349-6438
(800) 545-4505
www.crestedbuttechamber.com

Gunnison Country Chamber of Commerce
500 East Tomichi Avenue
Gunnison, CO 81230
(970) 641-1501
www.gunnison-co.com

Gunnison National Forest
Paonia Ranger District
P.O. Box 1030
Paonia, CO 81428
(970) 527-4131
www.fs.fed.us/r2/gmug/

Gunnison National Forest
Taylor River Ranger District
216 North Colorado Street
Gunnison, CO 81230
(970) 641-0471
www.fs.fed.us/r2/gmug/

Paonia Chamber of Commerce
120 Grand Avenue
P.O. Box 366
Paonia, CO 81428
(970) 527-3886
www.paoniachamber.com

22: Silver Thread Scenic Byway

Creede/Mineral County Chamber of Commerce
P.O. Box 580
Creede, CO 81130
(719) 658-2374
(800) 327-2102
www.creede.com

Lake City-Hinsdale County Chamber of Commerce
800 North Gunnison Avenue
P.O. Box 430

Lake City, CO 81235
(970) 944-2527
(800) 569-1874
www.lakecity.com

Rio Grande National Forest
1803 West US Highway 160
Monte Vista, CO 81144
(719) 852-5941
www.fs.fed.us/r2/riogrande/

Rio Grande National Forest
Divide Ranger District
Third and Creede Avenue
Creede, CO 81130
(719) 658-2556
www.fs.fed.us/r2/riogrande/

23: San Juan Skyway All-American Byway

**Cortez Chamber of Commerce
Colorado Welcome Center**
928 East Main
P.O. Box 968
Cortez, CO 81321
(970) 565-3414
www.cortezchamber.com
www.mesaverdecountry.com

Dolores Chamber of Commerce
201 Railroad Avenue
P.O. Box 602
Dolores, CO 81323
(970) 882-4018
www.doloreschamber.com

Durango and Silverton Narrow Gauge Railroad
479 Main Avenue
Durango, CO 81301
(970) 247-2733
(877) 872-4607
www.durangotrain.com

Durango Area Tourism Office
111 South Camino del Rio
Durango, CO 81302
(970) 247-0312
(800) 525-8855
www.durango.org

Mancos State Park
1321 Railroad Avenue
P.O. Box 1047
Dolores, CO 81323
(970) 533-7065
http://parks.state.co.us/Parks/Mancos/

Ouray Chamber Resort Association
1230 Main Street
P.O. Box 145
Ouray, CO 81427
(970) 325-4746
(800) 228-1876
www.ouraycolorado.com

Ouray Ice Park
P.O. Box 1058
Ouray, CO 81427
(970) 325-4288
www.ourayicepark.com

Ridgway Area Chamber Of Commerce
150 Racecourse Road
Ridgway, CO 81432
(970) 626-5181
(800) 220-4959
www.ridgwaycolorado.com

San Juan National Forest
15 Burnett Court
Durango, CO 81301
(970) 247-4874
www.fs.fed.us/r2/sanjuan/

Silverton Area Chamber of Commerce and Visitor Center
414 Greene Street

P.O. Box 565
Silverton, CO 81433
(970) 387-5654
(800) 752-4494
www.silvertoncolorado.com

Telluride Chamber of Commerce
P.O. Box 2113
Telluride, CO 81435
www.telluridechamber.com

Uncompahgre and Gunnison National Forests
2250 US Highway 50
Delta, CO 81416
(970) 874-6600
www.fs.fed/us/r2/gmug/

24: Flat Tops Trail Scenic Byway

Meeker Chamber of Commerce
710 Market Street
P.O. Box 869
Meeker, CO 81641
(970) 878-5510
www.meekerchamber.com

Routt National Forest
Yampa Ranger District
300 Roselawn Avenue
P.O. Box 7
Yampa, CO 80483
(970) 638-4516
www.fs.fed.us/r2/mbr

White River National Forest
Blanco Ranger District
220 East Market Street
Meeker, CO 81641
(970) 878-4039
www.fs.fed.us/r2/whiteriver

25: Grand Mesa Scenic Byway

Cedaredge Area Chamber of Commerce
P.O. Box 278
Cedaredge, CO 81413
(970) 856-6961
(800) 463-3041
www.cedaredgecolorado.com

Delta Area Chamber of Commerce
301 Main Street
Delta, CO 81416
(970) 874-8616
www.deltacolorado.org

Grand Mesa Byway Association
P.O. Box 122
Cedaredge, CO 81413
(800) 436-3041
www.grandmesabyway.org

Grand Mesa National Forest
2250 US Highway 50
Delta, CO 81416
(970) 874-6600
www.fs.fed.us/r2/gmug

26: Black Canyon South Rim Scenic Drive

Black Canyon of the Gunnison National Park
102 Elk Creek
Gunnison, CO 81230
(970) 641-2337
www.nps.gov/blca/

Montrose Chamber of Commerce
1519 East Main Street
Montrose, CO 81401
(970) 249-5000

(800) 923-5515
www.montrosechamber.com

27: Unaweep-Tabeguache Scenic and Historic Byway

Bureau of Land Management
Grand Junction Field Office
2815 H Road
Grand Junction, CO 81506
(970) 244-3000
www.co.blm.gov/gjra/gjra.html

Bureau of Land Management
Uncompahgre Field Office
245 South Townsend Avenue
Montrose, CO 81401
(970) 240-5300. www.co.blm.gov/ubra/index.html

Norwood Chamber of Commerce
P.O. Box 116
Norwood, CO 81423
(800) 282-5988
www.norwoodcolorado.com

Nucla-Naturita Area Chamber of Commerce
230 West Main Street
P.O. Box 425
Naturita, CO 81422
(970) 865-2350
www.nucla-naturita.com

Uncompahgre National Forest
2250 US Highway 50
Delta, CO 81416
(970) 874-6600
www.fs.fed.us/r2/gmug/

28: Mesa Verde National Park Scenic Drive

Cortez Chamber of Commerce
Colorado Welcome Center
928 East Main
P.O. Box 968
Cortez, CO 81321
(970) 565-3414
www.cortezchamber.com
www.mesaverdecountry.com

Mesa Verde National Park
P.O. Box 8
Mesa Verde National Park, CO 81330
(970) 529-4465
(800) 253-1616
www.nps.gov/meve

29: Rim Rock Drive

Colorado National Monument
Fruita, CO 81521
(970) 858-3617
www.nps.gov/colm/

Grand Junction Area Chamber of Commerce
360 Grand Avenue
Grand Junction, CO 81501
(970) 242-3214
(800) 352-5286
www.gjchamber.org

Grand Junction Visitor and Convention Bureau
740 Horizon Drive
Grand Junction, CO 81506
(800) 962-2547
www.visitgrandjunction.com

30: Harpers Corner Road

Dinosaur Chamber of Commerce
123 East Bronto Boulevard
Dinosaur, CO 81610
(800) 864-4405

Dinosaur National Monument
4545 East US Highway 40
Dinosaur, CO 81610
(435) 789-7700
www.nps.gov/dino

Rangely Area Chamber of Commerce
209 East Main Street
Rangely, CO 81648
(970) 675-8476
www.rangely.com

INDEX

ABOUT THE AUTHOR

Stewart M. Green is a photographer and writer based in Colorado Springs, Colorado. He travels the United States and the world working on projects for The Globe Pequot Press and other publications. Stewart has written and photographed many books for Falcon Publishing and The Globe Pequot Press, including *Rock Climbing Colorado, Rock Climbing Utah, Rock Climbing New England, Scenic Driving California, Scenic Driving Arizona, Walking Denver,* and *Rock Climbing Europe.* He has thirty years of experience as a photographer and is one of the world's leading climbing photographers. His work appears in many catalogues, advertisements, and national publications, including *Climbing, Rock & Ice, Sports Illustrated for Kids, Backpacker,* and *Outside.* View online galleries of some of Stewart's favorite images at www.stewartgreen.com and at http://climbing .about.com.